DEFINING WOMEN

The
University
of North
Carolina
Press
*Chapel Hill
& London*

DEFINING WOMEN

Television and the Case of

CAGNEY & LACEY

Julie D'Acci

791.457
D117

Library of Congress Cataloging-in-Publication Data

D'Acci, Julie

Defining Women: television and the case of Cagney and

Lacey / Julie D'Acci.

p. cm.

Includes bibliographical references and index.

ISBN 0-8078-2132-2 (cloth : alk. paper).—

ISBN 0-8078-4441-1 (pbk. : alk. paper)

1. Cagney and Lacey (Television program). 2. Television and

women—United States. 3. Women in television—United States.

I. Title.

PN1992.77.C24D33 1994

791.45'72—dc20   93-32536

CIP

The paper in this book meets the guidelines for permanence
and durability of the Committee on Production Guidelines for
Book Longevity of the Council on Library Resources.

98 97 96 95 94   5 4 3 2 1

Julie D'Acci is assistant professor of communication arts at the
University of Wisconsin–Madison.

TO FRAN

CONTENTS

Acknowledgments, xi

Introduction, 1

Chapter 1

Women Characters and

"Real World" Femininity, 10

Chapter 2

A Women's Audience, 63

Chapter 3

A Woman's Program, 105

Chapter 4

Negotiating Feminism, 142

Chapter 5

Female/Feminine/Feminist Audiences,

Spectators, and Readings, 168

Conclusion, 204

Notes, 211

Episode Script: "A Cry for Help," 259

Index, 325

ILLUSTRATIONS

Cagney and Lacey cocreators
 Barbara Avedon and Barbara Corday, 18

Tyne Daly and Loretta Swit as
 Mary Beth Lacey and Christine Cagney, 22

TV Guide advertisement for the *Cagney and Lacey*
 made-for-TV movie, 23

Loretta Swit and Tyne Daly as the original
 Cagney and Lacey, 24

Meg Foster in the original opening credits
 for the TV series, 26

The second Cagney and Lacey team
 discusses a case, 27

Meg Foster and Tyne Daly in the original
 opening credits, 36

Tyne Daly and Sharon Gless in the opening
 credits for the revised series, 37

Sharon Gless as the new Cagney, 40

Barney Rosenzweig and the cast
 of the Gless/Daly series, 50

National Examiner cover with photo of
 Tyne Daly and Sharon Gless, 53

People cover story on the breast cancer
 episodes, 56

Cover of 1985 Dell paperback by
 Serita Deborah Stevens, 60

Ms. magazine's 1987 Women of the Year, 61

TV Guide advertisement for

    "A Cry for Help," 89

Ethel Williams, Sharon Gless, Tyne Daly,

    and Judy Goldsmith, 101

Cagney and Lacey discuss a case, 123

Cagney and Lacey as "mature call girls," 133

The darlings of the women's movement, 146

"What do you know about it anyway, Sergeant?" 151

Conference in the "Jane," 186

Scene from "Power," 188

Two shots from "Who Said It's Fair?" 197

ACKNOWLEDGMENTS

I owe thanks to many people for their help, collegiality, and friendship during the research and writing of this book. My father, Anthony D'Acci, supported the project in countless ways. I am very grateful, and very sorry he never got to see its publication. Barney Rosenzweig, executive producer of *Cagney and Lacey*, generously granted me interviews and access to the program's set, production files, and production and staff meetings. Such cooperation is crucial to the study of television, and I applaud his openness to scholarly investigation. I also want to thank Barbara Corday, Barbara Avedon, P. K. (Patricia) Knelman, Terry Louise Fisher, Peter Lefcourt, Tyne Daly, Sharon Gless, Ralph Singleton, Stewart Lyons, Maury Harris, Ben Sobin, Eloise Robinson, Jo Corday, and the rest of the cast, crew, and staff of *Cagney and Lacey* for giving me interviews, information, and the opportunity to observe them at work. I offer special thanks to Barbara Corday and Barbara Avedon for granting me permission to include a script at the end of the book, and to the writers Chris Abbott and Terry Louise Fisher. I also thank Crystal Huston, Leslie Werner, and Diane Nassau at Orion Pictures and Azita Gorton at CBS for their help.

Barbara Hanrahan, David Perry, and Rich Hendel at the University of North Carolina Press have my great appreciation, and Pamela Upton my utmost gratitude for her expert copyediting and patience. Thanks also to Laura Moss Gottlieb for her skills as an indexer.

I am grateful to many friends and colleagues for sending me articles and press clippings, videotaping programs, granting me interviews, discussing the project, offering suggestions, and inviting me to present and publish papers. They include Helen Baehr, Cathy Shaker Breit, Robert Breit, Juliet Brodie, Maxine Fleckner Ducey, Gillian Dyer, Elizabeth Ellsworth, Lisa Freeman, Todd Gitlin, Timothy Haight, Teri Hall, Debbie Hanson, Henry Jenkins, Kathleen Levenick, Denise Mann, Elaine Marks, Biddy Martin, Tamar Mayer, Patricia Mellencamp, Carol Miller, Laura Stempel Mumford, Mary Beth Rhiel, Susan Searing, Lynn Spigel, Gabriele Strauch, Kristin Thompson, Sasha Torres, Marianne Whatley, Kathleen Woodward, and Nancy Worcester.

At many different stages, the manuscript profited from readers who provided incisive and thoughtful comments. They will no doubt recognize their contributions in the following pages and have my deepest thanks. Jane Feuer, Vance Kepley, Janet Staiger, Thomas Streeter, and David Thorburn all gave astute critiques and advice. John Fiske and Elaine Marks read with care, made many key suggestions, and offered an abundance of encouragement. Robert Allen's close attention to various drafts and his countless recommendations were utterly invaluable. His thoroughness and skill as a reviewer were nothing short of awe inspiring. My gratitude to David Bordwell is great indeed. He was an indefatigable reader and critic whose acuity and efforts helped shape the manuscript from its earliest conception. His boundless energy not only benefited the text but was a continual source of inspiration for its author.

Friends and associates have supported my work in more ways than they could ever know. I especially want to thank my colleagues in the television and film programs at the University of Wisconsin–Madison—John Fiske, Michele Hilmes, Tino Balio, David Bordwell, Donald Crafton, Lea Jacobs, Vance Kepley, and J. J. Murphy; Joanne Cantor and Mary Anne Fitzpatrick; the members of the women's studies program at the University of Wisconsin–Madison; the Console-ing Passions: Television, Video, and Feminism group; coeditors from *Camera Obscura*; former colleagues from the communications and women's studies programs at Loyola University of Chicago; and the graduate students in my seminars at the University of Wisconsin–Madison.

Three friends and colleagues warrant special mention. They have performed emergency readings, instant analyses, and editing feats; have given me their time, intelligence, and insights on more occasions than I could ever recount; and have kept me buoyed up with their remarkable wits. I am deeply grateful to Biddy Martin, Lynn Spigel, and Charlotte Brunsdon.

Finally, I owe immeasurable gratitude to Fran Breit, who has lived with this project for many years with complete equanimity and generosity. She has engaged in countless on-the-spot discussions, has listened patiently, has taught me about computers, and has given me boundless encouragement and aid. Her unstoppable and unparalleled humor has seen me through the ups and downs of such a long-term undertaking. There is really no way I can adequately thank her, but I dedicate this book to her with wholehearted appreciation.

DEFINING WOMEN

INTRODUCTION

      The late 1980s and early 1990s brought signs of trouble on many fronts: "Thelma" and "Louise" burst onto theater screens and made the cover of *Time* magazine; bitter fights erupted in the press and on television about feminist pedagogy and "political correctness"; Queen Latifa, Cindy Lauper, Aretha Franklin, Annie Lennox, M C Lyte, Madonna, and Salt-N-Pepa told it like it was on sound systems and music videos; Susan Faludi and Gloria Steinem appeared on TV talk shows and *Time*'s cover; activists stepped up their efforts in the battles over legal abortions and "family values"; Anita Hill, "Murphy Brown," and Hillary Rodham Clinton were omnipresent on home screens and the front pages of national publications; record numbers of white women and women of color fought for and won congressional seats in the 1992 elections; Sandra Bernhardt played an on-going role as a lesbian on *Roseanne*, and k. d. lang posed for a lesbian photo spread in *Vanity Fair*. The unsettling signals from on-screen and "real life" women spelled trouble for the categories "woman," "women," and "femininity"—full-scale, all-around "gender trouble."[1]

Perhaps these were signs of the return of the repressed, the resurgence of knowledges and desires that had gone underground during the Reagan and Bush administrations' backlash against the women's movements. Perhaps they were signs that such desires and knowledges had always been alive and well, kept vital by the continuous work of groups and individuals on the margins and the front lines. And perhaps they carried a warning that these troubles, these stirrings and shake-ups, simply will not go away.

This book deals with the cultural constructions of gender, the many troubles that underlie them, and U.S. television's place in the overall process. It investigates the "struggle over meanings"—specifically the meanings of *woman, women,* and *femininity*; the role of television networks, production companies, production teams, and publicity firms in generating and circulating these meanings; the ways in which TV viewers, the press, and numerous interest groups produce meanings and countermeanings of their own; and how all of these meanings clash and compete for social and semiotic space and power. The major questions I ask are these: How exactly do *woman, women,* and *femininity* come to have various meanings at a specific moment of history and culture? How do these different meanings serve the interests of the people and institutions producing them? How do they serve the interests of the television and advertising industries, or of TV viewers and social groups such as the women's movements? How do these meanings help to shape real human beings along particular lines or in particular ways? This book is also a "case study" of the U.S. television program *Cagney and Lacey*, because that series provides a crushingly clear illustration of the process I am examining: the cultural construction of femininity and the multifold battles over its definitions.[2]

The relationships among women and television are complex and often conflicted. For much of its history, U.S. prime-time network TV has considered young, white, middle-class women its primary target audience and the main consumers of the products it advertises. Millions of women of all classes, races, ethnicities, and ages (myself included) have watched and enjoyed TV almost every day of their lives. But television has also depicted women in ways that have been criticized by feminists for generating culturally dominant, conventional, and limiting meanings of femininity and gender. As Annette Kuhn says, "It seems to me that one of the major theoretical contributions of the women's movement has been its insistence on the significance of cultural factors, in particular in the form of socially dominant representations of women and the ideological character of such representations, both in constituting the category 'woman' and in delimiting and defining what has been called the 'sex/gender system.'" TV depictions, in other words, may have a very real correlation to our conceptions of what "woman" (as a notion produced in language and discourse) and "women" (as historical human beings) are and can be. They may take an active part in fashioning our social, sexual, and gendered possibilities and positions, as well as our behaviors and our very bodies.[3]

But how exactly are we to conceptualize the relationships among *woman, women,* and *television*? How are we to account for the social and cultural dominance of some definitions, representations, and enactments of femininity over others? This book conceives the whole process as one in which meanings are in constant tension, in which network television, its programs (or texts), its viewers, and its historical contexts are sites for the negotiation of numerous definitions and discourses, with certain ones achieving more power or "discursive authority" at specific moments and for specific participants than others.[4]

But this book also argues that the only way to investigate such power and such meanings is to observe them at work, to reconstruct and analyze their actual operations.[5] And for this reason it emphasizes what Christine Gledhill calls cultural "negotiation" involving each pertinent site—the TV institution, the TV text, the television audience or reception, and the social context. Such a focus illuminates the power of socially dominant "ideological" representations and definitions, as well as the simultaneous presence and power of socially subordinated, oppositional, and simply *different* ones. It traces how these many definitions interact, overlap, and clash within the individual sites as well as between and among them.[6]

This book, then, is based on the following assumptions: that social power is produced and exercised in myriad discrete instances; that power over meanings—its many shifts and struggles—may be analyzed and understood; that gender (like all aspects of the human subject) is not something acquired and settled once and for all at birth or shortly thereafter but is constantly in process, continually being shaped, enacted, and reconfigured; and that television (one of our culture's most productive technologies for generating images and meanings of masculinity and femininity) is a major participant in shaping the gender of its audiences. For these reasons, a specific example of the intersection of history, television culture, and definitions of femininity is worthy of extended investigation and analysis.

WHY *CAGNEY AND LACEY?*

Beginning in 1981, when it was first produced as a made-for-TV movie, *Cagney and Lacey* promised to offer a rich case study in the issues referred to above: the relationships among *woman, women,* and *television;* the battles over competing definitions of femininity; and the dynamics of representations, institutions, audiences, and contexts. At the time, the cultural definitions of *woman,* both in American society at large and in the representational practice of television, were multiple and open to debate. The traditional cultural meanings of femininity in a number of spheres (economy, labor, the family, and sexuality, to name a few) were being overtly challenged by discourses from the women's movements. Prime-time network television, in its overall quest for relevance and its specific attempt (begun in the late 1970s) to reach the "new working women's market," was generating portrayals of women that drew—in various ways and to varying degrees—on the new feminist consciousness, particularly that of the U.S. liberal women's movement.[7] Some of these depictions, such as those of the early *Cagney and Lacey,* were in sharp contrast to conventional images of women on television. As the 1980s progressed, however, the United States entered the throes of an escalating attack against the feminist movements of the previous decade, the tremors from which rocked and altered television's landscape.

A detailed study of the series helps to disclose the actual terms of cultural struggle over the meanings of femininity as it was played out on the field of U.S. prime time and its reception by various viewers from 1981 to 1988. Because the original *Cagney and Lacey* script was written in 1974 and offered (without takers) to every major movie studio in Hollywood, we can also gain insight into that earlier period as well. And because the program lived and died during a time in which television itself was experiencing enormous upheaval and change—the rapid growth of diverse cable channels, the emergence of FOX as a fourth commercial network, the sharp decline of the major networks' audience shares, the increasingly widespread use of videocassette recorders and remote controls, and the tendency to more tightly focus channels and more precisely target specific audiences (narrowcasting)—this study also illuminates the industry's massive reconfigurations in that era.

Furthermore, the issues contested during the late 1970s and the 1980s continue to bedevil network prime time and its audiences today. As noted earlier, the only way to understand how meanings, media, gender, and power actually interrelate and operate is to examine the details of a specific cultural instance. In that sense, my case study promises to furnish an important piece of the genealogy of women and television, illustrating how (during a particular and important moment) *woman, women,* and *femininity* were defined and constructed in the cultural sphere of fictional representations and interpretations, in the social sphere of audiences and consumers, and potentially even in the psychic sphere of human subjectivity.

A wide range of issues marks the series as an important benchmark for feminist and television studies. But first, by way of introduction: *Cagney and Lacey* was the first dramatic program in TV history to star two women in the leading roles. Conceived within the norms of the traditional police genre, it was about two white middle- and upper-middle-class female detectives in the New York City Police Department. Its creators were Barbara Avedon and Barbara Corday, its executive producer was Barney Rosenzweig, and Orion Television was the production company. Loretta Swit, Meg Foster, and Sharon Gless starred successively as Christine Cagney; Tyne Daly was Mary Beth Lacey. The program premiered as a made-for-TV movie in October 1981 and debuted as a series in March 1982, and its last original broadcast aired in May 1988 after it was canceled by CBS. At the end of its network run, first syndication rights were sold exclusively to the new women-targeted cable channel, Lifetime.[8]

I was originally attracted to *Cagney and Lacey* because it was directed at a working women's audience, constructed (after its first six episodes) as a "woman's program," and received by a large number of vocal women viewers.[9] It also generated representations of women that were different in numerous respects from customary ones: Its heroines were in-control protagonists who solved their own cases (both mentally and physically), were rarely presented as "women in distress" and were virtually never rescued by their male colleagues.[10] In addition to being active agents of the narrative, they were also the subjects, but rarely the objects, of sexual (heterosexual) desire. Christine Cagney, a single woman, had an ongoing sex life in which she often pursued men who interested her. Similarly, Mary Beth Lacey, a married woman, was cast as a sexual initiator with her husband, Harvey. Mary Beth was also the breadwinner of the family, while Harvey, an often unemployed construction worker, cooked and took care of the house and their two children.

When the program first aired, the actresses and the characters they played were in their mid-thirties; both were from working-class backgrounds, and there was a distinct minimization of glamour in their clothing, hairstyles, and makeup. Throughout the show's run, the two were depicted as close friends who took pleasure in one another's company and spent a lot of screen time talking to each other. Furthermore, much of the initial script material was drawn from the concerns of the early liberal women's movement in America. The first episode, for example, dealt with discrimination on the job and included a dialogue between the two protagonists about how Lieutenant Samuels, their commanding officer, was a "pig."

Cagney and Lacey was compelling to me because of its differences from conventional programming; it became even more so because of the reactions these differences generated in the press (both mainstream and feminist), in viewers, and within the television industry, and because of what happened to the differences over the course of the program's history. That history not only reveals numerous battles over how to define femininity but also makes plain the very "conditions of possibility" for representing women on television during the 1980s.[11]

Within its first two years, the series became the subject of intense public wranglings over often discrepant descriptions. The initial press reviews trumpeted such phrases as, "no racy 'Charlie's Angels' style glamour here." CBS executives, however, found the main characters "too tough, too hard, and not feminine." Letters from women viewers countered with enthusiasm and some amazement, "It's good to see smart, functioning, strong women" and "I enjoyed seeing a tough female." Harvey Shephard, vice-president of CBS programming, claimed, "They [the women's audience] accept a show with a woman in a traditional woman's role, like Michael Learned in *Nurse*, but not a woman in a man's expected role," while the publicity firm Rogers and Cowan advertised the series as "a television show that for the first time, takes an honest look at the lives of women who work." Elaine Warren of the *Los Angeles Herald Examiner* asserted, "*Cagney and Lacey* . . . genuinely wants to portray the sensitivity and strength of two women cops without a lot of airbrushed fantasy." The tabloid *National Examiner* warned, "Cagney and Lacey are female chauvinists . . . and they're poised to destroy the manhood of America." The *National NOW Times* (the organ of the National Organization for Women) wrote, "Those of us who . . . found the 'bitch' image of women on *Dallas*, *Dynasty*, and *Falcon Crest* wearying, discovered [in *Cagney and Lacey*] not the formula cops and robbers routine, but one of the few shows depicting credible women." Syndicated columnist Gary Deeb pronounced *Cagney and Lacey* "fraudulently feminist . . . a piece of filth that more often than not exploited females." And the British feminist journal *Spare Rib* concluded, "The women are required to retain their femininity while brutally combatting 'crime.' . . . Like any other police series, *Cagney and Lacey* serves to glorify the police force."[12]

The juxtaposition of these comments underscores many of the issues that have occupied feminist, poststructuralist, and cultural theorists for the past fifteen years: Meaning is multiple or polysemous, and the representations of Cagney and Lacey were interpreted and activated in many different and often conflicting ways by various viewers and institutions. "Woman" and "women" are not natural essences or coherent identities, but systems of differences and relations, social and cultural constructions.[13] Furthermore, "discursive authority" or hegemony over the definitions of *women*, *woman*, and *femininity* appeared to be crucial to social power: CBS, the women's movements, the mainstream and tabloid press, and women viewers themselves all had vested stakes in articulating and advancing their respective meanings. Female viewers seemed motivated from sheer pleasure and from a conviction that TV representations helped define the possibilities for women in their everyday lives beyond television. Finally, the juxtaposed quotations also point to the notion that meanings may not be divorced from the contexts in which they are made; they "do not reside in images" but are circulated between and among media texts, interest groups, the press, viewers, and the overall social and historical context.[14]

Because *Cagney and Lacey* was seen by all sides in this public struggle as producing TV depictions that were different from previous ones, an investigation of the series also led to an inquiry into network prime time's norms and conventions for women characters and into the crucial places of audience women and screen women in the overall functioning of nighttime TV. It furthermore widened into a study of television (which produces women as audiences, consumers, and representations) as what Teresa de Lauretis has called a "technology of gender," an institution that works to construct masculinity and femininity in numerous aspects of its textual and extratextual operations.[15]

But because I have chosen to zero in on *Cagney and Lacey* and its specific conjunctures of industry, reception, text, and context, I am not therefore automatically arguing against the work of such scholars as Raymond Williams, Nick Browne, John Ellis, Lynne Joyrich, James Collins, and Annette Kuhn, who urge that we study TV not so much as isolated programs but as "flow"—as *all* the available texts (commercials, "promos," and programs themselves), their constant accessibility and overlap via channel switching, their scheduling for continuous viewing, and their address to heterogeneous audiences.[16] I simply maintain that it is also essential to study individual series and their contexts, particularly those cases (such as that of *Cagney and Lacey*) in which audience members watch selectively and regularly, in which they plan and schedule, week in and week out, to view their favorite shows. In other words, as Charlotte Brunsdon has argued, it is important to not only retain the notion of the discrete TV text but to specify the particular way in which it may actually be viewed in any discussion or analysis of television.[17]

The chapters that follow present a detailed analysis of a specific example of prime-time U.S. network television. I have used many aspects of *Cagney and Lacey*'s history to illustrate my points, and I have focused primarily on the early period of the series's history, when the conflicts over its representations of women were most volatile, the pursuit of a working women's audience most ardent, and the response by women viewers most overwhelming. These chapters demonstrate the actual workings of the overall TV enterprise—the multifold aspects of its production, publicity, reception, and social context—and the ways in which its many players actively negotiated and vied for discursive power over defining *woman, women,* and *femininity.* One of my major aims is to examine the various discourses about femininity produced from different sites and by different players, and accordingly I have reproduced many examples from audience letters, articles in the mainstream and feminist press, publicity releases, production-team meetings, comments from network spokespeople, and other responses to the program.[18] These sources enable me to illustrate precisely how *woman, women,* and *femininity,* in a struggle specific to the 1970s and 1980s, came to be defined by traditional social discourses, discourses of the U.S. liberal women's movement, of the advertising and public relations industries, of prime-time television, of the mainstream and tabloid press, of numerous viewers, and of a variety of interest groups. They also show how particular definitions came to dominate at different times and at different points for the various participants in the struggle.

Each chapter spends a good deal of time examining institutional actions, exigencies, norms, conventions, and practices, because even though the book concentrates on the contestation of meanings—the continual process of negotiation at the levels of industry, text, and reception—it also delineates the powerful role of network prime time in constructing definitions and in shaping cultural representations, genres, narratives, audiences, spectators, and gender. It highlights the home screen's influence on the manner in which we view ourselves and the ways we enact the traditions of culture in our own bodies. But although the social and cultural force of prime-time network television and its texts is acknowledged and detailed, it is by no means seen as all-encompassing.

Chapter 1 pinpoints production and reception battles over *Cagney and Lacey*'s women characters in the areas of appearance, class, behavior, marital status, sexual and reproductive politics, sexuality, and all-around femininity. It traces these battles through an overview of the program's history, particularly in its first few tumultuous years. Chapter 2 turns to the negotiations surrounding the construction of a women's audience for the series. It lays out the circumstances that prompted the three major networks to attempt to lure working women to their TV sets during 1980s prime time, the actual ways in which CBS forged such a viewership for *Cagney and Lacey*, and the ways the press, the liberal women's movement, and the viewers themselves both constructed and defined a "women's audience" according to the terms of their own (rather than the network's) wants and understandings. Chapter 3 looks more closely at textual issues. It concentrates on the myriad negotiations that surrounded the production of a "women's program," and especially on how the police genre was transmuted as it incorporated two female—and, at first, feminist—protagonists and new definitions of femininity into a traditionally male-oriented form.

Because so many of the institutional, textual, and reception struggles over the series involved discourses from the women's movements, and because so many of the general battles over defining *women, woman,* and *femininity* grew out of the clash between the definitions of the women's movements and more conventional meanings, Chapter 4 investigates the tugs-of-war over prime time's representations of feminism and "feminist women" in the early 1980s. It then examines how *Cagney and Lacey*'s texts actually negotiated such representations over the course of 125 episodes. The final chapter focuses on both TV texts and reception by examining the relationships among *Cagney and Lacey*'s characters, or textual women, and women as audience members and spectators.[19] It demonstrates how the TV text may contribute to producing gender in its spectators and offers an interpretation or reading of the series. This reading demonstrates how a mainstream, commercial, realist text that has been subjected to all the demands and distortions of prime-time American television may nonetheless be part of a feminist project and a rallying point for pleasure and politics; how a text that is, among many other things, both troubled and troubling may also be positively trouble-making for traditional definitions of *women, woman,* and *femininity.*

CHAPTER 1

WOMEN CHARACTERS AND

"REAL WORLD" FEMININITY

During *Cagney and Lacey's* creation and the whole of its network run, the key players involved in production and reception continuously battled over what women on television should and should not or could and could not be. These players included those we would expect to be part of any negotiation of television's meanings—the TV network, the production company and production team, the television audience, the press, and various interest and pressure groups.

All these groups, of course, supported definitions of *woman, women,* and *femininity* that suited their particular interests, whether those were political, economic, cultural, "personal," or some combination thereof. Many network executives, for instance, wanted the show to include topical and relevant representations of women while they simultaneously hoped to preserve the conventional ways of depicting female characters. Despite the examples set by a number of 1970s sitcoms (which I discuss below), these conventions still presented women as primarily young, white, middle class, stereotypically "attractive," and domesticated. They specifically portrayed women as wives, mothers, heterosexual sex objects, subsidiaries of men, and as "vulnerable" and "sympathetic" characters; in addition, women were traditionally cast as the protagonists of situation comedies rather than prime-time dramas.[1]

In contrast, *Cagney and Lacey*'s independent production company, Orion Television (formerly Filmways), appeared at least somewhat committed to generating more innovative representations. Richard Rosenbloom, Orion Television's president, in fact had a reputation for producing the highest percentage of work written by women in Hollywood at the time. The series's production team (the creators, writers, producers, and main actresses), for its part, was powerfully influenced by the liberal women's movement and explicitly fashioned *Cagney and Lacey* (especially in its first few years) on early feminist terms. A significant segment of the women's audience for the series, as well as for other working women–targeted programs of the time, was looking for progressive, multidimensional, and "real" female depictions. (The oft-cited term *real* will be discussed at length in Chapter 5.) The mainstream press, as can be imagined, demonstrated extremely varied interests: One sector, very much affected by feminism, agitated for a wider range of women characters on television and, specifically, for roles shaped by women's movement concerns. Other media factions called for a return to "tried and true" femininity.[2]

Similarly, a number of interest and pressure groups weighed in according to their own stakes in divergent meanings and portrayals: The National Gay Task Force, for example, vehemently protested the network's effort to shield the series from connotations of lesbianism by replacing one actress portraying Cagney with another "more feminine" one. The National Right to Life Committee fiercely opposed Cagney and Lacey's support of a woman character who chose to have an abortion, while Planned Parenthood and the National Abortion Rights Action League (NARAL) applauded the program's embrace of reproductive rights. And spokespeople for the U.S. liberal women's movement generally and consistently championed the series for depicting "independent" working women and emphasizing the women's friendship.

Because the women's movements were such fundamental forces in U.S.

social history of the 1970s and 1980s, and in the controversies surrounding *Cagney and Lacey*, I need to say a few things about them here. The taxonomy of the different "camps" that I will draw upon has been well critiqued—among other problems, it tends to ignore the countless overlaps from camp to camp and to oversimplify a wide diversity of viewpoints. But because many feminists in the seventies and eighties defined themselves in relation to its terms, it warrants discussion. As I have already indicated, the camp that most influenced *Cagney and Lacey* is generally called the liberal women's movement. In America, this segment is associated with *Ms.* magazine, Gloria Steinem, and the National Organization for Women (NOW). Its primary emphasis, especially in the 1970s, was on equality under the law and in the labor force, with a focus on white, heterosexual, middle-class women; its programs for social change were oriented toward "reform" rather than a radical structural reorganization of American political and social life. In the late 1970s and the 1980s, due to the efforts of women of color and lesbians, the movement became more attentive to groups beyond the white middle class, and it also recognized the existence of structural reasons for women's oppression that required more than personal solutions. By and large, the movement has worked to train public attention on the social and cultural problems that women face involving wages, labor conditions, abortion and other reproductive rights, rape laws, women's safety, childcare issues, educational opportunities, female solidarity, and the importance of mass media in bringing about social change.

But feminism during the 1970s and 1980s was represented by other segments and theoretical approaches in addition to the liberal one. These various approaches have been profiled in other works, and I just want to flag four major positions—radical, cultural, socialist, and poststructuralist feminism. Many early radical feminists engaged in a sound critique of liberal feminism, made the oppression of women and the operations of patriarchy their central concerns, and favored the elimination of sex differences. But throughout the 1970s and into the 1980s, some radical feminists drifted toward a belief in a natural female essence. This approach, which came to be called cultural feminism, evolved into a celebration of, rather than a challenge to, "essential" sex differences. Associated with such groups as Women against Pornography, such feminism often valorized a biological femininity that was life- and nurturance-oriented and that was universally oppressed by a dominating and conquest-oriented patriarchy.

Socialist feminism, on the other hand, argued for the social construction of both femininity and masculinity and focused on such issues as the relationship between women's relegation to the domestic sphere and the maintenance of capitalism. Poststructuralist feminism argued for myriad differences within the seemingly coherent categories "woman" and "women" and for the notion that these concepts encompass a multitude of heterogeneous meanings produced in language rather than nature. Although liberal feminism plays the most active role in my case study of *Cagney and Lacey*, the other strands surface in some of the media and scholarly criticism I draw upon and discuss.[3]

THE REPRESENTATIONAL CONTEXT

Cagney and Lacey's earliest period, from its conception in 1974 to its production as a made-for-TV movie in 1981, seethed with conflicts over definitions of women and their many negotiations. But it was not the only project so beset. Generally speaking, representations of women in motion pictures and television programs were highly contradictory throughout the 1970s. Films such as *Alice Doesn't Live Here Anymore, Julia, The Turning Point*, and *An Unmarried Woman* expressed tensions between the emerging interests of the women's movements and more traditional notions of femininity. On prime-time television, a number of industry and social conditions combined to spawn a collection of amazingly paradoxical depictions. As Eileen Meehan demonstrates, by 1970 the A. C. Nielsen Company (which measures the television audience and publishes series "ratings") had changed its fixed group of designated Nielsen "families" from a sample that dated back to its surveys of radio audiences, replacing it with younger and more urban households. Also, CBS discovered that, although its programming was bringing in more total viewers than the other networks, its five "owned and operated" stations in New York, Los Angeles, Chicago, Philadelphia, and St. Louis were doing badly in ratings and revenues. The implications of this discovery, along with the Nielsen Company's changeover to a younger, more urban ratings sample, helped to alter the face of prime-time television.[4]

It is important to understand that Federal Communication Commission regulations at the time allowed each network to own five VHF-TV stations.[5] Called the "O and O's" (for owned and operated), these stations were responsible for a large share of the networks' actual profits and were located in highly lucrative metropolitan markets. Some CBS executives realized in 1969 that their schedule was heavily weighted with country programs such as *Green Acres, The Beverly Hillbillies, Mayberry RFD, Hee Haw, Petticoat Junction*, and *Gunsmoke*. These programs, although extremely popular in the United States at large, were not popular (or, because of ratings, were presumed to be unpopular) with the urban audiences of the O and O's—or, more precisely, with the newly designated Nielsen households. In a bold and internally contested move, CBS canceled its winning country schedule and oriented its programming toward what Jane Feuer has called "socially conscious sit-coms," and Todd Gitlin, "relevant" programming. Some network executives thought that these series would appeal not only to the desired eighteen-to-forty-nine-year-old, upwardly mobile target audience, but also to the *urban*, eighteen-to-forty-nine-year-old, upwardly mobile audience.[6]

The new socially relevant sitcoms were produced primarily by Norman Lear's Tandem and TAT Productions, by Mary Tyler Moore's MTM Enterprises, and by Twentieth Century–Fox (*M*A*S*H*), and Warner Bros. (*Alice*). The civil rights movement, the Black Power movement, the antiwar movement, the women's movements, and the accelerated entry of women into the labor force were all tapped for subject material. The effort to simply keep its programming up to date had already led ABC (in the late 1960s) into the social ferment of the times with such programs as *Mod Squad* and *Judd for the Defense*. (To some degree, NBC's *Julia* [1968] may also be seen as part of this trend.) But the push to attract specific upscale urban audiences intensified CBS's mining of thematic material that it thought would appeal to young, educated city dwellers. The move had enormous repercussions for the ways women were represented; programs featuring working women, African American women, older women, divorced women, single mothers, and working-class women filled the 1970s home screen. *The Mary Tyler Moore Show*, *Rhoda*, *Good Times*, *The Jeffersons*, *Maude*, *One Day at a Time*, *Alice*, and *All in the Family* were prominent examples of the new fare. Controversial women's issues such as abortion, rape, equal employment opportunities, and racial and gender prejudice were featured subjects. At least in some prime-time programs, "woman," "women," and "femininity" were no longer conceived solely in terms of young, white, and middle-class characteristics. Because this new "urban and sophisticated" programming was such a success at CBS, the other networks followed suit with a number of clones.[7]

However, as Lauren Rabinovitz, Serafina Bathrick, and Bonnie Dow have pointed out, these programs often produced contradictory and troubling representations of femininity and "independent" women, and most of the social issues raised were domesticated—that is, they were represented as contained and resolvable at the level of the family. With regard to their treatment of African Americans, Donald Bogle argued that these comedies "take authentic issues in the black community and distort them." Esther

Rolle, who played the character Florida on *Good Times*, quit the show because of differences with the producers over the portrayals, which she called "an outrage, an insult." And the National Black Feminist Organization charged that the representations of blacks and other "minorities" in these comedies were "slanted toward the ridiculous with no redeeming counter images" and that the programs gave the impression that black people did not perform effectively in professional positions. The issues raised by these series regarding both African Americans and women— problematic, delimited, racist, and sexist as they were—nevertheless became part of negotiated public discourse, introduced a measure of visible difference into television's repertoire, and challenged prime time's equation of women (since the 1953 disappearance of *Beulah* and *Amos 'n' Andy*) with white and upscale characteristics exclusively.[8]

Beginning in the mid-1970s and continuing into the next decade, different conditions in society and the television industry combined once again to generate even more paradoxical female characters. This time, pressure on the networks from groups such as the Parent-Teachers Association (PTA) to reduce incidents of televised violence led directly to the display of women's bodies as sexual attractions: "If you can't have Starsky pull a gun and fire it fifty times a day on promos," said Brandon Tartikoff (at the time vice-president of NBC's programming), "sex becomes your next best handle." Before this period, images of women on prime time had not been charged with the sexual display of motion picture imagery; instead, female TV characters were generally domesticated. However, from the mid-1970s to the early 1980s, female sex objects dominated the TV landscape in what is often called the "jiggle" era, or in the industry's noneuphemistic tag, the "T&A" ("tits and ass") period. It is, of course, no accident that these representations coincided with the ever-mounting backlash over the concerns and demands of the women's movements.[9]

One of the main paradoxes of this period is that, during it, women starred in more dramatic programs than at any other time in television history. Series like *Police Woman*, *Get Christie Love*, *Charlie's Angels*, and *Wonder Woman* are major offspring of that era. Each of these programs could be squarely classified under the jiggle category, and each promoted sensationalism by providing raw material for setting up the classic "woman in distress" situation. The women protagonists ultimately were either rescued by male colleagues or used superhuman capabilities to resolve their predicaments. Other jiggle examples include *Flying High* and *American Girls* (about stewardesses and reporters, respectively) and the women characters in *WKRP in Cincinnati* and *Three's Company*.[10]

Some television scholars have seen these programs as overt instances of the backlash against the women's movements, whereas others have read them as prime time's way of killing two birds with one stone and capturing both segments of a divided audience. As Todd Gitlin says of *Charlie's Angels*, the show "appealed at once to elements of the new feminism and its conservative opposition. The Angels are skilled working women and sex objects at the same time." The jiggle phenomenon, in the face of audience and interest-group protest, tapered off (at least in its most blatant form) by the early 1980s. But its complex and multidimensional legacy included the breaking of barriers to women—both black and white (*Get Christie Love* featured African American actress Teresa Graves)—as stars of TV dramas. It also introduced a "spectacle" aspect to the representation of female bodies—that is, a more explicit sexual dimension to the traditionally more domesticated woman, revealing her as sex and beauty object.[11]

GETTING NEW REPRESENTATIONS TO THE SCREEN

Cagney and Lacey came upon the scene in the midst of this history. Its first script, written in 1974, fell squarely within the conceptual terms of the liberal women's movement, in that it featured role reversals—women in a traditionally male profession and women in a standard, male, public-sphere genre. Historically and industrially speaking, its creators considered it an idea whose time had come. According to Barbara Avedon, Barbara Corday, and Barney Rosenzweig, *Cagney and Lacey* was specifically conceived as a response to an influential book from the early liberal women's movement, Molly Haskell's *From Reverence to Rape: The Treatment of Women in the Movies*. Avedon and Corday were engaged in the literature and politics of this movement, and both were in women's groups. Rosenzweig was "setting out to have his consciousness raised." They read Haskell's book and were intrigued by the fact that there had never been a Hollywood movie about two women "buddies" comparable to the men portrayed in *M*A*S*H* or *Butch Cassidy and the Sundance Kid*.[12] According to Rosenzweig, "The Hollywood establishment had totally refused women those friendships, the closest thing being perhaps Joan Crawford and Eve Arden in *Mildred Pierce*, the tough lady boss and her wise-cracking side-kick. So I went to my friend Ed Feldman, who was then head of Filmways [now Orion], and I said, 'I want to do a picture where we turn around a conventional genre piece like *Freebie and the Bean* with its traditional male situations and make it into the first real hit feminist film.'"[13]

Corday said, "Barney came to this conclusion not so much, at that time, as a feminist—because he was very new to all of those ideas then—but [he] came to the conclusion as a commercial producer, that it was *extraordinary* that there had never been a female buddy movie, and at that moment in history, it would probably be a great idea. He talked to me about it and I went to my partner, Barbara, and we talked about it. We conceived of it, all of us, as a feature, because that's what the buddy movies were, they were feature films."[14]

One of the main motivations behind *Cagney and Lacey* from its inception was the creators' notion that two women could, in fact, be represented as friends who worked and talked together, rather than as more conventional competitors. Both Avedon and Corday recalled that the relationship between the protagonists was modeled (if somewhat unconsciously) on their own eight-year relationship as writing partners and friends. As Corday said,

> We were women, we were partners, we were best friends. We were a lot of the things that we were writing about. . . . We spent a good deal of the eight years that we wrote together talking about our lives. . . . What we tried to get into the characters . . . was us. We didn't say we were doing it, or set out to do it, but there we were. . . . I'm more Mary Beth, Barbara's more Chris, but there are pieces of each of us in the other. . . . Barbara is very politically involved, very active in causes. I'm more conservative. . . . I finish her sentences for her. She's the one who races off as Chris does. I'm the one who says maybe we should talk about this for a minute.[15]

Ed Feldman at Filmways was, in fact, interested in the idea Rosenzweig had pitched to him, and he approved the "seed" money to hire Avedon and Corday as writers. Barbara Avedon recalled that, although Filmways was "excited" about the idea, its executives had difficulty understanding the view of women involved. They persisted in situating the characters in the film industry's context of women as spectacles and sex objects. According to Avedon, "They [Filmways] told us things like, when [Cagney or Lacey] rips her shirt back and shows her badge to the guys, they can all stare [at her breasts]. That was the level of consciousness, even though they were doing a women-buddy movie."[16]

Avedon and Corday prepared for writing the script by spending ten days with New York City policewomen. Avedon recalled, "The women cops we met were first and foremost cops. Unlike Angie Dickinson in *Police Woman*, who'd powder her nose before she went out to make a bust, these women took themselves seriously as police officers." Both Corday and

Publicity photo of Cagney and Lacey *cocreators Barbara Avedon and Barbara Corday. (© CBS, 1981)*

Avedon were convinced that the only way for *Cagney and Lacey* to work was for them to cast "strong, mature" women with "senses of humor"; because the script was thought to be so controversial for the time, they did not, however, consider mixing the races of the protagonists. They envisioned Sally Kellerman as Cagney and Paula Prentiss as Lacey.[17]

The creators all agreed that because they were dealing with potentially incendiary "feminist" material, their film would have to be, first and foremost, "entertaining." The original script, entitled "Freeze," was a spoof in which Cagney and Lacey uncover the existence of the Godmother, the female intelligence behind a brothel where men are the prostitutes and women the patrons. The major narrative device was the early women's movement notion of role reversals. Not only did the Godmother replace the Godfather and the prostitutes and patrons reverse roles, but, with regard to the protagonists, as Avedon said, "We turned every cliché over, even the unpleasant ones. We had Cagney say to a guy 'I'll give you a call sometime,' and then turn around and walk out insensitively. I really didn't like her very much for doing it."[18]

After getting the script financed by Filmways, Rosenzweig needed a major motion picture studio to pick up the project and do the actual production. He took the original property to every studio in Hollywood and received predictable "Hollywood" responses for the time, along the lines of "these women aren't soft enough, aren't feminine enough." Rosenzweig himself saw such responses as products of the studio heads' own personal views about femininity: "In those days," he said, "all the studio heads were males, and they didn't like [the *Cagney and Lacey* script]. They didn't think it was funny, they didn't think the women were feminine. It wasn't a conspiracy. Just from their own subjective point of view, they didn't think it was what America wanted to see because it wasn't something they wanted to see."[19]

Finally, Sherry Lansing (who was later to become the first woman head of a major motion picture studio, Twentieth Century–Fox) persuaded her boss at MGM, Dan Melnik, to make the movie. MGM said it would, but only if the well-known "sex symbols" Raquel Welch and Ann-Margret starred. (Their versatility as actresses was not yet widely recognized at this point in Hollywood history.) The other condition was a $1.6 million budget that, in true catch-22 fashion, prohibited the hiring of such high-priced actresses. The property, therefore, lay dormant for the next five years.[20]

In 1980 Rosenzweig decided to try again. This time he pitched the idea to the television networks as a pilot for a weekly series. Corday and Avedon reconceived the script, updating it and making it less of a spoof and more of a "realistic" crime drama. Because Corday, by this time, had taken a job as vice-president of comedy development at ABC, Barbara Avedon wrote the actual script herself. Although CBS declined to pick up the series, it decided to make the script as a less costly, less risky, made-for-TV movie, and Norman Powell in the TV movie department put it into development. The network also suggested that the producer cast "two sexy young actresses" in the leading roles. According to Rosenzweig, he told CBS, "You don't understand, these policewomen must be mature women. One has a family and kids, the other is a committed career officer. What separates this project from *Charlie's Angels* is that Cagney and Lacey are women; they're not girls and they're *certainly* not objects."[21]

During this impasse CBS, which had an outstanding "pay-or-play" commitment to Loretta Swit of *M*A*S*H*, asked Rosenzweig to cast her as Cagney. Avedon and Corday, who had recently worked with Sharon Gless on the TV series *Turnabout*, wanted her for the part; Avedon even said she had actually considered Gless the model for Cagney while writing the new script. But because Gless could not be released from her contract to Universal, Rosenzweig cast Swit as Cagney even though her *M*A*S*H* contract would preclude her availability should *Cagney and Lacey* turn into a series. Tyne Daly was cast as Lacey. Richard Rosenbloom, then president of Filmways Television and a staff producer at Filmways, joined the project as the movie's line producer, and Ted Post, who was known primarily as an action director, was hired to direct. The movie was shot in Toronto with a budget of $1.85 million; it was scheduled for broadcast on 8 October 1981 and was publicized in various ways by the women's movement, the network, and the mainstream press.[22]

The preproduction publicity trumpeted *Cagney and Lacey's* importance to the cause of feminism. Gloria Steinem at *Ms.* magazine had been sent a script by the creators and was so enthusiastic that she appeared with Loretta Swit on *Donahue* to plug the movie. According to one media critic, the two were so "reverential" that it "sounded as though they were promoting the first woman president."[23]

Steinem also featured Loretta Swit and Tyne Daly, in character in their police uniforms, on the cover of the October issue of *Ms.* The issue contained a feature article on *Cagney and Lacey* written by Marjorie Rosen, a well-known feminist film critic and author of *Popcorn Venus: Women, Movies, and the American Dream.* Rosen related the troubled history of the property, emphasized its importance for feminism, underscored the specific feminist characteristics she believed *Cagney and Lacey* brought into "distinctive focus," and ended with a pitch for a weekly series. The feminist characteristics especially applauded included the presentation of women as the subjects of narrative action and adventure in a traditionally male-dominated genre, as holders of traditionally male jobs, and as friends. Also emphasized were the movie's characterizations of women as autonomous, "individualistic," and "independent." Rosen concluded, "Watching *Cagney and Lacey*, it is virtually impossible *not* to think of its potential as a weekly series. For here's a rare TV movie that not only sports such surefire ingredients as crime, cops, and a pair of great buddies, but also maintains its distinctive focus on two highly individualistic, courageous, and thoroughly independent women—women we'd like to get to know better, and women who are worth visiting with again and again." At the bottom of the article appeared the message, "If you would like to see *Cagney and Lacey* expanded into a TV series, write to Richard Rosenbloom, Filmways, 2049 Century Park East, Los Angeles, California 90067."[24]

CBS's promotion department, having its own motivations and vested interests, publicized the movie according to a standard television practice called "exploitation advertising." This is a tactic, with precedents in the Hollywood film industry, in which a sensational—usually sexual or violent—aspect of a program is highlighted for the purposes of audience attraction. *Cagney and Lacey's TV Guide* advertisement filled three-quarters of a page. A large close-up of Loretta Swit, with her long blond hair, dominated the left side of the composition, while her clasped, outstretched hands held a pointed revolver that dominated the right. A significantly smaller, medium shot of the lesser-known (at the time) Tyne Daly in police coat, shirt, and tie appeared below the Swit close-up. On the lower far left of the page, underneath and smaller than the Daly image, was another shot of Swit lying on her back (presumably naked) with a sheet draped over her. One bare shoulder and arm and one bare leg, bent at the knee, were exposed. A man (also naked), depicted only from his waist up, was leaning over her, his arm across her body. The copy read, "It's their first week as undercover cops! Cagney likes the excitement. Lacey cares about the people she protects. They're going to make it as detectives—or die trying!"[25]

Various conceptions of femininity were set into play here, and it seems evident that CBS, in dealing with a movie about women in nontraditional roles, was careful to invoke not only connotations regarding the "new woman," but also more traditional notions as well. Cagney was shown as a cop with an aimed revolver, but also as a conventionally beautiful woman with eye makeup, lipstick, and long blond hair. She was also shown as a conventional object rather than subject of sexual desire. Lacey was shown in traditionally male clothing but was described in the conventionally feminine terms of "caring about the people she protects." And although they were both trying to "make it" as detectives, they were also stereotypical "women in distress" who might "die trying." The emphasis on stereotyped feminine behaviors and predicaments in an ad for a movie about women in new roles fulfilled the formula for exploitation advertising by suggesting sexual and violent content to the audience, while also reassuring

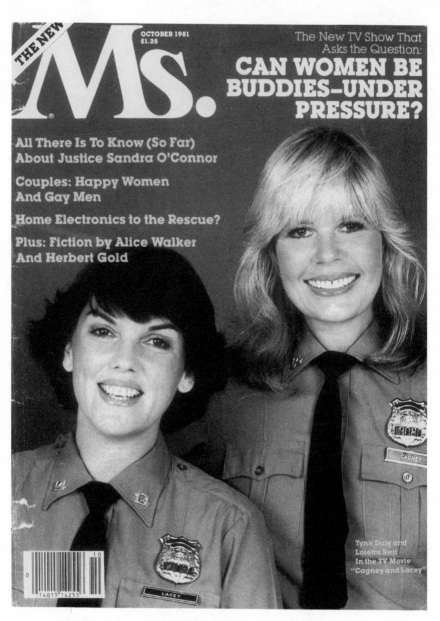

Cover of Ms., *October 1981, featuring Tyne Daly and Loretta Swit as
Mary Beth Lacey and Christine Cagney. (© Ms., 1981)*

it about women's traditional roles and positions in relationship to social
power. This initial industry ad illustrates the negotiation of differently
oriented interests in one cultural artifact. It furthermore exemplifies the
workings of what John Fiske calls a "secondary" or "second-level" text (any
publicity, review, or "official" public discourse about the "first-level" text,

TV Guide *advertisement for the* Cagney and Lacey
made-for-TV movie pilot. (© CBS, 1981)

Publicity still of Loretta Swit and Tyne Daly as the original Cagney and Lacey in police uniforms, before their promotions to detective. (© CBS, 1981)

or the program itself), which promotes, through the process of intertextuality, various readings or interpretations of the program. The ad thus demonstrates how the network fostered ambiguous or varied meanings of femininity both in a promotional "text" and in the potential audience.[26]

The *Cagney and Lacey* made-for-TV movie was also publicized in the mainstream press. In an article in the *New York Times*, published the day before the program aired, Barbara Basler interviewed three New York City policewomen who had seen a sneak preview. The article exemplifies both how the press joined in the struggle over meanings and the way in which "reality" got invoked in the process. Different participants in the history of *Cagney and Lacey* called upon "reality," "real life experience," or the experiences of "real policewomen" (and policewomen invoked their individual "real" experiences) as supports for their own particular notions of what the movie and the series meant for and about women. The title of Basler's article was "Real Women View the TV Variety," and the policewomen she interviewed basically praised the characters as "true-to-life," offering an "accurate portrayal of their jobs and problems." A few months later, however, Howard Rosenberg of the *Los Angeles Times* interviewed two Los Angeles policewomen who strongly challenged the "reality" of the representations ("it was two women trying to do exactly what men do") in favor of their own definitions of women and femininity. In relating the made-for-TV movie to women's lives on the police force, the Basler article generally demonstrated the ways that *Cagney and Lacey*, from the earliest moments of its history, generated discussion about the possibilities for women, not only in a television series, but also in the world beyond the TV frame.[27]

The movie aired at 8:00 P.M. on Thursday, 8 October 1981, and captured an astonishing 42 percent share of the television audience. (CBS had been getting a 28 or 29 share in that time period.) Within thirty-six hours, CBS was on the telephone to Barney Rosenzweig, asking him to start planning a weekly program. Gloria Steinem and the *Ms.* magazine staff had already lobbied members of the CBS board, urging them to make a series based on the movie.[28]

CONTROVERSIAL REPRESENTATIONS OF WOMEN

In the second phase of *Cagney and Lacey's* history, the television series starring Tyne Daly and Meg Foster (Swit's replacement as Cagney) aired from March 1982 to August 1982 (including summer reruns). These dates coincide with the period during which the network was most ardently courting and constructing a prime-time audience of working women. I will discuss this phenomenon in greater detail in the following chapter, but for now it suffices to say that the huge ratings success of the *Cagney and Lacey* made-for-TV movie appeared to convince the network that women-oriented programming that drew on feminist discourses and subject matter was a winning bet. But such a hunch, in the midst of the

Meg Foster in the original opening credits for the Cagney and Lacey *TV series.*
(© Orion TV, 1982)

Reagan years' opposition to the women's movements, only intensified the battlefield nature of the negotiations surrounding the production and reception of female television characters.

The series's first script was written by Avedon, Corday, and Rosenzweig and directed by Georg Stanford Brown. Filmways press releases for the premiere episode described the main characters as "two top-notch female cops who fight crime while proving themselves to male colleagues." This theme of women working in nontraditional jobs—in roles that called for rough action—and fighting sexism was, in fact, emphasized both in the publicity and in the episodes themselves. Keeping alive the link between the women's movement and the TV program, Gloria Steinem and *Ms.* magazine organized a reception for the creators and stars in early March.[29]

The very night and hour that *Cagney and Lacey* came to CBS, the series *9 to 5* (based on the hit movie of the same name that dealt with secretaries agitating for better working conditions) debuted on the rival ABC network. Gloria Steinem, speaking at a Hollywood Radio and Television Society luncheon a month earlier, had vigorously protested this scheduling, saying it might "split the audience and hurt each other's [the two

The second Cagney and Lacey team (Meg Foster and Tyne Daly) discusses a case on a park bench in a scene from "Bang, Bang, You're Dead," also referred to as "You Call This Plain Clothes?" (© Orion TV, 1982)

programs'] chances." The head-to-head competition, without a doubt, proved costly for both series in terms of ratings.[30]

Of the thirty-five press reviews I read on *Cagney and Lacey*'s premiere, most were favorable or had some good things to say. Most mentioned the feminist elements in the script: the "chauvinism" of the male detectives, Mary Beth and Harvey's role reversals, and working women's "juggling" of both personal lives and careers. "Tyne Daly," said one article, "is Mary Beth Lacey, wife, mother and breadwinner who juggles a tough career along with her family responsibilities. . . . Meg Foster is Chris Cagney, a single, attractive and ambitious policewoman who takes 'dead aim' on criminals and department chauvinists alike." Several qualified their support with comments such as "the show's message of female discrimination is too obvious and heavy-handed" and "the not-too-subtle message here is that women have to be twice as good to look equal with a man—a topic which could be the Achilles' heel of the series if pounded home too strongly." Many also pointed out the difference between Cagney and Lacey and other female television characters. Phrases like "no racy 'Charlie's

Angels' style glamour here," "mature women, not girls or sex objects," "not clothes horses à la Angie Dickinson," and "realistic crimebusting from the female perspective minus the giggle and jiggle," were common.[31]

Other pieces commented brazenly on the women's bodies, appraising them with regard to conventional television notions of glamour. "Ms. Daly," one of them claimed, "has a plain face, a schlumpy figure, a thick Eastern accent. She's not sexy on the outside. . . . Meg Foster is the better looking but far more of a tomboy than a sex symbol." Another noted, "While Foster and Daly are attractive, they look and act ordinary enough to be believable. . . . They are even occasionally permitted to look rumpled, discouraged, crabby." And another, "Past shows have had one token woman—with the exception of 'Charlie's Angels,' which featured a team of Wonder Women dressed and coifed from Rodeo Drive rather than DC Comics. Cagney and Lacey, on the other hand, are cops. They look like real people. They are cute rather than beautiful."[32]

For the next full year, such running commentary on the appearances of the two characters was standard in many press pieces. The practice demonstrates several things: First, the critics perceived a difference between Cagney and Lacey and other television depictions of women on the level of their bodies. This difference was, of course, produced through the televisual technique of mise-en-scène and related to the characters' sizes, shapes, hairstyles, makeup, clothing, gestures, and mannerisms.[33] However, the critical commentary also demonstrates a tendency to limit the perception of that difference to physical characteristics. By focusing on the actresses' bodies, the critics reproduced a traditional way of assessing the value of women, and this worked (in many instances despite the critics' apparent intentions) to contain the difference set into play by Cagney and Lacey. The phenomenon illustrates how difficult it is for females to escape being "pinned to" their biological difference or to get beyond the conventional equation of women with sex or sex object. It also demonstrates the presumed access to women's bodies, and the license to discuss and evaluate them, that television, film, and photographic images have helped to routinize.

Many reviews stressed the rapport between the two actresses and the friendship between two women characters. "It is the natural charisma which exists between Daly and Foster," read one, "which makes Cagney and Lacey a step above the norm. It is this caring for each other that allows the viewer to care for them." Another critic wrote, somewhat prophetically, "The two women are human beings, not just women, and as Simone de Beauvoir wrote, whenever women start acting like human beings they are accused of trying to be men."[34]

Despite the favorable press, and without much consideration for the fact that its program was pitted against *9 to 5*, which attracted the same audience, CBS wanted to cancel *Cagney and Lacey* after just two installments. The network did not, in fact, allocate any advertising money to promote the third episode in *TV Guide* (*9 to 5* had a half-page ad). There is no doubt that the first few episodes of *Cagney and Lacey* were a ratings disappointment to the network and failed to hold on to the large lead-in audience attracted by *Magnum, P.I.*, the program that immediately preceded it. But the high share garnered by the made-for-TV movie/pilot and the series's competition from *9 to 5* would normally have indicated a schedule change rather than cancellation as the networks' first strategy.[35]

The program's history suggests several reasons behind the push to cancel rather than to rearrange the series's position in the weekly lineup. The first involves the original ambivalence of executives in CBS's series development division. According to Rosenzweig, some were reluctant to support *Cagney and Lacey* as a weekly program from the beginning. "The thing you have to realize about *Cagney and Lacey*," he said, "is that it was not developed as a series, but as a movie for CBS. At CBS, there are series executives and there are movie executives. And not only do they not talk to each other in the hallways, they're in different buildings. Now remember that the series's people had all turned it down the first time around—it was developed by the movie people. So there was a whole group of executives at CBS who didn't want *Cagney and Lacey* to succeed." However, in another interview Rosenzweig said, "There were also people [at series development] who believed in it for a series."[36]

The show would have halted abruptly had not Rosenzweig persuaded Harvey Shephard, vice-president in charge of programming for CBS, to give *Cagney and Lacey* a *Trapper John, M.D.* rerun spot on Sunday, 25 April, at 10:00 P.M. Rosenzweig argued that *Cagney and Lacey* was an adult program requiring a time slot later than 9:00 P.M. Shephard reluctantly agreed but once again voiced CBS's ambivalence by telling Rosenzweig to "save his money" when Rosenzweig revealed that Filmways planned to spend $25,000 on new publicity for the show.[37]

Filmways took the financial risk anyway, sending Foster and Daly on a cross-country tour. In a week-long campaign organized by the Brocato and Kelman public relations company, Daly and Foster traveled to major urban areas and gave approximately fifty radio, television, and print interviews; included on the schedule was a Washington, D.C., television talk show interview with Tyne Daly and Betty Friedan "on the topic of women's rights."[38]

The 25 April episode of *Cagney and Lacey* pulled an impressive 34 share and ranked number seven in the overall ratings for that week. Despite that success, Harvey Shephard told Rosenzweig that many members of the CBS board (which was responsible for final renewal decisions) would consider the 34 share "a fluke." He said he would fight for the series's renewal only if Rosenzweig made a significant change in the program. The change was to replace Meg Foster as Cagney.[39]

At this point, other aspects of the network's dubiety began to surface. They were directly related to notions of femininity generated by the program and seem to be the most salient factors in CBS's hesitation. In a *Daily Variety* article dated 25 May 1982 and a *Hollywood Reporter* article from 28 May, Harvey Shephard spoke publicly about Foster's replacement. He was quoted in both articles as saying that "several mistakes were made with the show in that the stories were too gritty, the characterizations of both Cagney and Lacey were too tough and there was not enough contrast between these two partners." Several weeks after Shephard's statements appeared, an article in *TV Guide* revealed still other reasons for CBS's ambivalence and its decision to replace Foster. According to critic Frank Swertlow, *Cagney and Lacey* was to be "softened" because the network believed the main characters were "too tough, too hard and not feminine." The article quoted an unnamed CBS programmer who said the show was being revised to make the characters "less aggressive." "They were too harshly women's lib," he continued. "These women on 'Cagney and Lacey' seemed more intent on fighting the system than doing police work. We perceived them as dykes."[40]

There are undoubtedly many dimensions to this incident, but I will focus on only two here. The first is the presence, from the beginning of the series, of discourses that either associated Meg Foster with lesbianism or implied a lesbian overtone to the relationship between Cagney and Lacey. The second is CBS's claims that audience research indicated that viewers perceived the characters as "tough" and "masculine."

In the weeks surrounding the premiere of the series, there were straightforward references in the press to Meg Foster's earlier portrayal of a lesbian in the film *A Different Story*. Foster was, perhaps provocatively, quoted in an article in *US* magazine as saying, "I played a lesbian; it was my favorite role." Barbara Avedon recalled an event that occurred after Meg Foster's reading for the Chris Cagney part. According to Avedon, after a "brilliant" reading by Foster that "stood out head and shoulders above all the others," Avedon said to the assembled group, "She's my choice." An executive in casting, Avedon continued, "walked me out of the room with the other executives and said, 'She's trouble, she's a dyke, she can't carry a series.'" The executive, says Avedon, "was really a detractor from the beginning."[41]

In addition, Tyne Daly, in an article by Jane Ardmore, discussed what she called the "fear" that surrounded the concept of *Cagney and Lacey*. "We are," she said, "playing two women in what are customarily thought of as men's jobs; that's where the fear comes in." Ardmore continued, "Her [Tyne Daly's] first glimpse of fear occurred on the first episode of the series in which the two cops dressed up like hookers to go out on the street and apprehend solicitors. While they were dressing for the assignment, Chris Cagney came over and helped her partner with the clasp of her necklace. Somebody on the set said it looked 'seamy.' . . . She [Daly] and Meg were interviewed for *Entertainment Tonight*. . . . The first question was, 'What's all this stuff about a lesbian connection on the show?'" And finally, an article by Sal Manna in the *Los Angeles Herald Examiner*, written after the broadcast of the first three episodes, said, "Because nearly everyone is perplexed at the show's ratings failure, rumors have circulated that viewers were uncomfortable with the friendship of the two women, some even implying lesbianism."[42]

Whatever the connections among the above examples, it seems safe to say that homophobia, outright discrimination (at least on the part of the executive who maintained that the actress was a "dyke"), and associations of the series with lesbianism were operative from the outset. Apparently they gave CBS a way in which to voice its objections to the nonconventional and seemingly threatening depictions of women on the series. This would explain why the network rushed to cancel the program and then to demand Foster's removal as a condition of its reprieve. It would also explain why CBS gave more importance to comments it may have picked up in its audience research than to the conflicting comments from the press reviews quoted earlier.

New and expanded representations of women on TV could not, it seems, include even a hint of lesbianism. This taboo must, of course, be situated within the history of lesbianism's representation on prime time, but a few things are worth noting here. During the quest for "relevance" and socially "hip" subject matter during the 1970s, several programs aired episodes about lesbians, including *All in the Family* and *Medical Center*. Likewise, in the early 1980s, such prime-time programs as *Kate and Allie*,

Hotel, Hill Street Blues, St. Elsewhere, and *The Golden Girls* included lesbianism as a single-episode story line, and the daytime serial *All My Children* featured an ongoing lesbian character for several weeks in 1983. In the late 1980s, *Heartbeat* included as a regular a lesbian character, whose presence was instrumental in the show's cancellation by ABC after protests from religious groups. The main point here is that each of these "liberal" representations of lesbianism, in varying degrees (*Heartbeat* and *All My Children* tried to downplay this facet), underscored the "social problem" aspect of lesbianism and played off the notion of lesbianism as an "aberration."[43] That viewers might interpret the relationship between Cagney and Lacey as having homosexual overtones, or that two strong, recurring women characters might be perceived as "dykes" without the accompanying suggestion that "dykeyness" was a deviation from the norm, was something that CBS (at least in the early 1980s, on its prime-time schedule) simply would not chance. Such a characterization stretched the limits of difference regarding the representation of women well beyond the boundaries of TV's permissible zone.

The network's official explanation of Meg Foster's removal was that audience research had revealed objections to the characters. According to Arnold Becker, chief of research for CBS, a sample of 160 audience members had yielded comments about the women protagonists like "inordinately abrasive, loud and lacking warmth" and "they should be given a measure of traditional female appeal, especially Chris." But Becker also included his own personal opinion about the characters: "Even in the first show," he said, "when they [Cagney and Lacey] dressed like hookers, they weren't sexy looking—they were sort of like burlesque. . . . There's a certain amount of resistance to women being in male-oriented jobs. I think it's fair to say, in light of what has happened to ERA, that most people favor equal pay for equal work, but not women as truck drivers or ditch diggers or that sort of male work." He added that the allusion "to homosexuality" in *TV Guide* was "quite unfair." "Those tested," he said, "thought of Cagney and Lacey as masculine, not that they were lovers." It is also possible, of course, that the research survey inadvertently elicited particular responses from the viewers tested.[44]

The differential treatment given to the characters and the actresses during this incident underscores some of the specific dimensions of the network's anxiety. The *TV Guide* article said the married character played by Tyne Daly was being kept because CBS considered her "less threatening." The original Chris Cagney's nonglamorous, feminist, sexually active image and her working-class, single status manifested too many "non-feminine" markers, according to the network's definition of femininity. Cagney had no acceptable class, family, or marriage contexts that could contain, domesticate, or nullify those threatening differences.

The changes in the series and the firing of Meg Foster generated heated debates in the press and viewer letters over what constituted appropriate "femininity" (and "masculinity"). These debates referred to many aspects of the mise-en-scène: the characters' clothing, hairstyles, facial mannerisms, and the use of props such as cigarettes. They furthermore consistently referred to femininity and women's bodies as they appeared in the social world beyond the domain of the TV characters.

Howard Rosenberg of the *Los Angeles Times* began a satiric column on the issues raised by the incident with the questions, "What is feminine? What is masculine? What is CBS doing?" He then asked, "Are the old Cagney and Lacey too strident? Even too masculine? For the definitive answer," he continued, "I contacted Detective Helen Kidder and Detective Peggy York, partners in the Los Angeles Police Department." He quoted Kidder as saying, " 'I watched the show once and I was so turned off. They looked rough and tough, and they weren't terribly feminine, just in the way they dressed and acted. They were so, you know, New York. . . . Peggy and I wear good suits, nylons and pretty shoes, silk blouses, the hair, everything. Not that that keeps you from being a dyke.' " Rosenberg concluded with his own analysis of the characters:

> Although Cagney is the character to be softened, Lacey seemed to be far the toughest of the two. . . . Many of the symbols were conflicting, however. Cagney frequently spoke admiringly of men, which was good, but wore slacks more than Lacey did, which was suspicious. Yet, Cagney had pink bed sheets and longer and curlier hair than Lacey. . . . In Lacey's favor, there was a scene in which she sank amorously into bed with Hawvey [*sic*] and another in which she cooked breakfast for the family. Good signs. Yet she also dangled a cigarette from her mouth like Bogie. Cagney always drove, and Lacey didn't which could mean something. But Lacey talked without moving her mouth. Lacey convinced me, however, when she took off her skirt in one sequence, she was wearing a slip, not boxer shorts.[45]

Rosenberg's column was just one of many following the removal of Meg Foster, and numerous women reporters vented their outrage. Sharon Rosenthal of the *New York Daily News* wrote, "Not feminine enough? By whose standards? I wondered. Wasn't the whole point of the show to portray women on television in a new, more enlightened manner?" And

Barbara Holsopple of the *Pittsburgh Press*, writing about what the network wanted for the series, quipped, "Not tough cops, mind you. Nice feminine, good ones. Those yo-yos at the network were second-guessing us again."[46]

As Howard Rosenberg's interview with the two Los Angeles policewomen indicates, it is plausible and even predictable that a segment of viewers would find Cagney and Lacey problematic, some for the specific reasons mentioned by the network. The dominant viewer reaction in the letters I have seen, however, was critical of CBS; *TV Guide* also printed a series of angry responses to Foster's dismissal.[47]

Letters to CBS, to Orion Television, and to Rosenzweig's office fervently defended Foster and the series. "The program *Cagney and Lacey*," said one, "is being ruined. I have thoroughly enjoyed it: the actresses had good chemistry and I enjoyed seeing a tough female." Another read, "With Cagney and Lacey, Meg and Tyne, we at least have a program that shows two women doing a hard job, but we also see an honest and warm friendship. Their chemistry is just right. We can see they care for each other, there isn't much about a good friendship between women on TV. . . . It's nice to see two women enjoying this kind of relationship." And another, "I read in last week's *TV Guide* something about replacing Meg Foster for such reasons as she is too threatening? I don't understand where TV executives come up with such craziness. I get the feeling there's a card game at the Hillcrest Country Club called 'Let's go with the path of least resistance when it comes to women on TV.' There seems to be a NEED for all women TV stars to be a carbon copy of Cheryl Ladd. Where's the female Al Pacino? Where is the female Bobby de Niro?" Still another said, "Foster and Daly did a marvelous job of portraying strong, confident women living through some trying and testing circumstances. Too strong? Too aggressive? Come on! They are cops in the city. They aren't supposed to be fragile, delicate wimps." And a final one from England: "The excuse that Cagney and Lacey are too butch is pathetic. A policewoman in America let alone Britain not butch enough wouldn't last in the public streets."[48]

Two months after the removal of Foster, CBS may have, in the words of one reviewer, "shuddered a little" when a previously unaired Meg Foster/Tyne Daly episode, broadcast on 21 June, scored a 38 share and ranked number 2 in the week's overall ratings. However, the network continued to manifest its caution and discomfort with potentially controversial portrayals of women when it pulled the other new Foster/Daly episode (scheduled for 28 June) a few hours before air time. The network said it had received phone calls and letters protesting the episode, which was about a Phyllis

Schlafly–type anti-ERA spokeswoman whom Cagney and Lacey were assigned to protect. Even though the attempt to add the Equal Rights Amendment to the Constitution had already failed, CBS decided to avoid controversy by yanking the episode and airing it later in August. The network, furthermore, had asked Rosenzweig not to invite Gloria Steinem to appear on the show, as he had originally intended. Steinem, due to an overcrowded schedule, had already declined. In the *TV Guide* advertisements for these summer episodes, a considerable "feminization" of the images of Daly and Foster was evident, especially when compared to previous *TV Guide* advertisements for the show; longer hair, earrings, makeup, and more "feminine" clothing were prominent for both characters.[49]

BRINGING WOMEN BACK IN LINE

CBS's ultimate decision on *Cagney and Lacey* was that the series should be revised to "combine competency with an element of sensuality." Its solution was twofold: replace Meg Foster with someone more "feminine" and change Chris Cagney's socioeconomic background. Sharon Gless, whom one reviewer described as "blond, single, [and] gorgeous in the imposing manner of Linda Evans on *Dynasty*," was hired to replace Foster. The Gay Media Task Force, in light of allegations that the original characters were "too masculine," protested the replacement, saying that Gless's acting was "very kittenish and feminine."[50]

Instead of being from the working class, Cagney would now have been raised by a wealthy mother and grandmother in Westchester. Her father, a retired New York City policeman who had already been featured in the series, would be the divorced husband of that mother, and the marriage presented as a cross-class mistake. A new CBS press kit was issued to publicize the series in a different way. "Cagney and Lacey," it read, "are two cops who have earned the respect of their male counterparts and at no expense to their femininity." Furthermore, Cagney underwent a radical fashion change to accompany her class transformation. A network memo stated that "the new budget will include an additional $15,000 for wardrobe costs, the revised concept for character calls for Cagney to wear less middle class, classier clothes so that her upward mobility is evidenced." This revision must also be seen in relation to the history of television's skewed representation of class and to the advertising industry's decision, at this time, to target the upscale professional segment of the working women's market (discussed in Chapter 2).[51]

The new Chris Cagney was more of a rugged individualist than a femi-

Meg Foster and Tyne Daly in the original opening credits for the TV series.
(© Orion TV, 1982)

nist and was actually conservative on many social issues. Lacey more often espoused feminist positions and liberal politics. A CBS promo for the 1982–83 season made these new differences between the characters explicit and also foregrounded Cagney's heterosexuality. The promo began:

> *Mary Beth*: Ya know Chris, there've been some great women in the twentieth century.
> *Chris*: Yeah! And some great men. (dreamily)
> *Mary Beth*: Susan B. Anthony!
> *Chris*: Jim Palmer!
> *Mary Beth*: Madame Curie.
> *Chris*: Joe Montana . . . ooo, can he make a pass!
> *Mary Beth*: (lightly annoyed with Chris) Amelia Airhart! [*sic*]
> *Chris*: The New York Yankees!
> *Mary Beth*: Chris, can't you think about anything else than men?[52]

A comparison of the opening credit sequences for the Foster/Daly and Gless/Daly series also underscores the changes. The original opening featured the protagonists, in police uniforms, running through streets, down dark alleys, and up and down stairways and culminated with them standing—weapons drawn and arms outstretched—in the "freeze, police" position. The soundtrack was a sardonic jazz vocal called "Ain't That the Way."

Tyne Daly and Sharon Gless in the opening credits for the revised and recast series.
(© Orion TV, 1982–88)

The opening for the Gless/Daly series, by contrast, included whimsical scenes of Cagney and Lacey in plainclothes. They did chase a suspect down into the subway and apprehend him, but they also window-shopped and got "flashed" by a man in a trenchcoat. Cagney additionally jogged and bought a hot dog from a sidewalk vendor while Lacey, leaning up against the squad car, waited for her; they "toasted" each other with their coffee mugs and attempted to leave work for the day—Lacey in a bowling shirt and Cagney in a fur. The soundtrack was an upbeat, playful, instrumental melody.

THE STRUGGLE OVER FEMININITY: THE PRESS AND THE VIEWERS

The new and revised series starring Sharon Gless and Tyne Daly began its run in the fall of 1982 and generated a good deal of attention and enthusiasm in the press. The program's revisions make most sense when viewed in the context of the overall shifts in new television shows directed toward working women and drawing on feminism, and in the context of the general social and political backlash against the women's movements. During this period, as we will see in Chapter 4, many other burgeoning feminist-oriented programs also had their political edges completely blunted.

The mainstream press, in commenting on the Gless/Daly *Cagney and Lacey*, focused on the "changes" from the previous season. Many critics noted the general "softening" and "feminization" of the program. For example, one noticed that "the entire show this season appears less gritty than last year's style," and another remarked, "Some of the rougher, tougher edges are gone." Others discussed the diminution of the series's feminism: "The old CAGNEY AND LACEY coughed up alot of feminist smoke, heavy-handedly pitting its two female heroines against their male detective counterparts in a way that blurred the dramatic focus. . . . The clubbing approach of last season is gone. . . . Tonight's good-looking production depends largely on nuance."[53]

But the *Los Angeles Herald Examiner*'s Frank Torrez, who thought that the last two episodes of the Foster/Daly series had already deviated significantly from the first shows, disagreed with these assessments of the "new" changes and challenged the whole practice of network interference. Among other things, his comments demonstrate the many variations in viewer interpretations and analyses:

> This episode has virtually no 'feminist' dialogue in it, nor does it go out of its way to make the leads more feminine. . . . The whole idea of networks tampering with series after they're on the air rarely serves viewer interests. . . . 'Cagney and Lacey' has gone from stereotyped cops and robbers to being one of the better series on television. But it made that transition well before CBS executives fiddled with it. Fortunately, it has been able to maintain its quality level and integrity despite the interference.[54]

A large number of articles responding to Foster's replacement by Gless read like a semiotic register of the word *feminine*, and they serve (not always intentionally) to problematize its various meanings. Many singled out specific elements such as clothing, hairstyles, makeup, personality traits and behaviors, vocal qualities, and body movements as evidence for the presence or absence of femininity, although some also wrote of the nonconventional, potentially problematic character of the femininity embodied by Gless's Cagney. According to Gail Williams of the *Hollywood Reporter*, "If the series' executives wanted a 'softer' single woman costar, Gless could be a disappointment. She may be ultrafeminine in appearance, but Gless doesn't stint when it comes to evincing the appropriate toughness her part of an effective detective demands."[55]

Carol Wyman of the *New Haven Register* said of Gless's Cagney, "She's one of those people who is very pretty, and at the same time a jock, the kind of person who ruins her good stockings to chase a crook, talks loud when she gets drunk and gets impatient with a woman witness who cries too much." And Sharon Rosenthal of the *New York Daily News* wrote that Gless was "at a loss to explain all the fuss about predecessor Meg Foster's alleged 'lack of femininity,' saying only that she certainly wasn't about to start 'wearing lace' in an effort to appease CBS executives. Her costume? Sure enough: mannish trousers, a bulky sweater and a short suede jacket left rakishly unzipped."[56]

Contradictory interpretations of the new Cagney's femininity were, however, plentiful. "Not only is Chris Cagney now blessed with thick eyelashes and soft blond hair," read one article. "She dresses in clingy sweaters and silky blouses. That's not to say that she overdoes the feminine thing. She's just a more attractive, feminine character. Cagney's personality has changed too. She's not as tough as she used to be. She even cried in the last episode." And in a piece entitled "CBS Softens Show to Toughen Ratings," Candy Justice wrote of the "softening" not only of Cagney but also of Lacey: "Aside from changes in Cagney, Lacey also has changed some over the summer. Tyne Daly last year talked with a thick Brooklyn accent, wore her hair *very* short and wore little makeup. This year her hair is a little longer, with some soft curls to feminize her looks. Earrings and a bit more makeup have been added, and the Brooklynese has been toned down considerably. Now we'll have to wait and see if the feminine 'Cagney and Lacey' does better in the Nielsen ratings than the tomboy version."[57]

An article in the *Bryan (Texas) Eagle*, based on a mistaken version of the events leading to Foster's replacement by Gless (or written with an extremely dry sense of humor), provides a strong example of how a viewer's interpretation may be influenced by information that guides her or him to emphasize particular items in a program and deemphasize others. In this instance it reveals how assessments of femininity were derived not only from conventional markers of the feminine, but also from what the viewer believed to be public consensus on one actress as "too feminine" and the other as the countermeasure to that excess. "Meg Foster," the piece read, "a green-eyed beauty with exotic looks, was tabbed for Cagney when the series entered the schedule for a limited run last spring. But the producers felt that Foster was 'too feminine' for the role. Out with Foster, in with . . . Sharon Gless. Gless's hoarse voice and strong walk make her a natural as an authority figure. In fact, she once played a man in a woman's body [in the series *Turnabout*]."[58]

Sharon Gless as the new Cagney.
(Cagney and Lacey © *Orion Pictures Corp., 1988, all rights reserved)*

Gless herself, in most press interviews at the time and later, attempted to move the discussion away from comparisons between her femininity and Meg Foster's and from the "feminization" of Cagney. In one interview, playing explicitly on the language involved, she said, "The press has come to me and asked, 'Are you going to make the show more feminine?' And my flat answer is, 'NO, the show is feminine—it's about two women.'"[59]

Some articles that commented on the "feminization" of the program also noted changes in the relationship between the characters and the innuendo of lesbianism: "Miss Daly's tomboy quality was balanced by the introduction of a partner with more feminine characteristics than her original co-star. . . . This second-season rematch [is] perhaps more compatible with the network's definition of a conventional female relationship . . . [but] who cares if a cop is gay or not as long as he or she shoots *straight*." And, "Cagney and Lacey suddenly became adversaries, instead of buddies. This could be construed as a tactic designed to squelch any gay implications CBS apparently is convinced viewers associate with scenarios in which women work seriously together."[60]

Judging from audience letters, viewers were at first reluctant to accept Gless, but within two months a large and avid fan following began to develop. Two letters from viewers who had been angered by Meg Foster's removal exemplify these feelings: "To be honest with you, when you fired Meg Foster I swore never to watch your show again—but Sharon Gless has proven herself and won back the admiration I had for the show." And, "I thought Meg Foster and Tyne Daly were a great combination, but apparently some 'genius' of the male persuasion, obviously, decided that Meg Foster wasn't 'feminine' enough. My Gawd, should cops wear aprons and be pregnant? Gimme a break! However, *Lady* Luck was with you when you found Sharon Gless. I must admit that you did something right by putting her in the Cagney role. . . . She's extremely feminine with just the right amount of 'butch' to strike a very appealing balance."[61]

An ironic note here—and another strong testament to the operation of multiple and contradictory viewer interpretations or readings—is that according to published articles and viewer letters, Sharon Gless had at the time of the series's first run, and later, a large lesbian audience.[62] And this audience invested the Cagney character with unique meanings by drawing on a variety of nonconventional and nonpredictable strategies for viewing and interpretation. Taken in conjunction with the audience letters protesting the removal of Meg Foster and the press's comments on the appeal of the friendship between Cagney and Lacey, this development demonstrates that the network's investments in particular notions of "femininity" and the investments of at least certain viewers were squarely at odds. The potentially homoerotic overtones in the representations of the two women that formed the basis for the network's discomfort were, in fact, the foundation of particular audience members' pleasure. There was, of course, a continuum of responses, ranging from fans who found pleasure in the fictional representation of a close friendship between two women to those whose viewing strategies purposely highlighted the homoerotic nuances in the relationship.

The initial burst of articles on the "feminization" of the characters and the series was followed by a wide array of feminist-oriented pieces in mainstream newspapers that highlighted the importance of *Cagney and Lacey* to women. These hailed the series as "pioneering the serious role of women on TV" and "helping to break new TV ground." Many of the articles emphasized the notion that Cagney and Lacey, unlike previous TV characters, represented "real women." Elaine Warren's piece in the *Los Angeles Herald Examiner* entitled "Where Are the Real Women on TV?" read, "The single bright promise for women on TV this season is 'Cagney and Lacey' . . . which appears as though it genuinely wants to portray the sensitivity and strength of two women cops—without alot of airbrushed fantasy. The strains and rewards of two women working together give the show its definition." Judy Mann of the *Washington Post* wrote that the series was "a show of contemporary interest that portrays women as human beings . . . the heroines look and talk like real women and they have real working women's ambitions and problems." And Laura Daltry of the *Los Angeles Times* said that *Cagney and Lacey* portrayed an "encouraging partnership of sharp women . . . who hurl crooks up against walls, who keep each other on track, who sometimes disagree and don't speak to each other for days. The Gee-Whiz-women-in-men's-jobs! self-consciousness is delightfully absent. Rather, the series succeeds in something rare and wondrous: bringing a genuine women's sensibility to a rough job. They even shop for clothes on their lunch hour."[63]

Articles that stressed the difference between *Cagney and Lacey* and other TV representations of women and that continued the trend of commentary on the bodies of the characters/actresses and women's bodies in general were also prevalent during this period. Although not greatly different in kind from some of the earlier articles written about the Tyne Daly/Meg Foster series, this new crop was different in degree. They forcefully demonstrate a phenomenon in which cultural stereotypes, especially conventional television stereotypes, seem to work against women—certainly against the women who play the stereotypical roles, but also against women at large.

References to "sit-com bozos," "clowns," "buffoons," "busty bimbos," women who "jiggle" and "bounce," "sexpots," "dumb blonds," and "bitches" appear frequently and are used in offhand ways, apparently to make a graphic or colorful comparison with conventional television depictions or to provide humor. The fact that these phrases are used by supporters of *Cagney and Lacey* in touting the series's perceived advances over other TV representations dramatically foregrounds how naturally and unconsciously we equate woman with the body and how common it is to evaluate women's bodies and the stock behaviors of particular women's roles with impunity.

Most of the press reviews and articles on the Gless/Daly *Cagney and Lacey* were favorable and supportive, but a few were critical. One in the *Evansville (Indiana) Press* exemplified the social ramifications of TV's stereotypical depictions and definitions of women and spoke from a solid investment in those definitions. Written by Larry Wood, a seventeen-year-old, it dealt overtly with some of the effects of television's combination of feminism and "jiggle," and it negotiated discourses of the women's movement, traditional conceptions of femininity, and mid-1970s definitions of women as TV sex objects: "It's tough, let me tell you," began Wood,

> to be seventeen in the new world of feminism. Not so much when opening doors or addressing letters. More when watching a blonde in a tight skirt get into a car. After watching "Cagney and Lacey," the new series about policewomen, I've come to two conclusions: Feminism's fine. But there's something nicer about pretty feminists. . . . In the several years television has been promoting working women it's always concentrated on attractive women—women who looked like models but played lawyers instead. Angie Dickinson, television's first policewoman, was sexy, even flaunted it. . . . My style of chauvinism is not pretty, but maybe it explains why as fine a show as "Cagney and Lacey" can leave one unfulfilled.[64]

Such reviews notwithstanding, the first Gless/Daly season was met with widespread accolades. But despite the positive press, the series did not do well in the overall ratings and did only marginally well with a women-only target audience. (Its competition during much of the season was female-oriented prime-time movies). Consequently, CBS put the series on its cancellation list. In an effort to save it, Barney Rosenzweig coordinated a large letter-writing campaign in which the network and major newspapers throughout the country were deluged with thousands of viewer letters protesting the impending axe. The National Organization for Women and the Los Angeles chapter of NOW publicized the letter-writing campaign and urged their members to write. The Los Angeles chapter, according to state delegate Jerilyn Stapleton, had only two goals for the period: to get Ronald Reagan out of office and to keep *Cagney and Lacey* on the prime-time schedule.[65]

Virtually all the viewer letters from this outpouring mentioned the uniqueness of *Cagney and Lacey*'s women and the relationship between them. The writers repeatedly suggested that the protagonists were good role models for women and girls; that they were unique because they were "real" and "different" from all previous TV women; and that they were extremely important to the individual writer, the writer's friends and family, and the culture at large. Most fans related the series's depictions of women to their own everyday lives, often placing themselves in a particular social situation and at a particular point on the "feminism spectrum." Phrases such as "I'm a thirty-three-year-old nursing administrator," a "single working mother," a "married woman and mother who works inside the home," and "a feminist," or "not a women's libber—just a concerned woman," were common. Many of the letters echoed discourses of the liberal women's movement and demonstrated the workings of an "interpretive community" or a "community of heightened consciousness," as described in the work of such feminist scholars as Elizabeth Ellsworth and Jacqueline Bobo.[66] They also illustrated the many specific ways in which women fans were reconfiguring and redefining their notions of what it meant to be a woman.

Repeatedly, the writers said such things as, "It's good to see smart, functioning, strong women"; "It's a pleasure to see women in such active roles"; "It's one of the few programs that neither glamorizes nor degrades women"; and "At last women are being portrayed as three-dimensional human beings."[67] Long letters describing the particular significance of the series to the writers were plentiful. Wrote one viewer,

It's the only show on television I feel I can relate to. While I'm not a police detective, I do work in a high-pressure, fast-paced, male-oriented field. I am a twenty-six year old single woman, and a broker for a major Wall Street firm. I have worked on an institutional trading floor for the past few years, and I feel I've experienced the same kind of camaraderie AND conflict that I see between the characters on "Cagney and Lacey." . . . I think it's extremely important that "Cagney and Lacey" be given every fair chance to really succeed. It's a new concept in television and it may take some time for the audience to adjust to it. I believe "Cagney and Lacey" holds an especially important message for our youth on the changing role of women in our society.

Another wrote:

> My office alone contains six technical editors, RABID fans of "Cagney and Lacey." We're all highly paid, well-educated women in our forties with very different life-styles. Since we are "specialists" and work very closely with each other, each of us regards the others as "extended family," and we nurture and support each other in the best ways possible. We enjoy "Cagney and Lacey" because it contains so many moments that ring familiar in a woman's daily life. We see ourselves in it so often, even though OUR jobs are unbelievably unexciting. It's gotten so that Tuesday mornings are spent hashing over Monday night's episode. We're really addicted.

A letter that related TV's depictions of women to the possibilities for actual historical women read, "It's such an exciting show from a woman's point of view. Watching those two women makes one realize how much more attractive we are as women when we dare to be all our possible dimensions rather than the stereotypical images we have been taught to be and continually see on the screen. You have affected some of us profoundly."

The relationship between the two actresses and their characters and its effect on the viewers were discussed with equal enthusiasm. Tyne Daly and Sharon Gless were described as a "superb combination," a "winning team" who "together have great charisma" and "natural and genuine chemistry." "The vivid interaction of Chris and Mary Beth," wrote one viewer, "has actually made honest female relationships into major dramatic entertainment." Another claimed, "In the final analysis, it was the friendship between the two lead characters wherein lay the show's strongest appeal for me." One of the many male viewers who also protested the show's cancellation wrote, "I will miss watching the friendship between the title characters. Their arguments often evoked some in-depth soul-searching on my part. No other series has ever handled human relationships better."

Viewer delight in the series often stemmed from powerful identification with the characters. Said one fan, "People really do need their heroes and heroines." "To do away with Cagney and Lacey," continued another, "is an affront to our pleasure." Many writers spoke in detail of their strong connections to the protagonists: "I cannot remember EVER becoming so fond of continuing characters that I actually looked forward to being warmed by them week after week. In fact this show ruined all other viewing for me. It became my yardstick. Nothing else measures up. And I doubt that anything ever will."

The main factor in this sense of identification, for a great number of fans, appeared to be their perception that the characters were "down to earth," "normal," or more "real" than all previous TV depictions. One letter read, "An overdose of gloss and dazzle bores me as a viewer. It's as though I'm being forced to watch a party and knowing I wasn't invited, that I'm not a part of it. It's no fun to observe all the time. . . . Being able to see a little of myself in the women you portray is a nice thing for me—it's like having friends with whom there is empathy, and that's what I enjoy, that sense of involvement." Many others said such things as, "I feel like they are my friends, like they are people I know."

Tyne Daly's Mary Beth Lacey was often written of as the most "honest," "refreshing," "natural," "real," "believable," and "likable" woman character in television history. One viewer described her as "someone whose pain and frustration and warmth I feel and share." Lacey's relationship with her husband Harvey was described as the "best portrayal of a marriage I have ever seen."

Sharon Gless's Christine Cagney was repeatedly acknowledged as an unprecedented "role model." And her presentation as a single working woman—by choice and not by default—was specifically mentioned: "Chris," said one writer, "is a role model. She is single and fulfilled by that life style. Most single women in film and TV are seen as losers, incomplete, dependent or lacking somehow. 'Chris' is autonomous and knows where she is going." "Her character," said another, "is one of an assertive single woman who really enjoys her career. It's about time there was a television program which portrays women in this role."

Preteen and teenage girls, and a few boys also, wrote of their own identifications with the characters. Some girls described being completely caught up in the fiction: "My life is part of you. It's like I've known you for many years. You guys mean so much in my life. My hairdo I get done like Lacey's but the length of Cagney's. . . . My friend and I renovated part of my room into a detective's office—typewriter, maps, telephone, recorder etc. We went on strike. . . . We refused to eat supper unless my friend's mother called us Detectives Cagney and Lacey."

Despite the volume of viewer mail, and despite the fact that this mail came primarily from the desired target audience (upscale working women between the ages of eighteen and fifty-four), the program was canceled in the spring of 1983. After the cancellation, a widely syndicated column by Gary Deeb vitriolically attacked the series and its women on the very grounds for which most reviewers and fans had praised them, thereby touching off a letter-writing battle of its own. The program, according to Deeb, was a far cry from being "feminist" or important to women:

Here's a terrific quote: "I fear for the future of quality work for women in TV." Now what noble and talented human being could possibly have made that thoughtful statement? Why, it's none other than Sharon Gless, the co-star of "Cagney and Lacey," the horrible CBS female cop series that finally got put to sleep this month. Gless actually believes that "Cagney and Lacey" was a first rate, realistic drama, and that its cancellation spells doom for women-oriented programming on all three networks. What a crock. "Cagney and Lacey" was a piece of filth that more often than not exploited females and featured thoroughly implausible stories. Furthermore, the stars, Gless and Tyne Daly, were two of the phoniest and unappealing actresses on the tube. Good riddance to them and their program. And just as patriotism is the last refuge of a scoundrel, so is the embracing of the female flag the final argument to be used by a fraudulently feminist program that never could ingratiate itself into the consciousness of women viewers.[68]

In a fiery demonstration of the struggle over meanings, viewers responded to the newspapers in which "Deeb's Diatribe," as one paper called it, was printed.[69] One exemplary retort, lambasting Deeb's "feminism" and invoking that of the liberal women's movement, read:

I feel strongly that the vituperative tone of Gary Deeb's critique of "Cagney and Lacey" was uncalled for and unjust. I deplore the implied obscenities in his overemotional response to Sharon Gless's comment about the future of women role models on TV. She offered her point of view and does not deserve to have her show called "filth" as a result, nor to have her feminism labeled fraudulent. Perhaps he ought to keep his fantasies of what feminists think to himself until he stops trying to excuse his behavior by his "ingratiating" consciousness. Contrary to Mr. Deeb's point of view, the national NOW newsletter has found "Cagney and Lacey's" presentation of real dilemmas a refreshing, down-to-earth contrast to the polished purposelessness of women in most other shows.[70]

The exact reasons why Deeb found the series "fraudulently feminist" are not totally clear; the "exploitation of females" is one reason that I will examine closely in Chapter 3. But the fury of Deeb's attack is somewhat perplexing and his own "feminist" position difficult to assess.

In the midst of this controversy and public debate, several factors caused CBS to reverse its decision and bring the series back to life. First, the audience letters continued to come in. Second, after cancellation *Cagney and*

Lacey received four Emmy nominations, and Tyne Daly won an Emmy as best dramatic actress. Third, *Cagney and Lacey* scored number one in the ratings for the first week of summer reruns and remained in the top ten throughout the rest of the season. Nonetheless, CBS hedged its bets by reinstating the series with a very limited seven-episode trial run.

THE STRUGGLE GOES ON: THE PRODUCTION TEAM, THE NETWORK, INTEREST GROUPS, TV NEWS, AND THE TABLOID PRESS

Several important trends were evident in the period of *Cagney and Lacey's* history that began with the reinstated Gless/Daly series in the spring of 1984. First, television's portrayal of feminism, limited as it already was, underwent "mainstreaming." In other words, the strength of feminist views was severely diluted (as we will see in more detail in Chapter 4). This resulted in an increasing ambiguity about the meaning of feminism itself and programming that offered "something for everyone," depending on particular viewers' political positions and interpretations. Terry Louise Fisher (a producer/writer for *Cagney and Lacey* and cocreator of *L.A. Law*) described this as a shift from "political" issues to "entertainment value." During this period, some of the key players from the *Cagney and Lacey* production team, particularly Barney Rosenzweig, began to think more in conventional "network" terms and less in women's movement terms when it came to portraying the characters. This move sparked disputes among the production team over the women detectives' hairstyles, makeup, and clothing.[71]

Determined to assure the series's renewal beyond the limited seven episodes, Rosenzweig called for a general upgrading of the styles and "looks" of the two characters. He wanted a renovation of the Cagney look to include more "stylish, glamorous" outfits and a new hairstyle that would "move" and "bounce." Sharon Gless, reluctant to make her character "too frilly" and concerned about not being able to fix her own hair (she would have to arrive on the set a couple of hours early to have it done the new way), objected at first but finally conceded to the new coif. "You can have my hair for seven weeks," she told Rosenzweig, "but after that it's my own."[72]

For several months, Rosenzweig had wanted to change Lacey's overall appearance. Tyne Daly, who had designed the Mary Beth Lacey look by shopping with wardrobe designer Judy Sabel in the "sale" and "basement" sections of New York department stores, continually refused, however, to change the character's plain yet eccentric dress. Rosenzweig and Daly also disagreed over issues of makeup. These disagreements actually went back several months to an episode called "Burnout," in which Lacey has a breakdown and disappears for a day and a night. Because her character was supposed to have stayed up all night on the beach, Tyne Daly arrived on the set looking, according to Rosenzweig, "like death." He insisted that she go to makeup, she refused, and finally they compromised: she went to makeup but wore very little. "Burnout," interestingly enough, was the episode for which Tyne Daly won her first Emmy, and about which a woman journalist wrote, "Mary Beth was suffering from burnout and went AWOL. . . . She forgot to wear makeup. . . . She looked truly like a woman in trouble. A wife from *Dallas* would have perched on one of those sand dunes like someone in a Club Med travel poster."[73]

Battles over Lacey's hairdo were also frequent occurrences on the set. Rosenzweig would ask Daly's hairdresser to get to her between takes and tease and spray her hair. During one such incident, Daly shouted to the crew and staff, "Can anyone tell me why my producer wants me to look like Pat Nixon?" Furthermore, Rosenzweig and Daly had confrontations about Daly's weight, with Rosenzweig suggesting she be careful about putting on pounds and Daly incorporating whatever weight fluctuations she might have into her conception of the character.[74]

During this period, there were also negotiations and struggles at the level of script development. An episode involving Cagney's pregnancy scare (the last of the seven trial episodes, aired in May 1984) provides a powerful example. The script negotiations revolved around how to represent an unmarried woman's pregnancy, the whole issue of working women and childbearing, and the issues of contraception and abortion. A synopsis from my personal observations and notes gathered during February and March 1984 reveals some of the actual processes involved in the debates.

As conceived by Terry Louise Fisher, the story originally dealt with Cagney's discovery that she is pregnant. Fisher had struggled with how to resolve the pregnancy. Knowing that the network would never allow abortion as a possibility for Cagney, Fisher self-censored that consideration but was less than satisfied with resorting to the clichéd miscarriage route. After working on the script, however, she felt it opened up interesting possibilities. Then Tony Barr, an executive at CBS, rejected the script, saying that the network did not "want to shine the spotlight on pregnancy" and the problems of a pregnant unmarried woman.

Barney Rosenzweig, Barbara Corday (at the time, creative consultant for the series), Terry Louise Fisher (writer-producer), Peter Lefcourt (writer-

Publicity photo of Barney Rosenzweig and the cast of the Gless/Daly series. Standing, left to right: *Carl Lumbly (Petrie), Sidney Clute (LaGuardia), Al Waxman (Samuels), John Karlen (Harvey Lacey), Martin Kove (Isbecki).* Seated, left to right: *Sharon Gless (Cagney), Barney Rosenzweig, Tyne Daly (Lacey). (© CBS, 1984)*

producer), P. K. (Patricia) Knelman (at the time, coproducer), and Ralph Singleton (at the time, unit production manager) discussed various options at a meeting. CBS had suggested that they turn the episode into a "biological clock" story in which Cagney is faced with the decision of whether or not she will ever have children. Fisher felt that the biological clock angle was not dramatically sound because it would offer no "resolution" or "closure." She asked Rosenzweig if he would fight for the original story with the network. But Corday wondered if they wanted to fight at this point, thinking it would be better to hold off and do the episode the following season (if CBS were to renew the series)—in, for instance, the fifth show, so they could lead up to the situation by having Cagney become seriously involved with one person. Because the subplot of the script dealt with officers at the precinct preparing for the sergeant's exam, and because attaining the rank of sergeant was one of Cagney's immediate ambitions, Lefcourt suggested that the issue could be cast as a "my job or having a baby kind of choice." Fisher said she refused to do that to working women: "It sounds too much like waiting for Prince Charming to come." Lefcourt agreed, "You're right, the Cinderella story."

Finally, Rosenzweig suggested they leave the first act exactly as it was—Cagney *thinks* she's pregnant. In actuality, however, she is not. Because the network had seemed so adamant about not focusing on a pregnancy at all, Rosenzweig (in the midst of the meeting and in the presence of the participants) called Tony Barr with his compromise option. Barr agreed that Cagney could *think* she was pregnant, but only on the condition that Lacey accuse her of being totally irresponsible. A long discussion on how they would cast Cagney's irresponsibility then followed: "Should we say it was a night of passion?" "Cagney could say something like, 'I know it was my fault, I was acting like a teenager'; or, 'Well, it happens, I mean the diaphragm is not foolproof.'" Rosenzweig objected that "as the father of four daughters, I don't want to put down the diaphragm." The other four agreed that it was the only "safe method for women's bodies," and they did not want to portray Cagney as "being on the pill."

In the final episode, "Biological Clock," Cagney thinks she is pregnant but is not, and Lacey is only mildly accusatory. There is no mention of specific birth control technologies or how the "mistake" might have happened. There is no mention of what Cagney would do if she *were* pregnant, although Lacey strongly pushes marriage; Cagney seems to be developing a relationship with the "baby," and abortion is never mentioned as an option.

During this time, the producers and writers also were talking about where, in general, to go with the Cagney character. The discussions revolved around making Cagney more "sympathetic" and "committed," which would be accomplished by linking her romantically with one man. According to Terry Louise Fisher and Barbara Avedon, the word "sympathetic" is industry jargon used almost exclusively in connection with female characters, to describe female roles that evoke stereotypically "feminine" behaviors and situations. But the decision to make Cagney more sympathetic by showing her in a committed relationship with her boyfriend, Dory, was unpopular with viewers. During the "letters-from-viewers" segment on *60 Minutes,* one of the reporters actually read a letter that advocated the removal of Dory from the series.[75]

Cagney's single life and her sexuality were, however, continually troubling to the producers, writers, and network. According to a *New York Times Magazine* article, her "unmarried status does not hold appeal for CBS," which believed that "the only true states of grace for a woman are being married or actively looking for a spouse." Barbara Corday, in commenting on the problem, said, "We've been accused of Cagney being promiscuous, but she's barely what I consider to be a healthy active heterosexual female." And Tyne Daly, speaking about Cagney's and Lacey's sexuality and the network's investments in these issues, said that the CBS powers-that-be were nervous about the possibility that Chris "would be considered a sleepabout if she had a boyfriend every couple of weeks. . . . First they didn't want me [Lacey] to go to bed with my husband, and then when I begged and pleaded for us to have a little fun in the hay, they didn't want me to ever turn him down."[76]

In the spring of 1984, after the seven trial episodes, the series was renewed by CBS. During the 1984–85 season, Cagney was once again associated with some conventionally feminist actions. In one episode, in which she ends her relationship with Dory, she overtly rejects (in a long conversation with Lacey) the institution of marriage. In the same season, she files sexual harassment charges against a captain in the police department, urges Lacey to get a second opinion on a mastectomy treatment and consequently introduces the option of a lumpectomy, is the only one in her precinct to make the rank of sergeant, and continually emphasizes the importance of her career and her goal of becoming the first woman chief of detectives. In the face of critical and industry acclaim, a more secure place in the ratings (at least with target audience women), and the requisite changes in the characters' class and glamour, the network, it appears, became less skittish about the show's less-than-conventional representations of women.

The public struggles over *Cagney and Lacey* and definitions of femininity, however, showed no signs of abating during this period; many different voices in the political spectrum continued to comment on the program and its women. For example, the tabloid *National Examiner* printed a small color photo of Tyne Daly and Sharon Gless on its cover, captioned "Cagney and Lacey are shaming the men of America—say experts." The

National Examiner *cover with photo of Tyne Daly and Sharon Gless, captioned "Cagney and Lacey are shaming the men of America." (© National Examiner, 1985)*
1985)

accompanying article cited the conclusions of two mental health "experts" and of Martin Kove, a supporting actor in the series. It overtly criticized *Cagney and Lacey*—and feminism in general—for belittling men and adapted feminist language ("female chauvinists") to make its point. Most strikingly, it related the well-being of the United States and its international reputation to conventional definitions of femininity. "Television cops Cagney and Lacey," the article embarked,

> are female chauvinists . . . and they're poised to destroy the manhood of America, according to top psychologists who warn that the show is, in fact, a dangerous trendsetter that could lower the esteem of men around the world. "It's really a feminist show that makes all the men look like wimps or stupid or just plain bad," protested Martin Kove. . . . "It's appalling how many times I've been emasculated on the show. . . . They've taken away my pants and given me a tutu. My gun is rusty and there's dust on the trigger." CAGNEY AND LACEY has been . . . twice reprieved, largely due to the protests of women's libbers who closely identify with the two characters on the show. . . . Said clinical psychologist Dr. Henry Fairclough, "CAGNEY AND LACEY probably satisfies aspirations in women but it does involve its stars in improbable heroics, and challenges the masculinity of the actors." . . . Psychotherapist Dr. Harland Toft warned, "If that impression becomes pervasive overseas it could alter the view the rest of the world has about the U.S."[77]

In this interpretation, the new women characters were seen as downright dangerous in their capacity to shift social perceptions not just about femininity but about masculinity, and the emasculating threat of powerful women was indeed hysterically rendered.

Bridget Smith, in the British feminist journal *Spare Rib*, criticized the whole series on feminist grounds. Her challenge came from a radical, perhaps cultural, feminist point of view, which saw the program as ultimately defining and portraying women as male-identified agents of status quo power relations:

> "Cagney and Lacey" is proving very popular with many feminists. So WHY? Cagney and Lacey themselves are portrayed as whole characters, they are defined by their relationship with one another (both professional and personal), and not in terms of their relationship to men. The issues covered tend to be much more controversial than the overworked and stereotypical storylines usually found in "Cop" shows. The programme has tackled prostitution, breast cancer etc. However, despite

the fact that the series seems to be specifically relevant to women, "Cagney and Lacey" offers little to us. The BBC presenter introduces the programme as "Cagney and Lacey, fighting crime the feminine way." This sums up the inherent contradiction therein. The women are required to retain their femininity while brutally combating "crime." Their aggression is not part of their enlightened feminism but the result of their male defined training. Like any other police series "Cagney and Lacey" serves to glorify the police force. It may represent a different approach but the exercise remains the same.[78]

Smith's criticisms, as had Gary Deeb's before her, bring to the surface issues that contribute to the contradictory character of the series's texts and its femininity—"fighting crime the feminine way" and the "exploitation" of women—and that I will probe in greater depth in later chapters. But Smith and Deeb each also seize upon a contradictory textual aspect and apparently see that as revealing and bespeaking the total "truth" of the text. As I will show in Chapter 5, all the meanings of the text, including its meanings of *women*, *woman*, and *femininity*, may never be tacked down and decided once and for all, no matter how impassioned the critic's interpretation or how clear the analysis.

The contradictory aspects of the texts and the women characters were exacerbated by a number of episodes between 1984 and 1988, particularly those dealing with wife-beating, abortion, breast cancer, sexual harassment, date rape, and alcoholism. These programs simultaneously treated issues of enormous social importance to women and raised questions (explored in Chapter 3) about the use of "exploitation topics" in programs for and about females.[79] They both "cashed in on" and became part of intense public debates involving the institutional and social control over women's bodies and what women generally should and should not be. And they also brought several social interest groups and institutions into the overall discursive struggle over femininity and women TV characters.

A two-part program on breast cancer, from the 1984–85 season, and an episode on abortion, from 1985–86, offer interesting examples. Both episodes could be considered overt "exploitation" programs, and both were broadcast during ratings sweeps periods.[80] The breast cancer episodes, aired on 11 and 18 February 1985, centered on early detection, getting quick medical attention, and lumpectomy as an alternative to mastectomy. They remained well within the parameters of standard medical practice and did not critique the relationship between women and the medical institution, nor did they broach the topic of "disfigurement" in relation to the idealiza-

People *cover story on the breast cancer episodes, "Who Said It's Fair?" (©* People, *1985. "PEOPLE" Weekly is a registered trademark of Time Inc., used with permission)*

tion and fetishization of women's bodies. *American Medical News*, a publication of the American Medical Association, in fact printed a highly respectful article on the programs. And Barney Rosenzweig said he put aside "some of my prejudices about the medical profession, specifically because we did not want to get mired down in controversy. . . . We wanted to be very careful—we wanted to simply get the information out. And we felt in order to do that and serve our viewers, it was imperative to be as straightforward and non-controversial as possible."[81] Tyne Daly, however, in a cover-story article on the episodes in *People*, was overtly critical of the medical institution's relationship with women. She said that after some hesitation, she decided to do the part because "I realized that as long as there are women being led astray by the medical establishment, women getting hacked up into pieces, it's important that I tell the story."[82]

The episode about abortion, broadcast 11 November 1985, played a central part in the ongoing public battles over one of the most inflammatory social issues of the decade, and it further testifies to CBS's increased tolerance (however cautious) regarding some aspects of representing women. Entitled "The Clinic," the program centers on the bombing of an abortion clinic and Cagney and Lacey's support (after considerable debate between them) of a poor Latina's choice to terminate her pregnancy. In her book on advocacy groups and entertainment television, Kathryn C. Montgomery chronicles the history of this episode, revealing that for several months the producers, writers, network executives, and the Program Practices Department (often called the network "censors") had debated the script. Program Practices wanted to ensure that the script had "balance," preferably by having Cagney and Lacey take different sides on the issue of abortion.[83]

In the episode as it actually aired, Cagney (a Catholic) is initially reluctant but ultimately supports the woman's right to choose, and the strongest antiabortion arguments are made by her father, Charlie. Program Practices and the network executives, after calling for numerous revisions, were ultimately satisfied that the final version represented the balance they had envisioned. But Rosenzweig, seeking publicity, managed to stir up a fair amount of controversy around the script. He rallied the National Organization for Women, which issued "Action Alert" reports to its members about potential trouble over the episode, and he circulated videotape copies of the program itself around the country for local grassroots screenings. CBS executives were, of course, aggravated that the executive producer of the series was instigating trouble after they had gone to such pains to avoid it, and they were especially concerned that Rosenzweig was publicizing the program as "pro-choice."

Led by its public relations director, Daniel Donehey, the National Right to Life Committee (a group heavily invested in traditional definitions of women and their bodies) took Rosenzweig's bait and launched a protest several days before air time. The *Los Angeles Times*'s Howard Rosenberg noted that Rosenzweig had spun "controversy from straw," but antiabortion groups were already appealing to CBS to pull the episode, which the NRLC called a "piece of pure political propaganda."[84] When CBS, saying that it found the program to be "a fair and well-balanced view," refused to pull the episode from the schedule, the NRLC asked CBS affiliates to black it out. If an affiliate did not want to do this, it was asked to offer the NRLC air time for a half-hour film of the latter's choosing (such as the antiabortion film *A Matter of Choice*) or a half-hour to "put some of our folks on to rebut this." If none of these measures worked, the NRLC's next plan was to "call for a nationwide black-out of CBS during the balance of the month of November which is their rating month."[85]

As a promotional effort, Tyne Daly and Barney Rosenzweig flew to Washington, D.C., for a luncheon cosponsored by the National Abortion Rights Action League and Orion Television to "counter opposition" to the episode. According to Daly, "We feel we've done something very balanced. . . . I don't think I know a woman who hasn't struggled or knows someone who hasn't struggled with this issue." Planned Parenthood also organized a press conference about the episode in New York. John Wilke, president of the NRLC, and Barney Rosenzweig debated the topic on the *MacNeil/Lehrer News Hour*. To Wilke's charges that "this program is the most unbalanced, most unfair program we've seen in a number of years. . . . We did not hear a single right-to-life answer properly given," Rosenzweig answered, "A year ago we had an episode in which Christine Cagney believed she was pregnant, and never once considered abortion as an alternative. I didn't hear from the National Organization for Women or the Voters for Choice then about banning the show or boycotting us. I just got some rather nice letters from the pro-life people."[86]

One CBS affiliate pulled the show, and one, WOWT-TV in Omaha, Nebraska, offered equal time to the NRLC. Even after the broadcast, the political struggle continued: an antiabortion spokesperson suggested that "any further violence at abortion clinics would be on CBS's conscience." But in the *Washington Post*, Judy Mann praised the episode and the actions of CBS, saying of television that "no other medium is as capable of dramatizing and educating the public about some of life's most difficult experiences."[87]

In a scholarly article about the episode, written several years after it aired and apparently informed by aspects of liberal, socialist, and poststructuralist feminism, Celeste Michelle Condit raised questions about "The Clinic" and its feminist politics. She described it as breaking "new ideological ground" and inserting "new political codes into the public culture," but she also labeled it as a progressive rather than a radical text and said that it "favored the interests of career women but only marginally supported other groups of women." She went on,

> For women in poverty and women of color the program is more mixed. It explicitly affirmed the choices of a particular minority woman, but it did not deal with the ways in which poor women might fund abortion or contraception. It did not deal with the options provided by extended families or with the importance of motherhood in different cultures. It offered a sugary and unrealistic moral, "have an abortion so you can go to school and get off welfare," that may have appealed to latent racism in white audiences more than assisting poor women with real options. In the face of such silences, the Republican administration could continue its largely hidden work in pro-natalism by dismantling funding for family planning. From the perspective of these groups of viewers, this restricted presentation of abortion represents a serious political shortcoming of this episode.[88]

That the program was among the first in a number of years to confront abortion, that CBS worked so hard to make it "balanced," and that conservative discourses were currently on the rise, all undoubtedly contributed to such mixed, contradictory, and problematic meanings.

In both the 1984–85 and the 1985–86 seasons, *Cagney and Lacey* won the Emmy Award for best dramatic program. Tyne Daly won for best actress in 1982–83, 1983–84, 1984–85, and 1987–88, and Sharon Gless in 1985–86 and 1986–87. The series also won many other awards, including the award for best program given by the National Committee on Working Women in 1985 and the Humanitas Award in 1986.[89] In 1985 the "early lives" of the protagonists were novelized in a Dell paperback by Serita Deborah Stevens, called simply *Cagney and Lacey*. In 1986 the magazine *Channels* included *Cagney and Lacey* among its "Class of '86 Honor Roll"—seven recipients who "set the highest standards in the media." And in January 1987, Sharon Gless and Tyne Daly were featured on the cover of *Ms.*, along with ten other women, as women of the year. (Gless and Daly appeared in the top two positions after international woman of the year Winnie Mandela.)[90]

As this chapter has made clear, the negotiation of meanings of *women*, *woman*, and *femininity* took place among a variety of vested interests and with considerable conflict. We have seen how a number of players in the overall television enterprise vied for the primacy of their own definitions. And I would argue that CBS executives, in interfering with *Cagney and*

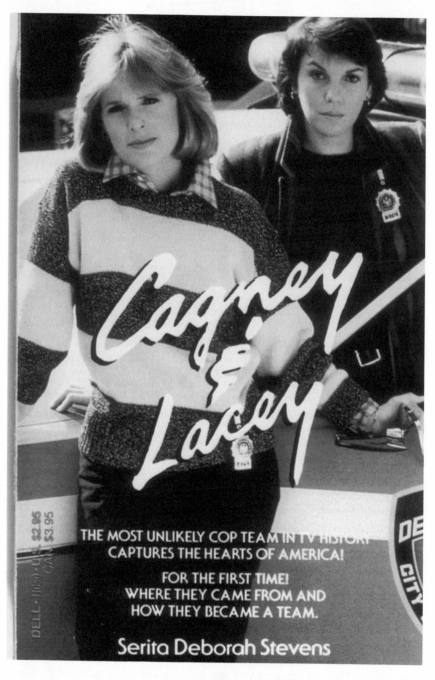

THE MOST UNLIKELY COP TEAM IN TV HISTORY
CAPTURES THE HEARTS OF AMERICA!

FOR THE FIRST TIME!
WHERE THEY CAME FROM AND
HOW THEY BECAME A TEAM.

Serita Deborah Stevens

Cover of Cagney and Lacey, *a 1985 Dell paperback by Serita Deborah Stevens that dealt with the early "lives" of Christine Cagney and Mary Beth Lacey. (Used with permission of Bantam Books, a division of Bantam, Doubleday, Dell Publishing Group, Inc.)*

Ms.

JANUARY 1987 ● $2.25

WOMEN OF THE YEAR

SHARON GLESS
TYNE DALY
JAN KEMP
MARGARET ATWOOD

SISTER DARLENE
NICGORSKI
SARABETH EASON
BARBARA MIKULSKI
DOLLY PARTON

MARY FRANCES BERRY
ANN BANCROFT
VICKI FRANKOVICH
LINDA WACHNER

0 140155 4

Ms. cover showing Sharon Gless and Tyne Daly as two of the magazine's 1987 Women of the Year. (© Ms., 1987)

Lacey's scripts and representations, achieved a certain amount of "discursive authority" of their own by delimiting the dimensions of class, "femininity," and feminism. This delimitation, however, by no means *contained* the differences of the characters on any of these levels—in production as well as reception: Tyne Daly, for example, continued to contest the issues of makeup, hairstyle, and costume, and Sharon Gless resisted letting the new Cagney become "frilly." Furthermore, some elements of the original Cagney characterization not only continued but were expanded upon in the revised and recast series.

The production team also continued to battle with network executives over how women could actually be represented on 1980s prime-time television, especially with respect to a single woman's sex life and her decisions on pregnancy and abortion. Similarly, the mainstream press (including syndicated columnist Gary Deeb), the *National Examiner*, interest groups (including the women's movements, the Gay Media Task Force, the National Abortion Rights Action League, and the National Right to Life Committee), and viewers continued to generate many different and often contradictory interpretations of the characters and definitions of femininity. Viewers, for one thing, continued to find in Cagney and Lacey's relationship the erotic dimensions that CBS had sought to squelch; Gless's large lesbian following, in fact, indicates that homoerotic interpretations of the women's friendship actually flourished.

It is important to note that many of the network's interventions were especially aimed at containing those aspects of the characterizations that challenged not only conventional definitions of femininity but also institutionalized differences among women—the differences that structure U.S. society. In this chapter the particular institutionalized differences were those of class and sexual preference. (Differences of race had been delimited from the outset). Later we will see that other interventions also focused on differences that posed a threat to what one CBS programmer referred to as "the system"—that is, differences involving "women's lib" and general female bonding. The following two chapters examine the process of struggle and negotiation as it worked to create a women's audience for the series and to construct the show as a "woman's program."

CHAPTER 2

A WOMEN'S AUDIENCE

How women were represented on TV and what did or did not constitute proper femininity were the subjects of a continual process of contestation and negotiation throughout much of *Cagney and Lacey*'s history. At the same time, the players in that drama also struggled to forge, define, and negotiate a "women's audience." CBS, Orion Television, and *Cagney and Lacey*'s production team and publicity firms all consciously undertook the construction of a working women's audience for the series; the press, the liberal women's movement, and particular women viewers themselves did the same, according to their own vested and variegated interests. On a more general level, prime-time network TV worked to produce gender—in this instance, to shape femininity—in its extratextual or second-level textual practices, including program scheduling, on-air promotions, *TV Guide* advertising, press releases, through-the-mail publicity, and promotional events. All these maneuverings make eminently clear the fundamental importance of women audiences to the functioning of network TV, especially in the late 1970s and early 1980s.

When I say that "audiences" and "the women's audience" were "constructed" by the industry for programs, I mean two things: First, network television sought to amass viewers already defined as women, in and by their social contexts, to watch particular programs—in other words, it sought to forge these viewers into an audience. But second, in forging this audience (by a range of publicity strategies, campaigns, program-scheduling tactics, and promotional methods), it worked to *produce* gender in its viewers, to affect what Annette Kuhn calls the human subject always in the "process of gender positioning," to shape human beings as "feminine," and to shape femininity along particular lines.[1]

Charlotte Brunsdon has written that publicity, scheduling, and ads *imply* a gendered audience.[2] Following Brunsdon's argument, I will demonstrate not only the *implication* but the *construction* of a gendered audience in and by these practices. Gender, in other words, was not produced in the relationships between spectators and television programs or primary texts only, but also in what have been called television's extratextual operations or its secondary texts; and the social lives and practices of TV viewers, apart from their relationship to television, were called upon and engaged in this process. For example, the publicity for *Cagney and Lacey* functioned almost exclusively in the field of social practices and discourses conventionally associated with women: women's magazines, the women's pages of newspapers, women's organizations, and women's department stores.

Women as audiences and women as consumers were not ready-made components for the functioning of the advertising and television industries in the late 1970s and the 1980s (indeed, they are not in any period); rather, they had to be continually fashioned, and in working to fashion them TV participated in the process of gender construction.[3] However, as the work of cultural studies continues to show us, many other factors come into play in any viewer's negotiation of the industry's addresses and "pitches," including the pitches that explicitly solicit women as feminine, as buyers, and as audiences. But how exactly have target audiences and consumers functioned in the history of network prime time? What has been women's particular place in this functioning? And why were women as target audiences and consumers so important to TV during the period under discussion here?

AUDIENCES AS CONSUMERS

When viewed as an economic institution or an industry, much U.S. television may appear to be an apparatus for producing audiences and consumers. ABC, CBS, NBC, FOX, and most cable networks stay solvent because they are able to sell particular viewers and the promise of others to advertisers.[4] The better the networks deliver on that promise, the more they can charge for advertising time. In a controversial and widely debated article, Dallas Smythe referred to these viewers as the "audience commodity"—"a non-durable producers' good which is bought and used in the marketing of the advertisers' product." The notion of an "audience commodity" relies, of course, on the related concept of "audiences as consumers." And as Smythe puts it, "The work which audience members perform for the advertiser to whom they have been sold is to learn to buy particular 'brands' of consumer goods, and to spend their income accordingly."[5]

In contrast, Eileen Meehan argues that what is actually bought by sponsors and sold by networks is not Smythe's "audience commodity," not all the consumer/viewers watching TV and presumably "represented" by A. C. Nielsen's ratings sample, but rather what she calls the "commodity audience." That commodity audience is conceived simply and solely as the group of "families" (or more precisely, the commoditized numbers abstracted from those families) that are metered and surveyed by Nielsen.[6] Meehan's distinction is undoubtedly essential to understanding the precise market for and functioning of the ratings systems. But if we bear in mind, as I think we should, that ratings carry with them not only an actual commodity exchange but a *promise* to deliver millions of empirical viewers and consumers to sponsors, the notion of television as a consumer-producing technology remains an apt form of description.

Programs, as we know, are the attractions by which such viewers are drawn into the enterprise, and there are two necessary components to the process: exposure to advertisers' commercials, and exposure to a panorama of products and particular ways of living. Clothes, cars, furniture, appliances, and other emblems of middle-class lifestyles and attitudes, are, for the most part, on constant display.[7]

WOMEN AS CONSUMERS AND TARGET AUDIENCES

Although television, as an apparatus for producing consumers, has predictably marketed to upwardly mobile women, men, teens, and children, it has always, from the earliest days of its history, considered middle-class women—primarily white ones—to be the main consumers of the products it advertises. A look at network television's top ten advertisers over a number of years demonstrates that it has been largely an advertising medium for goods sold in supermarkets (and, recently, fast-food franchises). American Home Products, Lever Brothers, Procter and Gamble, General Mills, General Foods, Johnson and Johnson, Pepsi, and Ford are among the giants of television sales. And as these advertisers see it, women are the ones who shop for such goods; throughout most of TV's history, even car commercials have been targeted primarily toward women. Women consumers, in fact, have been seen as the staples of the TV industry and as the major product sold (as commoditized numbers and as promised "real-life" humans) by the networks to advertisers.[8]

Because they are seen as TV's main consumers (and, at least by some, as its major program selectors), women have been a consistent target audience for network prime time throughout the medium's life span.[9] The networks' thinking on this subject was described in 1984 by Marvin Mord, ABC marketing and research vice-president: "In the early days, the whole family sat down to watch television together. Theory was that the woman controlled the dial in the evening, so others in the family came along for the ride." Several factors in the 1970s modified this adage, but women as target audiences remained fundamental to programming strategies and advertising campaigns throughout the 1980s. In fact, in the mid-eighties, according to CBS research vice-president David Poltrack, "three out of every four advertising dollars in prime time [were] aimed at women."[10]

From the early 1970s through the 1980s, target audiences composed of especially prized demographic groups (such as working women between eighteen and fifty-four or urban adults between eighteen and forty-nine) were called "quality" audiences.[11] Such a designation made it possible for programs to boast fewer total viewers and yet avoid cancellation as long as they drew in significant numbers of the desired "quality" ones. For example, *Cagney and Lacey* was able to stay on the air despite marginal overall ratings (it drew only mediocre numbers of gross audience members) because the producers could argue to the network that the program attracted a large quality audience—in this case, upscale working women between the ages of eighteen and fifty-four.[12]

The steady growth of cable throughout the 1980s and early 1990s has signaled far-reaching changes in the television industry. The competitiveness of FOX as a fourth network and Lifetime as one directed exclusively toward women; the heavy marketing to a youth audience in the 1990s, first by FOX and then by the three major networks; renewed advertising interest in the African American middle class; and the proliferation of channels targeted to specific audiences (Black Entertainment Television, the Nashville Network, the Cartoon Network, the Sci-Fi Channel, Spanish and Asian language channels, and home shopping, religious, and music-video channels)—all these trends show that the place of middle-class white women as prime time's major target audience may be undergoing a radical shift. The period of *Cagney and Lacey*'s introduction to and cancellation from the nightly schedule may, in fact, prove to have coincided with the three major networks' crises over retaining not only their most valued women's audience but also their hegemony over television in general; the same period, as well, may have heralded a total reshaping of the industry from broadcast to narrowcast contours. The next few years will tell us much more about television's reconfiguration; at the moment, though, it is clear that the late 1970s and the 1980s were a time in which the women's audience was still a major objective of CBS, ABC, and NBC.

IN SEARCH OF THE WORKING WOMEN'S MARKET

If, from its earliest days, the white, middle-class women's audience had been the linchpin of U.S. television, in the late seventies a number of things happened to make that group even more desirable to and sought after by the networks. Understanding the historical and institutional conditions that produced this phenomenon is crucial to understanding 1980s prime time, and the best place to begin is with the advertising industry's discovery of "working women" beginning in the mid-seventies.

As noted above, white, middle-class women have been the primary target group for U.S. advertisers since the early 1900s because they have been thought to exert the major influence over most of the nation's buying—especially items for the home. These items have included big-ticket purchases like home appliances and cars as well as faster-moving consumables like food or hygiene, health, and childcare products. In the mid-1970s, however, working women began to be recognized as an economic force in their own right. In the advertisers' view, the difference was that women, once seen as the major "influencers" over spending, were now seen as controlling much of their own disposable incomes.[13]

Although television advertisers also rediscovered the black middle class in the 1970s, their initial campaign for the "working women's audience" primarily conceived of its market as white (or they hoped—as has frequently been the case with U.S. advertising—to attract African American, Latino, and Asian American consumers in the general bid for white ones). The majority of cultural products generated during the early part of this campaign (films, magazines, and TV programs) were most pointedly directed toward white women and the representations were predominantly those of white females. For example, even though *Cagney and Lacey* featured a Latina as a district attorney and an African American woman as the precinct's beat reporter (both, however, appeared infrequently), it was not until the show's final season that an African American woman detective (played by Merry Clayton) was added to the regular character roster. And although Rosenzweig and the production team made an explicit effort to cast women of color in as many minor roles as possible, the overall consistent address to women of color was weak. It was actually not until the mid-1980s, with the introduction of Phylicia Rashād's Clair Huxtable (*The Cosby Show*) and Diahann Carroll's Dominique Deveraux (*Dynasty*), that prime time's quest for the working women's market began its concerted targeting of the African American middle- and upper-middle-class female audience.

The "neglected working women's market" (as conceived and racially delimited by the advertisers) spawned articles in *Advertising Age* and *Television and Radio Age* beginning in the mid-seventies and gaining in frequency and urgency in the late seventies and early eighties. The major problems addressed in these pieces were: advertisers were missing the boat by ignoring this burgeoning clientele; and they needed to develop dollar-efficient strategies to reach a market that was no longer a simple mass of "women between the ages of 18 to 49 or 18 to 54," but essentially a conglomeration of fragmented and continually shifting elements. "Every week," began an article in *Advertising Age*,

> marketers spend $6,000,000 in advertising on daytime television in hopes of reaching a mythical mass market—the comfortably familiar, domestically-oriented housewife, aged 18 to 54, with a family of 2.2 children and a husband who brings home the bacon, although he may not shop for it. In reality, this vine-covered scenario exists only in 5% of all households. Although we may be aware that 52% of all women now work outside the home, our marketing, media and creative strategies have been slow to change. . . . Demographically, the American woman is becoming an increasingly fragmented market. Divorce, changing family size, education, later marriage, employment and other factors keep even the fragments in flux. So it is increasingly difficult to reach this no-longer-mass market at reasonable cost.[14]

In 1979 Tina Santi, corporate vice-president of Colgate-Palmolive, New York (one of television's top advertisers), presented an early solution to these marketing problems: Target the "professional woman." According to Santi, although professional women were still a small percentage of total working women, they were "the *conspicuous consumers* . . . the role models [who] have an enormous influence on the 41,000,000 women who are wage earners today" (emphasis in original).[15] In 1982 Kate Lloyd Rand, the editor-in-chief of *Working Woman* magazine, summarized the general history of the phenomenon:

> When *Working Woman* first appeared in 1976, the idea of a working women's market was still so novel that there seemed to be no stereotype appropriate for it. That might explain why the first issue had not one but nine working women on the cover. How do you stereotype a working woman? With a steno pad? With coveralls? In a uniform? Carrying a briefcase? A housewife type with horn-rimmed glasses? By the end of the 1970's, however, advertisers, ever thinking upscale, had made the decision: She would be a dauntless, young and pretty vp, swinging along in a tailored suit and string tie.[16]

In the early eighties, two books by women in advertising agencies— *The Coming Matriarchy: How Women Will Gain the Balance of Power,* by Elizabeth Nickles with Laura Ashcraft, and *The Moving Target: What Every Marketer Should Know about Women,* by Rena Bartos—further rationalized the working women's market and had great impact on the production of women as consumers at the time. Nickles and Ashcraft's book proposed a solution to the market fragmentation problem by identifying and constructing a new type of woman. "Upscale," "professional," and "women's movement–influenced" (with regard to particular attitude characteristics culled from the language of the liberal women's movement and listed below) were all implicit qualities in the type. According to Nickles, although the *demographic* market of working women is a fragmented one, "Laura Ashcraft and I discovered unprecedented attitudinal and behavioral changes among women that have created a new *psychographic* market. . . . What we found was a woman we term the Go-Getter, and she is the woman who typifies the new mass market, accounting for 43% of all women nationwide. . . . The Go-Getter may or may not work outside the home. But even if she is a homemaker, *she thinks like a working woman*" (emphasis in original). Go-getters were "aggressive, self-motivated, goal-oriented and less influenced by the opinions of the men in their lives [than domestically oriented women]." Bartos's book divided women into similar categories.[17]

Whether or not advertisers continued to employ the stereotyped image of a "pretty vp, swinging along in a tailored suit," the pursuit and construction of the upscale, professional, self-motivated, individual-achiever woman became the industry's solution to market fragmentation and high-cost, multitargeted campaigns. By targeting to—and constructing representations of—go-getters, trendsetters, role models, and conspicuous consumers, the ad industry tried to reach and influence a large portion of the general women's market under its specific campaign for working women.[18]

"Working women," when used in the TV and advertising industries' phrases "working women's audience" or "working women's market," came to assume a meaning imbued with the psychographic and economic characteristics described above. It also, as mentioned earlier, assumed (but was not limited to) the meaning of "white," and my use of the phrase in the following pages must be read with these dimensions in mind. The entire phenomenon exemplifies advertising's insinuation into and co-optation of women's social, economic, racial, and cultural conditions (including discourses from the women's movements) to construct the categories "women as consumers" and "women as audiences," thereby shaping gender and race according to particular market-oriented specifications.[19] (As I said above, however, this is not to argue that historical women are simply and passively molded in massive numbers by such advertising practices).

The experimentations and proven successes of other media in attracting this new working women's market served to externalize television's risks. According to one critic, the television industry, "never one to venture out on a limb without plenty of company," took its cues about the availability and economic value of this audience from other culture industries. In the seventies and early eighties, for the most part a couple of years before network TV stepped in with both feet, many media had produced a whole variety of new cultural products directed toward the working women's market and employing a wide range of women's movement discourses. Those media with the best capabilities for narrowly targeting their audiences produced the greatest array and number of products: The magazine industry, for example, spawned a host of new publications during the seventies and eighties to challenge the domination of the more traditional "seven sisters" (*Better Homes and Gardens, Family Circle, Good Housekeeping, Ladies' Home Journal, McCall's, Redbook,* and *Woman's Day*). At least six of these new monthlies (*New Woman, Savvy, Self, Spring, Working Mother,* and *Working Woman*) caught on, developing sizable readerships and subscriber lists. *Ms.* and *Essence,* both originated in the early seventies and targeted to feminist and black women's markets respectively, had already developed into institutions of the liberal women's movement and African American women's culture.[20]

Cable television in the early eighties produced such programs directed toward "working women" as *Woman to Woman, The Eighties Woman, Sportswoman, Alive and Well, You! Magazine, Woman's Day, Working Mother, Sonya* (a program with psychologist Sonya Friedman), and *From Washington: Citizen's Alert* (national news stories of interest to women). And syndicated daytime television programs like *Donahue* and *The Sally Jessy Raphael Show* were capturing large shares of women viewers. In 1983 the Radio Advertising Bureau printed a brochure for its potential advertisers called, "Radio: It's Red Hot to Sell Working Women"; syndicated radio programs included *On the Move* (a program about "women on the move" such as astronaut Sally Ride), *Women in the Workplace, Coping With, Body Language,* and *Soap Talk*.[21]

In 1977 the motion picture industry made its most dramatic foray into the "new women's" pictures genre with the films mentioned in the previous chapter—*Julia, The Turning Point,* and *An Unmarried Woman. Alice Doesn't Live Here Anymore* had been a reasonable box office success in 1975; and during the late seventies and early eighties, the industry produced several other films targeted to the "new women's" or "working women's" audience—*9 to 5, Girlfriends, Rich and Famous,* and *It's My Turn.* (The motion picture industry, however, primarily continued to direct films to its steadier and more lucrative twelve-to-twenty-five-year-old market.)[22] As I discussed in Chapter 1, prime-time network television itself, from 1970 to 1978 (before TV's push for the *working* women's audience), had produced a number of "socially relevant" sitcoms that employed some women's movement subject material (often with great boldness, although always in the comedy genre) in order to attract an upscale urban audience—particularly upscale urban women.[23]

Recognizing the importance of the "women's audience" to its own economic health, and given the demonstrable successes of other media in attracting women as consumers, the television industry badly "wanted in" on the working women's market in the late 1970s and the 1980s. Two other factors contributed to TV's pursuit of this particular audience. First, the influx of women into the labor market was causing a drop in network daytime viewership; and second, with the massive changes beginning to take place in the industry, the commercial networks were starting to lose a noticeable share of their prime-time audience to cable. All of these conditions caused CBS, NBC, and ABC to focus on attracting women viewers to their own prime-time offerings. As early as 1976 (two years before the networks initiated their concerted quest for the new market), the A. C. Nielsen Company added "working women" as a demographic category to be surveyed and counted in order to demonstrate (or purport to demonstrate) what programs these women were actually watching.[24]

The introduction of two "women's forms" solved (initially) some of the industry's problems. The first was the nighttime soap opera inaugurated by *Dallas*—what one TV researcher called, "the single greatest programming discovery of recent years"—and the other a new crop of "four-hankie melodrama" made-for-TV movies. The "soapoperafication" of prime time and the made-for-TV melodramas were major victories for CBS and ABC in their quests for the working women's audience.[25] They were also phenomena that developed out of market, industry, social, and cultural conditions and, according to one television writer, were fueled by women viewers' wishes to see more women—in particular more older women—on their TV screens. In January 1983, *Newsweek's* Harry Waters concluded,

> The big sex switch is simply good business, or more precisely, a response to exceptionally bad business. With network audiences defecting to cable TV by the millions, programmers have decided that their prime demographic customer—the middle-aged female who usually controls the channel selector—must be courted more ardently than ever. And what she wants most to see, they've concluded, is women around her own age acting out her secret fantasies of power, wealth, and romance (just as the Joan Crawfords and Barbara Stanwycks did before Hollywood discovered Gidget).[26]

With the failure of two prime-time soaps—*Secrets of Midland Heights* in 1981 and *Flamingo Road* in 1982—and with their realization that the genre could not (even on TV) be cloned endlessly, television programmers began to cast about for other vehicles with which to lure working women viewers.

It was in the midst of these conditions that the 1981 *Cagney and Lacey* made-for-TV movie and the 1982 Meg Foster/Tyne Daly series came to the air. CBS apparently was willing to gamble that nonconventional representations of working women, women's movement discourses in dramatic scripts, and story matter involving problematic social and working conditions would attract the working women's audience. In the case of the *Cagney and Lacey* movie, the yoking together of "working women" and "feminism" was, in fact, a gamble with a big payoff for the network when the movie pulled in a 42 percent audience share.

Such a coup seemed to demonstrate that TV viewers were actually drawn in by overtly feminist subject matter, and that the time might be ripe to introduce feminist material on television in dramatic, and not just in comedic, forms. In the fall of 1982, several other programs targeted to working women were added to the prime-time schedule, including *Remington Steele, Gloria, It Takes Two, 9 to 5,* and, of course, the revised *Cagney and Lacey* with Sharon Gless and Tyne Daly. Each had as its primary subject matter, and target-audience hook, the social conditions of working women. Such issues as how to juggle a job and a family, career orientation and dating, discrimination on the job, lack of respect, sexual harassment, male chauvinism, dedication to the job, commitment to struggle, and female bonding were common to most of their plots. However, the poor representation of women of color also marked these programs as texts that not only contributed to defining "women" and "working women" as predominantly white but also linked feminism—particularly liberal feminism at this point in its history—primarily to the concerns of Caucasian, middle-class females. The onslaught against feminism that gained full force in 1982 would eventually have a pronounced effect on the future of such series.

DIFFERENT INVESTMENTS IN "AUDIENCE"

All the players who participated in constructing a working women's audience for *Cagney and Lacey* had their own conceptions of what such an audience actually "meant" and what it wanted from prime time. For CBS and its advertisers, the desired audience was as big a slice of the "audience commodity" as possible, including large numbers of working women but also significant shares of other upscale viewers as well. The networks, as we have seen, make their money by selling the audience commodity—or more precisely, as Eileen Meehan says, the "commodity audience"—to advertisers. They accept the ratings system as the only standard for determining the prices they can charge for this commodity; and they also conflate the ratings data with actual viewers and ascribe motivations and intentions to it.[27] With *Cagney and Lacey,* CBS initially acceded to nonconventional female portrayals in order to lure and satisfy the working women's audience. But it finished by proclaiming that the women's audience, when all was said and done, wanted only traditional depictions and was indeed turned off by any deviations from this norm. CBS's advertisers, who thought of the audience simply as a cluster of "consumers," were not especially interested in what it "wanted" but only in associating their products with a "safe," noncontroversial program.[28]

Orion Television, in contrast, appeared to conceive of the audience as a collection of eighteen-to-fifty-four-year-old, upscale, working women who were looking for a show about the "new woman." Of course, Orion's stake in the notion of "audience" included the network's "audience commodity," but in a different version that allowed a smaller number of concentrated "quality" viewers rather than a large number of total viewers.[29]

From the production team's point of view, the audience was a group of progressive viewers who were ready for more liberal and meaningful media representations. Since the made-for-TV movie's garnering of a 42 percent share, Rosenzweig had actually singled out the audience as the key factor in *Cagney and Lacey*'s existence: "We think," he said, "we've touched a nerve and hit onto something that people responded to. This show could be subtitled, 'You Asked for It,' because no one wanted the show BUT the public."[30] Rosenzweig later capitalized on the efforts of this audience to save the series and continued to be so convinced of the presence of large numbers of such viewers that, at the time the program was canceled, he was angling either to produce a motion picture for theatrical release or to sell the property to cable.[31] However, he also demonstrated a view of the audience more characteristic of "network" thinking when he charged that the women's audience had abandoned *Cagney and Lacey* in favor of made-for-TV "exploitation" movies.

The mainstream press, on the whole, railed at the network for its skewed views of audience preferences and its limiting adherence to ratings. When *Cagney and Lacey* was canceled during the 1982–83 season, the press by and large was outraged at CBS for axing the critically acclaimed program, and most writers believed that the women (and men) in the series's audience were looking for much more innovation and difference in prime-time television than the networks' constraints allowed.

The liberal women's movement, for its part, saw the audience as a political constituency of viewers who were influenced by feminism and who wanted the pleasure and power of seeing media reflections of their own "real life" struggles and situations. These reflections included women at work, women in nontraditional jobs, and realistic women's friendships. The audience envisioned by the women's movement also included viewers whose consciousnesses could be raised and for whom the characters of Cagney and Lacey could serve as "role models."

Finally, the many committed women fans saw themselves, not in relation to the network's and advertisers' sense of their viewing-and-buying capacities, but as individuals who were searching for new representations of on-screen women, particularly for characters who embodied the clashes between new and traditional definitions of femininity and who reminded them of themselves. Their conception of and investment in audience membership was essentially rooted in pleasure, identification, and politics. They applauded *Cagney and Lacey* as a show that at last met their needs, and they considered it "theirs."[32]

In the course of constructing and defining a "women's audience" and its wants, these players at various times acted independently of one another on behalf of their own interests, banded together, and engaged in public debates.

CONSTRUCTING A WORKING WOMEN'S AUDIENCE

The U.S. liberal women's movement and women in the mainstream press actually worked hard to build a women's audience for *Cagney and Lacey* in advance of the TV industry itself. Beginning when the made-for-TV movie first appeared, the women's movement saw the potential series as a force for the production of alternative and oppositional meanings. *Ms.* magazine, for one, tried to turn its readership into a target audience for the program. Remember that the October 1981 issue containing Marjorie Rosen's article on the forthcoming made-for-TV movie and featuring the cover photo of Loretta Swit and Tyne Daly as Cagney and Lacey also included the suggestion that readers contact Richard Rosenbloom if they wished to see the movie become a weekly series. Recall also that *Ms.* lobbied members of the CBS board to get the movie turned into a series and organized a reception for Meg Foster and Tyne Daly before the premiere episode, and that Gloria Steinem spoke to a predominantly female television audience on *Donahue* about the importance of the movie to women.[33]

Several articles in the mainstream press also touted the Foster/Daly series's political and feminist consciousness-raising functions. "Female [police] officers," read one, "believe they face discrimination in both the hiring and promotion processes and in the way they are perceived by colleagues, the public and the media. If a series like *Cagney and Lacey* makes even a small dent in that perception, its purpose will have been served."[34] The writings and actions of women's movement spokespeople and women journalists in the mainstream press not only forged an audience for the program but worked as second-level texts to situate it as a show "for women" and to encourage women's movement or "important-to-women" readings by viewers. In addressing its own audience or constituency, the women's movement was both assuming gendered subjectivity (i.e., assuming that most of its constituents were women) and working to effect or constitute femininity along particular lines—namely, those of a feminist awareness and a critique of conventional male/female roles.

The network, the independent production company, and the production team, however, did not engage very actively in building a women's audience for the original Foster/Daly series. Indeed, the 42 percent share from the made-for-TV movie/pilot might have led the network and producers to feel sanguine about their future audience prospects. Even the scheduling of the Foster/Daly show does not indicate that it was being situated as a woman's program or for a women's audience. Its position on Thursday nights at 9:00 P.M. EST, after the highly rated *Magnum, P.I.,* seemed to be determined by its genre as police program rather than as a strategy to reach women. After the show's bleak performance in this time slot, the third episode was scheduled (at Rosenzweig's urging) for Sunday night at 10:00 P.M. Although the series did significantly better in the new hour, its positioning there did not imply (except for the later, "more adult" hour) a special attempt to reach women.[35]

Everything changed, however, when the revised *Cagney and Lacey*, starring Sharon Gless and Tyne Daly, aired in the fall of 1982. A variety of strategies involving scheduling and publicity, subject material, and character portrayals was adopted. Engineered by CBS, Orion Television, Barney Rosenzweig, and the publicity firm of Rogers and Cowan, these multifaceted, across-the-board strategies were aimed at capturing the working women's audience they had missed the first time.

CBS programmers scheduled the revised series at 10:00 P.M. EST on Monday nights. The plan was to "counterprogram" against ABC's *Monday Night Football* and attract the working women's audience to CBS. Programmers hoped to build a loyal group of women viewers during the fall and early winter and retain it once the football season ended. Their strategy certainly demonstrates some of the ways in which television functions to solicit already gendered individuals, to constitute gender in its viewers, and to affect the material conditions and everyday lives of audience members along gender lines. For example, in many U.S. homes during the past two decades, men have watched football on Monday nights in one part of the house, while women watched CBS or NBC in another.

Since 1970, in fact, Monday nights had provided a major opportunity for CBS to attract a women's audience. But during the 1980s, the "ladies' night line-up" developed into a veritable working women's program block. In the first Gless/Daly season, *Cagney and Lacey*'s lead-in shows were *Square Pegs, Private Benjamin, M*A*S*H,* and *Newhart* (programs that already attracted a good share of working women). But as the decade progressed, the programs in the Monday night lineup became more pointedly and more uniformly oriented toward working women.[36]

CBS's promotion department also scheduled its "promos" for the Gless/Daly series to be aired during other CBS programs that drew in large numbers of women viewers, especially working women. The official promotional schedule for *Cagney and Lacey* for October 1982 shows that promos were broadcast during CBS's daytime soaps and game shows and, in prime time, during *Dallas, Knots Landing, Alice, Tucker's Witch, One Day at a Time, Archie Bunker's Place, The Jeffersons, 60 Minutes,* and the network's made-for-TV movies. In this strategy, we can see the way television works to construct and produce gender, for in this instance an audience gendered as women, already watching a TV product directed toward women, was being canvassed for other programs that would continue fashioning gender along similar lines. The content of the new "promos" was, furthermore, strategically reoriented. In *Daily Variety,* Rosenzweig announced that "CBS will promote the show differently, selling the relationship between the two women rather than the police action, and . . . the women's angle will be emphasized."[37]

Commercials for the first Gless/Daly season also left little doubt that a women's audience was being specifically targeted, especially when contrasted to those for the Foster/Daly run. The sponsors for the original series had included Gillette, Coca-Cola, Duracell, A&W, Upjohn, and Chrysler. For the Gless/Daly series, the list was much more closely tailored to women: Avon, American Home Products, Carnation, Sears, General Foods, Procter and Gamble, Toyota, McDonald's, Lever Brothers, Helene Curtis, Tampax, and Hanes.[38] The change in sponsors signals another way in which TV contributes to constructing gender categories and shaping masculinity and femininity. As we know only too well, many commercials for Procter and Gamble and American Home Products goods (for example) are pitched to audience women by on-screen actresses performing household chores. So programs aimed at women (characterized by representations and story lines that contribute to shaping gender and femininity along often stereotypical lines) feature commercials also aimed at women (which similarly contain stereotypical enactments), resulting in a double address (from two media texts) to engender their viewers as "feminine."[39]

The attempts to promote *Cagney and Lacey* as a women's program, to construct a working women's audience, and to secure high ratings involved a many-pronged publicity campaign. To coordinate the effort, Orion Television hired the firm of Rogers and Cowan Inc., as *Cagney and Lacey's* main publicists.[40] Because Rogers and Cowan's letters to Barney Rosenzweig offer detailed examples of publicity tactics, the actual process of building a working women's audience, and the workings of a relatively undocumented and influential segment of the TV industry, I will quote extensively from some of them below. The strategies outlined in these letters are also excellent illustrations of how the social lives and practices of TV viewers are called upon and engaged in forging audiences for programs.

Rogers and Cowan's conception of "audience," in the case of *Cagney and Lacey*, ultimately was that of a "working women's audience" in the meaning given to that phrase by the advertising industry and discussed earlier—that is, upscale, professional, primarily white women. And the firm appeared to envision this audience as one that had been influenced by feminism. In the *initial* Rogers and Cowan proposals, however, *working women* was somewhat less narrowly defined with regard to its "upscale" or class dimensions.

One of the firm's first ideas was to orchestrate a luncheon with *Cagney and Lacey's* stars and the women on the production team—Tyne Daly, Sharon Gless, April Smith (the producer at the time), and Barbara Corday—to honor working women. The event was to be a press and photo opportunity, with the particular aim of gaining publicity for the series in women's magazines and the "women's pages" of newspapers. It represented an attempt to situate *Cagney and Lacey* as a program for and about working women and to begin forming a working women's viewer base. To that end, the original concept—a luncheon in honor of women police officers—was reconceived (probably because of the growing emphasis on the upscale, professional woman) as an occasion to honor *all* working women.[41]

The *original* proposal read, "Taking stock of *Cagney and Lacey* we discovered we have a wonderful opportunity to salute the working women of Los Angeles." The luncheon, called "Cagney and Lacey Salute the Women Police Officers of Los Angeles," was proposed as follows:

> The women police detectives of the L.A.P.D. and the L.A. County Sheriff's Office will be invited. . . . Such an assemblage is press-worthy and will see print.
>
> Seated on the dais will be some of the most influential women in the city of Los Angeles and the State of California. They will attend this luncheon inasmuch as it will provide them with an opportunity to acknowledge their support of working women in general and women police officers in particular.

A list of "potential dais participants," including numerous prominent women, then followed. "The purpose of the luncheon, hosted by *Cagney and Lacey* stars Sharon Gless and Tyne Daly," continued the letter,

> will be to honor the working women of the 80's. An audience comprised of their on-screen counter-parts and a dais consisting of outstanding women achievers embraces the concept of working women in a flattering and dignified light.
>
> Tyne and Sharon are, indeed, working women. Together they represent both the single woman and the working parent and their roles as Cagney and Lacey notwithstanding, they are as qualified as anyone to discuss women's roles in society. As noted above, we think the event particularly news-worthy. . . . It will go a long way to positioning our show and our stars off the television pages and on to the important women's pages and magazines such as "Working Woman."[42]

A follow-up letter revised the luncheon plans; and these revisions fit in better both with the advertising industry's targeting of "go-getter" professional women and with *Cagney and Lacey*'s shifts toward presenting its characters as more upwardly mobile. They also parallel changes in the program that I will discuss in the next chapter—namely, its moves away from the "cop show" emphasis and from showing the characters in police uniforms.[43] The revised luncheon, according to Rogers and Cowan, would now be called "CAGNEY & LACEY Salute Working Women." "We have decided," the letter read,

> to approach this event from a much broader perspective and gather together a number of highly successful women from all areas of endeavor. We hope to create a forum to salute America's working women, emphasizing that there is at last a program on the air which addresses the specific needs and lifestyles of the female species. As such, the salute will not be directed toward the women of the Los Angeles Police Department alone, but toward all women who work. Representatives of the LAPD will, however, be invited to attend. . . .
>
> We have approached Gay Bryant, editor of *Working Woman* magazine, to enlist their editorial involvement and support. They reach the very audience we are targeting. Of course, this does not preclude any of the other press outlets we intend to pursue. In the event they lend the kind of support *Ms.* magazine did, we will distribute *Working Woman* to journalists across the country. . . . We want this luncheon to be a positioning tool for CAGNEY & LACEY. We do not expect it to make

the front page and that is clearly not our intention. We do expect "day and date" coverage. We also fully expect CAGNEY & LACEY to be around for a number of years and the good will generated here will be helpful now and will continue to be helpful down the line. . . .

Our invitation list includes the most important women in our community and in other communities. As you can see, we have stacked the deck with some well-placed female members of the press. While we do not know how many of these women will be available to attend, they were all chosen for very good reasons and each one can be a key to our real goal.

We are promoting an idea, a concept about the show that is important to communicate to our potential audience. Collectively, these women are influential decision-makers. Our effect on them and our ability to make them see what this show is really about will be important to the series' credibility and longevity. . . .

We want these people to meet April, Barbara, Sharon and Tyne and get to know the women behind the women of CAGNEY & LACEY. We want to get the word out that there is more going on here than cops and robbers. We feel that if we can gather a group of successful working women and encourage them to address their own common denominator with an eye toward improving the plight of working women everywhere, we will have achieved a great deal. We are hitting hard with this aspect of the show, and it is important.[44]

A second group of proposals involved TV, radio, press, and direct mail campaigns that appealed to a large, perhaps heterogeneous audience in a process Rogers and Cowan called "getting out the vote." Read one letter,

We call the nuts & bolts "getting out the vote." As long as the Networks measure our success by the numbers we will do everything we can to draw the largest possible viewing audience in the first critical six weeks and beyond. You are as familiar as we are with the wire services, the syndicated columnists, the talk shows (MERV, MIKE, JOHNNY, etc.), the Sunday supplements, and no less than a dozen other traditional television outlets. . . . We will work aggressively in this area. . . . We will coordinate our efforts with the entire CBS press department . . . and indeed get out the vote.[45]

Other media strategies, however, were directed at a specifically women's audience. One early idea, which still emphasized the police aspect of the series, provides a fascinating example of soliciting publicity aid from the network's owned and operated stations, or "O and O's," as well as of the blending of "news" and advertising. The proposal was called "Policewomen—Profiles in Courage." "Rogers & Cowan," says the letter,

will speak directly with the Station Promotion Managers of each CBS Owned & Operated station as well as the remaining top 17 U.S. markets in connection with a special week long "news-doc" (news documentary) about their city's policewomen. We will provide them with clips from the upcoming season of CAGNEY AND LACEY, and the opportunity to interview Sharon or Tyne in conjunction with the story.

Obviously Rogers & Cowan cannot dictate to CBS affiliates; what we can do is develop a scenario for such a week long look at their city's women in blue and suggest that such a story on working women is not only timely but is a legitimate news story. We will submit to station management that feature stories dealing with popular television program themes are well received by viewing audiences. (Witness the number of cruise stories prompted by the success of "The Love Boat").

In the event any of the CBS affiliates fail to pursue the idea, we will approach one or more of the independent stations in each market. Our basic plan is to have virtually every one of the top 20 U.S. markets running special features on women police detectives with a special slant toward CAGNEY & LACEY.[46]

Another idea sought to capitalize on the trend of using radio to reach the working women's market by promoting "an extensive campaign of on-air interviews with both Sharon Gless and Tyne Daly." First priority was given to syndicated radio shows that were willing to come and tape on the set, and both Gless and Daly did a battery of interviews for the CBS Radio Network, among others.[47]

The particular strategy that was absolutely crucial to amassing the working women's audience—and one that was relied on, throughout the history of the program, for maintaining audience contact—was that of publicizing the series in the "women's pages" of newspapers. Early Rogers and Cowan letters outlined the original intentions and tactics:

We will pitch telephone interviews with Sharon and Tyne to all Women's Page Editors at the daily newspapers in the top 70 Nielsen markets across the country. We're going to hit hard in this area, implying that it is incumbent upon them as working women to devote space to working women as embodied in CAGNEY & LACEY. Even though many of the Television Editors of these papers have already covered the show, our approach comes from a different angle and certainly presents a topic appropriate to a Women's Page. Also, we will supply canned editorial copy, stories from Sharon and Tyne themselves discussing their own roles as working women playing the parts of working women in a television series. These will be offered as "exclusive to your city" to daily newspapers in the top 70 Nielsen markets.[48]

Another often-employed campaign involved contacting women's groups by mail on a regular basis. Rogers and Cowan called this the "National Women's Group Mailing," and its design was conceived thus:

A list of national women's organizations is attached [260 organizations are listed]. We will mail a newsletter highlighting various aspects of CAGNEY & LACEY to each of them monthly for a six month period. They will be encouraged to include this information in any communications to their memberships. We hope to stimulate response to the show as well as gain attention for it.

While we don't expect it, it is possible that we may get a negative response from a group that finds fault with a particular episode. Even that does not frighten us. We feel that CAGNEY & LACEY would not be hurt by controversy. The show is strong enough that any small point one group doesn't agree with would be overwhelmingly supported by the majority of others.[49]

In mid-October 1982, Rogers and Cowan sent an initial letter to these groups. "[W]e . . . expect," the firm wrote to Orion Television, "the message delivered . . . which positions CAGNEY & LACEY as an important forerunner of honest, effective representation of women on network television—will elicit responses from these groups of caring, active individuals."[50] The actual letter employed women's movement language that focused on the importance of *Cagney and Lacey* to working women and the significance of having a show about women on such a male-dominated medium as television. It echoed traditional "network" thinking about audiences in saying that if *Cagney and Lacey* did not succeed, it would be because it had not "captured the imagination of the audience." It also made clear that in such a case the network would not gamble on this type of women's program again:

We are pleased to represent CAGNEY & LACEY, a primetime television show that, for the first time, takes an honest look at the lives of women who work.

Because it is the first show of its kind, the television industry will be keeping a watchful eye on CAGNEY & LACEY. If it fails to capture the imagination of the American viewing public, it may be some time before another dramatic series about women is seen on weekly television. While there have been a goodly number of solid roles developed for women in continuing series programming, they have been co-starring roles with men. Because this show's stars are *both* women, television executives will, unfortunately, characterize this show as a "female" series, even though shows about doctors, lawyers, and detectives, all of whom happen to be men, are never perceived as "male" shows. The importance of this show cannot be underestimated and it is because of its importance that we would like to bring it to your attention and to the attention of the members of your organization.[51]

The letter went on to describe the characters and their jobs, stressing that the dramatic focus was on relationships and reactions; it asked that the organizations publicize the series to their memberships and called attention to a press release included for reprint:

> Their [Cagney and Lacey's] occupation provides exciting storylines as they investigate crime in the fast-paced urban environment of New York City. The *real* story is the way they react to the pressures of their job, to each other, and to their friends and families, and the way people react to them. . . .
>
> It is our hope that you will watch for CAGNEY &'LACEY and alert your members to watch as well. If you agree with us that it is a worthy effort worth your support, we encourage you to write to CBS in New York, or your local affiliate, and tell them so. It will be this kind of feedback that will open the door to more shows of this caliber and more hours of television programming directed toward issues of importance to American women, presented in an honest and forthright way. A press release announcing the show is attached and we ask that you reprint it in any newsletter or other mailing to your membership. And, of course, we welcome any editorializing you may wish to add that will call their attention to CAGNEY & LACEY and encourage them to form their own opinions.[52]

Such women's groups as national and local NOW chapters responded by placing articles about the series in their own membership newsletters.

Yet a third proposal was called "CAGNEY & LACEY Salute to Working Women." This strategy was actually aimed at department stores, with a tie-in to a woman's magazine. It is a fine example of a double address to women in aspects of their lives already coded as gendered (reading women's magazines and department store shopping) in order to solicit and construct the further gendered audience for a women's TV program. According to Rogers and Cowan,

> In conjunction with the Promotion Directors of the Broadway Department Stores in Southern California, Carson Pirie Scott in Chicago, and Macy's in New York, we will develop a store-wide CAGNEY & LACEY Salute to the Working Women of America. We will effect a tie-in with "Working Woman" Magazine in conjunction with a salute revolving around a week long series of guest appearances by experts on fashion, beauty, health, investment, child care and other areas of specific interest to the working woman. This phase of the campaign will not take place prior to the premiere of the series on October 25th, but will be one of many on-going campaigns implemented to maintain a high level of awareness for the series. Once the three major markets have been completed we may opt to expand this promotion to such markets as Dallas, St. Louis, San Francisco, Boston and Philadelphia.[53]

The tie-in and support from *Working Woman* magazine never materialized. The reason probably derived from the "questionable" nature of *Cagney and Lacey*'s portrayals of women, even in the revised Gless/Daly version. The characters did not fit in with the images that the magazine was promoting, especially since it had shifted to target exclusively the upscale, professional working woman. A comment by Patricia Bosworth, arts editor for the magazine, in November 1982 (concurrent with the Rogers and Cowan letters), in fact read, "Right now prime time television is psychologically a very different place than it was in the 1960's and 70's. The role models are more realistic and gritty—compare the *abrasive* female cops Cagney and Lacey to Angie Dickinson's sleek 'Police Woman'" (emphasis mine).[54]

The bulk of Rogers and Cowan's publicity for the program fostered its association with the women's movement, though in a nonexplicit way. For example, although the words "feminist" or "feminism" do not appear in the firm's letters to women's organizations, the aspects of the program that are highlighted and the appeals to women in the audience are very much rooted in women's movement language and concerns. Their publicity releases, which spoke of women addressing their "own common denominator with an eye toward improving the plight of working women everywhere" and stressed *Cagney and Lacey* as "a show that is directed toward issues of importance to American women" and one that starred two women rather than a woman with a man, strengthened the program's identification with feminism and encouraged its feminist readings. The Rogers and Cowan campaign nicely demonstrates how the loosely organized, multileveled structure of network TV contributes to the multiple meanings and ambiguity of television representations. In this case the publicity firm, in its second-level texts, emphasized an aspect of the program that the network was choosing, at the time, to downplay and thus furthered the ongoing connection of the show with feminism.[55]

Despite the overall strategies for scheduling, promoting, and publicizing the series as a working women's vehicle and the myriad attempts to gather a large women's audience, *Cagney and Lacey* found itself in danger of cancellation at the end of the 1982–83 season. Television's practice of gender-programming figured strongly in the predicament: The series's average share for the six weeks during which it aired against ABC's *Monday Night Football* was a fairly respectable 27. A players' strike, however, truncated the football season that year, throwing a monkey wrench into the plans of CBS's programmers and proving nearly fatal for *Cagney and Lacey*. During the strike, ABC as well as NBC began to air made-for-TV movies, and the series's average share fell to a less respectable 22; at times it plunged to 18 and 19, and when pitted against *The Thorn Birds* on 28 March 1983, it plummeted to a gruesome 15.

"LAST-DITCH" EFFORTS

By March 1983, it was fairly clear that *Cagney and Lacey's* ratings would not satisfy the network's renewal board. In a "last-ditch" effort to corral the women's audience, Rogers and Cowan, Barney Rosenzweig, and Orion Television orchestrated a massive "Save *Cagney and Lacey*" campaign. Because CBS claimed it had used up all of its series-targeted budget, Orion footed the bill itself, just as it had picked up the tab a year earlier when trying to save the Foster/Daly series. Sharon Gless and Tyne Daly appeared on such programs as *The Tonight Show, Entertainment Tonight, Two on the Town*, and *PM Magazine* to solicit viewers. Advertisements for the season's final two episodes, to be aired in May, were placed in *TV Guide*. In late March, Orion ran full-page ads, featuring excerpts of favorable reviews, in *Daily Variety* and *The Hollywood Reporter*, and an all-out publicity blitz was planned for the week of 11 April.[56]

The goal was very specific: to gather a large women's audience for the last two episodes, especially the one on wife-beating, entitled "A Cry for Help," scheduled to air on 2 May. Sharon Gless and Tyne Daly took to the road (as Foster and Daly had the previous year): Daly went to Boston, Cleveland, and Washington, D.C., and Gless to Philadelphia, Chicago, and Dallas for a series of radio, TV, and print interviews. "We are shamelessly," said Tyne Daly, "asking people to watch and write letters."[57] Both actresses traveled to New York for such publicity events as a luncheon with the New York City Police Department, at which they donated $5,000.00 to the Police Bomb Victims fund. Photos of Gless and Daly presenting their check appeared in major newspapers throughout the country. Also scheduled were meetings and photo sessions with the police commissioner and with New York City mayor Ed Koch.

A major event on the New York stop, planned and coordinated with the U.S. liberal women's movement, was the previewing of "A Cry for Help," the episode on wife-beating. Previews like this one, as Susan Brower discusses, were a fundamental part of the overall publicity strategy for the series. (Brower also argues that *Cagney and Lacey*'s mediocre ratings and critical acclaim allowed it to be promoted as a beleaguered "treasure" that needed saving.) The episode was screened for an audience of women's movement spokespeople and representatives of various organizations, coalitions, and shelters involved with domestic violence and battered women; the screening was followed by a symposium discussion moderated by Gloria Steinem. The event received a good deal of press coverage, and it demonstrates one occasion on which different players, with different investments in *Cagney and Lacey*, banded together for mutual purposes as well as for their own individual ones. In this instance, the independent production company, the production team, and the publicity firm wanted to rally an audience in order to keep the show on the air as a commercial product; the women's movement wanted to rally the same audience as a forum from which to speak out against the epidemic of woman-battering and to save the program for its political and pleasurable aspects.[58]

As part of the overall campaign, Rogers and Cowan also sent a letter, signed by Sharon Gless and Tyne Daly, to women's pages editors of U.S. newspapers. The letter, which attempted to marshal both the women's press and women viewers on behalf of the series, employed women's movement terms and asked for the editors' aid in publicizing "A Cry for Help" to attract the all-important women's audience. "CAGNEY & LACEY," the letter read,

> was meant to be and is, a show principally about women, by women and largely for women. . . . Women have only recently become visible on the force so the examination of female officers themselves is new. But that's

where we focus, on the *woman*, not the guns, the explosions and car chases that are the gris [*sic*] for TV's mill.

Very often, we are approached on the street by working women and women officers, thanking us for an honestly refreshing hour of television and for heightening everyone's awareness of what women experience everyday. . . .

We know there is an audience out there for CAGNEY & LACEY. We know CAGNEY & LACEY is an important step for women on television and we are asking for your help to keep this program on the air. . . . We realize television is not your beat. But women's issues are. We cannot think of a more woman's-oriented story than the honest portrayal of two working women in partnership on television. . . .

It is our hope that you are familiar with CAGNEY & LACEY and would agree as to the importance of urging your readers to become involved. . . .

Our May 2nd episode, entitled "A Cry for Help" deals with wife beating, a subject finally gaining the attention it deserves. . . . Our portrayal of the problem could potentially help women who have gone through this terrifying experience. That is what we hope to accomplish with CAGNEY & LACEY. Not only do we want the show to be dramatically different, we want it to MAKE a difference. . . .

We don't want to be considered "an issue oriented program." But when we can integrate an important issue into a dramatic and entertaining hour of prime-time television, we believe it makes for better television.[59]

The women's movement also engaged in an all-out publicity effort to muster its constituency as an audience, presenting the series as "non-sexist" and the audience as crying out for this kind of programming. *National NOW Times* and *NOW L.A.* printed articles about the show and its impending cancellation and asked their readers to write on its behalf. Names and addresses of CBS officials were listed. Jerilyn Stapleton of *NOW L.A.* wrote,

CAGNEY AND LACEY, a non-sexist show about two New York Policewomen is in jeopardy of being cancelled due to "insufficient" Nielsen ratings. Evidently Nielsen boxes do not reside in feminist homes. Some of the problems that have contributed to the low ratings include being pre-empted with such marvelous shows as the Suzanne Somers Special, which made some regular viewers of CAGNEY AND LACEY extremely angry. Another problem was being pitted against other female

exploitation specials such as "Rage of Angels." Producer Barney Rosenzweig said he casts women and minorities in minor roles and bit parts
written for men every chance he gets. This further provides the audience
with more women being portrayed in non-traditional roles, not to mention more employment for women and minorities. To quote Rona
Barrett, "If CAGNEY AND LACEY leaves the airwaves, what's the
alternative? What's left in its place?" CAGNEY AND LACEY is a quality show that must remain on the air. Your letter could make that
difference.[60]

The female exploitation specials mentioned in Stapleton's letter
prompted Barney Rosenzweig to pursue the targeted audience in a new
way. Unilaterally, it appears, he decided to employ a tactic that produces
very stereotypical meanings about women. His particular angle on the
ratings problem was the relationship of women viewers to exploitation
programs. "The women of America," he said of the audience at this point
in the series's history, "deserted us; given the choice between us and a sexy
movie, they took the sexy movie." Hoping to compete with these movies,
Rosenzweig had "A Cry for Help" advertised in *TV Guide* with more of an
"exploitation" style than was typical for most *Cagney and Lacey* ads. He
said he had been urging CBS to employ this type of approach: "If I have
one complaint it's that [CBS] didn't know how to sell the show. At first, the
campaign was all screeching tires, guns drawn—it looked like 'Women in
Chains.' I pleaded with them."[61]

On 1 April the CBS print advertising department responded to Rosenzweig's plea in a letter that included a sketch of the proposed ad for "A Cry
for Help." "The logo," said the letter, "is similar to that used in your trade
ads. The look, as you can see, is anything but usual." The "look" emphasized violence and the process of attack. It was a full-page image of a
woman's face screaming in terror: the sleeve of her shirt was torn at the
shoulder, her body appeared to have been thrown to the floor, and diago-
nal action lines suggested rapid motion. A clenched fist appeared at the
upper right of the page. The copy read, "SOMETIMES HE HURTS ME
SO BADLY, I WISH I WAS DEAD. Who can a battered wife turn to,
when her husband is a cop? Tonight, a very special episode." When the ad
was actually printed in *TV Guide*, the image had been toned down to be
somewhat less violent, the fist in the upper right corner had been deleted,
and the copy did not include the opening (uppercase) line. This ad, nonetheless, was the first fully exploitative type to be used for the series (although the previous chapter described the exploitation ad used to promote

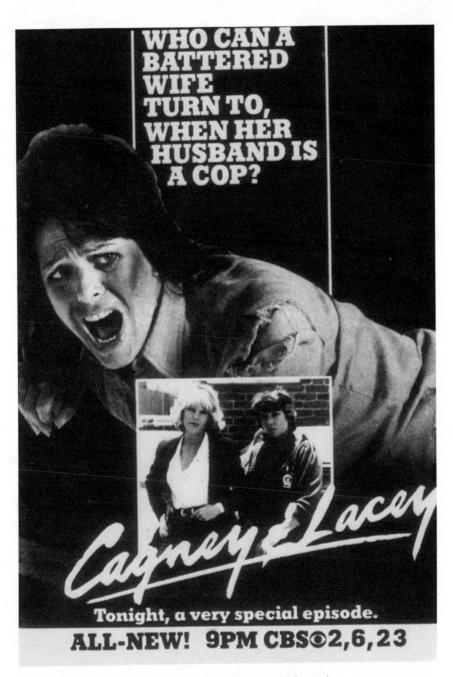

WHO CAN A
BATTERED
WIFE
TURN TO,
WHEN HER
HUSBAND IS
A COP?

Cagney & Lacey

Tonight, a very special episode.
ALL-NEW! 9PM CBS⊙2,6,23

TV Guide *advertisement for "A Cry for Help." (© CBS, 1983)*

the made-for-TV movie). At this point, Rosenzweig seemed to be primarily interested in securing the audience commodity, despite the fact that the "hot sell" advertising tactics defined women in ways at odds with the definitions "intended" by the program. Many Hollywood producers, however, describe this conflict as "part of the territory" of commercial television, especially in marketing an innovative and nonconventional movie or series.[62]

One of Orion Television's strategies for keeping the program on the air was to argue to the network that *Cagney and Lacey* delivered a substantial "quality audience," if not a large one overall. Hoping to build a case for renewal based on proof of this "quality," Orion had one of its staff members research the audience numbers. An Orion Pictures Company inter-office memo dated 27 April 1983 analyzed the ratings data and the viewing patterns of the prized women viewers. A note attached to the analysis read, "As hard as I tried to find a numbers story to put *Cagney and Lacey* in a more positive light, it just wasn't there. I am attaching a summary of what I did find after close examination of the data."

> The problems CAGNEY AND LACEY faced from the beginning of 1983 can be directly attributed to the dramatic change in orientation of ABC programming from men to women. During the six weeks of football this past season, CAGNEY AND LACEY was successful in delivering for CBS enough of the available women audience to achieve an average 28 share. However, I am sure ABC was aware of this adroit counter programming on the part of CBS and produced "Made Fors" [made-for-TV movies] that were targeted at precisely the audience which CAGNEY AND LACEY seeks to attract. Movies like WHO WILL LOVE MY CHILDREN, CONFESSIONS OF A MARRIED MAN, INTIMATE AGONY and GRACE KELLY (not to mention THORN BIRDS) were effective in reaching this audience. NBC was also trying to counter ABC's Monday Night Football and competed for that same audience with heavy women-oriented shows like LITTLE GLORIA, REMEMBRANCE OF LOVE, WAIT UNTIL MOM GETS HOME, RAGE OF ANGELS, and MOTHERS AGAINST DRUNK DRIVING. CAGNEY AND LACEY is being stifled by this onslaught from the other networks. . . .

Research indicates that the women were there. CAGNEY AND LACEY failed to capitalize on this availability of audiences. Look at the data:

TIME	NET	PROGRAM	18+	18–34	18–49	25–54	55+	House	Work
9:30–	CBS	Newhart	32	33	32	33	33	32	34
10:00	ABC	Movie	22	27	26	24	14	21	19
	NBC	Movie	27	20	23	24	36	27	25

HERE'S WHERE THEY WENT

TIME	NET	PROGRAM	18+	18–34	18–49	25–54	55+	House	Work
10:00–	CBS	Cagney & Lacey	27	25	29	24	24	27	27
11:00	ABC	Movie	26	33	29	29	16	26	26
	NBC	Movie	33	25	27	27	39	33	28

LOOK AT THE WOMEN WE LOSE

TIME	NET	PROGRAM	18+	18–34	18–49	25–54	55+	House	Work
9:30–10:00	CBS	Newhart	32	33	32	33	33	32	34
10:00–11:00	CBS	Cagney & Lacey	27	25	29	24	27	27	28

The memo also reports, however, that *Cagney and Lacey* actually "performed slightly higher than the average of all prime-time network shows, and certainly did better than the average with Total Women." The average network show airing between 9:00 and 11:00 drew in 761 women viewers per 1,000 households, whereas *Cagney and Lacey* drew in 822. Dismal as the numbers were, the fact that *Cagney and Lacey* did better than average with total women viewers could be used to make some kind of case.[63]

Despite all the attempts to save it, CBS did cancel the series in May 1983. But efforts to expand the audience did not stop with this setback; in fact, the interactions among various invested players only intensified. Both before and after the cancellation, CBS, the production team, and the mainstream press continued the public debate over their respective notions about the audience and that audience's tastes and preferences.

WHAT DOES A WOMEN'S AUDIENCE WANT?

As we have seen, the operative assumption governing network thinking at the time was that if an innovative program receives low ratings it is because the audience does not like the innovation—meaning, in the case of *Cagney and Lacey*, the series's new depictions of women. This viewpoint was articulated by Harvey Shephard of CBS, who explained the series's cancellation by saying that the show "turned off a sizeable number of women who, according to network research, were somewhat disturbed by seeing women in the traditional male role of police officer." In an earlier interview, Shephard said of the audience, "They accept a show with a woman in a traditional woman's role, like Michael Learned in *Nurse*, but not a woman in a man's expected role." Barney Rosenzweig indirectly responded in *TV Guide*: "What I'm sorry to see is people bringing up 'research' now that says women had a hard time seeing other women in traditionally male roles. What research? How many people did they talk to? I have my own research. I have thousands of letters, typewritten, intelligent letters—that say women loved the show." Tom Carson of the *Village Voice* also countered Shephard's allegations about the audience when he said that "*Cagney and Lacey* is radical only to the business types— who, let us remember, are still made rather panicky at the notion of a woman or women carrying an hour-long series." And Tyne Daly added, "The network is more nervous than the public. . . . The united front of two women on one show is especially threatening."[64]

A number of articles in the mainstream press emphasized the network's assumptions about audiences and their wants and the particular effect, because of these assumptions, that CBS's cancellation of *Cagney and Lacey* would have on future series of its kind. In familiar language, these articles stressed that the program was being evaluated by the industry as a test case for other shows and representations of its kind, and also as a test case for audience preferences. "If *Cagney and Lacey* is cancelled," wrote one reviewer, "some industry executives say it could be years before the networks try another series where women inter-relate in a meaningful, dramatically satisfying way." Arguing along the same lines, Rosenzweig predicted, "If CAGNEY AND LACEY fails this time around it will mean the end of any attempt to portray realistically drawn women on TV. If it succeeds then I think next year you'll be watching ten shows like it. If it fails we'll be pointed to as 'you can't do that.' If CAGNEY AND LACEY was STARSKY AND HUTCH and it didn't do well, no one would say, 'well, let's not do another show with men cops,' but this show's failing is going to doom any show that comes along with a woman in a less than traditional role."[65]

The interplay between Rosenzweig, the audience, and the press is a dramatic example of the confluence of different and overlapping investments in "audience" and the negotiations of these investments: Just as the series was canceled, the publicity blitz and the pleas to the audience for help were beginning to pay off. Letters from viewers began to pour in to CBS, Orion Television, and the *Cagney and Lacey* offices, and Rosenzweig, in the words of one TV critic, "brilliantly parlayed the support . . . in handball maneuvering with the network." This maneuvering can be summarized as follows: In March and April, when the first letters began to arrive, Rosenzweig answered most of them himself. His responses were variations on "Thanks for your letter, although to be effective it must be sent to CBS to either William Paley [address] or Bud Grant [address] or both. We too want the show to continue. The decision is Mr. Grant's and Mr. Paley's."[66]

By May and June, as the mail continued to come in, Rosenzweig developed a form-letter response. Sensing that CBS was casting a cold eye on the mail, he proposed a new tactic to the letter writers:

> Please excuse the form letter, but our offices have been inundated with mail asking us what our viewers can do to save *Cagney and Lacey* and we felt this was the only way we could respond to each of you. CBS too has received enormous amounts of mail, but our sense is that it is not reaching anyone with decision-making power. We therefore suggest that you write to either the editor of the *New York Times* [address], or the editor at the *Los Angeles Times* [address], as well as your local newspaper editors expressing your views regarding the cancellation of the series in the hope that a public outcry, published in the nation's press, will have some influence. You can also call CBS and register your complaints with Bud Grant's office in L.A. [phone number], or Tom Wyman's office in New York [phone number]. Thank you for your kind words and your support. Maybe together we can get Chris and Mary Beth back into the homes of the people who care about them.[67]

In mid-July, two influential members of the press, Lee Margulies of the *Los Angeles Times* and John J. O'Connor of the *New York Times*, wrote stories on the *Cagney and Lacey* audience letters, which by that time had deluged their papers. Both critics noted the wide geographical range represented by this mail and described it with such comments as, "Most of the letters were intelligent, well-written, and sincere, reflecting genuine hurt that a show that meant so much to them [the women fans] was being summarily withdrawn . . . and most of the letters came from women who found support and encouragement in seeing two strong-willed, career-oriented women portrayed on the tube." O'Connor described the sentiments expressed as "demonstrably passionate" and remarked that the same individuals who wrote to him actually had to write two letters (presumably an initial one to Rosenzweig) to vent their feelings. After the series's revival,

Rosenzweig and the staff of the *Cagney and Lacey* offices collected the names and addresses of the letter writers for a "fan club" file and continued to shore up the women's audience by publishing fan club newsletters between 1984 and 1987.[68]

A key group of players in this drama was, of course, the audience itself. The previous chapter used audience letters to explore the viewers' investments in representations of women and definitions of femininity. In this chapter, we will look at what they reveal about the writers' conceptions of themselves as audience members and of their part in creating a women's audience for *Cagney and Lacey*. Generally, the letters bespeak writers who understood how they fit into the economic operations of the TV industry and how they functioned as an "audience" in the network's definition of the term. However, the network's conception was not one in which the letter writers themselves invested. Many of them criticized and mocked the network's notion of audience and bemoaned the fact that, coupled with a devoted adherence to ratings, it resulted in such series as *The Dukes of Hazzard* (the program most often cited by letter writers as an example of the typical TV fare that won out over programs like the canceled *Cagney and Lacey*). But the writers did demonstrate a willingness to play within the network's rules for conceiving "audience" in order to make the case to CBS that they were the kind of viewers it wanted. In effect, they tried to capitalize on their own position and power within the overall television enterprise in order to achieve their own ends—the continuation of a treasured program.

The letters also shed light on the fans' own vested interests in being audience members and their efforts to enlarge their numbers. They reveal viewers who identified with the nonconventional meanings fostered by the program and its representations of women and whose interpretive strategies appear to have developed from what Elizabeth Ellsworth calls "collective alternative interpretations" and Jacqueline Bobo "a community of heightened consciousness," in this instance emerging from the discourses of the various women's movements. These investments and interpretive strategies appear to have produced a group of women fans who thought of themselves as active and tenacious audience *participants*—engaged in, and now struggling over, a program through which they could articulate some of the dimensions of their social lives. As Chapter 5 will show in more detail, the viewers in this particular instance constructed themselves as audience because their pleasure was worth not only a weekly viewing commitment but an all-out effort to preserve the object of their spectatorship.[69]

Many of the letter writers were disdainful of the network's conclusions about audience "wants." "Here's a show," wrote one, "on a par with *Hill*

Street Blues and with two of our most consummate actresses, and the powers that be have decided we, the public, are not ready to accept professional women capable of handling any emergency whether personal or otherwise. In heaven's name, why cancel shows of this calibre when we are inundated with such gems as *Three's Company* etc. etc." A large number attributed *Cagney and Lacey's* mediocre ratings not to the audience's rejection of women in new roles but to insufficient exposure time. Repeatedly, writers compared *Cagney and Lacey's* plight to that of *Hill Street Blues*, *Simon and Simon*, and *St. Elsewhere*, other nonconventional programs that took some time to gain a large following. They criticized CBS for not having the "guts" shown by NBC in championing its "quality" programs, or for not living up to its reputation as a network. One viewer wrote, "I do not understand why the most highly rated of the three major networks is not able to nurture a show of such excellence even in the absence of blockbuster ratings. Surely a high-quality show would enhance your reputation even more." "*Cagney and Lacey*," wrote another, "breaks some new ground. Give the public a chance to let the feel of it sink in."

Viewers often pointed to the "unfair competition" *Cagney and Lacey* faced from made-for-TV movies. One die-hard fan from Yonkers saw the series's high performance in the summer months as evidence of a strong and committed audience, arguing that viewers who had watched the TV movies during the regular season rejoined *Cagney and Lacey* during the summer, and perhaps even chose to view the movie with this plan in mind. The fan wrote, "I did not desert the program when NBC threw all those blockbuster movies against *Cagney and Lacey*. I watched those movies from 9–10 o'clock. At 10 o'clock I promptly switched to channel 2 [*Cagney and Lacey's* channel]. *Cagney and Lacey's* very high summer ratings were due to the return of all the viewers who watched those blockbuster movies. During the summer, they merely caught up with the shows they had missed during the winter."

Many writers were conversant with the industry's assumptions about target demographics, consumers, and ratings, and they incorporated that information into their letters, either to berate the network or to play its game. Said one viewer to Bud Grant of CBS,

> When are you people going to realize that all the wealth and power of consumerism is not necessarily in the hands of the 'Joanie-Loves-Chachi' crowd? That many of us women actually have IQ's above 75; that many of us are sick to death of your 'traditional' portrayals of us as brainless bombshells, simpering sycophants, or ancillary appendages to

men without whom we would cease to exist; and that as long as you continue to offer us this hogwash, you will continue to lose viewers.[70]

Another, from British Columbia, wrote, "For your interest in demographics, I'm 34, divorced, a teacher, and also watch *Masterpiece Theatre*, *60 Minutes*, *Donahue*, some Canadian programs, *and* a couple of soap operas." Another said, "We are retired but spend more money than the mentally immature individuals who follow *Dukes of Hazzard*. Don't your advertisers want to sell some big ticket items? Cater to us, too, please." And another pleaded with Rosenzweig, "Just tell CBS that I spend around $600.00 a month on food and I watch the commercials." One letter mocked the whole concept of audience ratings and "Nielsen families" and presented its own case for *Cagney and Lacey*'s renewal. "I am a NELSON family," the letter began.

What, you say, is a Nelson family? We are opposites of the Nielsen family. We have our favorite and entertaining shows, however, they are usually the opposite of the Nielsen family's and so the shows we like get "axed." Now, I usually don't write and complain (because the Nielsen's usually win out) but I would like to throw in my two cents worth about the black box and voice my opinion. CAGNEY AND LACEY is one of my favorite shows. I like the actors, the format of the show, and the friendship portrayed by Cagney and Lacey. But it is hanging by a slim thread because of the Nielsen's. Let's look at this logically: a. The show ranked a respectable 30 in the recent Nielsen's (playing against the second half of "V"). b. CAGNEY AND LACEY was only five shows behind REMINGTON STEELE which has been renewed and which has a very strong lead-in show THE A-TEAM (do I have to say more about the logics of the Nielsen's?). c. The show should have some time to recover from the rapid departure of Meg Foster. And finally, d. It should be given the benefit of the doubt a la SIMON AND SIMON which was very low in the ratings and which is now #8. . . . This Nelson is just asking to win one battle in the War of Ratings.

Many viewers recounted the actions they had taken to save the series, offered to continue to work for renewal in whatever ways they could, and proposed future plans. Their efforts also served to consolidate and further expand (from within, as it were) a working women's audience for the program. "A lot of my friends and I wrote to CBS," read one letter.

I want to do whatever is necessary to keep CAGNEY AND LACEY going. I am willing to volunteer my time. Tyne Daly and Sharon Gless and the show have a lot of people behind them who *really really care*! We are willing to do whatever we have to to let CBS know CAGNEY AND LACEY is *number one* as far as we are concerned. . . . I think CAGNEY AND LACEY stands up for women's rights and Tyne Daly and Sharon Gless are great at showing two professional women who are also friends. . . . I talked to many people and asked them to write letters, only one person said "no" and was against the show. Everyone else said they would write. . . . I also talked to some of the newspapers in the Metro area.

Another viewer from England, who coordinated a letter-writing campaign in that country, reported, "Since April of this year I have been trying to save the series *Cagney and Lacey*. The fans in England have written themselves or written through me. I have sent the letters on to CBS, Orion, and *The Chicago Sun Times*. . . . The series is or was always in the top 5 list in our charts, over 15 million people watched each week." Many other viewers reported that they wrote to *TV Guide*, local newspapers, and the networks.

A number of letters described *Cagney and Lacey* screening and letter-writing parties, the social character of the program's viewing, and the strengths of viewers' attachments:

After reading the article in the CHICAGO SUN TIMES about the series, I decided to organize a CAGNEY AND LACEY party. Everyone was asked to provide one piece of stationery. I'm providing the envelopes and postage. . . . Many of our group (close to fifty people) would have written anyway but this way it's more fun and we've all had a great evening discussing our favorite episodes and characters. . . . I am an avid fan of live theatre and I find it relatively easy to become involved with (and identify with) characters on stage. . . . But it's difficult to feel that same involvement from television because of distractions, commercials, and the fact that it's a video image, not live actors standing there in front of you. But somehow CAGNEY AND LACEY overcomes all of that to the point where I almost don't see our cat systematically destroying the furniture or don't hear the Pizza Man at the front door.

In describing another letter-writing party, a viewer commented, "Though none of us have written to any network before, we're writing now to save a show that none of us ever misses. It gives real emotions, and portrays women as human." Many other letters were attached to petitions listing anywhere from fifteen to three hundred names. "Enclosed," began one of these, is a list of people who are appalled at your decision to cancel the show *Cagney and Lacey*. We all feel that this is one of only a few shows on TV that is not insulting to one's intelligence. . . . *Cagney and Lacey* tries to show two people in a true to life situation coping with their work and private lives. . . . This show keeps your interest and is enjoyable to watch because of the terrific chemistry between Tyne Daly and Sharon Gless. They make a great team. . . . Let me say that the signatures on the enclosed copy range from age 22 on up and mostly under 49.

A petition from an office in Connecticut read, "The main topic of conversation during this morning's coffee break was the tragedy of the early demise of one of the few fine shows offered by CBS last season, *Cagney and Lacey*. It was the consensus of the group that CBS had done a disservice to its viewers, and we ask that your decision be reconsidered." Fifteen names followed. And another viewer promised, "I'll stand on a corner and get signatures. I'll buy all the products advertised. What will it take?"

Other letters offered suggestions for enlarging the viewing audience and saving the show. A woman from Delaware advised,

You have an enormous potential audience among college students. . . . A very effective, inexpensive campaign could be conducted via form letters to teachers of certain subjects (Women's Studies, Mass Communication, History of Television, for example) requesting them to ask their students to watch it once or twice. Each letter could result in anywhere from 40–200 new viewers. . . . CAGNEY AND LACEY can offer several discussion points for teachers. . . . If you decide this idea is worth trying, I will be glad to *volunteer* my help. I could do anything from simply preparing a mailing list to composing a form letter, to taking care of the actual mailing of a letter. I feel very strongly about the show and would like to do something to ensure its success this time around.

Viewers also boasted of getting friends and family to watch: "I bugged all of my friends into watching it and every one of them has thanked me for it." And others wrote of planning their social lives around *Cagney and Lacey* or viewing in groups. A letter from one of the program's male followers read, "We cancel all plans to see it and have often invited friends to see it with us, instead of going out." And a number of others described the formation of fan clubs like the British CLASS (*Cagney and Lacey* Appreciation of the Series Society) and *Cagney and Lacey* Watchers Club, which involved committed viewers who published their own newsletters. One U.S. viewer, Dorothy Swanson, wrote many letters to save the show and also got numerous other people to write. Swanson went on to form a group called Viewers for Quality Television that later—again by employing the letter-writing tactic—was the most instrumental force in returning the canceled *Designing Women* to the air in the spring of 1987.[71]

Another fan wrote to several of *Cagney and Lacey*'s advertisers "to persuade them to bring this show back on the air." Copies of three sponsor replies were enclosed in a letter to Rosenzweig, and these provide a provocative glimpse into another aspect of the TV enterprise. Judging by the examples of *Lou Grant* and *Heartbeat*, it seems that television advertisers are moved to act only when their product is associated with controversy rather than with programming applauded by viewers. *Cagney and Lacey*'s sponsors simply passed the buck back to the network. Procter and Gamble replied, "Control over the show's continuation or cancellation is in the hands of the network, and you might want to make your views known to them." Tampax said, "We will pass your comments concerning programming on to our advertising agency. However, as you probably realize, television networks base their decisions on ratings rather than advertising." Kellogg's, seeming to miss the point or bypass it, wrote, "Our intention is to participate in wholesome, entertaining radio and television programs and to talk about our products in an informative and pleasing manner. It's good to know that you feel we have succeeded."[72]

These audience letters are potent sources for understanding the viewers' conceptions of audience and of themselves as audience members. The outpouring of letters constituted a moment of public debate—the moment at which alternative and oppositional interpretation becomes actual collective political action.[73] The women's audience for *Cagney and Lacey* assumed a unique meaning—that of a collective force that inserted itself into the production process and influenced CBS to return a canceled series to the air. Given the banding together of the audience, Rosenzweig, and the press, the event also demonstrates how the different participants in the series's history collaborated to assert new notions of audience and of viewer wants. These notions, as we have seen, were quite opposite those of CBS (as voiced by Harvey Shephard above), which believed that the women's audience was invested in traditional representations only.

In the fall of 1983, when CBS agreed to resurrect the series for seven trial episodes to begin airing in March 1984, the press, the production team, and the women's movement were all publicly jubilant over their victory, and all singled out the women's audience as the critical force in saving the series. Such headlines as "Flood of Mail from Women Viewers Revives CAGNEY AND LACEY" and "Viewers Hollered Loud Enough to Be

Heard" were commonplace. The show's offices sent "I Helped Save CAG-NEY AND LACEY" bumper stickers to its fans and distributed the first issue of its *Cagney and Lacey* newsletter. The National Organization for Women's Los Angeles chapter sponsored a reception for the cast, producers, and writers that preceded a screening of the revived series's first episode, and invitations for the event were stamped in large red letters with the message, "WE WON! THEY'RE BACK."[74]

As noted in Chapter 1, the viewer letters alone would not have caused CBS to revive the series; the program was also getting high summer ratings and had saved CBS from a shutout at the Emmy Awards. *Cagney and Lacey* also had a few "friends in high places" who supported the show in various ways, and such bolstering is often crucial if an innovative and borderline (with regard to ratings) program is to succeed. For example, although many passages above may make him seem like the villain of the piece, Harvey Shephard, according to Rosenzweig, was a "good friend" of the program who "gave it extra nurturing"; Arthur Krim, president of Orion Pictures, was another fan who wanted the show saved. Orion Television's president, Richard Rosenbloom, was closely involved with the series from the beginning and was solidly committed to its longevity.[75]

CBS's scheduling strategy for the period of *Cagney and Lacey's* seven trial episodes in the spring of 1984 indicated an even more forceful targeting of the working women's audience. As a midseason replacement in the Monday night lineup, the network introduced *Kate and Allie*, also starring two women and aimed at working women viewers; *Scarecrow and Mrs. King* (a precursor to "couples" drama/comedies like *Moonlighting* that would target working women in the mid-1980s) was also part of the schedule.

The U.S. liberal women's movement maintained its joint efforts with *Cagney and Lacey's* publicity firm to rally women viewers. In April 1984, continuing a strategy of previewing episodes to important groups, NOW president Judy Goldsmith introduced Sharon Gless and Tyne Daly at a Washington, D.C., screening by the American Film Institute of a program on pornography. Mayor Marion Barry, citing the "positive and realistic presentation of the difficult and dangerous duties being performed by police women," had proclaimed 12 April Cagney and Lacey Day, and Ethel Williams, executive director of the D.C. Commission for Women, presented the actresses with an official proclamation of the event. According to an article in the *National NOW Times*, "the leaders of dozens of women's organizations paid tribute to the program and its stars." And several years later, when *Cagney and Lacey* was again in danger of cancellation in the spring of 1987, the *National NOW Times* published a half-page article

Ethel Williams, executive director of the D.C. Commission for Women, presents an official Cagney and Lacey Day proclamation to Sharon Gless and Tyne Daly as NOW president Judy Goldsmith looks on. (From National NOW Times, *May/June 1984, courtesy National Organization for Women, Inc.)*

about the program's beleaguered history and its enduring importance to the women's movement. "NOW," the article concluded, "is being called on once more for support, and for phone calls to local newspaper columnists covering media and to local CBS affiliate managers" (CBS president Bud Grant's address was included). The network, however, decided to renew *Cagney and Lacey* before a new write-in campaign gathered full force.[76]

MIXED MESSAGES ABOUT THE QUALITY AUDIENCE

Target audience considerations were among the major reasons for the network's revival of the series in the spring of 1984 and for its continued renewal of *Cagney and Lacey* until 1988. As one TV critic summed it up, "Clearly it made more sense to gamble again on a prestigious series that has shown ratings potential—and deals honestly with the growing force of working women—than to take all the risks of a brand new show." David Poltrack, CBS's vice-president for research, expressed perhaps the primary reason for the network's gamble in 1984: "The show made money for the network because it drew in a strong audience among women, making it attractive to advertisers. Its core audience, women 25 to 54, is the most saleable demographic segment. Now, by playing off the publicity and press attention, maybe some new people will try the show."[77]

For a 1985 *New York Times* article, Karen Stabiner interviewed Poltrack, Harvey Shephard, and Jerome Dominus (vice-president of network sales for CBS-TV) about the phenomenon of *Cagney and Lacey*'s ratings and audience. Stabiner wrote, "According to Poltrack a 2,600-family audience demographic sample compiled by the A. C. Nielsen Company shows that most of the women who watch CAGNEY AND LACEY are college educated and over 35; they make more money (more than $40,000 a year) and watch less television than the average viewer. About a third are men, most of them over 35, with a slight increase in male viewers between the ages of 18 and 49 after ABC's competing MONDAY NIGHT FOOTBALL ends its season." Stabiner further commented that CBS was especially interested in the series's popularity with an older, relatively affluent audience:

> Harvey Shephard says that the network has sensed a new interest on the part of advertisers in the older audience, people between 30 and 60, who really have the bulk of the buying power. . . . Jerome Dominus is even more plainspoken. He feels that the anticipated consumer potential of younger adults has simply not panned out, while the CAGNEY AND LACEY audience represents a stable, affluent wedge of the buying public. "Yuppies [Dominus says] are a marketing concept without legs. . . . They spend all their money on rent. I only wish I had more hours like CAGNEY AND LACEY to sell."[78]

These comments show that the notion of a smaller, "quality" target audience, with some new twists (in this case, the emphasis on older viewers), was given a strong show of support by the network. (And in fact, *Cagney and Lacey* managed to stay on the air for the whole of its history with marginal overall ratings: In 1984–85, the average rating was 15.9 and the share 26; in 1985–86 the rating was 15.4 and the share 26; in 1986–87 the rating was 15.1 and the share 24; and in 1987–88 the rating was 12.6 and the share 22.) Network affiliates also reported to Rosenzweig that they liked the series because it was "an intelligent show and a good lead-in for their local news." In other words, it delivered a good news audience to the affiliated stations. However, Barbara Corday (the program's cocreator and, at the time of this comment, president of Columbia Pictures Television) characterized the networks' view of the audience with a different slant: "I'm not sure the networks yet believe that you can spread this audience real thin. The attitude is, 'Hey, look at what they pulled off. They could *never* do it again.' "[79]

Similarly, a 1987 *TV Guide* column about *Cagney and Lacey*'s cancellation prospects summarized the networks' most persistent view of overall ratings and quality audience demographics: "In the plus column will be the show's prestige and its good demographics . . . but CAGNEY'S ratings [its gross audience numbers] are soft." And as Joseph Turow points out, CBS's championing of an older, affluent segment of the audience as prime demographic "quality" did not convince other networks or advertisers to follow suit. With the increased competition from the emerging FOX network, which pitched its programming to much younger groups, the three major networks joined the scramble for the youth audience that appeared to gain ascendancy with advertisers in the late 1980s and early 1990s. The lack of *Cagney and Lacey* clones underscores this trend, as does the fact that the series itself, because of mediocre ratings, was canceled once and for all in May 1988.[80]

Producing and delivering a desirable "audience commodity" is undoubtedly the major business behind the box. Since the 1970s, the notion of a "quality audience"—a deluxe group of, for instance, upscale young urban adults or working women—gave producers and independent production companies a way to sell the networks on programs that might not have large mass appeal. As "off-beat" a series as *Cagney and Lacey* might never have come to TV had it not been for the networks' active pursuit of the working women's audience and their search for different ways to reach and manufacture that group. But despite its partly institutional origins, the series was quickly taken up by the women's movement, by women viewers, and by the press, all of whom viewed their participation in different ways. They did not see themselves as swelling the ranks of the working women's market and audience, but rather, respectively, as a collective of feminist-oriented women looking for compatible mainstream representations, as a group of viewers (audience members, but also emotionally invested spectators) who enjoyed satisfying portrayals of women that echoed their own daily lives, and as a body of professional critics who were championing innovative television and arguing for a new conception of the relationship between ratings and audience preferences.

Social and historical conditions, however, influenced the institutional mandate to gather the working women's audience in complex and sundry ways. The 1980s backlash against the women's movements, for instance, eroded a lot of the general interest *Cagney and Lacey* and other shows of its kind might have continued to rouse, put enormous pressure on the series's representations and subject matter, and turned prime time away from programs with too overt a feminist slant. The networks developed other series like *Moonlighting*, *thirtysomething*, and the always reliable situation comedies, including *The Golden Girls*, *Kate and Allie*, *Designing Women*, and *227*, which attracted the working women's audience with far less risk.

And the increasing success of cable networks' narrowcasting to specific viewers has continued to upset conventional network strategies and notions regarding television audiences.

The idea of a quality audience responsible for introducing innovation and difference to the TV screen in the 1970s and 1980s was, of course, firmly rooted in class-based social divisions: "Upscale" was the indisputable touchstone of the "bottom line," and most "quality" programs featured solidly middle-class and upwardly mobile characters, mise-en-scène, and story lines. Series like *Good Times, All in the Family, Chico and the Man, Sanford and Son, Laverne and Shirley,* and *Alice* in the seventies and the convention-shattering *Roseanne* (with its working-class settings and characters and its iconoclastic woman lead) in the eighties and nineties, despite their unquestionable popularity, are nonetheless anomalies (and surely welcome ones) for the home screen.[81]

The impression that emerges over and over again in this discussion is one of the complex intermeshings of the whole TV enterprise, the dense network of players and motivations. On the one hand we have, as Ien Ang says, a demonstration of the power of the television institution; all participants have to "realize themselves" (and, I would add, their definitions and constructions of "audience") in relation to "given institutional constraints"—the needs and imperatives of advertisers, networks, production companies, and publicity firms.[82] On the other hand, women viewers, the women's movement and other interest groups, the press, and innovative members of the production team and the independent production company all constructed and defined the "working women's audience" for *Cagney and Lacey,* all according to their own needs and wants. And as the work of Ang and other scholars has also demonstrated, viewers' understandings of their activities as "audience" may be linked to issues of pleasure, desire, identification, narrative and genre fascination, diversion, or alternative and oppositional politics, for example, and may have very little or nothing at all to do with their consumption of the products advertised.

Furthermore the kinds of social positions the constraints of the TV industry have helped create for women (as consumers or as target audiences, for example) have also produced spaces for "women's culture"—shopping, escape into media fiction, or discussion and bonding around particular TV programs, to mention just a few. I am by no means saying that we should simply and uncritically celebrate these spaces and this culture, but rather that the relationships among all of these elements are dense and complex and can most fruitfully be analyzed as a process of ongoing tensions, of continual "up for grabs" negotiation.

CHAPTER 3

A WOMAN'S PROGRAM

As we saw in the previous chapter, the various players in *Cagney and Lacey*'s history participated in the construction of a women's audience, according to their sometimes divergent and sometimes overlapping needs and ideas. These same players also had active roles in developing *Cagney and Lacey* into a "woman's program"—although, as is probably obvious, such a concept is itself the product of struggle and differently oriented interests. *Cagney and Lacey* was always a "mixed form" or a "generic hybrid," but as the show evolved, its generic balance altered, making it less of a police genre and more of a "woman's form."[1] This change took place, of course, in the context of the series's attempt to reach a target audience of working women and its increased competition from female exploitation vehicles. The changes in genre gradually steered the show from physical action to talking, from "cop story" subject matter to woman's program subject matter. Similarly, the protagonists shifted from being primarily the subjects of rough police action to being more investigative detectives and more "conventional women" in ways that (at least in part) evoked the exploitation dimensions of that phrase.

The parameters of this chapter include not only institutional and social issues but also textual ones, and we will see how the contextual struggles and negotiations were also enacted very intensely at the level of the text itself, primarily because of the conventions and implications of the police genre. Nevertheless, the network's needs and constraints continued to affect these textual matters; in addition, the audience's interpretations of and investments in the text tend to complicate any pat conclusions we may wish to draw about what constitutes a "woman's program." The textual negotiations over *Cagney and Lacey*—specifically those involving newer discourses about women as autonomous individuals and protagonists of conventionally male TV drama and traditional discourses about women as wives, mothers, heterosexual sex objects, victims, and subjects of comedy— could result in interpretations of the program as either "progressive" or "regressive" (among other things), depending on what course one navigated through the text.[2] The arguments of this chapter make most sense when seen within the context of prime time's gender and genre history, but a few remarks will help situate them here.

GENDER, GENRE, AND TELEVISION

Although it is clear that the bulk of television advertising dollars has been aimed at women, the history of prime-time programming has been dominated by traditionally male-oriented stories and genres and by male characters—specifically white males. Beginning in the late seventies, it is true, women appeared on TV in somewhat greater numbers than at any other time in prime-time history. But between 1952 and 1977, males comprised roughly 70 percent, and often more, of the prime-time population. In 1976 the breakdown of characters by sex and race was 62.7 percent white male, 9.6 percent "minority" male, 24.1 percent white female, and 3.6 percent "minority" female. When the division of male and female characters is broken down into specific genres and specific narrative functions, the gender-based divisions in prime time become more complicated and pervasive.[3]

Throughout most of TV history, male actors and characters have starred in and been the active protagonists of dramas and action-adventure programs involving public-sphere stories and settings. The few women who were even a part of these dramas were most often mothers, wives, nurses, secretaries, romantic interests, or helpmates to the male heroes. Before the emergence of the "jiggle" series in the mid-seventies and the prime-time soaps of the late seventies and the eighties, dramatic programs were essentially a male preserve. Women, as stars and active narrative subjects, were usually limited to the situation comedy—the site of the family, the domestic, the private sphere, the home manager, and the consumer. (Surprisingly, though, male-led sitcoms also outnumber female-led ones by a significant margin in TV history).[4]

Between 1949 and 1990, there were only approximately 36 dramatic TV series (out of roughly 555) that starred women—in which, that is, a woman was the subject of the narrative action, the protagonist, and did not costar with a man. And these 36 shows included 7 programs that ran for as little as two months, 9 that ran under six months, and 7 that lasted only a year. In addition to the "jiggle" shows of the mid-seventies—*Charlie's Angels, Flying High, American Girls, Wonder Woman, Police Woman,* and *Get Christie Love*—the list included *Mama, The Bionic Woman, Nurse, Cagney and Lacey, Murder She Wrote, Heartbeat, The Trials of Rosie O'Neill,* and perhaps *China Beach.* Out of the above-mentioned 555 dramas, about 415 have starred men, while the remaining 100 or so have had men and women as costars.[5] Seen in this light, the innovative character of *Cagney and Lacey* is startlingly apparent, as is one of the many ways that TV has worked to construct gender—in this case by its gender-based allocation of genres, which has equated masculinity with serious, powerful, public action and femininity with domesticity, subsidiary status, and comedy.

Although this book continually emphasizes the multiplicity of meanings, this chapter will explore the hegemonic meanings that one dramatic genre—the police show—has historically *worked to* produce. Specifically, I will demonstrate how the struggles over defining femininity (and masculinity) involve television forms. Just as industry interventions, constraints, and extratextual practices contributed to the production of gender, a particular aspect of the text, genre, did so as well.

My basic argument is that the conventional meanings produced by the police program could not continue to be generated with two feminist women in the roles of police-protagonists. The genre, quite simply, could not hold. But how exactly did the program shift generically, and into what specific form did it develop? What are the implications of the changes in subject matter and the shifting of the program's depictions of women toward more of an exploitation format—a format in which women are often represented as victims? These are some of the questions this chapter seeks to answer, beginning with a detailed look at the police genre and its relationship to masculinity and femininity.

GENDER, GENRE, AND THE POLICE SHOW DRAMA

Television genres work to produce gender in a number of ways, some of which have been discussed above: First, they carve up the territory of TV into those programs involving male protagonists/stars and spheres of action and those involving females. Second, they target specific programs to men's audiences and specific ones to women's. Third, they initiate particular kinds of narrative structures that have gender-oriented implications.[6] Fourth, they work to produce particular meanings about gender in their textual operations (which is not, of course, to imply that a TV viewer invariably or uncritically adopts these meanings). And fifth, they work to constitute femininity and masculinity in their spectators.

Jane Feuer and Mimi White have pointed out the difficulties involved in defining television genres. One difficulty, as they have observed, arises from the mixed character of many present-day TV programs—the widespread blurring of genre boundaries. Lynne Joyrich and David Thorburn, furthermore, have described how all television genres have become suffused with melodrama, and Horace Newcomb and Caren Deming have noted the mixture of soap opera and melodrama in *Hill Street Blues.*[7] *Cagney and Lacey* certainly does not contradict these observations, and it is, in fact, the history of the show's generic mixing and matching that I am examining here. I do, however, assume and assert a continued degree of specificity and discreteness not only in the police genre but in other TV forms and genres as well. And I would argue that *Cagney and Lacey's* full-scale blending of genres was triggered by particular and discernible conditions on the levels of the text, the industry, and the general social context.

From 1982 to 1988, the series developed into a hybrid genre, from a more conventional police program (in the first Tyne Daly/Meg Foster episodes) to a combination of police genre, melodrama, soap opera, and comedy. These changes, and the consequent changes in the narrative dimensions of the episodes, were primarily motivated by gender. They worked to reassert more customary television notions of masculinity and femininity, which had been destabilized by the early episodes, and to produce definitions of women that the television industry hoped would attract larger numbers of female viewers. But the changes in the genre opened a new arena of clashes and negotiations centered around the questions of gender and made possible new pleasures and identifications for women viewers, however complex and problematic they might be.[8]

In order to understand *Cagney and Lacey* in these terms, however, we must first explore what I call the gender-oriented work of the conventional TV police genre by outlining and discussing the genre's norms. It is important, however, to note that I have limited my definition of police genres to dramatic television series involving the police per se and have excluded related programs, such as those with private detectives, district attorneys, and spies. I have also excluded police comedies and police "reality" and docudrama programs.[9]

GENERIC ELEMENTS

The series *Dragnet*, which ran from 1952 to 1959 (and was revived for a second run from 1967 to 1970 as *Dragnet '67*), is often considered the prototype of the television police drama. Although even before *Dragnet* there had been prime-time police series like *The Plainclothesman* and *Crime Syndicated*, and although the popular *Gangbusters* also premiered in 1952, it was *Dragnet* that developed and consolidated many facets of the early form. It introduced such elements as police department jargon and a heavy emphasis on police procedural (interviewing witnesses, interrogating suspects, keeping and researching police files), which contributed to the series's documentary style and its memorable realism. Another of the program's constitutive aspects was the police partnership or team: Sgt. Joe Friday (the Jack Webb character whose voice-over narration lent a further sense of "reality" to the narrative) was paired with several different male officers in the course of the series's two runs. Joe Friday solidly embodied the figure of the completely dedicated cop—a character with "no personal life and no interests other than police work."[10]

Also important in the genre's early development was *Highway Patrol* (1955–59). From a 1990s vantage point, this program seems atypical because of its nonurban setting (the highways of the western United States), but it added to the early genre a focus on action, including car, motorcycle, and occasional helicopter chases as well as physical fights and shootouts. Although Broderick Crawford's Chief Dan Matthews was the only regular character, other male officers aided him in his weekly pursuits.[11] Subsequent series produced in the late 1960s and throughout the 1970s contributed to and routinized many generic elements of the police drama, including squad room sets, squad car scenes, and violent action sequences.

Of the approximately sixty police series (as defined above) produced between 1952 and the early 1990s, most were dominated by Caucasian male actors and protagonists. Two, *McMillan and Wife* and *MacGruder and Loud*, featured married couples doing police work, although the "wife" in *McMillan and Wife* was not a member of the police force and was killed in a plane crash in the series's fourth season (out of five). Seven series showcased women protagonists, including *Police Woman*, the police-related *Charlie's Angels* (the "Angels" were former policewomen turned detectives), and *Get Christie Love*. But in these programs (with the exception of the short-lived *Amy Prentiss*) a white male always held the leadership position.[12] Of the other fifty-one shows, a few portrayed women as members of police teams, usually for short periods of time and in minor roles.[13]

The majority of these series, then, have focused on male actors and protagonists, usually in partnerships or teams. But the teams have included a variety of interpersonal arrangements. They might be twosomes in which an older veteran serves as mentor to a younger partner, such as in *Dragnet*, *The Line-Up*, *Hawaii Five-O*, *Kojak*, *The Streets of San Francisco*, *Dan August*, and *T.J. Hooker*. Or they might involve peers, as in *Adam-12*, *Starsky and Hutch*, *Delvecchio*, *CHiPs*, and *Miami Vice*. A few series have featured one man as the protagonist with subsidiary ones as commanding officers or squad members, including *Highway Patrol*, *Columbo*, *Toma*, *Baretta*, and *The Blue Knight*, whereas others, like *Ironside*, *The Rookies*, *Kojak*, *T.J. Hooker*, and *Hill Street Blues*, have portrayed precinct "families," in which the characters frequently interacted in the common squad room.[14]

Hierarchical structures and relationships in police programs have also varied. Occasionally the protagonist cop has harbored openly hostile feelings for his commanding officer, as in *Baretta*, but the main antagonisms are usually reserved for "higher-ups"—the police department "top brass" or the FBI. Kojak, for example, had a fairly amicable relationship with his commanding officer (they were once equals and partners), but he was often outraged by the interference and calculating careerism of the FBI agents who intruded in his cases.[15]

Even if the immediate superior was not the primary antagonist, there was usually some friction between him and the protagonist-cop, because the hero was often impatient with all bureaucracy and felt committed to and confident of his own course of action. He sometimes bent the law enough to capture the criminal or force confessions and information from witnesses.[16] But with the occasional exception of Baretta, he was not the "law in his own hands" loner of a Clint Eastwood movie. Although the male protagonist cops have been primarily white, several programs have starred or featured African American, Latino, and Asian American men: *Mod Squad* and *The Rookies* each featured an African American man (Clarence Williams III and Georg Stanford Brown, respectively) as part of the police team. The short-lived *Paris* starred James Earl Jones as a chief of detectives, and the equally short-lived *Ohara* starred the Japanese American Pat Morita as a lieutenant adept in the martial arts. *Miami Vice* and *In the Heat of the Night* each starred a black man and a white man as partners, *Hill Street Blues* featured two black police officers (teamed with white partners) and a Latino assistant commanding officer, and *Hawaii Five-O* had two Asian American officers as members of the police squad. *Starsky and Hutch* had an African American commanding officer who was a somewhat comic character, and the title character in *Hooperman* also had a black man as a partner.

Women, by and large, have been poorly represented in the majority of TV police shows; they have been, as Geoffrey Hurd says, "denied character." Policewomen in predominantly male series are frequently exploited for their sexual dimensions—showcased as sex objects or used within the narratives as bait for criminals. The opening credits of *T.J. Hooker*, for example, include shots of the male police officers running, sliding, jumping, shooting, and driving cars at high speeds. The shots of the female officer Stacy, played by Heather Locklear, show her in a bikini, lounging by a swimming pool, and in a low-cut dress, dancing provocatively into the camera. (There is one brief shot in which Stacy skims a police stick along the ground, tripping up a criminal.) Eve, the policewoman in *Ironside*, was used to "set up" male suspects and often functioned as the team's stenographer. The women characters in *McMillan and Wife*, *Hill Street Blues*, *Miami Vice*, *Hooperman*, and *Hunter* did, however, provide some alternatives to these stereotypical depictions.[17]

In addition to the police roles just described, recurrent women characters have also been featured as secretaries (as in *Hawaii Five-O*), as daughters (in the early episodes of *The Streets of San Francisco*, Lt. Mike Stone's daughter occasionally appeared), and sometimes as girlfriends of the protagonists (as in *McCloud* and *Hooperman*). The predominant roles for women, however, have been those for such nonrecurring characters as victims and as dangerous and "sexually excessive" women—alluring con artists and murderers, "tawdry" girlfriends of criminals, and prostitutes.[18]

The depiction of women as victims, both in series featuring male protagonists and in those featuring females, has been continuous and pervasive. This presentation generally divides victims into two categories, the first being "innocent" women. In the opening scene from a *Streets of San*

Francisco episode, for example, two women are folding clothes in a laundromat. A man pushes open the door, asks if one of them is Jennifer O'Brien, and shoots her point blank with a rifle. We later find out that she is a totally innocent victim who was killed as a way of getting revenge on her husband. Similarly, in *Hawaii Five-O*, a young, white, blond, and naive botany student, while on a field trip in a Hawaiian valley, is abducted and terrorized by a rapist/murderer who has escaped from custody. Or again, in the opening scene of another *Streets of San Francisco*, a young and "undeserving" woman comes home to her apartment to be raped and murdered by a male intruder whom she does not know.

The second category is that of women victims who are set up by the narrative as somehow "deserving" their victimization; the members of this group have had a number of different incarnations.[19] First of all, they might be "out of control" sexually. In a *T.J. Hooker* episode, for instance, four women who have made calls to a sex therapist's radio program are murdered. We find out that all of them talked to the therapist on the air about having or wanting to have extramarital affairs. The killer, at the episode's conclusion, says he murdered them because they were "nothing but married whores." The killer's psychological profile further blames women and their out-of-control sexuality for the situation: He is described as "unmarried, highly religious, product of the classic mother-figure who flaunted her sexuality but punished her children for it."

Another *T.J. Hooker* episode illustrates both a deserving woman victim *and* an undeserving policewoman decoy/victim: A character who has decided to run away from her husband and baby is kidnapped by a sadistic rapist/killer, and in the process of trying to capture the killer, a policewoman (undercover as a waitress) is also abducted. We see a shot of the policewoman with her hands chained to a bed post, her mouth gagged and her ankles tied together; her dress is slit up the side and most of her legs are exposed. When the woman who left her husband and child tries to escape from the rapist, he runs after her, knocks her down, shoots her in the stomach, and says, "Stupid slut." The policewoman is rescued by T.J. Hooker. Other characters might be shown in a more subtle fashion to deserve victimization: In *The Streets of San Francisco*, an "unsympathetic" woman—a shrill, alcoholic, "harpy" wife—is strangled by her husband; in another *T.J. Hooker* episode, a female Episcopalian priest, a woman struggling to be accepted in a traditionally male job, is brutally raped.

The representation of women's victimization has, furthermore, often been portrayed in a graphic and violent manner. An extended sequence from *The Streets of San Francisco*, for instance, begins with a woman iron-

starred or featured African American, Latino, and Asian American men: *Mod Squad* and *The Rookies* each featured an African American man (Clarence Williams III and Georg Stanford Brown, respectively) as part of the police team. The short-lived *Paris* starred James Earl Jones as a chief of detectives, and the equally short-lived *Ohara* starred the Japanese American Pat Morita as a lieutenant adept in the martial arts. *Miami Vice* and *In the Heat of the Night* each starred a black man and a white man as partners, *Hill Street Blues* featured two black police officers (teamed with white partners) and a Latino assistant commanding officer, and *Hawaii Five-O* had two Asian American officers as members of the police squad. *Starsky and Hutch* had an African American commanding officer who was a somewhat comic character, and the title character in *Hooperman* also had a black man as a partner.

Women, by and large, have been poorly represented in the majority of TV police shows; they have been, as Geoffrey Hurd says, "denied character." Policewomen in predominantly male series are frequently exploited for their sexual dimensions—showcased as sex objects or used within the narratives as bait for criminals. The opening credits of *T.J. Hooker*, for example, include shots of the male police officers running, sliding, jumping, shooting, and driving cars at high speeds. The shots of the female officer Stacy, played by Heather Locklear, show her in a bikini, lounging by a swimming pool, and in a low-cut dress, dancing provocatively into the camera. (There is one brief shot in which Stacy skims a police stick along the ground, tripping up a criminal.) Eve, the policewoman in *Ironside*, was used to "set up" male suspects and often functioned as the team's stenographer. The women characters in *McMillan and Wife*, *Hill Street Blues*, *Miami Vice*, *Hooperman*, and *Hunter* did, however, provide some alternatives to these stereotypical depictions.[17]

In addition to the police roles just described, recurrent women characters have also been featured as secretaries (as in *Hawaii Five-O*), as daughters (in the early episodes of *The Streets of San Francisco*, Lt. Mike Stone's daughter occasionally appeared), and sometimes as girlfriends of the protagonists (as in *McCloud* and *Hooperman*). The predominant roles for women, however, have been those for such nonrecurring characters as victims and as dangerous and "sexually excessive" women—alluring con artists and murderers, "tawdry" girlfriends of criminals, and prostitutes.[18]

The depiction of women as victims, both in series featuring male protagonists and in those featuring females, has been continuous and pervasive. This presentation generally divides victims into two categories, the first being "innocent" women. In the opening scene from a *Streets of San*

Francisco episode, for example, two women are folding clothes in a laundromat. A man pushes open the door, asks if one of them is Jennifer O'Brien, and shoots her point blank with a rifle. We later find out that she is a totally innocent victim who was killed as a way of getting revenge on her husband. Similarly, in *Hawaii Five-O*, a young, white, blond, and naive botany student, while on a field trip in a Hawaiian valley, is abducted and terrorized by a rapist/murderer who has escaped from custody. Or again, in the opening scene of another *Streets of San Francisco*, a young and "undeserving" woman comes home to her apartment to be raped and murdered by a male intruder whom she does not know.

The second category is that of women victims who are set up by the narrative as somehow "deserving" their victimization; the members of this group have had a number of different incarnations.[19] First of all, they might be "out of control" sexually. In a *T.J. Hooker* episode, for instance, four women who have made calls to a sex therapist's radio program are murdered. We find out that all of them talked to the therapist on the air about having or wanting to have extramarital affairs. The killer, at the episode's conclusion, says he murdered them because they were "nothing but married whores." The killer's psychological profile further blames women and their out-of-control sexuality for the situation: He is described as "unmarried, highly religious, product of the classic mother-figure who flaunted her sexuality but punished her children for it."

Another *T.J. Hooker* episode illustrates both a deserving woman victim *and* an undeserving policewoman decoy/victim: A character who has decided to run away from her husband and baby is kidnapped by a sadistic rapist/killer, and in the process of trying to capture the killer, a policewoman (undercover as a waitress) is also abducted. We see a shot of the policewoman with her hands chained to a bed post, her mouth gagged and her ankles tied together; her dress is slit up the side and most of her legs are exposed. When the woman who left her husband and child tries to escape from the rapist, he runs after her, knocks her down, shoots her in the stomach, and says, "Stupid slut." The policewoman is rescued by T.J. Hooker. Other characters might be shown in a more subtle fashion to deserve victimization: In *The Streets of San Francisco*, an "unsympathetic" woman—a shrill, alcoholic, "harpy" wife—is strangled by her husband; in another *T.J. Hooker* episode, a female Episcopalian priest, a woman struggling to be accepted in a traditionally male job, is brutally raped.

The representation of women's victimization has, furthermore, often been portrayed in a graphic and violent manner. An extended sequence from *The Streets of San Francisco*, for instance, begins with a woman ironing and listening to loud classical music while, unbeknownst to her, a man wielding a large knife breaks into the house. The subsequent scene shows a violent chase through various rooms, culminating in the dark basement, where the killer finds her hiding under the stairwell. During the sequence, we see many close-up shots of the knife underscored by terrifying music. Scenes of men with knives either attacking or attempting to attack women are indeed veritable clichés of the genre.

The "dangerous woman," beautiful and sexy but not what she seems to be, has also been a genre staple. Starsky and Hutch, for example, are often conned and fooled by such characters. In one instance, they are duped by an attractive witness who turns to them for protection, "comes on" to both of them sexually, and is finally revealed to be a party to the robbery under investigation and in possession of the missing money. Hutch says she has the "face of an angel and the heart of a con" and calls her a "dangerous little lady." In another episode, Starsky, while shooting at a criminal, accidentally hits and blinds a woman bystander. After many scenes of his guilty ministerings to her, we find out that she was an accomplice to the crime and the girlfriend of the perpetrator. In a *T.J. Hooker* episode, two beautiful women distract Hooker and his partner by dancing with them at a bar long enough for the partner's new Porsche to be stolen from the parking lot. *Hawaii Five-O* featured a dangerous woman as the beautiful daughter of an Asian crime boss, a woman who seems sweet and innocent but is actually trying to cheat her father out of four million dollars and has several people killed in the process. Another such character from *Hawaii Five-O* is the misguided daughter of a billionaire who pours large amounts of money into threatening and "questionable" revolutionary causes because she becomes sexually attracted to the revolutionary leaders. Many dangerous women are killed or end up in jail, although some, like the woman Starsky accidentally blinded, might be "saved" with the help and attention of the police hero.

Finally, women are cast as prostitutes or, as I mentioned above, as criminals' girlfriends. Prostitutes often appear in short scenes to give an urban "street" feel to the program, and they are usually characterized by Hollywood's markers of "street women": garish and "tasteless" clothes, hair, and makeup, poor posture, bad grammar, and the chewing of gum. Bumper Morgan, the hero of *The Blue Knight*, "looks the other way" for the "good" prostitutes on his beat.[20] But prostitutes may also function as informers and frequently have larger roles. In a *Starsky and Hutch* episode, for example, Starsky falls in love with a woman who, unknown to him, is a "call girl." After she is killed, Hutch breaks the news about her "past," and the disbelieving Starsky beats up on his partner, yelling, "Are you trying to tell me that my girl is a hooker?"

The repeated portrayal of females as victims, dangerous women, and prostitutes is all the more interesting because women have had very little other representation in the police genre, not even in the conventional role of the protagonist's wife. Most heroes have been single, divorced, separated, or widowed or have had offscreen marriages. The short-lived *Toma*, *Paris*, and *87th Precinct* were rare in featuring heroes with on-screen wives and families; and McCloud, Hooperman, and *Hill Street Blues*'s Frank Furillo were some of the few policemen with even a steady girlfriend. In fact, girlfriends of the heroes often end up dead; Starsky and Hutch each lost several in the course of that series's history. The TV police are, as Cary Bazalgette says, wedded to their jobs and in surrogate marriages with their partners.[21]

As for settings, almost all the police series between 1952 and the early 1990s, with the exception of *Highway Patrol* and *Kodiak* (which was set in the Alaskan countryside), took place in urban locations, often in large cities like New York, San Francisco, and Los Angeles. (*Hawaii Five-O* exploited both a city setting and the mountains and valleys of the Hawaiian landscape.) And virtually all the series have occurred in present-day time. Both of these generic aspects, of course, add to and extend the genre's "realism."[22]

A list, then, of the conventional generic components of the police series—or what Rick Altman has called the genre's "semantic elements"—includes cops (primarily white men in partnerships or teams), victims (who are often women), criminals (who are often men of color, although that is not the case in the examples I cited above), bureaucratic commanding officers or "higher-ups," squad rooms, police procedurals, violent police action (including car chases, physical fights, and shootouts), dangerous and "sexually excessive" women, urban locations, and present-day time settings.[23]

The male series vary with regard to the frequency with which they show car chases and other violent action. Programs such as *Dragnet* and *The Streets of San Francisco*, for instance, focused more on interrogation and police procedure. *Starsky and Hutch*, in contrast, included lots of physical and violent action (one episode spent nearly ten full minutes showing car and other vehicle chases), but unlike many of the other series, it also kept its primary narrative focus on the friendship between the two protagonists.[24] Male series, particularly since the 1980s, have also involved a mixture of generic forms. *Hill Street Blues*, for example, employed a narrative structure similar to the soap opera, *Miami Vice* included many aspects of music videos, and *Hooperman* blended comedy and melodrama.[25]

GENERIC "MEANING"

Ostensibly, the generic "meaning" of the police series (or what Rick Altman refers to as the genre's "syntax") is that police heroes protect the public and work to uphold social order. As John Dennington and John Tulloch put it, social order or the "Law" is seen as growing out of the popular consensus; that consensus is a dominant paradigm of social relations that involves a belief in social plurality, in the equality of all members of society, and the denial of social hierarchies. The cop or cop team are agents of this consensus who protect the public (the consensus members) from criminals and deviants. Violent police action is thus legitimated because the objects of the violence are outside the consensus, beyond the pale.[26]

I would argue that the classic TV police genre—as I have sketched it out—actually produced meanings not only about the protection of the public by the police, but also about male power, primarily white male power. The notion of the Law, although mostly implicit in the police show, may be used to articulate the connection between the police hero, general social order, and masculine supremacy.[27]

Three premises regarding the protagonist and the Law exemplify my claims: The first is that social order or the Law, as we saw above, is associated with the consensus. Even if never stated explicitly, it is generally assumed by the genre that the police protagonists are working in the interests of the public and the commonweal, as these interests have been institutionalized into laws (with a lowercase *l*). In the process of maintaining the Law, some cop/heroes work in close alignment with the consensus, whereas others work around and occasionally break laws. But whether the cop operates more on the side of the commonweal or on the side of his own assessments of right and wrong, the meaning of social order and the Law moves from its tacit identification with the consensus and institutionalized laws (as ideological as these notions already are) and becomes identified instead with the figure of the cop/hero. And this is the second premise that the genre produces: The Law becomes indistinguishable from the actions and individual moral code of the cop/hero. In other words, even though the hero may break or bend institutionalized laws, the larger social order or Law is tacitly redefined to agree with the moral vision of the individual police protagonist.[28]

This conflation of the Law and the individual hero is crucial to the operations of the genre, and it happens in several ways, but primarily through the overwhelming weight placed on the character development of the cop/hero and his construction as an empathetic protagonist. The TV cop in the United States, as I mentioned above, is almost never a cold loner like Clint Eastwood's Dirty Harry. On the contrary, he may be a lovable member of a squad room family or a public servant who "does all he can do with the obstacles of an apathetic public and wicked criminals." Despite his toughness, he is often, like Kojak, Baretta, or T.J. Hooker, shown articulating his moral code with emotion and feeling.[29] For example, in the *T.J. Hooker* episode cited above, in which a woman Episcopalian priest is raped, Hooker tells the priest that he cannot go to church because "I can't accept any man-made doctrine that prevents a person from doing what's right." When she asks, "Hooker, how can you make such a judgment?" he replies, "Inside here [pointing to his chest] is how I make it."[30]

As Cary Bazalgette shows, the cop character, especially in U.S. programs, is also made endearing, three-dimensional, and idiosyncratic by his association with props, costumes, and gimmicks: Kojak is totally bald, a flashy dresser, and eats Tootsie Pops; Columbo wears a crumpled raincoat; Baretta is completely disheveled and has a pet cockatoo; and Sonny Crockett sports a five o'clock shadow, a pastel wardrobe, and a pet alligator.[31]

In addition to the emphasis on character development, the conflation of the Law and the hero is further abetted by a focus on the body of the cop—his physical strength and prowess, which are often aided by weapons, technology, and cars. Starsky and Hutch, Baretta, T.J. Hooker, Steve McGarrett and Dan Williams from *Hawaii Five-O*, Sonny Crockett and Ricardo Tubbs from *Miami Vice*, to name just a few, all engage in feats of physical and technological derring-do. The cop is thereby shown as eminently capable of negotiating the dangerous space between social order and lawless disorder.[32] By and large, the meaning of the Law, although still loosely pinned to notions of the consensus, the public, and institutionalized laws, becomes more abstract as the character of the cop/hero becomes more concrete and equivalent to the Law itself.

This makes possible the third premise regarding the meaning of the Law in the genre: The cop hero and his moral code become the stand-ins for the Law as male power. This force, exchanged between men and exclusive of women, then becomes the basis of social order—what Jane Gallop has discussed as "the biologistic reduction of the Law of the Dead Father to the rule of the actual living male" and "living males' imposture as the Law."[33] The narrative separation of the male cop or cop team from significant relationships with women and the dedication to the profession of policing render the figure and the body of the cop "worthy" of articulating such an abstract notion of Law. This is especially noticeable in contrast to the figures and bodies of women in the genre who, when represented at all, are often laden with materiality as victims, sex objects, and prostitutes or as sexually excessive, out of control, and dangerous females.

WOMEN AS PROTAGONIST COPS

Obviously, putting women into the traditional police genre role of cop and the Law demands a number of problematic and sometimes impossible negotiations. The problems are only exacerbated by the fact that substituting the female for the male body disturbs not only conventions of the police genre per se, but also general cultural codes of masculine activity and feminine passivity as well as conventional codes of appearance, figure movement, and spheres of action for women in TV dramas.

Historically, as we have seen, women really began to appear as stars and protagonists in the network police genre beginning in 1974 with *Police Woman* and *Get Christie Love*, followed in 1976 by the police-related *Charlie's Angels*. (Although, as early as 1957, Beverly Garland starred as a policewoman in the syndicated *Decoy*, in which a *Dragnet*-style voice-over accompanied the action.)[34] A confluence of social and industry conditions produced some of the specific negotiations that characterized these 1970s programs: Pressure from interest groups such as the PTA to reduce TV violence had led to displays of women's bodies as TV titillation; new discourses from the women's movements were being taken up by a variety of series; and more dramatic programs starring women as protagonists (most, but not all, as sex objects) were produced than at any other time in television history.

The specific tensions surrounding the replacement of the active male body (the Law's equation with male power) with that of the female were negotiated by these programs in a number of ways. The female cop was usually allied with a male mentor, a father figure or "brother" cop. *Police Woman*'s Pepper Anderson (the Angie Dickinson character), for example, was linked with Lt. Bill Crowley, her superior officer, and Detective Christie Love (the Teresa Graves character in *Get Christie Love*) with Lt. Matt Reardon, Capt. Arthur Ryan, and Sgt. Pete Gallagher. (Most of the women police officers in predominantly *male* police programs—with the possible exceptions of *Hill Street Blues* and *Hooperman*—were also represented as allied with and protected by the men on the team or in the partnership.) In other words, it was always the male cop who could successfully negotiate the disordered space between victims and criminals, and the female who was produced as the weaker extension of the male Law, primarily as a father-identified daughter.[35]

The women cops also often ended up as objects of the rough action rather than participants in it—classic "women in distress" who had to be saved by their male colleagues. Furthermore, they were portrayed as sexual spectacles: the opening credits for *Police Woman*, for instance, included shots in which Angie Dickinson's legs were isolated and fetishized in the frame. But perhaps the most interesting negotiation of these tensions was the construction of the female cop's body as a re-creation or reinvention of the genre's own sexually excessive women. Both Christie Love and Pepper Anderson frequently went undercover as decoys, disguised as prostitutes, criminals' girlfriends, and seductresses. And Charlie's Angels often acted as bikini-clad lures for jet-set criminals. Posing as sexual bait and as decoys was, in fact, probably the major police duty performed by these female cops, and in this way women's excessive sexuality was regularly displayed by the protagonists, but it was also harnessed in the service of the (male) Law rather than disrupting or threatening it.[36]

All of this is not, however, to foreclose on possible alternative readings or interpretations of these programs. They may also offer pleasure to female viewers by showing women as protagonists in public-sphere domains of action and, as Diana Meehan says of *Charlie's Angels*, as members of a "supportive female group."[37] They also need to be studied in much more detail to ascertain the specific ways in which the various generic tensions were resolved in each. (The fact, for instance, that Christie Love was an African American policewoman calls for an extended analysis of the series's negotiation of gender and race issues.)

Cagney and Lacey, as we know, came to TV under different industry conditions than these programs of the mid-seventies, and with different investments in particular definitions of femininity and gender. Television's "T&A" period—in its most blatant form, at least—was over by the early eighties. The first half of the new decade was characterized instead by the television industry's concerted effort to attract target-audience women in prime time and particularly to capture the new working women's audience. According to the producer/writers, the *Cagney and Lacey* made-for-TV movie was designed as a standard police drama with a "realistic" approach to the subject matter. The action and talking elements were both emphasized, but an "action director," Ted Post, was hired. And although Rosenzweig insisted that it was a show about two women who just happen to be cops ("We're not *Starsky and Hutch* in drag"), the movie and the first series episodes employed many conventions of the police genre, including police procedural, violent action, a New York City setting, present-day time, and antagonistic commanding officers. *Cagney and Lacey's* particular "twist" was in its role reversal—two women were the stars and protagonist cops, and the focus was on the buddy relationship between them.[38]

Both textually and extratextually (or in second-level texts), the movie and its characters were situated as explicitly feminist, and the tensions regarding women, the Law, and the police genre were greatly exacerbated and much less easy to negotiate than in the series of the 1970s. Displaying active, autonomous, feminist women in a buddy relationship was the fundamental objective of *Cagney and Lacey,* and therefore the protagonists could not be depicted as sex objects, nor could they be rescued by the male police officers. Furthermore, their primary bond was with each other rather than with a male commanding officer or partner. The historical routes for channeling women into the genre were simply not navigable in this case.

The *Cagney and Lacey* movie and the early series episodes used an incendiary combination of overt feminist dialogue (about discrimination on the job, sexism, and women's oppression), violent crimes, and women protagonists who functioned as the subjects rather than the objects of rough police action. In both the movie and the first episode, however, Chris and Mary Beth, like their seventies predecessors, went undercover as prostitutes. But even though it resorted to this cliché and the corollary meanings about women that it generated, *Cagney and Lacey* also put a somewhat different slant on the topic. For example, in the made-for-TV movie, Lacey becomes part of a prostitutes' group that is fighting to establish a union for protection and financial autonomy; she identifies with the fight, links it to her own, speaks out against the lack of police protection, and gives a pitch for labor organizing.[39]

The feminist orientation made for especial volatility. When Lieutenant Samuels, the commanding officer of the precinct to which Cagney and Lacey have been assigned, hears of their promotion to detectives, he responds, "Terrific. Last year blacks, this year broads. Will someone explain to me why guys with families are getting laid off and broads are getting promoted?" Such dialogue highlighted a major contradiction in the representation of women cops as agents of the consensus and enforcers of laws and intensified the tensions of putting women into the conventionally male genre: Sexual difference, along with race and class, is, of course, a repressed element of the consensus paradigm—something that is overlooked and excluded when we speak of society as nonhierarchical and pluralist.

Although institutionalized laws have often sanctioned women's exclusion, sequences such as Lacey's involvement with the prostitutes' organizing efforts and her frustrations, as a woman, with the police underscored still another tension: Whereas, on the one hand, laws have commonly been used to exclude women, on the other (problematic as this notion is), they are sometimes the only protection and recourse available to females; but they are not always enforced on women's behalf. Putting two feminist women in the genre, in other words, posed some strong challenges to the fundamental ideology of the status quo.

But even though *Cagney and Lacey* disturbed the genre and produced many differences in its initial representations of women, it generated traditional portrayals as well. Both women were actively heterosexual, and Lacey's primary commitment to her family was explicitly emphasized. "I'm a mother, wife, cop," she says to the gung-ho Cagney, "with the emphasis on the mother, wife." Her nurturance, pacifism, intuition, sensitivity to people, and ambivalence about her job were, in fact, among the fundamental ways the series dealt with the troubles caused by associating the culturally "empathetic woman" with the images of cops and violence. (Cagney, on the other hand, identified with her father Charlie, a former cop; she was less ambivalent about her role as law enforcer and often had to be convinced by Lacey of the various and complicated sides of situations.)

Despite its bow to conventional elements, *Cagney and Lacey's* differences and challenges to genre and gender norms were interpreted as threats by CBS. This attitude is reflected in the comments quoted in Chapter 1, wherein a network programmer complained that the characters were "too tough, too hard, not feminine," "too harshly women's lib," and "more intent on fighting the system than doing police work," finishing with, "We perceived them as dykes."[40] It appears that the series undermined the gender-specific meanings of the Law produced in the conventional police genre. Two feminist women as police protagonists, as subjects of aggressive physical action, neither objectified by nor aligned with a father/protector male cop, were seen as structurally transgressive. The bonding between them was seen as a harbinger of "deviance" and disruption, rather than as a sign of professional dedication to the Law (as it is with the male teams).[41] The substitution of female for male bodies both laid bare and threatened the very equation of the Law with male power that the genre had worked so hard to produce.

The previous chapters have described how, as a result of CBS's interference with the series, Meg Foster was fired and replaced by Sharon Gless, Cagney's class background and wardrobe were upscaled, and both characters were "feminized." In addition to these changes, the narratives also underwent the first of several major shifts, characterized by the increasing incorporation of melodrama, soap opera, and comedy—historically forms more closely associated with women and women-oriented programming than was the police genre. This transition, of course, fits in with Rosenzweig's public announcements that the "women's angle" would be emphasized and the relationship between the characters, rather than the police action, promoted. As noted earlier, the revised program was heavily advertised as a show *for women*; it was specifically aimed at a working women's audience and was scheduled in the Monday night "ladies' line-up." A new "Bible" that laid out the series's dogma for future writers made further evident the revised direction. "*Cagney and Lacey*," it read, "is a police show, but the crimes are a background to the people who commit them and the people who solve them."[42]

A format guide for the structuring of episodes, which had first been developed for the original series, was now actually implemented, and these guidelines clearly illustrate the new generic and narrative bias. It is the combination of stories described therein that I call "episode structure":

1. Episodes will consist of an "A" story; a "B" story; a "C" story; and "Runners" (aka running gags).

2. Ideal breakdown is as follows:
   "A" story—20 to 22 pages in length
   "B" story—18 to 22 pages in length
   "C" story—approximately 8 to 10 pages in length
   Runners—approximately a total of 9 pages.

3. By definition, the "A" and "B" stories will be constructed so that they are of equal or near equal importance.

4. All stories and runners should be blended and integrated into teleplay structurally so that no single act is "top-heavy" with one story and no other story is lost.

5. Of the "A" and "B" stories, only one should be a straight cop story.[43]

It is clear from this format that the cop story was intended to occupy roughly one-third of the total script pages; it did not necessarily have to be the primary or "A" story, and both it and the other main (noncop) story had to be balanced with regard to their overall importance in the episode. The six episodes from the original Foster/Daly series did not adhere to these guidelines—the "A" and "B" plots for the premiere episode, for instance, were both fairly conventional cop stories. Although a couple of the other original episodes came close to the guidelines, it was not until well into the first season of the Gless/Daly series that the format prescribing a more mixed form was fully actualized.

As *Cagney and Lacey* was transformed from a police drama to a combination police genre/melodrama/soap opera/comedy, each element of the episode structure—the cop story ("A" or "B"), the noncop story ("A" or "B"), and the "C" story—was affected, including changes in subject matter, in generic elements, and in the relative importance of the particular story in the overall episode.

In the cop story segments, the subject matter generally shifted from more traditional police genre material, such as thefts, murders, and drug rings, to "women's issues" and such women's program material as rape, wife-beating, incest, and pornography.[44] If the subject of a show did involve more traditional police material, the story line usually also was given a twist that implicated Cagney, Lacey, or another principal character. In other words, the story might change from one that followed Cagney and Lacey's *investigation* of a shooting to one that showed their *implication* in a shooting, or to one that involved them getting shot. More whimsical subject matter was also incorporated. In one show, for example, Cagney becomes obsessed with capturing a world-class jewelry thief, and they develop a mutual admiration; in another, Cagney and Lacey and two male detectives go undercover on a TV game show, disguised as fruits and vegetables. The changes in the cop story segment most often involved a move away from police action sequences and the types of behaviors, props, and settings typical of the genre (Cagney and Lacey chasing a getaway car and shooting a bullet through its windshield; Cagney, Lacey, and street-gang "hoods" circling one another in a mutually threatening way; bank robbers, in ski masks and carrying sawed-off shotguns, pulling a heist; prominently featured alleys and city streets; graphic display of the victims and perpetrators of various crimes) in favor of scenes featuring police procedural, people talking about the crime that has been committed, and shots of Cagney and Lacey doing more humdrum, sanitized detective work.

*Cagney and Lacey discuss a case at their desks. (*Cagney and Lacey,
© *Orion Pictures Corp., 1988, all rights reserved)*

By way of illustration, consider the first episode of the Foster/Daly series, "Bang, Bang, You're Dead" (about the killing of prostitutes), which aired in March 1982. The murder scenes contain many conventional generic elements: there is a shot of the killer, knife drawn, crawling through a window into a prostitute's room; a grizzly shot of a murdered prostitute in a bathtub, her face and torso covered with a sheet but her bare legs and one bare arm draped over the sides of the tub and covered with blood; shots of the killer slashing with a knife at Foster's Cagney (disguised as a prostitute) and of Cagney kicking him in the groin, bringing him to the floor, and kneeing him in the chin. A fall 1982 episode from the Gless/Daly series, entitled "Hotline," used a similar story—the serial murders of women. In this episode, however, neither the actual murders (of which there are three) nor the murder scenes are shown on film. They take place offscreen, and we are told about them in shot/reverse shot expository dialogue sequences that occur in the squad room.[45] We never see a weapon or the killer *as* killer, although we do see him twice in his everyday role as a delivery boy.

As the mise-en-scène of crime and rough action gave way to that of crime *investigation*, scenes of the protagonists roughly dealing with "seedy johns" in the red-light district, as they do in "Bang, Bang, You're Dead," became scenes in which they interrogate suspects, talk to Lieutenant Samuels and the other detectives about the case, talk to families and friends of the victims, and go through photos and records. As the series progressed, the two women often got computer assistance and talked to the coroner and the district attorney. In addition to furnishing "clues," all these talking scenes provided often humorous interactions with various characters, and they took place in increasingly domesticated settings. (Although cost-control measures were always a consideration for a program that, in the fall of 1983, cost between $776,000 and $837,000 per episode, and over a million dollars by 1986, I found no evidence that cost was a motivating factor in the change from the mise-en-scène of a cop show to that of a woman's program.)[46]

The above, of course, describes general trends. Some conventional generic props, behaviors, and settings did, in fact, remain in the cop story segments throughout the series's history. A number of episodes, for example, began or climaxed with Cagney and Lacey giving chase on foot through city streets, up and down stairs, or along rooftops, drawing their weapons, and sometimes forcibly apprehending suspects. And the two-part season and series finale in May 1988 involved a "no holds barred" shootout. Traditional police-genre plots still formed the basis for some episodes, but, by and large, they were increasingly outnumbered by woman's program subject matter or by standard cop story material that additionally implicated the main characters or involved whimsy.

The noncop story segments were similarly transformed. First, the non-cop story consumed more script pages and screen time and enjoyed greater relative importance as the series progressed. It was often the "A" story, and in several episodes it was virtually the *only* story. Its subject matter, like that of the cop story, began to focus more on such woman's program, women's issue topics as Cagney and her boyfriends, Lacey and her kids, Lacey's minor "nervous breakdown," abortion, pregnancy, breast cancer, sexual harassment, drug abuse, alcoholism, and psychological therapy. The non-cop story might also be totally comedic: Cagney and Lacey are assigned to take the actress playing "Detective Deedee"—a glamorous TV police officer who captures criminals by saying "hold it, big boy"—on patrol with them; or Cagney and Lacey organize a police department party, have a Lucy and Ethel–type food fight while preparing in Lacey's kitchen, and do a "showgirl" routine as entertainment at the party.[47]

The "C" stories, which often involved the male members of the detective squad, similarly developed into ones that drew on woman's program subject matter about relational, "sensitive" men. They variously dealt with such topics as Lieutenant Samuels's problems with his wife, his son, his weight, and a new girlfriend; Detective Petrie's discovery of his wife's extramarital affair, his attachment to his baby daughter, and his ethical stands on labor strikes and South African apartheid; Detective Isbecki's relationships with women and his devotion to his mother; and Detective LaGuardia's health food diets and his infatuation with Lacey's mother-in-law.[48]

DEVELOPMENT OF SCRIPTS AND EPISODES

The general trends described above can be followed in detail at the textual level as they worked to produce a woman's program. The six original Foster/Daly episodes, as I have indicated, were heavily weighted toward the conventional police genre in terms of subject matter, the relative balance of cop and noncop stories, and established generic elements. In addition to the premiere episode, in which the "A" story was about the serial murders of prostitutes and the "B" story about Cagney and Lacey cracking a drug ring, subsequent episodes involved a Chinese gang bank robbery, an "illegal alien" import ring, and a street-gang stabbing.

The use of standard police show topics and conventional generic elements was especially noticeable in comparison to later episodes. In one of these original programs, for example, Lacey is badly and visibly beaten up, and in another both protagonists are attacked by a suspect with a blowtorch. The final two original episodes featured material more associated with the conventional woman's program (child abandonment and the protection of an anti–Equal Rights Amendment activist), but they also emphasized many routine police genre elements. Only two of the six original shows had well-developed noncop stories—one in which Chris and Mary Beth appear as uninvited guests at a precinct party from which they have been purposely excluded, and one in which Harvey Lacey, despite dizziness from inner-ear problems, rescues a neighbor-boy's pigeon from a roof ledge while his panic-stricken sons look on. (A script comment sheet from Rosenzweig on the latter episode stated that the Harvey/pigeon story needed to be tapped for its "warmth" potential.)[49]

April Smith, who had been the executive story editor for CBS's recently canceled *Lou Grant*, was hired as producer for the revised series in which Sharon Gless replaced Meg Foster, and the writing staff she assembled sharply reflected the conception of the show as a mixed generic form and the new push to emphasize the "women's angle." She brought in Robert Crais, a writer from *Hill Street Blues*, Frank Abatemarco, who had written two Robert Conrad pilots, and Jeffrey Lane from the daytime soap opera *Ryan's Hope*. Smith's tenure as producer was a transitional period for *Cagney and Lacey*, and the thirteen episodes she supervised show a range of diversity regarding subject matter, generic conventions, episode structure, and the relative importance of the cop and noncop stories. Also evident is the effect of the individual writers and their television backgrounds.

Five of the thirteen programs leaned toward the standard cop story or a standard cop story that also directly implicated Cagney and/or Lacey. Some of the Smith shows were, in fact, almost exclusively cop story. In acknowledgment of the pressures, especially at this point in the series's history, to follow the format guidelines and *not* overemphasize the cop story segment, Smith attached the following memo to the script treatment for the first Gless/Daly episode. The script, titled "Witness to an Incident" (by an out-of-house writer, Paul Ehrmann), dealt with Cagney and Lacey's differing versions of a crime they both witnessed.[50] "We are aware," Smith wrote,

> that the "A" story [the cop story] in this treatment now takes up most of the show. It's an interesting, action-filled yarn that poses some fundamental questions about police work and police perception, but it does need other story support. We intend to explore the rift between Cagney and Lacey in their personal lives: with Harvey, possibly with a neighbor/friend of Cagney's we would like to introduce. Also, we will round out the community/police conflict we have only initiated here. Those will become our "B" and "C" stories.[51]

The actual filmed episode was still overwhelmingly cop story–oriented (although the effects of the incident on Cagney and Lacey are explored). The season's second episode, "One of Our Own," written by Robert Crais and April Smith, similarly accentuated the cop story. Crais, it will be recalled, had come to *Cagney and Lacey* from *Hill Street Blues*.

More than half of the thirteen scripts, however, incorporated woman's program subject matter in both the cop and noncop story segments. "Beauty Burglars," the season's third episode (written by Patt Shea and Harriett Weiss), for example, delivered the first balanced, fully developed, woman's program–oriented noncop story, which involved Lacey's upcoming participation in the wedding of a wealthy friend. However, the seventh episode, "Mr. Lonelyhearts" (by Jeffrey Lane), was the first one in the series's history that could truly be called more a woman's program than a police program. Both the cop or "A" story (a polygamy scam perpetrated by a young, beautiful woman on elderly men) and the fully developed "B" story (Cagney's decision to be celibate and how she dealt with a new boyfriend) could be considered woman's program topics. Traditional police genre elements were minimized (in this instance, the crime itself was not violent), and procedural detective work was underscored. In their subject matter, episode structures, and generic elements, both "Mr. Lonelyhearts" and another Jeffrey Lane script ("Affirmative Action"), also produced by Smith, foreshadowed the trend of future episodes. The fact that Jeffrey Lane came to *Cagney and Lacey* from the daytime *Ryan's Hope* suggests that the series was consciously and explicitly incorporating aspects of soap opera into its form. April Smith's own script for the series's tenth episode, "Recreational Use," put the "B" story focus squarely on Cagney's stormy romance with the cocaine-addicted Sergeant Dory McKenna.

Another change evident during Smith's tenure as producer was the alteration in narrative structure. Although each of the episodes employed an overall closed, classical narrative structure, some "C" story lines began to take on more continuous, serial forms. Gradually the "B" stories followed suit, and both began to display an open narrative pattern characteristic of soap operas. This development did not become truly significant, however, until the 1986–87 season, with the continuing story line about the alcoholism of both Cagney and her father, Charlie. The change contrasts markedly with the practice of the original series, which had been to keep even the "sub-'C'" narratives classically structured. (A note from Rosenzweig on one of the original six Foster/Daly scripts, for example, read, "We should step out of the Charlie [Cagney] romance carefully so that even though it is an *off-stage story* it progresses with a beginning, middle and end" [emphasis mine].)[52] The episodes also began to include more open-ended cop stories, in which all the pieces of the puzzle did not come together and were not followed up in subsequent shows.

In late December 1982 April Smith left the series, along with Crais, Abatemarco, and Lane. Apparently major problems had developed between her and Rosenzweig over their different conceptions of the program. According to Rosenzweig, Smith wanted to do "think-pieces" like those done on *Lou Grant*, and according to Rona Barrett, she wanted to deal with "heavier social issues." (Smith herself, although she offered encouragement on my project, declined to be interviewed, saying she wanted to put this phase of her professional life behind her.) Steve Brown and Terry Louise Fisher (a former Los Angeles assistant district attorney and writer, who went on to cocreate *L.A. Law*) were hired in January 1983 as the new producer/writers to complete the season's remaining nine episodes. (Actually, in speaking about the production and writing of both April Smith and the Brown/Fisher team, Rosenzweig commented that, as executive producer, he served the function of bringing their work "back to center." According to him, they all wrote scripts that, for TV, were "too political" and "too far left.")[53]

This Fisher/Brown period marked a turning point for the series in its approach to genre and to subject matter, which began to include complex and topical "women's issues" that were actually major social problems. (Of the nine episodes Fisher and Brown produced during this time, five were heavily weighted toward the noncop story segment and involved women's issues. Three leaned toward the cop story segment—two were typical police stories and one was mixed.) "Open and Shut Case," the first episode written by the new team, is about an African American woman who has been gang-raped by four men (their races are unspecified), and who has spent two full years in the courts at four separate trials. At the time of the story, the convicted rapists are in the process of overturning their convictions, and the woman is being subpoenaed to begin the testifying process all over again. This mainly noncop story, which revolves around Cagney and Lacey's friendship and solidarity with the woman, is weighted equally with the cop story about ethnic feuds—the framing of a Turkish man in the stabbing and eventual death of an Armenian, and the legal system's lack of concern with solving the case. Brown and Fisher's second script, entitled "Date Rape," is about the violent rape of a white woman who "picks men up at bars"; a Terry Louise Fisher/Chris Abbott script from later in the same season was "A Cry for Help," the script about wife-beating discussed in Chapter 2. Other woman's program episodes from this period concerned the death of a nameless bag lady ("Jane Doe") and Lacey's emotional breakdown ("Burnout").

CONTEXTUAL PRESSURES, EXPLOITABLE ISSUES, AND WRITING A MELODRAMA

The deliberate move toward topical, exploitative, women's issues stories was, of course, spurred on by considerations of gender—considerations motivated by the need for a women's audience—and resulted in representations that the industry felt would attract that audience. The movement was explicitly encouraged by Orion Television's report, mentioned in Chapter 2, on *Cagney and Lacey's* ratings or "numbers" performance. The report recommended that the series go in the direction it had already begun to take, particularly under the production/writing team of Fisher and Brown; it also made explicit some of the contextual pressures that influenced the changes. The report concluded: "We can prove that CAGNEY

AND LACEY achieves a 27 share or better when it is *not* faced with this competition [from the female-exploitation made-for-TV-movies]. However, this indicates the show must be *thematically* strengthened. This can be done by re-orienting the show around those themes that have been so successful against us, or by paying closer attention to contemporary women themes and less to cops and robbers."[54]

A letter from Barney Rosenzweig and Richard Rosenbloom to CBS, written just before their 1983 renewal meetings, further clarified the series's new direction and invoked the exploitation advertising examined earlier. It began:

> In the plethora of information being assembled and disseminated for scheduling meetings in the past few days, a very interesting discovery has quite possibly been overlooked. For the first time this year, "CAGNEY & LACEY" took on an ABC Television Movie on its own terms and came out the victor. LEGS, a high-budget, typically ABC, female-oriented, exploitation film lost by more than 10% of the total audience to episode #21 ["A Cry for Help"] of "CAGNEY & LACEY." Furthermore, that same night against "V," one of the most successful miniseries of the year, "CAGNEY & LACEY" held to its season average and performed better than any other show on CBS' schedule for the night.
>
> "CAGNEY & LACEY" #21 was not an exceptional episode. True, it had an exploitable theme: wife battering. But then, "CAGNEY & LACEY" has had many exploitable issues: date rape, child abuse, celibacy as an alternative to promiscuity, erotic hotlines, sexual harassment, etc. What made episode #21 different was that it was the first and only time that "CAGNEY & LACEY" was promoted and advertised in the same exploitative fashion as an ABC Television Movie. No squealing tires, no "freeze, police," but an advertisement aimed at that very specific 18–48 [*sic*] year old female audience. We at "CAGNEY & LACEY" are encouraged by this experiment. We know we can continue to devise female-oriented, exploitative themes. It took a while to discover our problem. In fairness, we didn't know we had one until football was over and the onslaught of female-oriented television movies began. We now know how to combat them. We've got the evidence. Now, we ask for the opportunity.[55]

When, after being canceled, the series was revived for seven trial episodes in the spring of 1984, the practice of developing exploitable stories aimed specifically at target audience women predominated. Terry Louise Fisher became executive story editor/writer, and Peter Lefcourt (who had written two previous episodes for *Cagney and Lacey* and was a writer/ executive story editor for *Scarecrow and Mrs. King*) was hired as the new producer.

The seven trial episodes reflected the pressures that those involved with the series felt to compete for the target audience women and get picked up for a full season in the fall. Women-oriented exploitation topics were prevalent, but they explored fewer complex social problems. As Terry Louise Fisher said at the time, "Last year was much more political than what we're doing this year. This year it's more entertainment values."[56] The plots for six of the seven episodes revolved around a male-stripper club and wife murder; pornography; Cagney's pregnancy scare; illegal baby selling; Lacey blaming herself for Cagney's getting shot; and Cagney's love/hate relationship with a bounty hunter who competes with the detectives to capture a criminal.

A major indicator of the series's evolution into a woman's program was the strong trend during this period toward "talking episodes." During a writers/producers meeting in February 1984, Peter Lefcourt commented that he thought of *Cagney and Lacey* not as a cop show but as a "melodrama." Both he and Terry Louise Fisher thought the variant drafts of "The Baby Broker," the script on which they were currently working, revealed a "process of distillation" that would culminate in the arrival at "quintessential *Cagney and Lacey*."[57] The script in question, in this instance, was one in which Chris and Mary Beth investigate the case of a baby who is abandoned when her wealthy parents find out she is deaf. The detectives discover that the parents had actually bought the baby from a baby broker for $35,000, and that the broker's "M.O." (modus operandi) is to scout out indigent pregnant women in welfare lines. Lacey takes the baby home, and Cagney goes undercover as a pregnant welfare mother. The Laceys decide to adopt the child, but the biological mother, who has been tracked down in the course of the investigation, wants her back.

This script, written by Terry Louise Fisher, went through three major drafts followed by four additional revisions. In the first two drafts, Cagney and Lacey enter the apartment of the wealthy adoptive parents and, with weapons drawn, arrest them. There are several long sequences in which Cagney and Isbecki (one of the male detectives) pose as an "expectant" welfare couple, one in which Cagney chases and captures a thief in the welfare lines, and one in which Cagney and Isbecki trap and capture the baby broker. By the third draft, however, the scene of Cagney and Lacey apprehending the adoptive parents had been deleted, no thief was chased through the welfare lines, and Cagney and Isbecki are shown only briefly on their undercover assignment. Even the scene in which Cagney and Isbecki nail the baby broker had been dropped. What remained were scenes of Mary Beth and Harvey Lacey talking about the baby, Chris and Mary Beth talking about the case and the baby, Lieutenant Samuels telling Lacey not to get involved, and Lacey confronting the biological mother. According to Lefcourt and Fisher, the script at this point captured the quintessential *Cagney and Lacey*—the emphasis was on the *effects* of the crime and, in this instance, the audience never even saw the perpetrator. One week before the program was actually filmed, a brief scene in which Cagney and Isbecki (in their undercover roles as the expectant welfare couple) "set up" the baby broker in his office was restored to the script. Nevertheless, the changes in the development of this one episode demonstrate how the actual writing process during this time tended to whittle away the police genre elements, instead fashioning a talking program—what the writers/producers described as writing a melodrama.

In another interview, Terry Louise Fisher spoke further about this phenomenon: "How does catching the bad guy impact on these women? How does it affect their spiritual, personal, and emotional lives? Instead of just showing Chris and Mary Beth doing heroics, they often sit around and talk about how this affects their gut. Women *do* sit and think, 'What does this mean?'"[58]

In a scholarly study on "discourse patterns" in *Cagney and Lacey*, Judine Mayerle reported that, as the series progressed, there was a gradual shift in "personal discourse" screen time involving Cagney and/or Lacey from 25 percent to 50 percent. Furthermore, producer/writer Patricia Green noted in the fall of 1985 that *Cagney and Lacey* had reached the point where "what happens in the personal lives of the two characters is considered first in the development of new story lines, with the traditional law-and-order action developed as a supportive framework." Since the seven trial episodes in the spring of 1984, the series, although always a "mixed form," had tilted heavily toward melodrama, soap opera, and comedy. In a biting roast of the series, a *Vogue* magazine review even concluded, "They shoot straight and they're nurturing too. These little ladies can do it all. Cagney and Lacey, ace detectives bucking the prejudices of male cops, are really just TV's updated packaging for that old feminist anathema, the 'woman's picture.'"[59]

In the four seasons from fall 1984 through spring 1988, the episodes continued to mix police genre and woman's program forms.[60] Many of them drew heavily on women's issues and women-oriented subject matter, including child molestation, child pornography, incest, abortion, wife-beating, and kids and drugs. The autonomous, active subjectivity of the protagonists was increasingly modified by more conventional female depictions and by stories that evoked more familiar roles. During this same period, Lacey's status as a wife and mother was given a good deal of screen time in stories involving her family: her younger son has trouble reading, displays an interest in pornography, and takes up with a friend who smokes marijuana; her older son commits vandalism, enlists in the Marine Corps, is mistakenly thought to have been killed in a helicopter crash, and later visits home. The 1985–86 season included continuing story lines that dealt with her pregnancy (coinciding with Tyne Daly's real-life pregnancy) and the birth of her daughter. Many "B" and "C" stories dealt with Harvey and Mary Beth's relationship—their minivacation in a hotel with a swimming pool, their purchase of a new house, the vandalism of the house, and Harvey's business upsets and successes.

Similarly, Cagney's short- and long-term relationships with men were given much more screen time than they had been in earlier programs. "B" and "C" stories concerned her various boyfriends—a lawyer, a police detective, a Scandinavian ski instructor, a writer, a district attorney who gets killed, and a working-class plumber; in two programs she receives and considers marriage proposals, and in another she has a serious affair with a disability rights activist who has paraplegia.

Several "A" stories of this period cast Cagney and Lacey as victims, representing a significant departure from earlier portrayals of the characters: Two episodes dealt with Cagney's sexual harassment by a captain on the police force, several others (with continuing story lines) led up to and exposed her severe alcoholism, and two episodes in the final season involved her rape by a man she had dated.[61] Two episodes also centered on Lacey as the "victim" of breast cancer, and a subsequent one on her possible discovery of a new tumor.

Although humor had always been an element in the series, the four seasons between 1984 and 1988 frequently showed the characters as the subjects of comedy. Several "A" stories, which were essentially the only stories in their particular episodes, were totally comedic. In one, for instance, Cagney and Lacey return to the police academy for a refresher course and are involved in a series of humorous incidents; in other episodes mentioned earlier, they go undercover on a TV game show disguised as a tomato and a banana, escort "Detective Deedee" around in their squad car, have a slapstick food fight in Lacey's kitchen, and perform as showgirls for a department party. On two other occasions they dress up as "mature call girls" and go to Los Angeles on a totally capricious case.

Cagney and Lacey as "mature call girls." (© Orion TV, 1987)

I have argued that in substituting the female cop team for the male one in *Cagney and Lacey*, the police genre could not hold. The series became a hybrid, a combination of police drama and more traditionally women-oriented forms. In the textual operations of this hybrid genre, women were produced in a number of different and often contradictory ways—as active gender-transgressive cop/heroes (although in modified form after the network's interference), as autonomous protagonists, as a father-identified single woman, as a nurturing mother, as victims (of rape, violence, sexual harassment, cancer, and alcoholism), as heterosexual love interests, and as traditional female TV comics.

Although I can only decry what I see as the degeneration of the female hero and the recovery of traditional femininity, I also think (unlike the *Vogue* piece quoted above) that *Cagney and Lacey*'s edge or bite came from the very tensions produced and negotiated in the combination and clash of police genre, melodrama, soap opera, and comedy. The focus on talking, families, and domesticity, the adherence to conventional gender roles typical of soap operas, the heightened emotions surrounding the battle of good and evil that characterizes melodrama, and the taming and domestication of women's power found in most situation comedies—as well as the presentation of women's culture and friendships—were entwined with depictions of women as managers of the social order, and enforcers of the Law. The

Law and women's concerns became bound up with one another, producing a hybrid form that was irreducible to a division between police genre and woman's program.[62]

Such an intertwining challenged the equation of the Law with male power. But furthermore, the combination of and conflict between different definitions of femininity ensured that sexual difference was not repressed in the representation of Cagney and Lacey. The two women, in other words, were not presented as "substitute men," but neither were they simply "not men," the binary opposites or "others" to a preeminent male subjectivity.[63] As we will see in Chapter 5, the mixture of genres and the mixed meanings of femininity and gender plainly illuminated the conflicted position of socially and culturally constructed women in 1980s Western patriarchal culture. They also disturbed the established boundaries of feminine subject positions, on the levels of both the women characters and women viewers.

However, we cannot simply rest here in our analysis of the program, because, as we have seen, *Cagney and Lacey's* history, like much of dramatic women's programming on prime time in the late 1970s and the 1980s, also included the practice of exploitation. It was a key factor in the series's development from a standard police drama into more of a woman's program and was fundamental to its presentation of mixed meanings concerning femininity. In other words, the very mixture that produced *Cagney and Lacey's* sharpest challenge to male supremacy was arrived at by employing a practice that constructed women (among other ways) as victims. The practice is not easily dealt with or dismissed, and its nagging problems and implications must be examined in more detail.[64]

EXPLOITATION PROGRAMMING

As I pointed out in the preceding chapter, many people in the television industry, especially from the late 1970s through the 1980s, considered exploitation programming an inevitable mainstay of prime-time television, especially for programs directed toward women. They believed that it simply was not possible to attract a large number of viewers without exploitation topics, and they attributed this to the tastes and entertainment desires of the audience, especially the women's audience. From their point of view, the use of exploitation subject matter was part of the territory of popular commercial TV programming, and, with an innovative program like *Cagney and Lacey*, it was just one of many tactics necessary to keep the series on the air. Others in the industry saw the practice as a lure for attracting large audiences to shows that presented serious, socially responsible treatments of contemporary issues. *Something about Amelia*, the 1984 made-for-TV movie about a father's incestuous abuse of his daughter, for example, was considered at the time to set a new standard for exploitation vehicles. The subject matter was "hot," and the movie brought in not only high ratings but also critical acclaim for its "sensitive" and "important" treatment of incest. The combination was one that others in the business were hoping to replicate.[65]

For the *Cagney and Lacey* series, as we have seen, exploitable or promotable programs developed, at least in part, to combat the other networks' women-oriented movies, which were competing for the same target audience. They also comprised part of the general effort to make the program and its depictions more conventional and to emphasize its "women's angle" dimensions. From one point of view, the use of exploitation material literally cashed in on—and subjected to the demands, constraints, and distortions of television—issues that were enormously complex and traumatic for women. But from another standpoint, numerous women viewers found *Cagney and Lacey*'s handling of these issues important and most welcome. Several such episodes also won awards and praise from social programs, rape crisis centers, and battered women's shelters. The reception of these shows and others like them certainly makes the tangled and contradictory character of exploitation programming apparent. Below I will look more closely at some of the tangles and at some of the audience letters responding to the exploitation episodes. But let me begin by making plain some of the problems I, as a feminist cultural critic, find with the practice.

Television distorts and makes problematic the notion of "women's issues" in a number of ways, including its representation of them as originating and resolvable at the level of the personal, the private, and often the domestic. The social origins and dimensions of the problems and the need for fundamental structural changes are usually not addressed, although some programs may refer to women's shelters or groups and crisis centers. But Laurie Schulze, in discussing the exploitation dimensions of made-for-TV movies, comments that even the "pedagogical stance" adopted by "made-fors" may actually have a "domesticating function." The references to institutions and professional services and the statistics presented can, she warns, serve to reassure us that solutions are available and that "the problem is being handled."[66]

Also, even though the problems dealt with in these programs have profoundly serious implications for many women, the networks' designation of a group of issues as "women's issues" is highly troubling on several counts. For one thing, TV's criteria for choosing these issues is, as we have seen, skewed toward subject matter that can be tapped for its sensationalism. Whereas other potential issues, such as low wages or discrimination based on race, class, age, appearance, disabilities, and gender, are also crucial for women, they may lack exploitation potential and are perhaps more difficult to reduce to an individual level. (In other words, the *social* dimensions of racism or wage discrimination are harder to repress.) Additionally, television's selection of potentially sensational (usually sexual or violent) subjects as its designated "women's issues" tends to produce and reproduce the notions of women as victims and as sexual objects—the very notions that some of the programs purportedly intend to dispel. And furthermore, the casting of major social atrocities like rape, woman-battering, incest, and sexual harassment as "*women's* issues" tends to "contain" them, consign them to the domain of "belonging to women," and once again obscure their more general social, power-oriented, and structural characteristics.

These implications were not totally lost on the press or on some members of *Cagney and Lacey*'s production team. John J. O'Connor of the *New York Times*, while basically praising the series as "indisputably a class act," also said that "*Cagney and Lacey* hasn't yet found the perfect balancing mechanisms for dealing with subjects that are still considered sensational or controversial. . . . It's not that any of this is completely objectionable. It's simply that the wheels of exploitation can be heard grinding off camera." More pointedly, in speaking about the exploitation dimensions of the breast cancer episodes, Tyne Daly revealed, "The show's writers thought the breast cancer story line was so juicy. I wish it wasn't so juicy. I just wish it wasn't juicy anymore in our society to see women threatened." She added, "I didn't want to see the victimization of Mary Beth. I signed on to play the hero not the victim. And sort of as a general rule of thumb, I don't want to play the victims. I'm not mad for women-in-jeopardy as an art form."[67]

Although there are obviously dangers and many contradictions in exploitation programs directed at women, some of them may perform important social functions. As Laurie Schulze says of the "issue of the week" made-for-TV movie, they may serve to open up "the site of an immense and intense ideological negotiation, limning . . . the more salient and disturbing phenomena on the social agenda." Furthermore, she continues, they "may very well lay bare more conflicts and contradictions in the culture's ideologies of masculinity and femininity, and of the family, than they lay to rest." The immediacy of the conflicts and contradictions stirred up by *Cagney and Lacey*'s women's-issue episodes was demonstrated in an outpouring of letters from viewers and social interest groups. The program was praised for giving such issues a large public forum and for communicating to women in the audience that their experiences were not isolated ones. A male viewer, upon hearing of the series's cancellation in 1983, wrote, "The issues the show dealt with such as rape, wife abuse, and drug abuse were all handled in a superior manner and greatly enlightened viewers on these topics. The show deserves a much better fate than the one that has been bestowed upon it." A female viewer said, "Keep the show on the air with its provocative topics which need to be aired. Violence against women on TV shows seems to be increasing rather than decreasing."[68]

Rape crisis centers, hospital programs, and women's service organizations expressed their appreciation for the series's treatment of rape in Fisher and Brown's "Open and Shut Case" and "Date Rape." A letter from the physician in charge of the emergency departments at a women's hospital, also a member of the hospital's rape intervention program, said, "On Monday evening February 21st I watched the *Cagney and Lacey* program on Rape. I was impressed with the directness and sensitivity with which a large number of issues were addressed. I think the program was a valuable introductory document on the subject of rape—a subject so often neglected on network television. It was especially valuable to consider the issue from the perspective of the many characters on the program. . . . I applaud your efforts." The director of an urban program on women's safety wrote about "Date Rape":

I would like to express our great admiration and appreciation for the superb job you did on a subject that is very important, usually ignored and commonly misunderstood. You portrayed with accuracy, clarity and sensitivity all the attitudes surrounding this complex issue, ranging from the skepticism and/or downright disbelief on the part of those who hear about such an incident to the feelings of frustration and self-doubt of those who suffer through it, causing them to wonder if they somehow precipitated the assault and thus hesitate to report it or seek counseling. It is extremely difficult for a television program, especially in an hour format, to impart information on a complex social problem without resorting to a lecture—or, on the other hand, to create an effective episode without glossing over the more subtle, emotional aspects of the topic in the name of dramatic action. Somehow you managed to do it, and we are grateful for the work and thought you must have put into such an accomplishment.

The various responses to "A Cry for Help" (the episode about a cop who beats his wife) provide further examples. Remember that "A Cry for Help" was the first *Cagney and Lacey* episode to be advertised in *TV Guide* in a wholly exploitative manner, and that Barney Rosenzweig and Richard Rosenbloom cited it to CBS as an example of a ratings-successful, "female-oriented exploitable theme." Remember also that the episode was pre-screened at Lincoln Center, during *Cagney and Lacey*'s 1983 publicity blitz, for a number of women's groups and social service organizations involved in the prevention of violence against women. The episode and stars Sharon Gless and Tyne Daly were introduced by Judy Goldsmith, president of NOW, and the screening was followed by a panel discussion moderated by Gloria Steinem.

At least two lengthy articles about the episode appeared in the main-stream press, one by Beverly Stephen of the *New York Daily News* and one by Virginia Castleberry of the *Dallas Times Herald*. In addition to talking about the program per se, both described women's shelters and hotlines in their areas and gave telephone numbers for them. "It's not every day," wrote Castleberry, "that television deals with the issue of battered wives. But, social service experts will tell you, women are abused in their homes every day in cities such as Dallas. And in the real world as on the TV show, there are places for battered women to turn." (A listing and a discussion of the services in the Dallas area follows.)[69]

A viewer letter on this episode read, "Please consider running your program again that was aired last night on the subject of a battered cop's wife. . . . I have a personal reason for wanting to see it—someone near and dear to me has this problem. Her husband controls his temper at work and of course has a greater anger when he is home. He has threatened to kill her if she were to tell on him etc. She is afraid and has three children and no job. She feels trapped." Another letter, which picked up on Cagney's reve-lation in the episode that she had once been abused by a boyfriend, said, "This week we *felt* what she [Cagney] endured in having once been beaten up by a boyfriend. I wouldn't be surprised if the courage Cagney showed in getting out of that situation immediately, ends up helping some battered wives to find their own courage."

A director of a women's shelter also responded:

On behalf of the organizations and employees who provide support services to battered women and their children, I would like to thank you for your recent episode of CAGNEY AND LACEY that dealt with the issue of domestic violence. The program's strong points were its realism and discussion of myths about spouse abuse. The conclusion of the show was excellent in that it depicted the victim's struggle as only beginning. While leaving a violent situation is difficult, remaining away is even more difficult as it involves much work on the victim's part. . . . Everyone associated with the production is to be commended. . . . Making the community aware of domestic violence is one of our program goals. Your show has helped us in this respect.

And the executive director of a commission on violence against women offered, "CAGNEY AND LACEY has helped to dispel stereotypes that are harmful to survivors of sexual assault and domestic violence. CBS has performed an important public social service in presenting such programming."[70]

"Open and Shut Case" (the episode about rape, the problems of prosecution, and female solidarity) won the American Women in Radio and Television Award for 1983. And both "Open and Shut Case" and "A Cry for Help" won the 1983 Humanitarian Awards from the Los Angeles Commission on Assaults against Women.

Examined together, the viewer and interest group responses (including NOW's) to women's-issues programs, the industry's wholehearted pursuit of exploitation topics, my own regard for the series's handling of some of these topics (which I will discuss in the following chapters), and my own and others' problems with exploitation programming directed toward women all help illuminate the tensions created in bringing feminism and complicated social issues to television. The various reactions underscore the claim that different participants in the overall television enterprise engage in television (produce it and interpret it) from divergent interest-based positions and with disparate investments and wants; any given program may produce mixed and conflicted responses in any one viewer. But they also illustrate the power and perils of industrially produced mass culture—the many troubles that shape it, that it looks for to keep itself "popular," and that it both perpetuates and may help put to rest.

I have argued that *Cagney and Lacey* evolved into a "woman's program." But this end was achieved through a process of institutional, textual, and reception-oriented negotiation. We have seen that, on an institutional level, many struggles resulted from the representation of women as feminist police detectives in a stereotypically male genre, and that most of them were inflamed and exacerbated by the Reagan years' backlash at feminism. The networks hedged their bets by alternately giving (some) and taking (more) in their attempts to portray the "new woman." In the textual negotiation of new and old discourses about women, the police genre (because of its history, norms, and institutional and cultural expectations) was forced to give way and transmogrify.

The industrial and textual negotiations resulted in the taming and harnessing of some of *Cagney and Lacey*'s perceived transgressions, producing a series that the ratings and conventional wisdom on women's programming seemed to prescribe. Although the show was always a hybrid form and always produced multiple meanings about its women characters, the negotiated changes steered it toward the "woman's program" category in the stereotypical sense of the phrase—a show that starred and was targeted toward women, and one that generated traditional depictions of women, showed women as victims, and exploited sensationalistic or "hot" subject matter.[71]

But as we also saw, there was considerable negotiating done at the level of reception—in viewer and interest group readings and interpretations of the series. So it was not only the institutional and textual agitations that produced a woman's program, but audience activity as well. And this factor, of course, poses a number of quandaries. The audience letters quoted in previous chapters indisputably prove that a number of women fans found Cagney's and Lacey's *original* incarnations in the Foster/Daly series appealing, fascinating, and a welcome addition to prime time. It is also clear that the series was of special interest to them *as women* because it embodied the conflicts of traditional and new discourses about femininity. For those reasons, the original series too (long predating the transformations I have described in this chapter) might be called a woman's program. But some of the changes that took the series more in the direction of exploitation nonetheless produced episodes that were likewise admired by many audience women, not necessarily for their sensationalistic dimensions but because the issues raised were pertinent to the fans' lives, their friends' lives, their own struggles with social problems, and the clashing of ideas about what it meant to be a woman.[72]

Furthermore, the writing of feminist scholars on such topics as soap operas, melodrama, and situation comedies demonstrates convincingly that conventional women's programs do not necessarily produce conventional meanings about femininity. In a different but related vein, Constance Penley's, Henry Jenkins's, and Camilla Bacon-Smith's work on women fandoms of *Star Trek* throws into further question the too-easy correspondence between particular types of story materials and genres and particular groups of gendered viewers. This is not to argue that there is, after all, no such thing as a "woman's program" or that the phrase is totally meaningless. Industry practice, history, and everyday life tell us differently. It is simply to say that the phrase supports enormously different definitions, investments, and wants.[73]

But the troubling relationship between what are generally considered "women's programs" and exploitation topics will most certainly continue to haunt us. The simple fact that many women's histories and social situations are shaped by conventional forces of inequality, subordination, "victimization," harassment, and stereotypical valuations as sex and beauty objects makes it virtually impossible to pry those elements apart from representations involving and directed toward women.[74] Just as Chapter 2 showed that "women's culture" and institutional constraints regarding audience considerations are complexly imbricated, we see here that troubles, terrors, comforts, and empowerment can be both bound into and unleashed by women's programs in ways that plainly serve network and advertising needs but also those of viewers who are gingerly negotiating the minefield of television reception.

NEGOTIATING FEMINISM

In using the case of *Cagney and Lacey* to probe how *woman,*
women, and *femininity* were defined in the overall television enterprise of
the 1980s, we come squarely up against the ways feminism was actually
handled in the program. *Cagney and Lacey* is unique in television history
because it dared to go where no program had gone before (or has gone
since)—that is, intrepidly into the territory of feminism, to a degree un-
matched on prime time. Such daring caused it to be dubbed "the darling of
the women's movement" by the mainstream press. But as we glimpsed in
Chapter 1, anyone familiar with feminist theory and criticism over the past
twenty years knows only too well that "feminism" is a hotly contested term
with widely varying meanings, polarized "camps," and often conflicting
theoretical premises. *Cagney and Lacey* essentially drew from and engaged
with liberal Western feminism, especially the American liberal women's

movement of the early 1980s. In thus situating itself, the program became a forum for the active negotiation of a number of discourses: the social critiques, analyses, jokes, and new definitions of women that stemmed from the liberal women's movement; the hostility toward feminism that coincided with the debates over and defeat of the Equal Rights Amendment (ERA) in the United States; and "common sense" status quo definitions of femininity deriving from a range of entrenched institutions and practices. At a textual level, the series also experienced the general tendency of more "radical" programs to become, after some time on the air, more open or "popular," to foster more ambiguity and consequently more varied audience readings—or, from another view point, to cast a wider net in order to reach not only the preferred target audience (in this case, upscale working women) but a range of other viewers as well.[1]

Cagney and Lacey did not venture into this relatively uncharted women's movement territory alone. In the fall of 1982 (when the Gless/Daly series premiered), many programs flirted with feminism. And this historical moment (which was quite literally just that) marks the very point at which women's movements gains, having filtered into widespread popular consciousness, were abruptly set back by retrenchments spearheaded by the Reagan White House. In October of that year, Elaine Warren of the *Los Angeles Herald Examiner* wrote:

> On paper, a quick scan of the new fall series makes it look as though Gloria Steinem has seized control of the corporate suites at the networks and taken command of the airwaves. Among the new shows are those pivoting around: A housewife who goes to law school and becomes a hard-driving assistant district attorney (*It Takes Two*—ABC). Three office secretaries who take flak from nobody, least of all their boss (*9 to 5*—ABC). Two women cops who patrol the streets together and explore the boundaries of friendship (*Cagney and Lacey*—CBS). A young attractive private detective who heads her own agency using a fictitious male name (*Remington Steele*—NBC). This was supposed to be the season in which television grows up and discovers real women. On paper—maybe. But what might have once been good intentions have been subjected in the meantime to network processing which blends, chops, dices and pulverizes fiber into mush better than anybody's Cuisinart. The results are dismally disappointing. . . . Only one *Cagney and Lacey* attempts this goal in a whole-hearted, courageous way.[2]

Warren went on to criticize the other programs and their treatments, and her comments on *9 to 5* and *Remington Steele* are particularly pertinent here. They plainly show how new economic discourses about women and work, the vigorous reassertion of traditional assumptions about women as sex objects and appendages of men, and network beliefs about conventional prime-time femininity fermented together in television texts directed toward a women's audience. "At its inception," said Warren, "*9 to 5* made the bold promise to champion the cause of secretaries and fight sexism on the job. And with Jane Fonda as executive co-producer, who could doubt the sincerity of its goals? *What*, then, are the three secretaries in the show doing parading in lingerie in the very first episode of the fall season?" The response to this question came from the show's coproducer, Bruce Gilbert:

> The subject matter was at the request of the network. . . . However, I don't want to use that as an excuse, because the fact of the matter is, the storyline was a real phenomenon taken out of the newspapers, based on a secretary who is raising two children, having a lot of trouble making ends meet, who is given the opportunity to sell "Lovewear." It's a reality of life that many women are supplementing their incomes—particularly clerical workers—by taking on these outside jobs. . . . We still show sexism in the office.

The dangers of bringing such a complex, contested, and pervasive issue as sexism to early 1980s prime time (under the stewardship of Jane Fonda or anyone else) and the hazards of invoking a "reality" basis for representations are, of course, dramatically underscored in Gilbert's response.

Warren's critique of *Remington Steele* revealed similar tinkerings with the show's original conception. The premise was that a woman detective (Laura Holt, played by Stephanie Zimbalist) opened up her own detective agency. But because an agency run by a woman was attracting few clients, she invented a fictitious male head-detective named Remington Steele and then joined forces with a bumbling, inept, but handsome former thief who pretended to be her creation. As Warren described it, "Since the pilot episodes for the show were screened for the media earlier this year, Zimbalist's tough-guy image has undergone significant changes: She has come to depend on Steele in traditionally feminine, vulnerable ways—cuddling up to him at trying moments—and her overall strength of character has been noticeably diluted."

Michael Gleason, executive producer of the program, denied that there had been deliberate changes and asserted that Zimbalist's vulnerability was part of the show's "twist." "The thing that I love about Stephanie Zimbalist and the way she plays Laura Holt," he continued, "is that the stereotype has always been Joan Crawford with the padded shoulders—you know, a terribly hard, tough lady who always lost her femininity as she rose to the top. Stephanie Zimbalist/Laura Holt never loses her femininity. And I think that's a wonderful statement to make." On the other hand, Michael Burstin, vice-president of dramatic series development at NBC, said of the series's changes, "I think it was partially her own [Zimbalist's] interpretation, rather than anyone at the network's request." He also said that "almost everyone involved with the show is unhappy with the new slant, and is working toward getting it back the way it was." Whatever the exact derivations of the changes in *Remington Steele*, the show never returned to "the way it was"; if anything, it went more in the direction flagged by Warren. The other new working women series, *Gloria* and *It Takes Two*, were similarly criticized in the remainder of Warren's article.

Although Elaine Warren singled out *Cagney and Lacey* as the only show of the 1982 lot that actually dealt with "real women" in a "wholehearted and courageous way," we have seen many instances in which its nonconventional characters were readjusted back to more customary norms. This chapter will probe some institutional, contextual, and textual negotiations involving the series and feminism itself, not just in 1982 but throughout its run.

HOME-SCREEN FEMINISM

We have seen that throughout its history *Cagney and Lacey* was publicized, promoted, and championed by the U.S. liberal women's movement and by many other feminists. As late in the series's run as January 1988, *TV Guide* featured on its cover a drawing of Sharon Gless and Tyne Daly as their popular characters, with a feature-story title and credit reading, " 'Why I Consider *Cagney and Lacey* the Best Show on TV,' by Gloria Steinem." I have argued that this promotion and support helped cause the series, from its earliest days, to be received and understood (at least by some viewers) as a feminist program; and I have suggested that this perception was fostered through the process of intertextuality—that women's movement–oriented publicity and discussions functioned as secondary and tertiary texts that influenced future readings of the primary text, *Cagney and Lacey* itself.[3]

It is obvious that feminism found vigorous engagement, not only at the level of secondary and tertiary texts but also at the level of the primary ones. And although CBS was able to curtail its more pointed representations, the network's discursive authority was by no means total. Until the

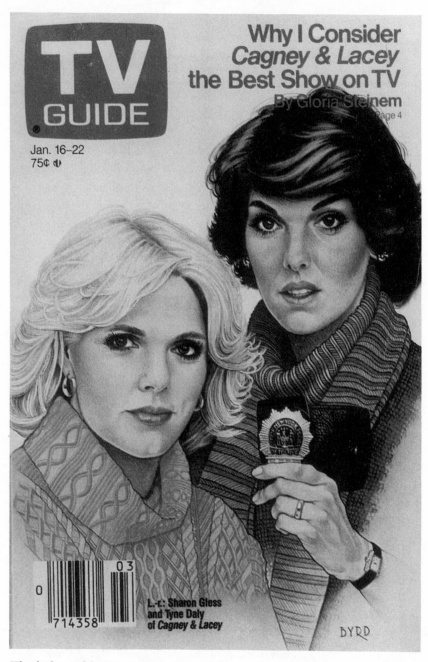

Why I Consider
Cagney & Lacey
the Best Show on TV
By Gloria Steinem
Page 4

TV
GUIDE

Jan. 16–22
75¢ ¢)

L.-r.: Sharon Gless
and Tyne Daly
of *Cagney & Lacey*

BYRD

The darlings of the women's movement. (Artist, Byrd, reprinted with permission from TV Guide® *Magazine,* © *News America Publications Inc., 1988)*

series was canceled in the spring of 1988, feminism (in some form or other) continued to be an influence in the narratives, and viewers certainly persisted with feminist readings and interpretations. None of this is to claim, however, that all—or even most—feminists would call *Cagney and Lacey* a feminist program. But more about that later.

There are undoubtedly many routes one could take in analyzing the series's handling of women's movement discourses, but in the following pages I will discuss three main ways in which such discourses were treated and how they were transformed in the course of a seven-year history.

EXPLICIT GENERAL FEMINISM

Riding the crest of the women's movement in the late 1970s and very early 1980s, the *Cagney and Lacey* movie and original Foster/Daly series generated what I call "explicit general feminism" (usually with a liberal slant). This included dialogue and scenes that straightforwardly addressed discrimination against women in both the public and private spheres, stories structured around topical feminist causes, and the use of unequivocal feminist language and slogans. It also included the conflation of issues involving gender, race, and to some degree class, as well as political analyses of stereotyped masculinity and status quo feminine roles.[4]

Despite Rosenzweig's public declaration that they were not "carrying the banner of feminism," it is clear that the production team set out to include women's movement language, situations, and jokes in the movie and first six episodes. Commentaries and memos on various drafts of the scripts actually bespeak efforts to be blatantly and "correctly" feminist; those pertaining to the sixth and last Foster/Daly episode, "Better than Equal," provide noteworthy examples. The show tackled a fiercely contested public issue—the 1982 attempt to add the Equal Rights Amendment to the U.S. Constitution—and involved the two feminist detectives in an assignment to protect Helen Granger, an anti-ERA activist modeled on the notorious Phyllis Schlafly. On 10 March 1982, two weeks before the series even premiered, Rosenzweig sent a memo about the first draft of "Better than Equal" to Fred Freiberger (the show's producer at the time). It began: "I think we should be a bit stronger *politically*—hipper stuff. We need to research on something more for Granger to 'say,' for her to 'speak' about. What Granger says and what C&L respond to should be on a higher plane than this first grade primer approach to ERA. . . . If necessary, let's contact Steinem office for material. This episode has an opportunity of being one of our better ones, but we've an obligation to be sharp here" (emphasis in original).[5]

Rosenzweig also included an example of the kinds of quips he thought they should use: "*Cagney*: 'I keep waiting for that houseworker in the ring-around-the collar commercial to tell her old man to wash his neck!'" A followup interoffice memo, written on 21 March by P. K. (Patricia) Knelman (the series's associate producer and later its coproducer), addressed Rosenzweig's concerns and provided research for the rewrites. Her memo was a five-page, single-spaced summary of the history and content of the ERA. It went on to outline the "Stop ERA" positions put forward in the *Phyllis Schlafly Reports* newsletters and the positions of other anti-ERA groups. (We should also recall that this was the episode in which Gloria Steinem had been invited to guest star.)[6]

All the original shows contained many explicit feminist lines, gags, and runners. Although some may come across as heavy-handed and didactic—and were criticized as such by the mainstream press—they set a tone for the series and its reception; from a 1990s perspective, their boldness for prime-time drama is noteworthy.[7] In the first episode, "Bang, Bang, You're Dead" (about, as we saw, the serial murder of prostitutes), the leitmotif is the protagonists' attempts to prove themselves capable cops despite their gender. They have put a key piece of the crime puzzle together—all the murdered prostitutes wore crosses. Lacey wants to tell their commanding officer, Lieutenant Samuels:

> *Lacey*: Let's ram this down Samuels' throat.
> *Cagney*: Are you kidding? Not yet. We're hugging this to our little old female bosoms.
> *Lacey*: Come on, Chris. You can't do that. He's the boss.
> *Cagney*: I know . . . but he's very busy right now. Let's leave him alone. We'll tell him later on.
> *Lacey*: Chris, we don't really have to be twice as good to be equal.
> *Cagney*: Says who?

In the same episode, the two detectives, in "hooker gear," meet one of their street informants, who cracks, "If you don't mind my saying so, you dress a little flashy for cops."[8] To which Foster's Cagney retorts, "Well, you see, when you're doing a man's job, you don't want anyone to think that you've lost your femininity." (It is, of course, woefully ironic that CBS later used virtually the same language to force Foster's removal from the program.) And later in the show, when an intractable Samuels refuses to give the women interesting assignments, confines them to "john detail" (the entrapment of men soliciting prostitutes), and will not acknowledge them as full members of the squad, the dialogue (with accompanying stage directions) was written as follows:

Samuels: Cagney, will you get on with your job and let me talk to my men?

[Cagney elaborately turns to Lacey and with great interest begins a new tack.]

Cagney: That certainly was a delicious stew you made last night, Mary Beth. Could you give me the recipe?
Lacey: Well first, you have to buy a pig.

[Samuels glares at them.]

Cagney: Buy a pig? I didn't know you could buy a pig in this town.
Lacey: Oh, you can buy a pig almost anyplace in this town. You don't want an old pig, or a fat pig, you just want a nice succulent . . .

[Samuels interrupts them.]

(As the series progressed, the Samuels character, while retaining some bluster, softened considerably and became more of a "sensitive man" like the sympathetic male characters in women's programs such as soap operas; and many future episodes dealt with his "deep-down" vulnerability and tender-heartedness.)

Struggles against racism, and to some degree classism, were originally portrayed as congruent with the fight against sexism; although the two white women were often cast as the enlightened teachers of their male colleagues, the African American Detective Petrie bore the weight of representing his entire race, and race was sometimes subsumed under gender. Petrie was depicted as politically sympathetic with Chris and Mary Beth's battle for equality. When the white Lieutenant Samuels, as quoted in the previous chapter, snarls upon hearing of Cagney and Lacey's promotion and commendation from police headquarters, "Terrific. Last year blacks, this year broads. Will someone explain to me why guys with families are getting laid off and broads are getting promoted?" Petrie curtly fires back, "Maybe they had seniority." In the made-for-TV movie, Loretta Swit's Cagney says to Petrie, "Interesting how it comes in the same package—sexism and racism." And in "Better than Equal," when the protagonists are reluctant to guard the Schlafly-based character, Petrie says to them, "Boy, you guys are sure touchy about that woman." Meg Foster's Cagney responds, "How would you feel if you were guarding the head of the Ku Klux Klan?" to which he concedes, "I'd leave my gun at home." Later, in an argument with all the male detectives about the ERA, Lacey says, "Petrie, the Constitution said that all men are created equal . . . then they added the amendment to include blacks. Well, when your baby comes, if it's a girl, don't you want her to be equal, too?" "Yeah," he answers, "I sure do."

This linking of racism and sexism was, in fact, an explicit intention of the production team. In the series "Bible," Petrie's character description plainly stated, "Marcus Petrie is Cagney and Lacey's friend in court. Having been on the receiving end of racism and white supremacy, he is sensitive to their struggle to be accepted as members of the team—equals."[9] But the overt political links among the three diminished as the series progressed, and Petrie and Sharon Gless's Cagney actually developed an edge of hostility, which in the later episodes appeared to derive from individual differences. Petrie was portrayed as sensitive, mild-mannered, precise, and liberal, and Cagney as insensitive, cocky, obstreperous, and politically regressive. White feminist movements certainly have been guilty of perpetuating racism in many ways, and some of *Cagney and Lacey's* early attempts to analyze racial and gender discrimination in tandem demonstrate just a few of these ways. But the gradual unraveling of all ties between sexism and racism in the program evidences (at least in part) the burgeoning conservatism in U.S. society at large, which fought to turn back not only the gains of the women's movements but those of African Americans at the same time. The displacement of issues deriving from uneven social power onto the foundation of individual differences and personal style hints at the direction television feminism would take as both the 1980s and *Cagney and Lacey* wore on.

For example, in the highly acclaimed "The City Is Burning" (a 1987 episode on racism impelled by New York's Howard Beach incident and written by African American screenwriter Samm-Art Williams), Cagney, who is in charge of the investigation, walks into the squad room and declares that the case has been solved and the murder was not racially provoked. To the group of detectives who for much of the episode have been hurling racial, anti-Semitic, and ethnic slurs at one another, she says, "Okay, listen up all you crackers, wops, niggers, chinks, spics, micks, kikes, and polaks. Did I leave anybody out? Good. That's the last time I want to hear any of those words in this place." She then declares that there was no racial motivation to the murder: "[It was] nothing but a hot car deal gone sour. That's it. There was nothing racial about it." To which Petrie, trembling with uncharacteristic rage and emotion, replies, "Thank you, Judge

"What do you know about it anyway, Sergeant?" A scene from "The City Is Burning," with Carl Lumbly as Petrie and Robert Hegyes as Esposito. (© Orion TV, 1987)

Cagney. . . . What do you know about it anyway, Sergeant? What do you know about names that can cut. Would you like to be called a spoiled honky bitch? Or how about lush? . . . Does that measure up to gook or hebe or coon? Would you like to explain that to my daughter, Lauren? That's what I did last night."[10]

Although the scene is among the most hard-hitting and powerful of the series, it clearly demonstrates the dismantling of the Cagney character's (and the program's) original conception of race and gender as at least partly related facets of social stratification. By the time this episode was written, the dismantling had already taken place, and the Cagney character had long been a politically obtuse one. Throughout the series's history, on the other hand, Petrie and Lacey continued a fairly warm friendship, which in "The City Is Burning" includes bonding against racism. However, their friendship increasingly came to seem more related to Lacey's liberal and expansive qualities (and perhaps the extratextual knowledge that the actress was married to African American director and actor Georg Stanford Brown) and Petrie's open and socially committed ones than to the overt political bonding of the original relationship.

In the early 1982 episodes, class as well as race was linked to feminism. In "Better than Equal," for instance, Lacey confronts the Schlafly-based activist with: "Most women aren't as lucky or as privileged as you are, Mrs. Granger. . . . How come so many women support themselves and their children if the law's so terrific? . . . If every woman was as liberated as you are, there'd be no need for a feminist movement." However, feminism itself also was occasionally criticized during this period. Notwithstanding the production team's attempts to forge links among race, class, and gender oppression, one such criticism was directed at the women's movement's own racism and classism. In an episode called "Street Scene," Chris and Mary Beth show up uninvited to a baby shower at Detective Petrie's house. The wives of the male detectives are, we have been told, unhappy about having their husbands working with two women. Cagney and Lacey's feminism is a well-known fact among the assembled group, and just before their unexpected entrance, Bonita Velasquez, a Latina and the pregnant wife of one of the male detectives (both characters, incidentally, disappeared from future episodes), is relating a story. We catch her in mid-sentence: ". . . 'You can afford to be a feminist, honey,' I told her. 'All I got going for me are big bazooms.' " As is much too evident, here, however, the dialogue ends up, in a shocking and degrading way, producing the very racism, classism, and sexism it set out to expose and challenge.

Conventional masculinity, in the early episodes, was directly linked to sexist structures and cultural practices. In "Better than Equal," Samuels asks the protagonists what they have against the Schlafly-based character, and Lacey responds, "It's politics." Samuels retorts, "All that Gloria Steinem feminist stuff, right?" to which Lacey retorts, "Helen Granger doesn't want women to be equal with men because she thinks men should take care of women. But the truth is, until women are liberated, men really won't be, either." When Detective Isbecki joins in with, "If you ask me, it's all bull," the feminist Foster/Cagney inquires, "Wouldn't you like to not have to be so macho all the time?"

Other issues that became completely disassociated from a feminist analysis in later narratives—such as Cagney's father-identified daughterhood— were, in the early episodes, also given a women's movement nuance.[11] In a Foster/Daly episode called "Pop Used to Work Chinatown," the relationship between Cagney and her father, Charlie, yielded a critique of gender roles:

Cagney: C'mon down to Clancy's with me. Charlie wants me to join him for a drink.
Lacey: A drink? You mean a drunk.
Cagney: He's feeling a little lonely. All he wants is to hoist a couple with

his number one son, and tell it like it was when he was a cop. What's the harm in that? . . .

Lacey: . . . Look, Chris, I like your dad. He's a charmer. But what do you want to be his son for? What's wrong with being a daughter?

Cagney: And daughters are supposed to whip up homemade stew for Daddy, while sons get to belly up to the bar with him.

As noted in previous chapters, the original Foster/Daly series was, in fact, considered "too women's lib" by the network, and the renovated Gless/Daly one significantly toned down its feminism. The diminution of explicit discourses did not, however, garner much attention in the press—either mainstream or feminist. Some headlines such as "CBS Softens Show to Save Ratings" acknowledged the changes, but much of the mainstream press, as we saw in Chapter 1, still seemed to perceive the women's movement material in "sledgehammer" terms: "The clubbing approach is gone," announced one review, while another, quoted earlier, contended that "the message of female discrimination is too obvious and heavy-handed . . . [and] could be the Achilles' heel of the series if pounded home too strongly."[12]

Several viewer letters from my sample touched on this issue. One evidenced initial reluctance about the explicit feminism: "I've enjoyed *Cagney and Lacey* since its beginning. Didn't particularly care for its title—envisioned two female macho cops, twirling revolvers, flashing their badges, and shouting, 'I am woman.' But I watched it . . . and I liked it." Another was overtly critical of CBS's opinion about the series and its call for revisions. The writer unabashedly protested: "How can a show be 'too women's lib?' For once a series focused on women and their relationships. It resembles the rationale that terminated the series *Universe* because it was 'too intelligent.' "[13]

It is obvious, from excerpts cited in this and the preceding chapter, that even though the made-for-TV movie and the Foster/Daly series featured explicitly feminist subject matter, dialogue, and jokes, they also included some material that was troublesome and offensive from feminist points of view, among them: the sensational serial murders of women; racist, classist, and sexist slurs; graphic portrayals of women as victims; stereotyped depictions of prostitutes; an overly didactic approach; and white women as enlightened teachers about racism. Some feminists, as we have seen, also found the characterization of the two heroines as police-identified and violent indefensible.[14]

The explicit feminist discourses disappeared in the first half of the new

Gless/Daly season in the fall of 1982. The "Bible" clearly spelled out the modifications. It also underscored the shifts in genre discussed in the previous chapter. "Sexism," it declared,

> is a texture to the series, rather than a weekly issue. First and foremost, Chris Cagney and Mary Beth Lacey are good cops, professionals; not standard bearers. Their response to the continuing *unconscious* chauvinism in the precinct is one of the running themes. It is a show about transition—working it out in the work-place—in this new age of consciousness. It is also a show about two women who happen to be cops, rather than two cops who happen to be women." (emphasis in original)[15]

Furthermore, when April Smith was hired as the producer for the revised series, she was quoted in *Variety* as saying she had no desire to turn the program "into a Women's Lib vehicle." With this comment, Smith followed in the footsteps of Barney Rosenzweig, who said the show was not "carrying the banner of feminism," and prefigured later remarks of Sharon Gless, who publicly disavowed that the series was feminist.[16] Also, one of the episodes during the Smith half of the first Gless/Daly season, evocatively called "Affirmative Action," introduced to the precinct a new white woman detective who was in the job "for the money" and who failed horribly at her duties.

The foregoing must be seen in light of the fact that prime-time network programs considered radical for their times (such as *Cagney and Lacey* and *Hill Street Blues*) have tended, for a whole range of reasons, to become gradually more mainstream as their seasons go forward and as they have worked to promote themselves to a wider audience than may have initially been attracted to them. But it is the details and conditions of this gradual mainstreaming that are so crucial to understanding the precise workings of industrial popular culture. *Cagney and Lacey*'s turn away from (and in some cases repudiation of) explicit feminism can only be truly appreciated within its specific social context: early 1980s America and the decade's severe backlash against women's rights.

As Susan Faludi describes the period, women's entry into higher-paying jobs suddenly stalled, pay dropped in many heretofore promising occupations, and the number of women in elected and appointed political positions declined. The status of low-income women plunged drastically, child support from divorced husbands went down by 25 percent, the number of women seeking refuge in domestic shelters rose 100 percent, and, since the seventies, reported rapes virtually doubled and sex-related murders climbed 160 percent. Antiabortion furor and violence, furthermore, rose to a frenzy, and it became widely acceptable to speak out against women's rights and to disavow feminism. Given such conditions, the series's mutations, especially those related to its women's movement heritage, took on wide-ranging significance.[17]

When explicit feminist discourses were reintroduced to the program with the scripts written and produced by Terry Louise Fisher and Steve Brown (beginning in January 1983), they most often involved the women's-issue topic of the episode (including rape, date rape, and wife-beating). Such discourses were usually (until well into the 1984–85 season) spoken by the Lacey character.

WOMEN'S-ISSUE FEMINISM

Cagney and Lacey's turn to "women's-issue" feminism brings up a number of points touched upon in the previous chapter. This type of feminism was confined to such issues as sexual assault, sexual harassment, and wife-battering. It usually had an exploitation dimension—a sexual or violent component—to its presentation, but it was also well researched by the production team and rendered in ways that many affected women and feminist agencies found acceptable and helpful. Although it was channeled into women's issues and consequently was less encompassing than what I have called explicit *general* feminism, it was sometimes flagged by the narratives as feminist. Even if it was not, its widespread recognition as a women's movement analysis of the particular topic made it a fairly apparent representation of feminism. This trend was unequivocally lambasted in *Vogue* magazine: "The two detectives roam New York City saying, 'Aaahhh, kiss off!' and 'Button it, will ya?' as they fight crime. But the crime they fight is not ordinary crime. Specifically, it's crime relating to women. New York seems to be crawling with creeps growling, 'Say, dere's some a 'dem women's libbers. Let's *git* 'em.'"[18]

One of my basic points is that the abandonment of explicit general feminism was predominantly characterized by a backing away from feminist positions that, although basically liberal, critiqued structurally inequitable social and economic conditions. Thereafter the program's feminism was associated with particular issues that, though they actually signaled major social problems (which *Vogue's* lampoon-style review did not set out to acknowledge), were presented as *specific to* women rather than to society as a whole. The representation of feminism changed, in other words, from a criticism of institutional inequities (sexism, racism, and, to a lesser degree, classism) to an examination of women's issues (or what the industry imagined as such issues) that had the potential for dramatic intensity and exploitability.

Just as the original Cagney character challenged the limits of appropriate gender definitions for television, the original *Cagney and Lacey* threatened the borders of social power hierarchies and the limitations on what social issues and treatments were acceptable subjects for 1980s network prime time. (The female detectives were seen as "more intent on fighting the system than on doing police work.") The channeling of feminism into episodes dealing with "women's issues" contained the threat to the "system" posed by more explicit and more wide-ranging feminism and by two feminist protagonists. Despite the interference of network executives, however, feminist meanings (although transformed) continued to be produced by the program and interpreted by viewers.[19]

Of the series's 125 episodes, 14 could be considered women's-issue exploitation programs, as I will describe that category shortly. An additional 36 (for a total of 50) were also exploitation episodes directed at the women's audience, but these did not necessarily involve "women's-issues"; they did not follow the format I will outline or involve widely recognized feminist discourses and positions. Of *Cagney and Lacey's* 14 major women's-issues programs, 4 dealt with rape, 2 with wife-beating, 2 with sexual harassment, 1 with abortion, 1 with incest, 2 with child molestation, and 2 with breast cancer. The additional 36 exploitation episodes primarily treated subjects that were less intense than the women's-issue episodes. They centered around topics that the TV industry considered of magnetic power in attracting women: pornography, child pornography, a male stripper club, an erotic hotline, baby brokering, a bigamy scam, Cagney's pregnancy scare, Lacey's emotional breakdown, Cagney's alcoholism, the birth of Lacey's baby, Cagney's marriage proposals, Lacey's being taken hostage, and Cagney's getting shot, to name some.

The remainder of the 125 programs were divided among police episodes, comedy episodes, and some primarily "political" episodes (El Salvador hit squads, toxic waste dumping, Lacey's nuclear weapons protest and arrest). But most of them (and most of the 125 generally), it should be remembered, were characterized by a *mixture* of police story, women's story, and comedy elements. Because the 14 women's-issue episodes were so important to viewers, and because they formed a key part of the series's engagement with feminism, they require some elaboration.

The treatment of feminism in these programs, although confined to the particular women's issue at hand, was nonetheless fairly overt and fell into a discernible pattern. This pattern was initially developed in the first episode dealing with rape, Fisher and Brown's "Open and Shut Case," which aired in January 1983. The second episode on rape, "Date Rape" (another 1983 script by Fisher and Brown) further expanded upon it and forms a prime example.

There are basically four elements to the pattern. First, general popular misconceptions and myths about the crime or the issue and the woman "victim's" relationship to it are exposed.[20] These misconceptions or "different sides" are often voiced by the men in the squad—Isbecki, Coleman, Samuels, Esposito, Newman, and occasionally LaGuardia. Petrie is usually on the feminist side, but more because of his character's sensitivity and insight than from explicit feminism.[21] Cagney (except when she herself is the victim) is often, for the first half of the narrative, on the side of popular misconceptions. Lacey, the most consistent spokesperson for feminism in the episodes, is almost always on the side of progressive women's movement views. (Even when Cagney is the victim, Lacey more fully articulates the feminist position about how the situation should be analyzed and what should be done.) However, in the breast cancer episodes (in which Lacey is the victim), it is Cagney who pushes her partner to consider alternative treatment and a second opinion. And in "A Cry for Help," Lacey is at first oddly reluctant to believe that one of her male co-workers could be a wife-batterer, evidences uncharacteristic mistrust of the allegations, wonders about the wife's "part" in the situation, and implies that a woman should simply leave a violent domestic situation. In this instance, Cagney (who reveals that she was once beaten up by a boyfriend) and Lieutenant Samuels (whose former partner was a wife-batterer) take the women's movement positions. Harvey Lacey is usually also on the feminist side but may occasionally express a myth or misconception, as in "A Cry for Help," when he maintains that there is something wrong with any woman who will not leave an abusive relationship.

Second, the brutalities, hassles, and inequities of the law enforcement and prosecuting systems are emphasized in references to vicious questioning by defense attorneys, trials that go on and on, and insensitive and cruel interrogations by members of the police department. Third, the woman victim's own guilt, internalizations, self-blaming, isolation, fear, and paralysis are also made clear. This position may be taken in dialogue spoken by the victim herself or by another woman in the narrative who has previously had a similar experience. Fourth, the episode usually culminates with a show of women's solidarity, demonstrating the need for women to band together to stop abuses and to shatter the myth of a victim's isolation. The solidarity may be manifested by other women who come forth to testify against the criminal, by both protagonists' strong support of the victim at the end of the episode, by Cagney and Lacey's fierce commitment to capturing and prosecuting the criminal, and by references to women's shelters, centers, and support groups.[22]

Some examples from "Date Rape" will make the pattern of women's-issues feminism clearer. The episode involves a white woman, Carole Mitchell, who picks up a man at a bar, invites him to her apartment, asks him to leave at the end of the evening, and is then raped by him. She comes to the precinct and asks to talk to women detectives. The fallacies about date rape and the general callousness of the men in the police precinct (and, by implication, of many men in general) are exposed in the following dialogue: Sergeant Coleman goes over to Cagney and Lacey after Carole Mitchell leaves and says, "Hey, what did she want? Come on, I got a bet with Isbecki. I say it was rape. He says it was non-support or a battered wife." Isbecki then grabs the interrogation report from Cagney's desk and reads, " '. . . picked him up at a bar and took him home.' You know what this smells like to me? A one night stand that never called back." To which Coleman adds, "Sure, the chick gets upset, turns him in to the cops to get revenge." A general repartee among the men follows:

> *Isbecki*: I mean, women are always saying "no"—sometimes they mean "yes," but usually they mean "maybe." Am I wrong?
> *Petrie*: I think you're over-generalizing.
> *Samuels*: You know who Thelma's [his former wife] favorite hero of all time is? Rhett Butler. So romantic she said. So how come when Rhett Butler throws Scarlett down on her bed that's romance? But when some poor slob does it, that's rape?

To which Lacey replies, "With respect, sir, if you don't know the difference between rape and romance then you've got a serious problem." At Lacey's exit, Coleman quips, "It's her time of the month? Or what?"

Throughout most of the episode, Cagney is less than supportive of Carole Mitchell, focusing instead on being accepted by the "guys." At one point she spews out more distortions about date rape and women's responsibility:

> *Lacey*: Hey, Chris, you don't believe her. You don't think that it was rape.
> *Cagney*: Mary Beth, listen to me. This is not something that I could say in front of the guys. I go out a lot. You know that. I also say "no" a lot.

Lacey: Oh yeah? Well, my goodness.

Cagney: The point is when I say "no" they get that I mean "no."

Lacey: I can't believe that you said that. Since you never have been raped that means that Carole Mitchell could not possibly have been raped either?

When Cagney and Lacey get a potential rapist's profile from a male police officer in charge of records, the officer says to them, "I don't think he's your boy. M.O. is different. Parker likes to do it in alleys. He likes to humiliate his victims." To which Lacey fires back, "Oh, I see, as opposed to rape being done in their own homes which is not humiliating." And the officer retorts, "Excuse me! I thought you were a cop, not some Gloria Steinem."

The insensitivities of the police department and the hassles and brutalities of the judicial and legal systems are further underscored by Samuels's counsel to Cagney and Lacey about not working too hard on the case. "You want my advice," he says, "don't knock yourselves out. . . . Even assuming, for argument's sake, you've got a case here, it's a waste of time looking for the perp. There's no conviction percentage. No jury is going to buy a woman going out on a date with a guy and then hollering rape." And when Carole Mitchell becomes infuriated at what she feels is judgmental condescension from Chris and Mary Beth, she shouts, "I thought women cops would be different, but they're not—just pigs in dresses." To which an equally incensed Cagney retorts, "Wait 'til you see what a defense attorney would do to you."

In "Date Rape," the guilt and self-blaming of the victim is largely voiced by a second woman who, the protagonists discover, has also been raped by the same man they are hunting. The second woman is a theatrical agent who had represented the rapist (an opera singer) several years earlier. She tells the detectives that she had asked him out to dinner, and he wanted to have sex: "When I said 'no,' he went berserk, beat me up, and raped me." She continues, "I kept going over and over it in my mind and wondering was it something that I'd done? Had I lead him on? Well, finally, it was just easier to forget it and try to pretend it never happened." Carole Mitchell herself articulates the rage and alienation felt by many victims when she confronts the women detectives: "Oh look at you two—you're standing there so busy judging me—because I pick up guys in a bar. . . . Where else am I supposed to meet someone. . . . What am I supposed to do, sit home and wait for Prince Charming to come knocking at my door? . . . What you really think is that I'm a tramp and that I don't have the right to say 'no.'"

The turn toward women's solidarity comes when Carole Mitchell is raped and brutalized again by the same man. Chris and Mary Beth visit her in the hospital and, after leaving the building, Lacey pounds her fists on the squad car and shouts, "What's happening to us, here? . . . The woman told us she was scared of him and we didn't listen. All we listened to was the guys' smutty jokes, and all we cared about was our lousy conviction percentage." "You don't mean US," says Cagney, "you mean ME. . . . I'm not wasting time feeling guilty, Mary Beth. I'm going to find that bastard and I'm going to nail him." The two finally capture the rapist in a scene of physical action and aggression that manifests their rage. The rapist punches Cagney in the mouth and knocks her to the floor. Lacey leaps on top of him, lands him, and, with her pistol aimed, says, "I told you not to move. . . . I don't need much of an excuse." Such action and physical display, although offensive to some women viewers, appeared to tap into others' fantasies of power and revenge because it offered the satisfaction of seeing women accomplish physical feats usually reserved for male heroes, "get even" in the face of victimization and oppression, and act autonomously on their own and other women's behalf.

Although these women's-issues episodes were perceived as exploitation opportunities by some people involved with the series, and although they presented knotty problems for feminism (for example, by showing women, including the protagonists, as victims, or by implying that the problems had neat solutions and that everyday, "normal" life went on despite them), they also addressed such topics as social inequities, violence against women, and women's bonding in struggle. Furthermore, as the audience letters indicated, the episodes met important and deep-seated needs in a number of viewers.

The other thirteen women's-issues episodes followed a similar pattern, with variations according to the particular subject being portrayed. (Lacey's breast cancer episodes, for example, had no "criminal" but nonetheless laid out various myths and misconceptions about its topic, probed some short-comings of the medical establishment, examined the implications of wom-en's fear and aloneness, and offered a strong image of women's bonding.) The feminism in these episodes was sometimes manifested through refer-ences to women's centers and women's shelters. But as I mentioned above, even when a script was not explicitly feminist, general audience recognition that the treatment of the subject resulted from a women's movement inter-pretation and intervention made the feminism at least fairly obvious to many viewers. At times Lacey's equation with feminism in these episodes was straightforward and unambiguous, as when her colleague compares her to Gloria Steinem in "Date Rape," but it increasingly came to be subsumed under her generally liberal (but not specifically feminist) character. It is to this displacement of direct feminist positions that I now turn.

AMBIGUOUS OR TACIT FEMINISM

As the series progressed, its feminist affiliations became much more muted and oblique, transmogrified into what I am describing as "ambiguous" or "tacit" feminism that appeared to derive not from a social movement but from the life experiences, lifestyles, and behaviors—the overall bundle of traits—of the individual characters, particularly the protagonists.[23] It also was not labeled as "feminist" by the narratives. Just as Terry Louise Fisher said in 1984 that the series had moved from "political" causes to "entertainment values," so coproducer Shelley List and story editor Kathryn Ford claimed a few years later that their policy with regard to feminism was to avoid hard-line statements that would alienate the audience.[24] On the level of narrative, this change of emphasis included making "radical" politics a matter of characterization and equivocating about the program's feminism. Some viewers, that is, could read this tacit feminism as a women's movement critique, whereas others might see it as a natural outgrowth of independent, intelligent, spirited individuals who happened to be women. The details of how this change actually happened and worked itself out in the texts are themselves fascinating testaments to the complexity of popular culture and to the ways it contains, homogenizes, and defuses its subject matter, yet stays open by continuing to support and suggest a multiplicity of viewpoints.

As one example, throughout the series, Sharon Gless's Cagney fires a continuous barrage of wisecracks at the John Wayne–identified Detective Isbecki. Her barbs are sharp critiques of masculinity and consequently reverberate with the language and sensibilities of the women's movement. But Cagney considers herself more of a rugged individualist than a feminist, and her jeers are not explicitly linked (even by association with a feminist character) to a women's movement analysis of sexism. Cagney is flippant and swaggering with Isbecki because her personal history has encouraged such character attributes as cockiness, quick wit, and a belief in her own superiority. Of course, in their interpretations of the characters and stories, particular viewers may—and often do—read tacit feminism as an *explicit* depiction.[25]

Both Chris and Mary Beth possess traits, backgrounds, and behaviors that could be readily *interpreted* as feminist. Whereas the Swit and Foster

Cagneys were declared and active feminists, Gless's Cagney takes what could be called antifeminist positions in a number of the narratives, at least initially. But she is also, as the above example suggests, associated with actions and behaviors that many would consider independent, empowered, or liberated. She is self-sufficient and lives alone in a Soho loft, which she bought with money inherited from her mother. She has rejected her mother and wealthy grandmother's plans for her future by becoming a New York cop like her Irish, working-class father. She is proficient in a number of activities, some of them traditionally male-dominated; for example, she plays pool and poker better than most of her male opponents. (She is actually a card sharp, and for one episode a professional dealer was hired to double as her hands in a poker game.) She is a knowledgeable New York Yankees fan, plays softball, jogs, drives sports cars, and identifies herself with cultural heroes. (Her loft is decorated with a large movie poster that reads "Cagney—*Blood on the Sun*" and a "sculpture" made from her former yellow Corvette.) Before acknowledging her alcoholism in the 1987 season, she prides herself on the fact that she can drink most men under the table. She also graduated from Barnard, spent her junior year in Paris, and has well-developed hobbies and accomplishments, such as photography and fluency in French. She occasionally wears haute couture yet often sports a Yankees jacket, and she is opinionated, raucous, and a jokester.

In the realm of male/female relationships, Cagney is most often an active sexual subject in control of her desires and wants. She has many sexual relationships in the course of the series's run, but she also goes through a period of avowed celibacy. (In intimate scenes with men, however, she is occasionally represented as "kittenish" and somewhat passive.)[26] One of her main "feminist" positions is a rejection of marriage on the grounds that it is not the right thing for her. She does receive proposals of marriage from two of her long-term boyfriends—Dory, a detective and former cocaine addict, and David, an American Civil Liberties Union lawyer. In both of these instances, Cagney's rejections of marriage are cast by the narratives as testaments to a woman's right to remain single and still be "healthy." After she breaks up with Dory, she and Lacey (an inveterate advocate of marriage) have a lengthy discussion that begins in the women's room at the precinct and concludes at a bar, in the course of which Cagney lays out the reasons that marriage is not for her:

> *Cagney*: I don't like what I've become. It's not me. It's not what I
>   want. . . . There are some nights I just want to go home and take off

my makeup and wash my hair and eat yogurt, read a trashy book. But, I don't know, lately, that's not true, every night, Mary Beth, every night I leave this place, I go home, I clean up the apartment, I doll myself up, and then I go fussing in that damn kitchen like I was Betty Crocker.

Lacey: Well, Christine, Dory's a very demanding man. Now, you have to talk to him, and get him to understand.

Cagney: No. It isn't Dory. Dory doesn't even care. It's me. I'm doing the stuff I think I'm supposed to do.

Lacey: Now I'm not following this at all. If you don't want to do it and Dory doesn't care, then why do you do it?

Cagney: I tell you, Mary Beth, I feel like I'm suffocating. I do. I have these crazy tapes that keep playing around in my head like old reruns of *Ozzie and Harriet* . . .

Lacey: He's not the right man.

Cagney: What is the RIGHT MAN?

Lacey: Well, he's out there, Christine, now you have to believe that.

Cagney: Mary Beth, you're not getting it. I'm 38 years old. It's no accident that I've never married. I like my life. My life works just fine exactly the way it is, and I'm not getting married because I'm supposed to.

Lacey: I agree with you a hundred percent.

Cagney: From your mouth?! You're saying it's all right to be single?!

Lacey: Well, Chris, what I'm saying is that you should never settle.

Cagney: You are not listening to me. I'm not talking about settling. I'm talking about liking my life the way it is. There's nothing wrong with my life because I'm single.

Three seasons later, in telling David she cannot marry him, Cagney invokes basically the same explanations: "I'm forty-two years old, David. If I'm not ready to get married now the chances are I never will be. I like my life the way it is. . . . I don't know if I ever wanted a husband and children and two cats and a backyard." When David asks, "Why are you so afraid?" Cagney replies, "You're not listening to me. Fear has nothing to do with this. We just want different things. You can't make me less than I am just because I don't want marriage."

One of Cagney's other main "feminist" orientations is an unwavering commitment to her work as a detective. When another male suitor, a playwright, wants her to go to London with him on the spur of the moment, she says, "You've got to understand, I've got a job—not just a job, a career." He replies, "Chris, how much of yourself can you give to your work? Don't you think you deserve to pamper yourself a little bit—to *live* a little?" And Cagney rejoins, "I don't think you understand. I *like* my work." But Chris is not simply dedicated to and engrossed in her job; she is aggressively and unflinchingly ambitious, and her publicly declared goal is to be the first woman chief of detectives. For many seasons she talks about becoming a sergeant, and she finally is, in fact, the only one of her precinct to attain the rank.[27] She is not at all demure or humble about the achievement or the authority required. When Lieutenant Samuels goes out of town for a few weeks, Cagney, assuming she will take command, moves her things into his office, sits in his chair, leans back, puts her feet up on his desk, and then calls Lacey in and toasts her with a coffee mug, saying, "The sweet smell of success—to us."

Some of the tacit feminism associated with Cagney, especially in the area of work, has an ambiguity that can make her read as explicitly feminist. As I suggested, this ambiguous feminism is usually shown to derive from Cagney's ambition, determination, and her commitment to fighting for what she thinks she deserves because she considers herself "the best"—and often is. But her feminism is not always so couched, and occasionally a less veiled feminist discourse breaks through. In the scene just described, the police department, without Cagney's knowledge, has brought in another lieutenant—a man—as Samuels's replacement. (In a subsequent episode, however, this new lieutenant fails so miserably that Cagney has to take the reins and restore order after all.) When, several episodes later, she finally confronts Samuels about the incident, her outrage at the department for passing her over is expressed in charged terms: "There's another agenda working here, Lieutenant," she says, "and you know it. It's called the old boys' network." Samuels challenges her, saying, "If that was true you wouldn't have made sergeant," to which she replies, "I took a test and I passed it. They couldn't keep me from being a sergeant." Samuels suggests, "You could have been assigned to a desk," but Cagney retorts, "And for that I'm supposed to be eternally grateful and keep my mouth shut. After all, I've done pretty well, don't you think? For a girl?"

In another episode, Cagney takes temporary command of the squad and, at Inspector Knelman's insistence, has to ask the pregnant Lacey (who wants very much to keep working) to take maternity leave. She puts it to Lacey this way: "The men officers outnumber the women thirty to one. We fought the department, we fought the union, we won the kind of benefits that we deserve, so take the win, Mary Beth. . . . Look, I know Knelman's being a pig."[28] Her perpetual jibing at machismo also makes her, at times, appear to be a radical proponent of not only women's rights but women's superiority. When, for instance, Isbecki's bachelor party is being planned, she announces, "There's nothing more sophomoric than a group of guys contemplating their hormones." And she tells Isbecki, "The last place I want to be is at your homage to homo erectus."[29] Even though, in most of the instances cited, Cagney's "feminism" may be primarily motivated by character traits, it is equivocal enough that at times it seems more rooted in the larger social women's movement and thus more explicit. Such a multiplicity of meanings encourages, enables, or at the very least readily permits feminist interpretations that go beyond the particular delimitations of the text, specifically a text bound by the knowledge that Gless's Cagney is *not* a feminist, and one that went to some lengths to tone down its overt feminist aspects.

The Lacey of the later series, too, exhibits traits and engages in activities that could be interpreted as "feminist," yet are not directly indicated as such by the narratives. Her relationship with Harvey, for example, throws into question the social construction of gender and conventional male/female roles: he is the primary caretaker of the house and the kids, and she is often the main (and at times the only) wage earner.[30] Although generally maternal, Mary Beth can also be an aggressive participant in rough physical action, and she leaves no question as to her own personal and nonconventionally feminine power. In addition to examples already discussed, in the breast cancer episodes, she runs down a fire escape, jumps from the bottom rung to the street, takes a flying leap to tackle a suspect, and says, "Freeze, you bastard, or I swear to God, I'll take you out of the game." She can play "bad cop" and take a hard line in interrogating witnesses, and she is resourceful and clever. In various episodes she "talks" suspects into the precinct house, talks a little girl off a roof ledge, and distracts Isbecki from a claustrophobia attack when the two are trapped together in an elevator. She is also a sexual subject and often initiates sexual activity with Harvey.[31] Her body, too, manifests aspects that could be read for their feminist dimensions (at least from some feminist points of view). Her clothes are practical and seem to be chosen for comfort, and she is at times heavier than is conventional for female television stars. Tyne Daly has, in fact, said that "Mary Beth Lacey gives hope to overweight women everywhere."[32]

Some of Lacey's lines even have a radical feminist inflection. In an episode on child pornography, during which her twelve-year-old son buys a porn magazine and the Laceys argue over its possible effects, she quite pointedly says, "I don't want my son to grow up thinking a woman's body is a piece of meat. It's degrading to me. It's degrading to women's bodies."

In other dialogue, however, we can glimpse the trend toward a more muffled politics. In a 1987 episode, for example, Lacey and Cagney are in a stakeout van videotaping potential criminal activity. Cagney says, "Nice and steady. Hold him in frame. You sure you're in focus, Mary Beth?" To which Lacey replies, "You're not Alfred Hitchcock, here, Christine . . . *I'm* manning the camera. [pause] Womanning. [pause] Personning." Such dialogue serves to signal the more "humanist," as opposed to "feminist," direction that coproducer Jonathan Estrin said the series took in its last few years.[33]

Much of Lacey's feminism in the Gless/Daly series, as we saw above, was manifested in the women's-issue programs, in which she appeared completely conversant with and took women's movement positions on rape, incest, sexual harassment, and abortion. And as the following chapter will show, her liberal politics and biography generally lead her to take women's movement stances (although not marked as such) with regard to women and poverty, single mothers, and women's friendship.

CONSIDERING THE VARIOUS REPRESENTATIONS OF FEMINISM

The explicit feminism of the *Cagney and Lacey* made-for-TV movie and the Foster/Daly series made absolutely clear that the positions of the characters and of the narratives as a whole emerged from a social and cultural movement of women who set out to have political influence over their own material conditions. This type of feminism also pointed to the institutionalized, structural inequities of gender, race, and to some degree class. Furthermore, many of its dimensions—Cagney and Lacey's struggles with discrimination on the job and with the men in the precinct and their own declared and hard-hitting viewpoints as feminists—were unique and much too short-lived on prime-time TV. But there were, as we saw, dangers and problems in negotiating this explicit feminism on mainstream commercial television.

In addition to the problems discussed above, there were also difficulties related more specifically to the constraints of 1980s network prime time drama itself. As we know, television at that time rarely depicted explicit feminism in its series and consequently did not offer an array of competing and conflicting feminist positions. Such a situation fostered the assumption that the "feminism" or the feminist position being portrayed was all inclusive—that is, that it delineated the universe of women's movement views. Prime time in the 1980s, furthermore, demanded a feminist perspective that could be rendered in broad and accessible strokes and was part of everyday popular discourse. Liberal feminism appeared to be the logical and perhaps only candidate for such depictions, and so, from the outset, feminism's dimensions and differences were severely restricted.

That explicit feminism (even though delimited and at times offensive) actually came to the TV screen in a dramatic series format was, however, a remarkable occurrence. And without the legacy of its initial attempts, *Cagney and Lacey* would most likely not have exhibited the possibilities for continued feminist readings. This legacy was simply the commitment to pursuing some form of women's movement inquiry, the continuation of overt feminism in the women's-issues episodes, and the tacit or ambiguous feminism that camouflaged itself at the level of characterization.

Cagney and Lacey's original handling of feminism was too controversial for mainstream, prime-time TV, and through institutional and textual negotiations it became less socially general and less explicit. The shift to women's-issues feminism had both problematic and positive aspects, neither of which can be ignored. As we have seen, the women's-issues shows tended to ratify the notions that feminism and social atrocities like rape, wife abuse, incest, and sexual harassment were female concerns and could be restricted to historically constructed women. They also exploited such issues for their sensational dimensions and produced women as victims. From another point of view, however, they gave the issues widespread exposure and reassured women in the audience that they were not alone in their experiences. The turn to both women's-issue feminism and feminism disguised at the level of characterization doubtless allowed a program that portrayed women's movement material to remain on a popular mass medium during the throes of a conservative backlash, and it resulted in a text that some viewers could read as "feminist" and others in different ways.

The following chapter will examine Annette Kuhn's notion of "openness" as a way of accounting for the shifts in *Cagney and Lacey's* representation of feminism that I have described here. This concept provides a way of accounting for the fact that 1980s prime-time network TV was ultimately governed by the imperatives to address a large heterogeneous audience, to offend as few members of that audience as possible, to amalgamate progressive and reactionary voices, and to encourage multiple readings of programs. So despite the downplaying and constriction of feminism and despite the network's discursive authority over its more explicit representations, feminist fragments continued to find negotiations in the texts, and political readings of the series survived and thrived. It is to the terrain of feminist readings and feminist spectators that we now turn.

FEMALE/FEMININE/FEMINIST AUDIENCES,

SPECTATORS, AND READINGS

Many of the negotiations over and shifts in the representations of feminism examined in the last chapter were provoked by social and institutional pressures resulting from the backlash against feminism. They were also prompted by a tendency, evident in network prime time of the 1970s and 1980s, to gradually render potentially controversial programs more ambiguous or open to multiple interpretations—in other words, to make them accessible to more audience members and consequently more profitable. We have seen throughout this book how the production team, faced with network charges that the series was "too women's lib," worked to tone down its feminism, and how the explicit feminism of the early episodes was later channeled into "women's issues" programs or subsumed under character traits rather than maintaining its overt social and political character. We have also seen that, until the last gun was fired, the liberal women's movement persisted in championing and publicizing the series, and that throughout its history viewers continued to read the series in out-and-out feminist ways. Such readings were based at least in part on what I have called the "tacit or ambiguous feminism" of the characters, which was readily interpreted by some viewers as unabashedly feminist. The conversion to ambiguous feminism also helped to illustrate how different viewers could identify with the characters in different ways, and how they could take up different spectator positions depending, for one thing, on where they situated themselves on the "feminism spectrum."[1]

Because I am concerned with the struggles over defining *woman*, *women*, and *femininity*, with the politics and power of which definitions achieve discursive authority at particular junctures in history and culture, and because my focus is television, I must at this point address a number of questions: How exactly could an industrially produced mainstream text like *Cagney and Lacey* play a significant part in female fans' efforts to reconceive and redefine themselves as women in 1980s U.S. culture? In what ways did the program speak to feminine (and feminist) spectators or subjects? And given the series's gradual downplaying of feminism, the many structural and narrative maneuvers to bring the characters back in line, and the program's status as a realistic police program with aspects of melodrama, soap opera, and comedy, how is it that so many viewers continued to read it from feminist perspectives?

By asking these questions, I am not implying that *Cagney and Lacey* in fact *is* a feminist text, or that such a designation would be possible, productive, or even wise. The task for feminist critics, as Susan Sheridan puts it, is "not to identify a feminism within the text . . . but rather to invent strategies of reading in tune with . . . feminist aims." Generating and underscoring some of these reading strategies is indeed one of my main concerns. But as the previous chapter demonstrates, I am also making claims about the text itself, one of which is that *Cagney and Lacey*'s direct incorporation of women's movement discourses made it the subject of immediate interest and debate among a good number of feminists. Which is not, of course, to suggest that all feminists found or find the program compelling.[2]

The many textual ambiguities in the series's representations of feminism undoubtedly invited a diversity of readings by the feminists who did watch it, and who continue to watch it in reruns. (Beverley Alcock and Jocelyn Robson, for example, called it a "fundamentally reactionary text, . . .

pleasurable perhaps but not progressive.") These same ambiguities, as a few audience letters reveal, also allowed the text to be enjoyed by viewers who explicitly described themselves as *not* feminists. For its part, the British fan club CLASS (*Cagney and Lacey* Appreciation of the Series Society), although it undoubtedly had some women's movement–oriented members, refused to call the program "feminist" because it considered the label too "limiting." Nevertheless, I believe that *Cagney and Lacey* negotiated the types of discourses and produced the kinds of representations that may have helped large numbers of viewers, many of them self-identified feminists (among whom I include myself), to "make productive use of the contradictions of our lives." Comments by women who wrote letters on behalf of the program, women journalists in the mainstream and feminist press, and feminist scholars from different segments of the women's movements all offer evidence that the series met otherwise unsatisfied viewer needs.[3]

In this chapter I will argue that *Cagney and Lacey* addressed and called out to feminine and feminist spectators, and that as a mainstream realist text, it indeed lent itself to numerous readings, including feminist ones. I will, in fact, also offer my own feminist reading of the text. But first I need to delineate and discuss the debates in media studies over spectators and social audiences, texts and contexts, and to examine the specific ways in which a realist mainstream text may actually address feminine subjects and admit feminist readings (as well as the ways in which some *Cagney and Lacey* fans actually interpreted its realism).

TEXTS, CONTEXTS, SPECTATORS, SOCIAL AUDIENCES

At this point some thorny theoretical issues emerge and must be addressed—the point at which we confront the relationships of the text, the textually addressed spectator/subject, and the social audience, each of which is discussed below. And in this effort to bridge the divide between media texts and their social contexts, we come to the textual/contextual crossroads, where textually "deterministic" and reader-oriented avenues of criticism have a somewhat hazardous intersection.[4]

A major debate in media studies centers around who or what has the greater power—the industry, the text, the context, or the viewer. This debate, of course, extends to issues of gender and, as applied to my particular case study, raises such questions as: Did mainstream film and network television of the 1970s and 1980s, with their investments in particular and limiting definitions of *woman* and *women*, have the power to produce movies and programs that addressed their spectators according to the terms of those limiting definitions? Did the textual operations of cinema and television construct specific definitions of femininity (including woman as the object of the male gaze and the camera's look, as sexual spectacle, as passive being, as "not male," as the domesticated "other" to a preeminent masculine subjectivity), and, furthermore, were they the most influential force in determining not only how a viewer would interpret those definitions, but how she would "subjectively absorb" them into her own experience and enactment of gender? Did social contexts (including that of the family) and the many discourses that comprise them have the real power to "gender" subjects before those subjects ever encountered the discourses of media texts—and with more force? Did viewers, by producing multiple readings or interpretations of films or programs, have the ability to choose, reject, or negotiate the text's address and so escape the potential impact of its gender (among other things) address? Can holding in tension aspects of each of these positions offer sharper answers to these questions?[5]

Annette Kuhn has grouped scholarly work on women's genres into two camps—one that emphasizes contexts (often TV studies), and one that emphasizes texts (often film studies). The work underscoring contexts, whether tacitly or overtly, posits a female viewer (whom Kuhn calls a "social audience" member) who is already formed, by social and cultural discourses, as an a priori gendered subject, as already male or female. The work emphasizing texts, on the other hand, overtly posits a feminine subject (a "spectator") who is constructed (among other ways) in and by the operations of the text. The stress here is on the text's ability to address or interpellate its spectator as feminine (or as occupying a feminine subject position) and, by so doing, contribute to the ever-ongoing process of gender and subject construction. In defining the social audience, Kuhn writes, "Constructed by discursive practices, both of cinema and TV and of social science, the social audience is a group of people who buy tickets at the box office, or who switch on their TV sets; people who can be surveyed, counted and categorized according to age, sex, and socio-economic status." In defining spectators, she says, "Social audiences become spectators in the moment they engage in the processes and pleasures of meaning-making attendant on watching a film or TV program."[6]

Obviously we need a theory of texts and contexts that accounts for both social audiences and spectators (whether or not we ultimately choose to describe the concepts with those particular terms). And for this reason, Kuhn proposes the model that I summarized in the introduction and have used as my general analytic framework: "Both spectators and social audience may . . . be regarded as discursive constructs. Representations, contexts, audiences and spectators [may be] seen as a series of interconnected social discourses, certain discourses possessing greater constitutive authority at specific moments than others. Such a model permits relative autonomy for the operations of texts, readings and contexts, and also allows for contradictions, oppositional readings and varying degrees of discursive authority."[7]

This model permits us to acknowledge and analyze the power of texts—and of the industries producing them—to address their spectators as "gendered" along particular lines, the power of spectators to actively make meaning of texts, the power of social audience members to negotiate both texts and contexts, and the power of contexts to function in the shaping of audiences, spectators, reading strategies, and representations. It also allows us to theorize about how discursive authority or the hegemony of some meanings over others both occurs and alters in different time periods and places, or for different participants in any specific instance of media and meanings.

The particular social audience for *Cagney and Lacey* emerged through the efforts of public relations firms, the network, the production team, the women's movement, and the fans themselves. It assembled to watch the series in homes throughout the United States, Canada, England, and many other countries. Some people viewed with "families" and friends, others in large groups. Many fans were committed to watching regularly and planned their schedules and social events accordingly. But as we have seen, this conglomeration of viewers conceived of itself as an audience very differently from the television network that may have contributed to gathering it. The women fans tuned in week after week because the program offered them many moments of recognition and pleasure and mobilized some of the conflicting discourses regarding what it meant to be a woman in the 1980s Western world. The social audience may initially have been drawn to the series by disparate means (TV promos, women's pages of newspapers, *Ms.*, TV talk programs, NOW newsletters, radio interviews, *TV Guide* articles, friends, channel switching, and happenstance). But once these women fans entered into the show's "regime of pleasure" and identifications, once they answered its address, their continued production of themselves as a social audience was inextricably entwined with their positions as textual spectators.[8]

For its part, the series's address offered spectators unparalleled delight "as women" and had everything to do with the textual figures of the women involved—the protagonists whose point of view organized scenes, whose voices enunciated the plots, and whose desires motored the narratives. The intertwining of social audiences and spectators is also apparent here because, as Christine Gledhill says, textual figures or representations of women are sites for the negotiation of "what women's history tells us about femininity lived as a socio-culturally differentiated [contextually produced] . . . category," as well as for the negotiation of discourses that define femininity in traditional (patriarchal) terms.[9]

The concept of "negotiation" is, in fact, Gledhill's specific way of bridging the gap between socially and textually produced subjects, between social audiences and spectators. As we will see, this leap is possible for her because women viewers take active roles in negotiating the discourses of the text and, consequently, how the text may position them, but also because the textual figure of "woman" is conceived in two ways: first, as a "patriarchal symbol," and second, as a "site of gendered discourse, drawn from the specific socio-cultural experiences of women and shared by women, which negotiates a space within, and sometimes resists, patriarchal domination."[10]

Textual representations of women, in other words, are not just conventional or stereotypical constructs shaped by patriarchal imperatives ("cut to the measure of the patriarchal Unconscious") that might address a feminine spectator as the "other" to a predominant masculine subjectivity (as simply a nonmale); they are also imbued with meanings from the lived social and historical experiences of specific groups of present-day women.[11] They are sites of textual negotiation, and, at least in part, they echo the social experiences of particular women audience members and go on to reverberate in the everyday discursive network of that social audience. Said another way, the figures of women in the text and the feminine spectator both are potentially constituted in relation not simply to patriarchal discourses, but to discourses from women's history. Discourses that constitute the social audience, then, overlap in the text with discourses that constitute spectators, complicating the distinction between social audiences and spectators, contexts and texts.[12]

Throughout this book I have demonstrated the many ways in which *Cagney and Lacey*, on a textual level, actively negotiated the competing and conflicting discourses involving femininity that strongly affected the everyday lives of millions of women at the time. These discourses emerged from traditional (patriarchal) "common sense" definitions of *woman* and *women*, from the conventional structuring of classical narratives, genres, and mise-en-scène, from the women's movements, and from what Gledhill describes as the historical experiences of particular groups of women.[13]

Furthermore, the *Cagney and Lacey* texts actually worked to address feminine and female spectators, and specifically those spectators who were themselves shaped by the conflicting discourses of late 1970s and 1980s Western culture. The show was, after all, developed to appeal to the new working women's audience—a group born out of and into the contradictions defining "femininity" at the time. Within these parameters, however, it offered many different places for its spectators to occupy and accommodated feminist-oriented positions, positions between feminist and traditional ones, and nonfeminist positions, to name a few. The texts, in other words, admitted "a range of positions of identification," and, furthermore, "within the social situation of their viewing, audiences [could] shift subject positions as they interact[ed] with [them]."[14]

This chapter also demonstrates how some of the letter writers in my sample (most of whom were apparently white, middle-class women) responded to, took pleasure in, and negotiated textual subject positions as well as textual meanings based on the myriad facets of their everyday lives, histories, contexts, and previously constituted subjectivities. (As I have, however, mentioned at many points throughout this book, the text's specific address to women of color was weak, and although some women of color—as well as some lesbians—undoubtedly took up positions offered by the text, their doing so most likely demanded more effort and more psychic mobility than was required of many white, middle-class, heterosexual women viewers.)

Much of *Cagney and Lacey's* uniqueness sprang from the way it offered spaces for feminine spectators and the ways it mobilized a wide range of pleasures for many of its female viewers. Few mainstream, industrially produced films and television programs have done these things, and when they have (as in *Cagney and Lacey's* case as well), the texts and representations of women are utterly fraught with ambiguity, tension, contradictions, and hazards. Because representations of women are so riddled with conflicts, it is equally important to understand how particular popular realist texts may have numerous readings and appropriations.

FEMINISM, REALISM, AND MAINSTREAM TEXTS

During much of the 1970s, feminist media scholarship basically rejected mainstream realist texts for producing and perpetuating patriarchal meanings about women. Avant-garde works and feminist "counter practices" in films, literature, and video art were seen as the alternatives that would engender new definitions, new feminist culture, and feminine subject positions. But since the later seventies, feminists also have been reappraising popular conventional texts for their subversive, oppositional, and pleasure potential. How exactly, then, may *Cagney and Lacey*, as a mainstream *realist* text, be read as feminist and be said to address a feminine subject?

In *Women's Pictures*, Annette Kuhn describes a variant of fictional realism that she calls "new women's cinema." The phrase refers to the films I mentioned in Chapters 1 and 2, which were targeted at the new working women's market in the middle to late 1970s—films such as *Julia, Alice Doesn't Live Here Anymore, Girlfriends*, and *An Unmarried Woman*. According to Kuhn,

> The pleasure for the female spectator of films of this kind lies in several possible identifications: with a central character who is not only also a woman, but who may be similar in some respects to the spectator herself; or with a narrative voice enunciated by a woman character; or with fictional events which evoke a degree of recognition; or with a resolution that constitutes a "victory" for the central character. The address of the new women's film may thus position the spectator not only as herself a potential "winner," but also as a winner whose gender is instrumental in the victory: it may consequently offer the female spectator a degree of affirmation.[15]

In her discussion of *Girlfriends* and *Julia*, Kuhn also talks about the "openness" that structures these particular texts as somewhat of a departure from classical Hollywood realism. She sees the openness as particularly appropriate for new women's cinema because "feminism is controversial," and "openness permits readings to be made which accord more or less with spectators' prior stances on feminist issues." Kuhn argues that although the openness in new women's cinema deviates from classic realism, it essentially *reworks* rather than destroys classical textual operations. Furthermore, even though new women's cinema may be a source of affirmation for feminine spectators, she claims that basically it buttresses the institutional and ideological operations of dominant cinema and, consequently, of patriarchy.[16] Although I appreciate Kuhn's hesitations about the progressive potential of "new women's cinema" and realism in general (for reasons I discuss at the end of this chapter), I would specifically argue that particular popular realist texts, such as the ones she discusses and also *Cagney and Lacey*, may nonetheless be read for their feminist dimensions, address spectators as feminine, and convey considerable subversive power to many of their viewers.

Cagney and Lacey has many of the characteristics Kuhn ascribes to the realist new women's cinema. We saw in Chapter 4 how the series became more open in its representations of feminism, changing from an explicit general feminism to a "women's-issues" variety and, more pointedly, to feminism that was submerged in individual characterization. In this way, from the industry's point of view, the program's potentially controversial feminist orientation would alienate fewer segments of the audience and would be available (open) to more varied readings. Chapter 3 showed that as *Cagney and Lacey* developed, its narratives grew more open-ended—that is, all the problems did not achieve resolutions. Also, the representation of the friendship between the protagonists was open enough that lesbian viewers were able to read homoerotic overtones in the relationship. But additionally—and these are crucial points—the women-oriented realist texts Kuhn discusses offered female spectators the pleasure of several kinds of identification: the fictional events might evoke a degree of recognition; the gender and other traits of the protagonist might be similar to those of the spectator; and the narrative voice was enunciated by a woman character. They also may have offered the spectator affirmation because of the way the text addressed and positioned her as "a winner whose gender is instrumental in the victory."

Such pleasures, identifications, and affirmations point to specific ways in which *Cagney and Lacey*'s texts similarly offered particular subject positions to their viewers and addressed or called out to their spectators as feminine and potentially as feminist. They also fueled a strong sense of alternative and oppositional power in a good many women fans. If we accept Christine Gledhill's arguments, their force may actually owe much to the very realism that feminist critics once may have thought to be mired down in patriarchy and the status quo.

Gledhill's account of the intersection of realism and melodrama in mainstream film and television texts, in fact, stretches our understanding of realism's subversive potential for feminism. In her words, "the modern popular drama . . . exists as a negotiation between the terms of melodrama's Manichaean moral frameworks and conflicts [the struggle between good and evil] and those contemporary discourses which will ground the drama in a recognizable verisimilitude [realism]." Gender representation is at the heart of the whole enterprise because the "realistic" elements incorporated into the text to make it relevant and credible often involve the "figure of woman." Here Gledhill distinguishes between woman as "patriarchal symbol" and woman as a "site of gendered discourse, drawn from the specific socio-cultural experiences of women and shared by women." She argues,

When popular cultural forms, operating within a melodramatic frame-work, attempt to engage contemporary discourses about women or draw on women's cultural forms in order to renew their gender ver-isimilitude and solicit the recognition of a female audience, the negotia-tion between "woman" as patriarchal symbol and woman as generator of women's discourse is intensified. While melodrama orchestrates gender conflicts on a highly symbolic level to produce the clash of identities that will adumbrate its moral universe, the codes of women's discourse work in a more direct and articulate register to produce realist and gendered recognitions.[17]

This "more direct and articulate" register of the codes of women's dis-course is the one in which I argue that many *Cagney and Lacey* fans oper-ated, both in responding so wholeheartedly to the characters and narra-tives and in claiming, as they did, that they were more "real" than other TV representations. I also believe, more specifically, that at least some of the "codes of women's discourse" accessed by the fans were very much rooted in liberal women's movement understandings and analyses of the time. Furthermore, I would argue that the clashes between women's move-ment discourses, "women's discourse" (in Gledhill's sense of the phrase), and traditional (patriarchal) discourses produced the unique "charge" that made the representations seem so potent and so "real" to many letter writers, engendered such intense identification, and underpinned the spe-cific feminine spectator and subject positions offered by the text. Notwith-standing its many criticisms, then, "real" turns out to be a charged and salient category for fans.

TEXTUAL WOMEN AND "REAL WOMEN" FANS

The multiple and competing discourses about what women should and should not be were negotiated textually in *Cagney and Lacey*—espe-cially at the sites of the women characters—in ways familiar to the letter writers in my sample from their own everyday lives: the frazzled Lacey, try-ing to juggle both motherhood and a full-time job, packs the wrong lunch for her kids; the work-identified Cagney battles the prejudices against unmarried "career women" and spends a lot of time defending her decision to remain single. (The writers, in fact, often contrasted these familiar clashes with what they described as unrecognizable elements in the "lives" of other women characters on, for example, *Dallas* and *Dynasty*.) The fictional textual negotiations thus were directly related to many of the fans' own "real world" negotiations, helped make sense of everyday gender troubles, and provided practical aid and inspiration for day-to-day life. That both the letter writers and the show's protagonists were "1980s women" and that the narrative voice was spoken by women characters were certainly crucial factors in the spectators' achieving such complete affirmation and identification.[18]

In this context, it is not difficult to see why so many letter writers described the protagonists as "real."[19] And within such a framework, the term may escape some of the perils of "reflection theory" and "positive image analysis" that have proved so problematic for feminist media studies.[20] *Real women*, in this sense, may connote not only fictional sites for the negotiation of recognizable ("real") discursive conflicts, but also a contrast with conventional patriarchal representations and predictable television depictions. The term may, in other words, bespeak a way of defining women in relation to other historically and culturally produced definitions.

In writing about the characters as "real," many fans drew explicitly on analyses of the liberal women's movement. As I just mentioned, to them "real" meant women who were different from traditional feminine stereotypes, who were, for one thing, fully functional in the public sphere—engaged in work outside the home, confronting the problems of a male-dominated labor force, and juggling both work and home lives.[21] Joyce Sunila, a *Los Angeles Times* reporter and obviously a regular viewer, wrote that, on *Cagney and Lacey*, "the real problems of the day are struggled with"; these real problems included "women adjusting to work designed by and for men with which they are often out of sync and sympathy." Another woman wrote about the characters, "They are able to get more *realistic* emotions in one episode than most series get in an entire season. As a woman who owns her own business, the realities that this program depicts of having to balance your ambitions and goals for your career, along with maintaining a personal life are acted and written excellently. They can easily be related to" (emphasis in original).[22]

Real also referred to women characters who were not sex symbols or overly glamorized, who challenged established male/female roles (which defined what both men and women could and could not be), who were substantive, complex, and down-to-earth, and who had a strength not typical of most television women. "I know I speak for all women," wrote a fan,

when I say that it's about time there has been a television show which portrays two real and human women who are successful as police detectives. They may not be infallible or shaped like Suzanne Somers, but not many of us are and some of us don't want to be. Therefore, we prefer to watch a show which has as its stars people like ourselves living probable and possible lives. I also believe this show is not popular just among women but among men intelligent enough and self-assured enough not to feel threatened by female success.

And another wrote,

> There is one regular show which I always make time for—it's something I enjoy, not in the way one enjoys reading the Sunday comics, but more in the way one enjoys the Op-Ed page—it's intriguing and a reflection of aspects of my own life. It is *Cagney and Lacey*.
>
> *Cagney and Lacey* is appealing because it is good lowkey drama, with nuance and substance. It doesn't "prettify" people or situations, and it allows the principals depth, unpredictability and (yes, I'll go ahead and say it) even an unfashionable tinge of masculinity.

Numerous fans commented on television's part in producing and circulating conventional, limiting, and potentially oppressive representations. They discussed how particular programs fostered definitions and meanings that badly needed changing, and how *Cagney and Lacey* helped articulate the new ways in which they were explaining and understanding themselves as women. These new articulations were, again, often described as "real" or like themselves. One viewer, for example, said, "My background is that of a businesswoman and I am currently a bank officer. I find little or no entertainment in the many shows ('fluff' shows) featuring women as brainless, helpless, uninformed or dependent upon men for their every decision. *Cagney and Lacey* offers women who are independent and responsible adults in the real world with problems in real life situations." And another, "*Cagney and Lacey* is the only show on TV I care to watch. Guess I don't have to tell you TV is male dominated, with one adventure starring men after another. . . . When I watch these two women working together and being friends, fighting, loving and surviving it's so believable. . . . I love it when Mary Beth's feet hurt or she packs the wrong lunch for the kids. . . . So sad it is that your show is so unique to TV. I can think of no other show I've ever seen that's had real women, ordinary, living, breathing women as its stars."

In addition to the sentiments already echoed, many of the fans, as we saw in Chapter 1, asserted that Cagney and Lacey's relationship was crucial to their involvement in the program and to the program's success in creating meanings for them. This corroborates and extends Gledhill's claim that female media friendships draw on codes from the subculture of women, inform the representations of women with meanings that challenge patriarchal conventions, and prove enormously important to some female members of the viewing audience.[23] They play a key part in making the representations seem "real." According to one viewer, "There are so many things to like about *Cagney and Lacey*, but the thing that grabbed me and others I'm sure is that Chris Cagney and Mary Beth Lacey are so real. They work together and they're friends. It's so refreshing and sadly, so unique. There wasn't much I cared to watch on TV before your show came along. All women were given was a choice of adventures with hunks or roles as bitches or airheads. And when it came to dramas for TV, forget it, the woman was a victim or a tramp."

Frequently the letters integrated many of the issues set forth above. One of them, written jointly by a woman and a man, said,

> *Cagney and Lacey* is one of the best shows on TV, in that it accurately portrays the difficulty of being on the police force as well as the stress of managing both a full-time career and a marriage and children.
>
> *Cagney and Lacey* is an excellent show in that it is humorous, has excellent plots, and is a fairly true representation of life. Most importantly, though, it is the only show on television today which is an honest and thorough example of the roles which women, whether single or married, play in our society today. The women in your show are expected to be, and are able to be the equal of their male counterparts. They are not left to assume only lesser, more "feminine" traditional roles.

Other viewers described how the series realistically addressed both female power and oppression. "It's time now," declared one, "to show women with strengths and be realistic about problems in a patriarchal society."

The letter writers' characterization of the program and characters as "real," then, may be said to derive from women's movement analyses of the time, from the pleasures and identifications that accompany the spectatorship of a realist text whose "woman" draws on codes of women's experience as well as patriarchal conventions, and from the recognition of the conflicting meanings involving the women characters within the series. *Real women*, in this light, may be read as a phrase with which the fans could differentiate themselves from and critique traditional standards of femininity. As a description, it may be viewed as explicitly relational, seen as a contrast to conventional and patriarchal representations, stereotypical

TV representations, razzle-dazzle glamour women, subservient women, or women as bitches, airheads, victims, and tramps; it may also be viewed against shifting social discourses, expectations, and possibilities. It also illustrates one of the ways in which a mainstream, realist, 1980s TV text addressed feminine spectators and provoked feminist readings.

TEXTUAL WOMEN AND FEMININE SPECTATORS: IDENTIFICATION, DESIRE, SUBJECTIVITY

In the following pages I will deal with *Cagney and Lacey* as one large text from the beginning to the end of its run. My purpose is to foreground some of the ways that this realist police show/melodrama/soap opera/comedy and its textual figures of women negotiated "women's discourse" (in Gledhill's sense of the phrase): how they manifested feminine desire, point of view, narrative voice, and subjectivity; and how they addressed feminine spectators—mobilizing identification and feminine desire. I am interested in illuminating these aspects of a series about which a teenager wrote, "It gives me confidence in myself to know that I can do just as well as boys in sports and other things," and about which women viewers said: "When I saw Cagney I knew she was who I wanted to be like and I started slowly and, well, I have changed. I speak my mind now and I even got up enough courage to try my hand at my own photography business"; or, "Each week she somehow gives me the courage to be myself more around others and to strive for something more in my life." Of Lacey, one also offered, "She gives me hope and strength to do two jobs (marriage and my work), and I learn so much from how she copes."

In my reading I will focus on two textual aspects—the friendship between the women protagonists and the mixture of police genre and women's forms—to illustrate my points. As are all readings, mine is selective in the specific elements that I choose to highlight or ignore based on my investments in the discourses being negotiated, in the meanings my theoretical perspective brings to the fore, and in the ways secondary texts (specifically the comments of fans, critics, and production team members) influence my interpretation. Other viewers would come up with many different interpretations depending on which discourses they emphasized and which courses they charted through the text.

Poststructuralist feminism, which underpins much of my project, argues for the constructed and relational character of woman, women, and human subjectivities—in other words, it claims that categories of gender and identity gain meaning from their relations to other constructed categories and other human subjects, and that both "woman" and "women" are products of history and culture rather than of nature. It also argues for the political and historical importance of strategically deploying the "fiction" of women's identity, agency, and solidarity, given the array of social and cultural struggles in which historically constructed women often find themselves.[24] In this reading, then, when I speak of women as subjects rather than objects of desire, as autonomous agents, and as independent from men (to single out a few phrases), I am specifically situating these constructions as historically produced in relation to those that, for example, define women as objects, as "others" to a preeminent masculine subjectivity, and as subservient and dependent upon men for existence and meaning.

IDENTIFICATION WITH WOMEN BUDDIES

From the series's conception, the friendship between Cagney and Lacey both motivated and structured the narratives; it was also the terrain on which many of the negotiations involving *women, woman,* and *femininity* found expression. Even though Harvey and Mary Beth's relationship was given a large amount of screen time and was important to many viewers, the relationship between the protagonists was unquestionably the heart of the movie and the series. It was a vital element in many fans' pleasure, and members of the press also cited it as fundamental to the program's appeal.[25] It was one of the primary means by which the series incorporated what Gledhill called "subcultural codes of women's lived experience" to make the drama topical and realistic, and it was one of the elements that infused the sign "woman" with dimensions other than patriarchal ones. From the beginning, as we have seen, the production team was totally convinced that female friendship was a fundamental aspect of many women's lives and would form the perfect hook for "gendered recognition" and the lure for large numbers of viewers. For spectators, it was indeed a potent source of identification.

Cagney and Lacey's relationship manifested an alliance and solidarity between (and by extension among) different women; and within its terms, female bonding was situated in and to some degree emerged from the difficulties of negotiating a male-dominated workplace and society. This unusual television representation allowed the notion that even women's friendship was constructed in relation to historical conditions and events. Also, the differences between the characters were often explicitly underscored and thereby opened up to potential exploration by viewers.

The portrayal of women's friendships on TV is, of course, not recent or unique to *Cagney and Lacey*, but other examples have mostly appeared in situation comedies: Lucy and Ethel, Mary and Rhoda, Laverne and Shirley, Kate and Allie, the "Golden Girls," Sugar and Spice, and the women on *Designing Women* and *227* are prominent examples. Women's friendships in TV dramas, on the other hand, have been scarce indeed, with *Charlie's Angels*, *Heartbeat*, and *China Beach* offering a few possible instances. The fact that *Cagney and Lacey* included consistently "serious" as well as humorous aspects of women's relationships was one of the things that made it rare in TV history and especially prized by some women fans. As we have seen, the friendship was also one of the things that made the series seem "real" because it accentuated an important aspect of many present-day women's social experiences. The friendship spanned 125 episodes, incorporating many dimensions that form both a background for and an important part of my reading.

First and foremost, Cagney and Lacey talked. They talked about how their police cases affected them and about their lives outside of work. Because their talking processed so thoroughly the details and implications of both the cop story and the noncop story, it became at times a virtual commentary on the episode's stories and how those stories affected the two protagonists. Much of the conversation, however, was strictly about "personal" issues; as we saw in Chapter 3, Judine Mayerle's research showed that by 1985 most episodes contained as much as 50 percent "personal discourse" time involving Cagney and/or Lacey.[26] If one of the characters would not talk about some aspect of her personal life, as when Lacey was unwilling to discuss the return of her long-lost father, the refusal itself became a narrative issue. The places in which the conversations took place were standard and recurrent. The favorite spot was the women's room at the station house, and it was here that many of the protagonists' most intimate and intense exchanges occurred. They also talked in the women's locker room, the squad car, while walking down streets, and occasionally on the firing range. Cagney sometimes dropped in at Lacey's apartment— and later, house—to discuss things, although Lacey rarely did likewise.

Cagney and Lacey's bonding was cemented in many other ways: They joked, carried on a running banter, and were sarcastic with one another; they exchanged meaningful looks as commentaries on what was going on around them; they traded pointed barbs and the occasional competitive volley; and they fought, sometimes seriously. They were also playful with each other: While the two are conducting an investigation at a high school, for instance, Lacey, to Cagney's amazement, stops in the corridor and performs a spontaneous cheerleader routine. Their playful dialogue in the

Foster/Daly series included such exchanges as Cagney (in "hooker" disguise) asking Lacey, "Do I look sexy?" and Lacey replying, "Irresistible." Or Cagney, "wired" with a microphone, inquiring of her partner, "Would you like to say a few words into my cleavage?" On police cases, the two sometimes dressed up and went undercover; in various episodes they masqueraded as prostitutes, pharmacy clerks, factory workers, and art aficionados.[27] Occasionally they shopped together and also occasionally doubledated. Frequently one or the other was shown in a reverse shot, looking either incredulous, amazed, or proud in reaction to her partner.

Their relationship also had "caretaker" dimensions. During Lacey's breast cancer ordeal, it was Cagney who convinced her partner to explore the lumpectomy option and who (along with Harvey) was in the hospital room both before and after Lacey's surgery. During Cagney's bout with acute alcoholism, Lacey replaced Cagney's boyfriend at her partner's loft, stayed the night with her, and was the only one who could convince her to get help. When Cagney was hospitalized after getting shot in the line of duty, Lacey spent many hours visiting and ministering to her. And Cagney, who had attended Lamaze classes with Mary Beth and Harvey in case she had to fill in at the birth, sped Lacey to the hospital for the baby's emergency delivery. There was a physical dimension to their relationship as well: In various episodes they embraced and kissed one another and fixed each other's hair and makeup. Lacey also tied Cagney's tie, massaged her feet, and blew into and held her hands when Cagney said she was cold. During intense arguments, furthermore, they shoved and pushed one another in rage. Their mutual importance was explicitly acknowledged— Lacey, for example, named her baby "Alice Christine" (for her mother and for Cagney)—and at one point they went together to a police department psychiatrist to work out some of their partnership problems. Finally, many of the episodes' freeze-frame endings featured a shot in which both characters appeared together in the frame.

The talk, play, intimacy, anger, and overall interchange between the two women were repeatedly invoked by fans, not only as "realistic" but also as sources of unparalleled viewing pleasure and as a surefire way of distinguishing *Cagney and Lacey* from male cop shows. A teenage viewer put it this way: "I'm 14 years old and think the show is great; having two realistic leading women who laugh, cry, act tough (and sometimes crazy) together. I have never really been a fan of police shows, whose characters are macho and don't let anything bother them, but yours is different because of Chris and Mary Beth's friendship."

In the following sections, I will read this relationship for some of its "realist" discourses, which emerge from and speak to the social and economic conditions of at least part of the women's audience, and for some discourses that may work to engender desire. I turn first to notions of solidarity and difference.

SOLIDARITY

Cagney and Lacey's representation of solidarity bespoke the historical importance of women's bonding during a period that saw both advances and retrenchments for the women's movement; it also involved the negotiations that accompanied women's full-scale entry into the labor force, especially in nontraditional jobs. We have already seen that work-related scenes were singled out for praise as evidence of the program's and the characters' "realness" and were valued by its women fans. Chris and Mary Beth were the first female detectives in an initially hostile all-male precinct.[28] Their bond grew out of these conditions and gained complexity from the mutual support that they made necessary.

The layout of the precinct house actually inscribed topographically the two women's relations to these material conditions (and the discourses that structured them) and to one another. It was divided into spaces for specific types of interactions and mapped out their social and hierarchical dimensions. The large squad room, in which all the detectives had desks (Cagney's and Lacey's faced one another), was the space for general group conversation. It was also the place where the protagonists deliberated (across their desks) about police cases. The commander's office, a small, glassed-in cubicle in one corner of the squad room, was the space for dialogue, primarily about police work, among Lieutenant Samuels, Cagney, and Lacey, or among the three of them and one of the top brass—Inspector Knelman or Inspector Marquette. (Encounters in this office were occasionally personal—Samuels, for instance, might ask Cagney for tips on dating behavior, or Samuels and the two women would talk about his problems with his son.)

So far, the precinct's design and its implications for the chain of power and general squad interaction are quite similar to that found in male police series such as *Kojak* and *Hill Street Blues*—a separate space for the commanding officer and a large common room for everyone else. In *Cagney and Lacey*, however, it also delineated some of the tensions of male/female relationships in a male-dominated workplace, in that the women had to "get away" to talk freely and privately. They often escaped into the women's room—their personal, appropriated conference room on the margins of the institution (the margins on which, Teresa de Lauretis says, women's

Conference in the "Jane." (© Orion TV, 1985)

discourse operates under patriarchy).[29] Whenever either of them wanted to exit for a private moment in what the writers and scripts referred to as the "Jane," she would signal the other by saying, "Conference, Mary Beth," or "Conference, Christine." (The Jane was off the squad room through a set of doors next to Samuels's office.) This somewhat unusual conversational venue also served to distinguish the women detectives' conversation from that of their counterparts in male-buddy series. Male buddies tended to talk in more properly institutional or institutionally related spots—primarily the squad room or squad car—and to discuss work-oriented items and events.

The episode cited in the previous chapter, "Power"—in which Cagney, on Inspector Knelman's orders, forces Lacey to take maternity leave—is a good example of how the pair's partnership in a traditionally male job undergirded their friendship. Banished to her apartment, Lacey tells Harvey how much she wishes she could be at work to support Cagney while she is temporarily in command. Back at the precinct, Cagney is tormented by the male detectives, who try to undermine her authority and take advantage of her, and by Inspector Knelman's intrusions and interference in her decisions. At a certain point in the episode, the precinct setting described above takes over. We see a shot of Knelman railing at Cagney in the commander's office, followed by a long shot of the squad room filled with detectives, with Knelman storming out of the office and through the larger room. In the back center of the frame we see Cagney alone in the glassed-in space. She is alienated from the detectives in the squad room, with whom she has taken a hard line, and is deflated and discouraged by Knelman's invective. The camera cuts to closer shots of Cagney as she picks up the telephone, calls Lacey at home, but gets no answer. She then walks out of the office. The next shot is a long take, long shot profile of Cagney alone in the women's room, looking down at the floor.[30] Lacey's absence from this scene makes dramatically clear the character of the partners' friendship, the solidarity and support born of and sustained by their struggle in an overwhelmingly male place of work. It also underscores the crucial place of female bonding in the fray and the quality of their private talking space, which is quite literally "on the margins of the institution."

The many scenes in this private space are, in one way, a source of the series's greatest strength, part of its transgressiveness and ambition. As viewers, we find ourselves not only in the conventionally "male" generic squad room but also in the nonconventional "Jane." In this marginal other space, we are directly addressed *as women*, and femininity is confirmed. For many female fans, the space seems "normal" despite its violation of genre norms. But as in so many aspects of this program and most popular culture directed toward women, the representation is forged in contradictions and cuts at least two ways. One of the reasons that the moments in the Jane are so familiar and loved is because we are used to seeing women not only talk and bond but do so in private places; used to seeing them steal away to interior space while men command the public spots—used to seeing women in the bathroom. With this aspect of the series, we have one more demonstration of the "on one hand *this* and on the other *that*" of mainstream addresses to feminine spectators, of industrial culture directed at women, and of the overall conflicted positions of *woman, women,* and *femininity*.[31]

Later in "Power," the protagonists' recurrent solidarity born of the alienating work conditions is again demonstrated. After a day of put-downs, threats, and orders from Inspector Knelman to close a case she "knows" is not correctly solved, Cagney visits Lacey at her apartment. She says, "I cracked the case tonight. I was right and everyone else was wrong. This job is hard enough for a man, Mary Beth. You add the flack they give a woman and it's almost impossible. Maybe I'm just not cut out for it. Or maybe I have to settle for being a great detective." To which Lacey replies, "Knelman—you're better than he is, Christine. You're smarter than he is. You've

Scene from "Power," with Michael Fairman as Inspector Knelman and Sharon Gless as Cagney. (© Orion TV, 1985)

got more nerve than he does. . . . You can go as high as you want to in this department, Christine. And you'll be doing it for all of us—make up for the Knelmans."

The characters' solidarity, in addition to being shaped by their relationship to work, was in other episodes structured by such social traumas as Cagney's rape and sexual harassment and by threatening situations with social and political dimensions, such as Mary Beth's breast cancer or Cagney's alcoholism. In other words, their bond could be said to derive from some of the conditions that produce the category "women" and many of its inhabitants in late-twentieth-century Western countries, and thus it functioned as a powerful source of viewer identification.[32]

DIFFERENCE

In addition to solidarity, Cagney and Lacey's friendship was also characterized by differences. Such differences, of course, may work to signal that women's history is lived in a multitude of ways and is structured by myriad and often conflicting social discourses and conditions. They also tap deeper into the verisimilitude or realism that Gledhill discusses because they permit a wider display of "women's experiences" and "women's culture," as well as a wider spectatorship. And although the presence of *both* Cagney and Lacey and the interaction between them seemed to be the fundamental source of many viewers' involvement with the program, the characters' differences allowed various audience members to identify more closely with one or the other. A thirteen-year-old fan summed up the phenomenon in this way: "I always like Chris Cagney better, my mom says it's because I have the same 'HOSTILE' personality. Her favorite is Lacey. I figure that's why we like the show—something to please both of us." Because the narratives did not let the differences stand as simple markers of "character contrast" but actually spent a good deal of time probing them, the general notion of difference—especially of differences between and among women—was readily accessible to viewer scrutiny and consideration.

Differences or contrasts between characters are, of course, mainstays of television dramaturgy that have divergent functions and meanings for the television networks, for genres and narratives, and for spectators. The networks use differences to appeal to a wide range of audience members and so increase their viewer base; genres and narratives use them to exploit contrasting behaviors, appearances, and motivations, thereby achieving dramatic "depth" and "richness"; and spectators get to identify with and take pleasure in various personalities, behaviors, beliefs, races, classes, ages, and so forth. Some of the social differences explored by *Cagney and Lacey* were those involving marriage, motherhood, professional ambition, feminism, class, politics, and personality or subjectivity. All these differences, of course, as we have seen many times throughout this book, were also quite circumscribed, and their delimitation helped perpetuate the conventional equation of "women" with whiteness and heterosexuality.

Although heterosexuality was unquestionably the norm on the show (in later seasons, however, a gay man was introduced as Cagney's next-door neighbor), the characters' differing positions on marriage (and motherhood), which remained consistent from the 1981 pilot movie through the 1988 final season, permitted the negotiation of both culturally established and more unorthodox discourses. They not only offered feminine spectators different options for identification, but they also provided some critique of traditional assumptions that a woman's value was derived from an institutional relationship with a man or as a childbearer or caretaker. Lacey (despite her nontraditional husband/wife relationship with Harvey) was a strong proponent of marriage as the ideal state for a woman and, right up until a 1988 episode in which she finally "gave in" and acknowledged her partner's right to a different view, was always encouraging Cagney's serious involvements with men.[33] Cagney persisted in wanting to remain single and offered a number of impassioned reasons why. But her attitudes toward male/female roles were a conflicted and somewhat paradoxical mixture: Her problems with men and her perpetual jibes at macho masculinity coexisted with her continual heterosexual couplings and her oftentimes submissive, "needing to be taken care of" behavior in scenes of physical intimacy. In the case of both characters, the contradictions made possible a sharp critique of customary ways of conceiving male/female relationships and women's "worth."

The partners' differences on motherhood functioned in a similar way. Lacey was not only an actual mother but maternal in general. She nurtured the men in the squad as well as casual acquaintances, gave out health tips and cold remedies, spent the night at the precinct to provide company to a jailed teenage girl who was deaf, brought groceries to hungry welfare-hotel children, planned to adopt an abandoned baby, and was generally "good with" children on police cases.[34] She often played a mothering role with Cagney and, in fact, on an initial trip to a psychiatrist to work out problems with her partner, inadvertently listed the name "Christine" when talking about her children. (The psychiatrist asked if Christine was her daughter.) Cagney, on the other hand, was much more ambivalent about maternity, and although she probed what not having children might mean to her, she also mused to her partner, "You know, sometimes the thought of never having my own child is like an ache. I'm afraid that I'll disappear from the gene-pool for all eternity. My life would be meaningless. But most of the time, I don't feel that way."

Related to these differences in marital and motherhood status were the pair's professional differences. The "mother/wife/cop" Lacey, although wanting to be a sergeant, was less career-oriented than her partner because of her nuclear family status. Cagney, who was totally ambitious and wanted to be chief of detectives, identified with her retired-policeman father and built her self-concept on this identification. The depictions of a less ambitious, maternal (mother-identified) woman and a highly ambitious, father-identified daughter, of course, conformed to the two classic psychoanalytically based options for women, but they also highlighted the differences that produce male and female possibilities and aspirations under patriarchy. The portrayal of Cagney made room for spectators who defined themselves in ways outside the tried-and-true canon for TV wives and mothers. But Lacey's sometimes ferocious aggression on the job (among other behaviors and traits) also challenged the more traditional aspects of her otherwise maternal portrayal.

Other significant differences, which afforded a negotiation of discourses rarely seen on the home screen, were those of politics and class, and the relation between the two categories was often plainly foregrounded. Cagney, who actually revealed in one episode that she was a Republican, was blinded by class privilege to the social conditions of women who could not "help themselves." In one episode, for example, while she and Lacey investigated a crime in a rundown welfare hotel, she pronounced haughtily, "The nobility of poverty is giving me a headache"; in another, she scorned the striking uniformed police officers and crossed their picket lines. Her upper-middle-class background (she was raised in a Westchester "mansion" by her grandmother and mother and attended Catholic schools), which was repressed in her fierce identification with her working-class father, Charlie, explained many of her hardnosed attitudes toward class issues to viewers, if not to the character herself.

Lacey, a "latchkey kid" raised by a single, working-class mother who (after her mother's death) struggled herself as a poor young working woman, was a political liberal. Her upbringing, according to the narratives, had taught her the interworkings of class and politics. And her liberal-to-leftist leanings were mainly portrayed as the result of her individual background and experience: solidarity with laborers and factory workers (her mother had worked in a factory), a pro-choice stance on abortion (Lacey herself had an abortion before she met and married Harvey), and active support for single, working-class mothers. However, although the narratives rooted Lacey's political positions in her personal history, thereby individualizing their wide-ranging social dimensions, not all her political beliefs were so embedded. In one episode, for instance, she agitated against nuclear waste dumping, and in another she was arrested in an anti–nuclear weapons demonstration.[35]

The narratives' use of class to probe the characters' socioeconomic differences sometimes verged on the ludicrous as they incorporated "realistic" details to spark audience interest and, from the industry's point of view, audience recognition: Cagney ate croissants from Michel's, while Lacey got donuts from Mel's. In the opening credit sequence, Cagney left work in a fur coat while her partner sported a bowling shirt.[36] Cagney spoke impeccable French when they ordered out in "fancy" restaurants, while Lacey fumbled with the pronunciation and was shocked at the actual food to which the words referred. In fact, Lacey often had difficulty pronouncing complicated names and spoke in a heavy New York accent with occasional grammatical flaws; during an episode in which the two went undercover as art gallery patrons, Cagney was shown to be "in her world" (she and her mother had toured galleries on Saturdays when she was a child), whereas Lacey did not know how to dress the part and made one social gaff after another.[37]

Mary Beth and Harvey got excited over such purchases as a vibrating lounge chair, a dining room dimmer switch, a microwave oven, and a new refrigerator. They drank beer out of cans, watched television at night, and ate large quantities of pasta, pizza, and lasagna. When going to a convention in Florida, they fantasized about the "rum drinks with the umbrellas," and "their song" was Sonny and Cher's "I've Got You, Babe." But despite this Hollywood-inspired conception of the working class and its members' tastes, Lacey often used the class difference between her and Cagney to soundly criticize a stratified social system.[38] And throughout, discourses of the upper middle class and conservative politics (Cagney) and those of the working class and liberal politics (Lacey) were continuously and vigorously negotiated in the interactions of the two characters.[39]

The final difference I want to highlight involves what might be called personality types but what I describe as the different "subjectivities" of the protagonists. As may be obvious, Lacey was portrayed as a stable and coherent character and was at times valorized by the narratives as the normal and moral ideal for women. Cagney, in contrast, was always a "subject in process," and although she often started out an episode taking a "conservative" position but ended up "enlightened," she never achieved the integrated "self-knowledge" or unified subjectivity of her partner. Such a difference allowed spectators to identify with a protagonist who was at times fairly noncoherent.[40]

In writing about Cagney, the press often alluded to her complex mixture of traits and behaviors. Michael Ryan of *People*, for example, called her "ambitious, competitive, sometimes cruel, often humorless," and Karen Stabiner of the *New York Times Magazine* quipped, "She's an ambitious driven wiseacre." The *Los Angeles Times*'s Howard Rosenberg exclaimed, "Gless really cooks as Cagney, a character that just knocks me out. She is funny, vulnerable, angry." And Fred Robbins, quoting Tyne Daly, wrote that Cagney was "the newer, the more exciting, the less-easy-to-define one. She represents a change in women in the country now."[41]

The fact that Cagney was difficult to define, that she did not achieve a sense of "wholeness" or integration in the narratives, prevented her from solidifying into a normative ideal, as the Lacey character often seemed in danger of doing. On the one hand, of course, this irresolution could be troublesome, because Cagney was the single, ambitious, and in many respects nonconventional woman. On the other hand, it worked to keep open and permeable the definitions of *woman, women,* and *femininity* and even the notion of human subjectivity. In Cagney one encountered a conflicted character whose subjectivity could easily be seen as arising from relationships with other subjects and discourses. Her equivocal connections to men and to male/female roles were a case in point, as were her contradictory positions on class—her identification with her working-class father and rejection of her wealthy mother and grandmother on the one hand, and her scorn for labor and the struggling working class on the other. Some of this inconsonance was related to the production team's problem, discussed in Chapter 1, of not knowing "where to go" with Cagney—troubles compounded by the network's skittishness about portraying a single, sexually active woman, the attempts to make her more "sympathetic," and the commitment to keeping her single and dedicated to her work. It was also related to the decision, following the Foster/Daly episodes, to make the character more upscale.

In the 1987–88 season, Cagney grew more "self-reflective" than ever before. After struggling to admit that her father was an alcoholic, and after his death and her own plunge into severe alcoholism, she began to achieve some "self-insight." At Alcoholics Anonymous meetings she was able to admit to weaknesses and aspects of herself that she had, to that point, refused to acknowledge. Nonetheless, in a 1988 episode in which she took over the precinct after the breakdown and failure of Lieutenant Thornton (a temporary male replacement for Samuels), she was shown as still very much "in progress." In the episode, a woman named Ann asks Cagney to be her AA sponsor. Cagney's own sponsor, Jo, warns that she does not think Cagney is ready for the responsibility. Flattered and impressed that Ann (a psychiatrist) has asked for her help, Cagney ignores Jo's advice and becomes Ann's sponsor. Later, cocky and swaggering as ever, Cagney tells Lacey about Ann: "She's boozed up, burned out, and all mine. She's a therapist. Can you imagine? How'd you like to have your shrink cry through your sessions with you?" To which a wary Lacey replies, "I hope it works out, Chris." And Cagney retorts, "What do you mean HOPE? This is HISTORICAL, Mary Beth! Talk about acceleration! I mean, I'm moving through this [AA] program like a house on fire!"

Throughout the episode, Cagney also takes a self-righteous attitude toward Lieutenant Thornton, who "broke down" in the line of duty, and is cold and distant with Donna, her father's former girlfriend, whom she has always spurned. On Jo's advice, Cagney asks Donna out to dinner to "make amends." When Donna joins her at the restaurant, Cagney acknowledges that she has not always been kind and has said hurtful things. She then blurts out, "So I wanted to apologize for what I said. It's important for me to apologize, and I do. That's all. I apologize. All right? Now I better go." A baffled Donna says, "What about dinner?" and Cagney replies, "I don't think it's going to work out. Besides, I already ate." In the next scene, a self-congratulatory Cagney says about the meeting with Donna, "I was generous with an enemy."

The "always in progress" subjectivity and the "bad girl" dimensions to her character may have elicited spectator identifications with Cagney rooted in the wish to transgress the boundaries of appropriate femininity, the very boundaries that were so hotly contested during the 1980s. The fact that Cagney flagrantly defied stereotypes of the feminine (demure, passive, conciliatory, pleasing, kind, nurturing, and modest) and contrasted sharply with the more feminine Lacey made, of course, for a complex and compelling textual negotiation.

The exploration of the protagonists' various differences, then, worked to flag some of the competing social discourses and conditions that comprised the category "women," demonstrating that femininity was defined and lived in disparate ways, but this exploration stopped short of probing differences based on ethnicity and race. The differences it did underscore, however, may have called into question by many viewers the category "women" and its social constructedness. And the portrayal of a complex women's friendship may have stimulated a broader inquiry into all the differences that structure *women, woman,* and *femininity.*

DESIRE

The relationship between the two women detectives was obviously fundamental to viewer identification in ways that raise important questions. Although some fans appeared to identify more with one character than the other, many indicated that they identified with aspects of each and, furthermore, that the friendship between the characters was a crucial element in the text's possibilities for identification. This leads us to the question of desire and an examination of how it may have played itself out in the text and its spectators.

As I have suggested several times, many viewers interpreted Cagney and Lacey's relationship using strategies derived from particular lesbian reading practices. In other words, realist textual discourses were encompassed within a reading that specifically enhanced the involvement and desires of some lesbian viewers. I maintained in Chapter 1 that viewers responded in varying degrees to the homoerotic overtones in the protagonists' relationship, and some purposely enhanced those overtones to increase their viewing pleasure. The series's lesbian viewers, indeed, exploited the text's ambiguity or openness to intensify their identification, delight, and desire. They produced imaginative readings that transcended the boundaries of the inscribed relationship, going beyond and reconfiguring for their own purposes what was "actually" there, actually presented in the realist text.[42] The program was nothing short of "cult" viewing for lesbians worldwide.

A number of lesbian viewers, in fact, wrote and submitted to the producers scripts that developed the latent homoeroticism between the characters. A lesbian comedian did a stand-up routine in Provincetown, Massachusetts, that included such lines as, "Would it hurt the ratings if once, just once, when Cagney and Lacey are in the women's room, Chris would lean over and kiss Mary Beth on the lips?" The routine went on to fantasize all sorts of erotic encounters between the two. And an article by Walta Borawski in *Gay Community News*, which criticized *Cagney and Lacey's* handling of AIDS, recalled the episode in which a furious Lacey pushed Cagney up against the wall of the women's room. Borawski commented in general that "the liberal politics of the series get more than a bit entangled with mainstream expectations" and then continued, "It's like the time Lacey punched Cagney out in the women's bathroom and everyone acted like sex had nothing to do with it." Before the series's cancellation in the spring of 1988, apparently spurred on by lesbian interest in the program, writer and story editor Kathryn Ford had, in fact, written a "spec" script involving lesbianism.[43]

Many scenes between the two women, particularly those containing expressions of physical intimacy, were singled out by lesbian viewers and "canonized" in informal repertoires that cast a lesbian slant on potent mainstream depictions.[44] These same scenes might be recalled by other women for their manifestations of close female friendship, but not necessarily with homoerotic dimensions. For example, in discussing the ending of the two-part episode on Mary Beth's breast cancer, Jackie Byars describes the sequence in which Cagney comes into the hospital room right after Lacey's surgery:

> The visual conventions normally used to signify heterosexual romance are repeated in the display of the women's friendship, indicating that formal cinematic and televisual conventions are not gender-bound. These conventions can be used to display maternal love as well; they express closeness and affection. Harvey bends over Mary Beth as he announces Christine's presence. To the sounds of a waltz that punctuates the scene and emphasizes the women's friendship, Christine replaces Harvey, bending over Mary Beth and taking her hand, and, as the sequence ends, Mary Beth and Christine settle into a *mutual gaze*: the frame freezes dramatically, drawing attention to their closeness, as it draws the audience into their relationship. (emphasis in the original)[45]

This sequence, which can be seen as underscoring a deep friendship between two heterosexual women, can also be read by numerous lesbian viewers as signifying unabashed desire in the sexually coded look between the protagonists.[46] In such moments, in which desire for and identification with the women heroes is eminently available, the texts may actually

Scene from "Who Said It's Fair?" part 2, with Sharon Gless and Tyne Daly as Cagney and Lacey. (© Orion TV, 1985)

address lesbian spectators. Lesbian viewers, of course, will always do innumerable things to turn mainstream culture into "lesbian texts"; will always exceed and explode the limits of "what's there"; will always exercise and inscribe lesbian desire. It is this issue of desire that I want to examine more directly.

The intensity of all women viewers' involvement in Cagney and Lacey's relationship most likely incorporated aspects not only of identification but also of desire (even if operating unconsciously). It is fairly safe to say that viewers identified with Cagney, Lacey, or both. But the large percentage of two-shots and shot/reverse shot sequences that linked the protagonists together in the frame and set up an ongoing relay of looks among the two characters and the spectator surely also drew on and evoked desire.[47] There was a continuum of response to the homoeroticism in the relationship between Chris and Mary Beth, but I see the text (within the historical context of film and television conventions) as eliciting desire in *all* of its spectators.

A couple of points should be clarified here: There is no doubt that the series's production team worked very hard to underscore the heterosexuality of its protagonists—especially after the 1982 controversies over lesbian innuendoes. Mary Beth and Harvey may have had the most active sex life of any married couple on TV. (This is all the more interesting because, in the original made-for-TV movie, Harvey had a problem with impotence.) And Cagney, as we have seen, was usually involved in either a long-term or a short-term relationship with a man. Both characters' interactions with men were highlighted events that occupied more screen time as the series progressed and the cop story segments diminished in overall importance. But this emphasis on heterosexuality did not prevent the text (within, of course, the historical context of lesbian and feminist politics) from evoking in its women spectators both identification with and desire for the women characters, leading into a critique of heterosexism itself.

The representation of solidarity between the protagonists, the narrative exploration of the differences between them, and the evocation of both identification and desire in the audience worked, then, to address feminine spectators as subjects constructed in conflicting discourses with regard to femininity, marriage, motherhood, politics, class, feminism, and sexuality. A viewer's own investments in and relation to these discourses and material conditions surely had the strongest influence over the spectator positions she assumed. The text's address, in other words, was simply one facet in the overall workings of numerous other discourses, practices, environments, and events.

GENERIC MIXTURE AND FEMALE SUBJECTIVITY

In Chapter 3, we looked at the specific discourses negotiated in the course of the series's generic shift from a fairly standard police drama to a combination of police program, melodrama, soap opera, and comedy. We saw that in some respects, the main characters were depicted as active and autonomous narrative protagonists—subjects of dramatic action and of desire—and were thus different from conventional representations of women on TV, while in other respects they more closely resembled traditional television women. The combination of cop and noncop story segments and the transformations in the subject matter of both produced a particular mixed form and necessitated highly complex and problematic negotiations involving women and femininity.

Not only could the conventional police genre not hold, but the ultimate ideological work of *Cagney and Lacey's* mixed form might be seen as revalidating earlier types of TV women and stereotypical femininity. Cagney and Lacey could be presented as active agents, but only on the condition that they also appear as a host of other things: mothers, nonthreatening comediennes, victims of rape and harassment, "victims" of their own bodies (breast cancer), and prey to "weaknesses" (alcoholism). As I claimed in Chapter 3, this ideological work might, in fact, have echoed some of the "intentions" of the network (although not conceived or strategized by CBS in this particular way).[48] But the ideological recuperation of traditional depictions was surely not the only thing happening in the series. The mixture of realism with police program and "woman's program" stories produced a fictional negotiation of the complexities, tensions, and incompatibilities experienced by women in the United States during the renaissance of the women's movements and the subsequent backlash that led to a sudden retrenchment in their discourses and gains; in other words, *Cagney and Lacey* offered a narrative, televisual negotiation of women's agency as well as women's objectification, containment, and repression.

I would argue that the representations of women's subjectivity, continually interwoven with representations of conventional femininity and women's friendship, addressed and constituted spectators as feminine subjects in powerful ways. The depiction of female subjectivity (even when modified, distorted, and to some degree repressed) also tapped into the experiences of many women viewers, reverberating with their own fictions and hopes of self-realization. The series's final episode, when viewed in relation to the overall history of the narratives, offers a potent example of this point. Some viewers objected to this episode because of its unabashed violence and the derivative character of a season finale that seemed more like a cliffhanger from *Dallas, Dynasty,* or *Falcon Crest* than a *Cagney and Lacey* ending. Nonetheless, it provides an apt demonstration of my arguments.

The two-part show was unlike any previous *Cagney and Lacey* episode. It was virtually all cop story (with a few brief scenes chronicling the mutual attraction between Lacey and an FBI agent), but it was more akin to a hybrid mystery/spy thriller than a conventional police program. It is interesting, of course, that after transmogrifying into a "women's program," the series in its final show returned to a conventionally "male" genre choice. Like several of *Cagney and Lacey*'s later narratives, the story involves an exposé of the U.S. government's implication in clandestine activities and cover-ups. The protagonists are sent upstate by the New York Police Department, on what we discover is essentially a sacrificial mission, to apprehend the banker/financier of one of the Reagan administration's international arms deals. The man they take into custody turns out to be an FBI decoy, who was sent on the expedition by his department because he is a "troublemaker" and therefore also expendable. Cagney, Lacey, and the FBI agent—all of them live bait—are driving a nondescript, low-powered station wagon back to the city. They are chased by a BMW 735i containing a team of three professional hit men dressed in black jumpsuits, black leather boots, and black wraparound sunglasses and armed with large, high-powered automatic weapons. Cagney, who is driving, pulls into the yard of a rambling farm to elude them. She and Lacey, carrying small revolvers, go into the barn, and the FBI agent (who has an automatic weapon) goes into the house.

The BMW tracks them into the yard, and one of its occupants gets out of the car and enters the farmhouse. We then hear rounds of gunfire and see the house's windows being blown out. The full-scale shootout that ensues occupies four minutes of screen time and employs such techniques as slow-motion photography during some of the most violent killing. The wounded FBI agent stumbles out of the house and collapses on the ground, but he has managed to kill one of the hit squad. The two women, still in the barn, dodge round after round of gunfire from the two remaining hit men, who are now right outside its doors. As the men open the barn doors and prepare to storm inside, the FBI agent rises up from a bloody heap behind them and guns one of them down. The other swings around to return the volley and, at this point Cagney and Lacey appear in the open barn door side by side. Their pistols are aimed at the back of this last gunman. (Lacey is wearing a wraparound blue skirt with a floral print blouse and—in a detail of gendered verisimilitude—her slip is showing.) They fire simultaneously and take the remaining hit man down.

The codes are glaring: Two women with revolvers and a clunker of a car are instrumental in wiping out a sophisticated hit squad armed with state-of-the-art weaponry and transported by the ultimate top-of-the-line driving machine. The women do get help from a "sensitive" man who is also armed with an automatic weapon but who dies in the line of duty. The plot encompasses a complete fantasy of female agency, subjectivity, solidarity, and power, all accomplished with symbolic and material markers of "femininity"—small guns, a low-powered family car, a flowered blouse, and a wayward slip.

When they return to the precinct, the protagonists are changed characters. They are absolutely humorless in the face of the squad's congratulatory banter about the "Cagney and Lacey mini-series," which would star Sally Field or Sigourney Weaver as Lacey and Glenn Close as Cagney. They are far less respectful of Lieutenant Samuels's rank. They receive a sudden promotion (engineered by Inspector Marquette, the NYPD's culprit in the affair) to Major Case Squad in order to keep them quiet about the department's complicity in the government cover-up. When the real banker/financier allegedly commits suicide, they decide not to let their investigation stop but to take the story to Lynn Sutter, an African American ace reporter who has been featured in past episodes.

At the conclusion of the program, an exchange between Cagney, Lacey, and Lieutenant Samuels invokes the protagonists' conversations in the women's room, their "place on the margins," and consequently the ways in which they have negotiated the patriarchal world of the precinct and the department. It also emphasizes Cagney and Lacey's solidarity, not only with each other but with other women. Earlier in the episode they had been preparing to paint the women's room. At the conclusion, they ask Samuels's advice about pursuing the investigation, and he responds by saying, "Paint the women's room." At their bewildered reaction, he continues, "You're asking me for advice. I'm giving you advice. . . . You paint the women's room and you put yourselves in a 'win win' position. . . . You paint the women's room so that when the *Times* prints the story that you're going to give Lynn Sutter, either you're going to leave a legacy for whoever comes here after you've gone on to Major Case, or, in the very likely event that Marquette pulls the promotion, then you at least have a freshly painted toilet here at the Fourteenth."

We have already seen that women fans found Cagney and Lacey especially "real" because they were not typical TV women but were, rather, "assertive," "the equal of their male counterparts," "not left to assume only lesser more 'feminine' roles," and "independent and responsible adults." The portrayal of feminine subjectivity and female protagonists who were in solidarity with one another undoubtedly plugged into both the realities and fantasies of some women viewers' own agency and subjectivity. And they may have offered many women an analysis of their conflicted status in 1980s Western societies as well as actual empowerment.

FEMINIST READINGS AND FEMINIST SPECTATOR POSITIONS

As a mainstream, realist, industrial TV program, *Cagney and Lacey* cannot be analyzed in the way one would analyze a film or video produced as "counterpractice" by a feminist filmmaker. The institutional analysis I have presented in this book makes that clear, I think. Nonetheless, the feminist discourses surrounding the circumstances of the series's production, the ways in which its narratives negotiated the complexities and incompatibilities of women and patriarchy, and its importance to millions of women in the viewing audience make it amenable to the kind of feminist analysis I have espoused here.

The viewers themselves wrote, "I love the show, I love the acting, I love the writing. Yes, I am a feminist, and I don't usually care for cop shows. *Cagney and Lacey* is just right. It's the show for me." Or, "It is television at its most effective as an instrument of education and/or social reform. Committed to a feminist perspective, it influences without being dogmatic." Another fan concluded simply, "*Cagney and Lacey* stands up for women's rights." Other admirers, writing from feminist points of view about the decision to cancel the series, queried, "Is this male chauvinism at work? Are the two female stars too strong for male egos to accept?" and, "It would be difficult to believe you yielded to nervous male egos threatened by the efficiency of Mary Beth Lacey and Chris Cagney—or would it?"

In the same way that Cagney and Lacey, the characters, negotiated patriarchy by their conversations on the margins and in the chinks of the institution, *Cagney and Lacey*, the series, operated on the margins of prime-time television's ratings from 1982 to 1988. It was the only program of its kind, and its ardent support from large numbers of women fans indicates that it filled a gaping hole in viewer needs.

The spectator positions offered by the programs were, as I have argued, multiple: Some women, for instance, may have taken up a position that understood the agency and active subjectivity of the protagonists as deriving from rugged individualism, personal character traits, and personal history. Others, among them the letter writers I just cited, may have accounted for the same depictions in more feminist ways. Especially because they negotiated feminist meanings, *Cagney and Lacey*'s texts held out positions of viewer intelligibility and identification and addressed their spectators not simply as feminine subjects, in whom conflicting discourses about woman competed, but also as "feminist" ones struggling to resolve the same competing discourses.

In suggesting this, I do not mean to imply that feminine or feminist subjects are palpable substances or essences; rather, I have tried to demonstrate how a specific moment in history and culture may shape femininity and feminine subject positions along particular lines. *Cagney and Lacey*'s specific addresses to audiences and spectators and its unique women characters incorporated aspects of femininity and women's culture that were current at the time. Large numbers of women viewers identified with the characters and believed that the program played a part in reorienting and redefining their senses of what it meant to be a "woman."

Said another way, the textual figures of Cagney and Lacey were not just negotiations of conventions from the histories of patriarchy and of film and television depictions of women; they stood for something in excess of the assumption that woman is the object against which the masculine subject can define itself. Following Christine Gledhill, we may see this excess as the incorporation of women's discourse into the textual figure of woman. That incorporation, as we have seen, was at least in part a strategy of the television industry to solicit the women's audience. But in the overall process, the textual figures did not simply draw in the social audience but also hailed and called out to feminine spectators, who identified with the protagonists and took up positions offered by the text. The identification with Cagney or Lacey or both, in other words, may have mobilized new discourses about femininity and feminism, and the textual females may have played a part in the continuous definition and redefinition of "women" and "woman" by their viewers.

In addition to the possibilities for new definitions, new understandings, and a reconceiving of personal and social power, there will always be dangers for those of us who enter into the regimes of pleasure created by popular stories and protagonists.[49] No matter how skilled we are as negotiators or how nimble in occupying our mobile spectator/subject positions, we are always skirting trouble when it comes to identifying with female characters in mainstream texts—the trouble of being defined and positioned by discourses not of our own choosing (conscious or unconscious). But this, of course, is a risk that describes and defines a good measure of our everyday lives and some keen moments of our pleasure.

I will not claim that *Cagney and Lacey*'s "problems" do not exist, but I hope that I have showed to some degree how a mainstream, realist, and problematic (from feminist points of view) text may have had a part in addressing and accommodating feminine, feminist, and perhaps even lesbian subjects and may be read for its feminist dimensions and effects.

CONCLUSION

As I come to the end of this project, a number of things seem clear to me. One is that we will be wrangling for many years to come over television's utopian and dystopian possibilities and its status as a good object or a bad one, a vehicle for social empowerment or for status quo ideology. As Patrice Petro has said of mass culture (and as most of this book testifies), we might want to begin with the assumption that it "is neither intrinsically 'progressive' nor 'reactionary,' but highly contradictory."[1] When it comes to *women, woman,* and *femininity,* Petro's statement seems to be absolutely on target. The tight interweaving of institutional constraints and women's "lived experience," of prime-time TV's construction of femininity and women's understanding of themselves *as* women, are impossible to pick apart. As we have seen, the whole enterprise is one of continual negotiation and renegotiation, in which the networks and advertisers may at times define many of the terms, but they never have the final word.

But pointing out the contradictory character of TV is only the first step. As the work of Lynn Spigel demonstrates, we need to spend more time analyzing the historical moments from which television texts emerge and in which they and their viewers participate. As Mary Beth Haralovich says, "[It] is the work of history to explore the degree to which [the] social context is itself composed of opposing tendencies" and to show how a text "intersects with and articulates the contradictory orientations of its context" and provides spaces in which "contemporary women spectators negotiate their subjectivities within their own herstories."[2]

Furthermore, it seems clear that we must continually ask of the contradictions in television: For whom are they contradictory? If the subversive power that I detect in 1980s prime-time network TV derived from the clashes and incommensurabilities it produced and from the ways it helped me as a viewer to understand and negotiate the contradictions of my own life, what of viewers whose "lives" were simply not depicted? Has fictional network prime time been contradictory, in that sense, for Latinos, Asian Americans, Native Americans, Americans with disabilities? Has it been only minimally contradictory for African Americans, gays and lesbians, the elderly, the working class, and the poor? Or has the contradictory character of prime-time fiction been bound by its constraints on race, ethnicity, class, age, and sexual orientation? Even though it seems certain that viewers identify, on the level of fantasy, with characters who differ from themselves in all of these dimensions, have some viewers had to "scrap" a lot more than others to partake in whatever utopian possibilities the medium might offer?[3]

With regard to masculinity and femininity, it seems clear that network prime time has been what Teresa de Lauretis described as a technology of gender—and what I have discussed in this book as a social and symbolic system that produces women as consumers, target audiences, representations, and spectators. It is a powerful force in and shaper of our cultural, psychic, and everyday lives as gendered human beings.

But U.S. prime time is also clearly a discursive system in a hegemonic society, one that can best be analyzed (as Annette Kuhn and Christine Gledhill, among others, have respectively argued) in the terms of Foucault and Gramsci. In this sense, viewers do not passively conform to its shaping influences but actively interact with its discourses. Because, in such a model, gender definitions (as all definitions) are in constant flux and process, and because power comes not from the top down but from throughout the entire social formation, both gender and television are in a constant and vigorous state of negotiation.

These negotiations, struggles, readings, and interpretations, as we have seen, involve both pleasure and power. Fictional practices meet and negotiate with social ones in a number of ways; for instance, *Cagney and Lacey* and its characters helped women fans not only reconceive themselves as women but also cope with and change aspects of their daily lives, and in this manner a mainstream text was used for feminist and political ends. This point begs many questions, but I believe that more distinctions need to be made between alternative and oppositional social potential and viewer pleasure (not that they cannot and do not often go together). The alternative and oppositional potential of a cultural product (in this case, a TV program) requires, it seems, the presence of political coalitions—with *Cagney and Lacey*, these were the women's movements and gay and lesbian interest groups, among others. (With Jacqueline Bobo's work on *The Color Purple*, they were the Black Power and civil rights movements and the tradition of African American women novelists and scholars.)[4] Into the discourses and articulations of these groups, we as viewers can pull the discourses of the text, and it is these groups that can also translate our negotiations into social actions and material change.

Viewer pleasure, although it is probably a prerequisite for any mainstream representation to have counterculture potential, is also a complicated story of its own, and one that deserves much more of our attention and research. All viewing pleasure is, first of all, not necessarily oppositional or "progressive." It may be "regressive," support the status quo, or have nothing at all to do with battles for social (or even semiotic) power. And we cannot forget that the pleasure taken in mainstream texts by underrepresented social groups, such as *Cagney and Lacey*'s lesbian fans, emerges from representational deprivation, and that it is essentially a case of rifling through popular texts and simply "making do."

But from my point of view, the production of counterhegemonic readings, even when these readings are shaped by and contribute to the work (both semiotic and social) of actual coalitions and interest groups, is not enough. We must, I think, figure out how to have a real impact on television itself. Although the institutional history I have presented in this book makes clear that network prime time operates with a well-defined set of economic imperatives, it is also clear that "open" texts are crucial to its functioning (perhaps increasingly so), that audience pressure has been a force in shaping its fictional depictions, and that the presence of women, feminists, people of color, and gays and lesbians have indeed affected the prime-time fare of the last twenty years.[5]

Although Barbara Corday has spoken about the difficulties women face in trying to change television from within (due to its structure of constraints and economic exigencies), the involvement of many women and feminists in the production of *Cagney and Lacey* had a considerable impact on the series and its possibilities for feminism. (In the same way, Herman Gray argues, the presence of black production team members shaped such programs as *Frank's Place*, to which I would add *The Cosby Show*, *227*, *A Different World*, and *In Living Color*.)[6]

Cagney and Lacey provided not only jobs for women but a potential forum for feminine, feminist, and alternative discourse. Seventy-five of the 125 scripts were written or cowritten by women (Patricia Green won an Emmy for the second part of the breast cancer program "Who Said It's Fair" in 1985), and 104 of the 125 episodes credited one or more women as producer or supervising producer. When P. K. Knelman, as coproducer, is added to this list, all 125 episodes involved at least one woman in a producer or coproducer capacity.[7] Women also served throughout the series's history as creative consultants, executive story editors, executive story consultants, and first assistant directors. Although this percentage is not as high as the ones for writers and producers, 29 of the 125 episodes were directed by females, and Karen Arthur won an Emmy for directing the episode "Heat" in 1985. And in addition to providing two of the few leading dramatic roles for women in prime time, the series tried to offer a good share of its minor roles (some recurrent) to women, especially (although it could have done much better in this regard) to women of color.[8] The assistant district attorney was a Latina; the precinct's beat reporter and the police department psychologist were played by African American women; and, as mentioned in Chapter 2, an African American woman, Merry Clayton, joined the cast in 1987 as Detective Verna Dee Jordan.[9] Among other minor female roles, there were parts for several older women judges and for a woman head of a nuclear technology department, a woman head of a social services department, and an elderly woman con artist; a recurrent role was that of the precinct's "bag lady," Josie.[10] Furthermore, African American directors Bill Duke and Georg Stanford Brown were enlisted to direct a number of episodes, Brown winning an Emmy for "Parting Shots" in 1986.

It seems particularly necessary to work toward and agitate for a greater representation of difference in all the mass media given the cultural retrenchment on feminism and the battles over nonconventional femininity manifested on our home screens in the 1980s and early 1990s. ABC, for example, canceled *Heartbeat* in 1989 after religious watchdog groups protested the series's lesbian characters; NBC, besieged by the same groups in early 1991, assured advertisers and the public that it had no intention of continuing a story line on *L.A. Law* involving a possible love relationship between two women characters. Later in 1991, however, NBC (fearing it was losing viewers to more daring cable channels) announced it would continue stories about its bisexual (or "flexible") female character and even featured her in a lesbian relationship in a December 1991 episode, but the network soon dropped both the story line and the character.

In the summer of 1991, the Network Television Association (a trade group representing ABC, NBC, and CBS), also fearing the loss of viewers to cable, had urged marketers not to be "intimidated" by boycott organizations and not to pull their sponsorship from controversial programs.[11] And in the fall of 1992, *Roseanne* introduced recurring lesbian characters on the program; the story line, however, quickly atrophied. In the face of these developments, I believe it is vital that we generate ways of intervening in the popular struggle over meanings. Especially as the political tenor of the United States shows signs of moving away from the ultraconservatism of the Reagan and Bush years, it becomes particularly important not to concede television and its representations to the discourses and energies of the New Right.

In addition, although I think that individual textual, audience, and industry analyses will remain crucial to the field of media studies, my work on this project has convinced me that we must also continue to engage in studies that seek to incorporate all three. Janice Radway's *Reading the Romance*, for example, has been an influential work in cultural and feminist studies because it brought the romance novel into such an inclusive framework, examining the ways in which various aspects of production and reception, text, context, and history functioned interdependently. In television, the interworkings of textual representations, narrative and generic norms and conventions, audience constructions, industry imperatives, spectator positionings, viewer readings, and contextual forces reveal the dense complexity of the whole enterprise and allow us to see more clearly the innumerable aspects that fashion the phenomenon. Such interworkings furthermore enable us to understand more fully the multiple ways in which *women, woman,* and *femininity* are defined and contested and to analyze the power-based investments of institutions and individuals in this ongoing struggle. They allow us to realize how power and meanings are produced and how they actually operate in specific instances of history and culture.

As I have pointed out more than once in the course of this book, *Cagney and Lacey* poses numerous "problems" for a feminist analysis like mine: the "feminization" of the characters on the level of their bodies, the general "reconventionalizing" of women in the course of the series, the gradual "victimization" of the protagonists, the use of exploitation topics, the diminution of explicit feminism, the circumscribed nature of the differences that were portrayed (especially the fact that Cagney and Lacey are both white), the valorization of heterosexuality at the expense of other sexual orientations, and the offering of feminist and feminine spectator positions that always skirt close to ideological recuperation and co-optation, to name several. But I set out to demonstrate why and how the series could nevertheless be read as "feminist." How such readings—and the power they may have unleashed and generated—are incorporated into social and televisual change is the stuff of future history.

One final point that strikes me is that there is a great deal of pent-up anger over gender troubles—especially those troubles that involve conflicting meanings of *women, woman,* and *femininity*—seething beneath the surface of much contemporary Western life. The popularity of *Thelma and Louise* and the rash of "girls with guns" movies in the early 1990s, the outrage and bitterness that swirled around Anita Hill's testimony before the Senate and its aftermath, the storm over Dan Quayle's attack on single mother "Murphy Brown," and the rage and frustration expressed on the subjects of rape and safe abortions are only a few examples.[12] As television opts more and more for topics that it can play as alluring spectacles but that many people experience as the quotidian pain and terror of everyday life, we must be clever and energetic in inventing new ways of looking at and analyzing the medium. We must also think anew about coalitions that will help us deal with TV's power and pleasures and with its potential for influencing politics and social change.

NOTES

INTRODUCTION

1. The phrase "gender trouble" comes from Judith Butler, *Gender Trouble: Feminism and the Subversion of Identity* (London: Routledge, 1990). Butler uses it to launch a full-scale inquiry into the indeterminacy of gender. The examples I cite here (the troubles occupying "feminine" subject positions in late-twentieth-century Western culture; the troubles "between the sexes"; the troubles surrounding women's bodies, images, power, and sexuality; and the troubles that females in patriarchal culture continue to create) arise because of the ways gender has been cast culturally in masculine/feminine and male/female binaries, with the first term gaining its preeminence from the "other." All the "troubles" I invoke, in other words, cry out for the major dismantling of "gender" offered by Butler. For the race dimensions of some of these "gender troubles," see Tricia Rose, "Never Trust a Big Butt and a Smile," *Camera Obscura*, no. 23 (May 1990): 108–31; Michelle Wallace, "Women Rap Back," *Ms.*, Nov./Dec. 1990, p. 61; Toni Morrison, ed., *Race-ing Justice, En-gendering Power: Essays on Anita Hill, Clarence Thomas, and the Construction of Social Reality* (New York: Pantheon, 1992); *The Black Scholar* 22, nos. 1–2 (1992).

2. In using the word *television*, I am primarily referring to U.S. prime-time network TV—specifically, narrative programming broadcast between the hours of 8:00 and 11:00 P.M. Eastern Standard Time by the three major networks, NBC, CBS, and ABC; I also refer mainly to the 1980s. An analysis of women, femininity, and television would be different in the context of state, public, or community-financed systems; or of nonnarrative or (to a lesser degree) narrative daytime commercial television; or of particular prime-time programs on FOX or the various cable networks.

The notion of the "struggle over meanings" has been developed by Stuart Hall and other cultural studies scholars. They include in this notion the assumption that dominant and powerful groups try to "naturalize" their own specific and vested meanings into the general understandings of the culture at large—to make them seem like obvious, agreed-upon "common sense." See Stuart Hall, "Signification, Representation, Ideology: Althusser and the Post-Structuralist Debates," *Critical Studies in Mass Communication* 2, no. 2 (June 1985): 111; and Hall, "The Rediscovery of 'Ideology': Return of the Repressed in Media Studies," in Michael Gurevitch, Tony Bennett, James Curran, and Janet Woollacott, eds., *Culture, Society, and the Media* (London: Methuen, 1982), p. 73. For a history of cultural studies, see Hall, "Cultural Studies and the Centre: Some Problematics and Problems," in Stuart Hall, Dorothy Hobson, Andrew Lowe, and Paul Willis, eds., *Culture, Media, Language* (London: Hutchinson, 1980), pp. 15–47; and John Fiske, "British Cultural Studies," in Robert C. Allen, ed., *Channels of Discourse, Reassembled: Television and Contemporary Criticism*, 2d ed. (Chapel Hill: University of North Carolina Press, 1992), pp. 284–326.

Some of the material for the case study itself comes from the production files of Barney Rosenzweig, executive producer of *Cagney and Lacey*, and from my own observations over a three-month period between January and March 1984. During this time I visited on the set and locations for the series and sat in on general production meetings, cast readings, meetings with producer-writers and directors, with producer-writers and actresses, and with the main production team, which at the time included Barney Rosenzweig, Terry Louise Fisher, Peter Lefcourt, P. K. (Patricia) Knelman, Barbara Corday, and Ralph Singleton. I also observed in the editing room and screening lab (viewing daily footage) and in the postproduction screening room, and I conducted interviews and had discussions with many of the participants.

3. Annette Kuhn, *Women's Pictures: Feminism and Cinema* (London: Routledge and Kegan Paul, 1982), p. 4. The phrase "sex/gender system" comes from Gayle Rubin, whose definition is quoted by Kuhn: "The set of arrangements by which a society transforms biological sexuality into products of human activity, and in which these transformed sexual needs are satisfied" (Rubin, "The Traffic in Women: Notes on the Political Economy of Sex," in Rayna Reiter, ed., *Toward an Anthropology of Women* [New York: Monthly Review Press, 1975], p. 159).

This distinction between *woman* and *women* comes from Teresa de Lauretis, who writes: "By 'woman' I mean a fictional construct, a distillate from diverse but congruent discourses dominant in Western cultures. . . . By *women*, on the other hand, I will mean the real historical beings who cannot as yet be defined outside of those discursive formations but whose material existence is nonetheless certain. . . . The relation between women as historical subjects and the notion of woman as it is produced by hegemonic discourses is neither a direct relation of identity, a one-to-one correspondence, nor a relation of simple implication. Like all other relations expressed in language, it is an arbitrary and symbolic one, that is to say, culturally set up" (de Lauretis, *Alice Doesn't: Feminism, Semiotics, and Cinema* [Bloomington: Indiana University Press, 1984], pp. 5–6). But as note 13 below makes clear, "women" is not a self-evident category of nature but also a notion produced in language and discourse.

4. For a discussion of the "performance" of gender, see Butler, *Gender Trouble*, pp. 24–25, 134–41. The "discursive authority" formulation is from Annette Kuhn, who writes: "Representations, contexts, audiences and spectators [may be] seen as a series of interconnected social discourses, certain discourses possessing greater constitutive authority at specific moments than others. Such a model permits relative autonomy for the operations of texts, readings and contexts, and also allows for contradictions, oppositional readings and varying degrees of discursive authority" ("Women's Genres," in Christine Gledhill, ed., *Home Is Where the Heart Is: Studies in Melodrama and the Woman's Film* [London: British Film Institute, 1987], p. 347). Kuhn, of course, is drawing on the work of Michel Foucault.

In the pages that follow, I profile the major social discourses regarding femininity that operated in the representations and reception of *Cagney and Lacey*; give a theoretical and empirical account of the institutions and individuals invested in these discourses; inquire into the production of texts, readings, and contexts; and point to the varying degrees of discursive authority that ensued at particular moments and places in the series's history and for particular participants.

5. Kuhn, again drawing on Foucault, says, "Since the state of a discursive formation is not constant, it can be apprehended only by means of inquiry into specific instances or conjunctures" ("Women's Genres"). In referring specifically to Foucault's notion of power, she also writes: "If power relations . . . can neither be directly observed nor theorised in advance, how can they be investigated? How can something so dynamic and fluid ever be subjected to inquiry? At an abstract or a general level, in fact, it cannot: it has to be seen in operation, for power relations can only be analysed at work in specific social and historical 'instances'" (Kuhn, *Cinema, Censorship, and Sexuality, 1909–1925* [London: Routledge, 1988], pp. 7–8). Kuhn also refers to Robert C. Allen and Douglas Gomery's call for a "Realist" approach to history (as developed by Roy Bhaskar and Rom Harre). The object of such historical study, according to Allen and Gomery, "is not the historical event in itself, but the generative (causal) mechanisms that brought that event about" (Allen and Gomery, *Film History: Theory and Practice* [New York: McGraw-Hill, 1985], p. 16). All of this is not to argue that my reconstruction of the instance in question (or the generative mechanisms that brought it about) is the only one possible.

6. The notion of *negotiation*, which traces its lineage from Antonio Gramsci, Stuart Hall, and David Morley, refers to the actual jockeyings among individuals and institutions to achieve authority, or at least some place for their own meanings, in a particular discursive field at a specific point in history and culture. See Stuart Hall, "Encoding/Decoding," in Hall et al., eds., *Culture, Media, Language,* pp. 128–38; David Morley, *The "Nationwide" Audience: Structure and Decoding* (London: British Film Institute, 1980), pp. 156–62. For Gramsci's notion of hegemony, which undergirds much of the work on negotiation in cultural studies, see Antonio Gramsci, *Selections from the Prison Notebooks,* ed. and trans. Quentin Hoare and Geoffrey Nowell-Smith (London: Lawrence and Wishart, 1971). Christine Gledhill has recently proposed a comprehensive theory of negotiation involving a tripartite analysis of institutional, textual, and reception contexts ("Pleasurable Negotiations," in E. Deidre Pribram, ed., *Female Spectators: Looking at Film and Television* [London: Verso, 1988], pp. 67–68). My case study of *Cagney and Lacey* follows Gledhill's outline. It examines the different stakes in different meanings of femininity at all three levels and the negotiations that have resulted from their intersections and collisions.

Prime-time network television is a loosely structured institution comprised of different (and fairly autonomous) segments with different stakes (economic, cultural, and "aesthetic," to name a few) in the overall enterprise. In the course of this book, I will enumerate the ways in which such segments as the advertising industry, the television network, the independent production company, the production team (made up of producers, writers, actors, and actresses, among others, all of whom exercised varying and often significant degrees of control), and the publicity firm had stakes in and struggled over often conflicting definitions of femininity. The struggles were especially acute because the historical period covered here was one in which prime-time television attempted to deal with general social and cultural changes involving women, with discourses of the women's movement, and with institutional innovations that focused on women both as target audiences and as representations (many of them, as we will see in Chapter 1, motivated by attempts to reach the newly "discovered" and produced "working women's market").

At the level of the *TV institution*, then, I identify from the outset various sites of what Volosinov calls "differently oriented interests" that contribute to the polysemy, multiple meanings, or, in Volosinov's term, the "multi-accentuality" of TV's female depictions. (See Hall, "Rediscovery of 'Ideology' "; V. N. Volosinov, *Marxism and the Philosophy of Language* [New York: Seminar Press, 1973]. See also Robert Stam, "Mikhail Bakhtin and Left Cultural Critique," in E. Ann Kaplan, ed., *Postmodernism and Its Discontents: Theories and Practices* [London: Verso, 1988], pp. 116–45.) Prime-time TV to some degree exploits this polysemy, keeping its meanings of femininity relatively open in order to strike responsive chords in a wide variety of audience members with a host of different viewpoints and visions. But network prime time has also operated within a well-defined set of economic and institutional practices and conventions that have served to mediate social meanings along particular lines in particular historical periods. (The various participants and organizational levels mentioned above negotiate these meanings in many different ways, only intensifying the institutional tensions I am probing herein.)

The *TV text*, as David Morley describes it, is a site of numerous intersecting social discourses (see Morley, "Changing Paradigms in Audience Studies," in Ellen Seiter, Hans Borchers, Gabriele Kreutzner, and Eva-Marie Warth, eds., *Remote Control: Television, Audiences, and Cultural Power* [London: Routledge, 1989], pp. 16–43). But, as mentioned in the preceding note, it is more specifically a site of social discourses that are *mediated* by the institution of television—affected and shaped by prime time's economic imperative to produce consumers and audiences, as well as by its aesthetic and formal norms and conventions involving genre, narrative, mise-en-scène, camerawork, sound, and editing. (*Mise-en-scène* refers to what has been "put in" the shot. It designates setting, costumes, props, lighting, figure movement, and facial expression. See David Bordwell and Kristin Thompson, *Film Art: An Introduction*, 4th ed. [New York: McGraw-Hill, 1993], pp. 145–85.)

Such a conception of the TV text allows me to demonstrate the specific ways in which network prime time in the 1980s drew on social discourses regarding femininity and fashioned and delimited its portrayals along particular lines. This concept also clearly shows that television, as a social and symbolic practice, is not a neutral vehicle for the "reflection of life" or for the nonhierarchical, pluralistic representation of sheer heterogeneity—of all different classes, races, ethnicities, bodies, ages, sexual orientations and preferences, abilities, disabilities, and so forth. It furthermore implies that TV texts may contribute to "gendering" their spectators according to particular historically based (and therefore fluctuating) norms. But I hasten to repeat that, even though delimited and constrained, TV definitions of *woman, women,* and *femininity* are never univocal but always open and subject to sundry readings and interpretations. (Television texts include not only programs but also on-air commercials and promotional spots.)

TV viewers, also the sites of multiple social discourses, actively negotiate the discourses of the text and may be shaped and constituted by them along the axes of gender, class, race, sexuality, and so forth. Chapter 5 deals with these issues in more detail. For television texts and viewers as sites of intersecting social discourses, see Morley, *The "Nationwide" Audience*, pp. 156–62.

7. Television's quest for the working women market, beginning in the late 1970s, will be discussed in Chapter 2.

8. *The Nurses* (1962–65), on CBS, starred two women (Shirl Conway and Zina Bethune) as titular protagonists. The actual episodes, however, often had male-doctor leads. The title of the series, in fact, changed in 1964 to *The Doctors and the Nurses*.

Cagney and Lacey's syndication rights through September 1992 were sold to the cable channel Lifetime, and sales to basic cable, WTBS, or TNT were prohibited for the term of the Lifetime agreement. No sales to WGN were permitted through 31 August 1989 (information from "Orion Television Syndication 'Cagney and Lacey' Fact Sheet," supplied courtesy of Keith Merryman, Orion Television).

9. As we will see, especially in Chapter 3, *Cagney and Lacey* changed from being more of a police program to being more of a "woman's program"—more of a soap opera/melodrama/comedy. It always, however, remained a mixed form. In using the phrase "woman's program," I am simply referring to the types of programs that have become associated with and targeted toward women by television networks.

10. At the conclusion of the made-for-TV movie that introduced the series, Loretta Swit's Cagney is put into a "woman in distress" situation and is rescued by the squad (most of whom, with the exception of Lacey, are men). Representations of the protagonists as classic "women in distress" (who cannot fend for themselves and are rescued by men), however, are very much downplayed in the Foster/Daly episodes. The Gless/Daly series does have a few sequences in which the cliché figures—Lacey is rescued from a high beam by her husband Harvey in one scene and is taken hostage in another. Mimi White cites two instances in which Cagney is represented as "trapped" or "caged" by the framing and the mise-en-scène ("Ideological Analysis and Television," in Robert C. Allen, ed., *Channels of Discourse, Reassembled: Television and Contemporary Criticism*, 2d ed. [Chapel Hill: University of North Carolina Press, 1992], pp. 181–87). White finds this problematic for the series's representation of women's subjectivity. By and large, however, the characters are not regularly presented as classic "women in distress," in need of help from male colleagues.

11. The program's history makes plain what Michele Barrett describes as "an indication of the bounds within which particular meanings are constructed and negotiated in a given social formation" (*Women's Oppression Today* [London: Verso, 1980], p. 107).

12. Beverly Stephen, "Policewomen: TV Show on the Case," *Los Angeles Times*, 11 Apr. 1982; CBS executives quoted in Frank Swertlow, "CBS Alters 'Cagney,' Calling It 'Too Women's Lib,'" *TV Guide*, 12–18 June 1982, p. A-1; viewer letters, Rosenzweig files; Shephard quoted in Lee Margulies, "Campaign to Save Cagney and Lacey," *Los Angeles Times*, 20 July 1983; Rogers and Cowan letter to national women's groups, 20 Oct. 1982, Rosenzweig files; Elaine Warren, "Where Are the Real Women on TV?," *Los Angeles Herald Examiner*, 31 Oct. 1982, sec. E; Mark Carlisle, "Cagney and Lacey Are Shaming the Men of America," *National Examiner*, 2 Apr. 1985, p. 21; Toni Carabillo, "Cagney and Lacey Fight for Survival—Again," *National NOW Times*, May 1983, p. 8; Gary Deeb, "Tube Watch," *Syracuse Post Standard*, 30 May 1983; Bridget Smith, "*Cagney and Lacey*," *Spare Rib*, no. 161 (Dec. 1985): 31.

13. Recent work on the convergence of poststructuralism, postmodernism, and feminism has led to a rethinking of many one-time "fundamental" feminist categories. See Judith Butler, "Contingent Foundations," in Judith Butler and Joan W. Scott, eds., *Feminists Theorize the Political* (London: Routledge, 1992), pp. 3–21, for a critique of fundamental or foundationalist categories.

As we have already seen, this theory has questioned and exploded the notion of the fixity of meaning. Meaning is, rather, multiple or polysemous; it is not tacked down in a one-to-one correspondence between words and objects, signs and referents. Such theory has additionally argued that *woman, women,* and *femininity* are discursive constructs, notions produced in language and representation, and that the meanings attached to these categories are the products of history and culture rather than of nature. For dismantlings of the category *women*, see Hazel Carby, "White Women Listen! Feminism and the Boundaries of Sisterhood," in Hazel Carby et al., eds., *The Empire Strikes Back: Race and Racism in 70s Britain* (London: Hutchinson, 1982), p. 213. For a discussion of Carby's points, see Elizabeth Weed, ed., *Coming to Terms: Feminism, Theory, Politics* (London: Routledge, 1989), p. xviii. See also Butler, *Gender Trouble*; and Denise Riley, *Am I That Name?: Feminism and the Category of "Woman" in History* (Minneapolis: University of Minnesota Press, 1988).

Chandra Mohanty, furthermore, contends that "the assumption of women as an already constituted and coherent group with identical interests and desires, regardless of class, ethnic or racial location, implies a notion of gender or sexual difference . . . which can be applied universally and cross culturally" ("Under Western Eyes: Feminist Scholarship and Colonial Discourse," *Feminist Review*, no. 30 [Autumn 1988]: 64). And as Biddy Martin says, *women* as well as *woman* can "mask the operations of white, middle-class, heterosexual 'womanhood' as the hidden but hegemonic referent" ("Lesbian Identity," in Bella Brodzki and Celeste Schenck, eds., *Life/Lines: Theorizing Women's Autobiography* [Ithaca, N.Y.: Cornell University Press, 1988], p. 79). In summarizing the overall position, Denise Riley writes, " 'Women' is a volatile collectivity in which female persons can be very differently positioned so that the apparent continuity of the subject of 'women' isn't to be relied on" (*Am I That Name?*, p. 2).

Other feminists have attempted to demonstrate that "nature," even with regard to sex and gender, is composed of innumerable differences, which are only organized by language into two binary and conventional categories. The divisions *male* and *female* totally disregard, among other things, the many "biological" overlaps (hormones and secondary sex characteristics, to name a couple) in culturally designated men and women. See Ruth Bleier, *Science and Gender: A Critique of Biology and Its Theories on Women* (New York: Pergamon Press, 1984); Anne Fausto-Sterling, *Myths of Gender: Biological Theories about Women and Men* (New York: Norton, 1979); Suzanne J. Kessler and Wendy McKenna, *Gender: An Ethnomethodological Approach* (Chicago: University of Chicago Press, 1978); Sandra Harding, *The Science Question in Feminism* (Ithaca, N.Y.: Cornell University Press, 1986); Evelyn Fox-Keller, *Reflections on Gender and Science* (New Haven, Conn.: Yale University Press, 1984); Sandra Harding and Jean F. O'Barr, *Sex and Scientific Inquiry* (Chicago: University of Chicago Press, 1987); Donna Haraway, *Primate Visions: Gender, Race, and Nature in the World of Modern Science* (London: Routledge, 1989).

Poststructuralism, likewise, has exploded the notion of a unitary, noncontradictory, fully present human subject. Rather, the human subject is a mass of contradictions; it is comprised of conscious and unconscious processes and is continually constructed by and in its relations to other social subjects and discourses. Although they have greatly stimulated theoretical inquiry, all of these arguments have also posed a disturbing problem for feminism because they have been read as signaling the "deaths" of subjectivity, agency, and identity (*woman* and *women*) before "women" historically have been able to assume them. See Biddy Martin, "Feminism, Criticism, and Foucault," *New German Critique*, no. 27 (1982): 14–18; and Tania Modleski, *Feminism without Women: Culture and Criticism in a "Postfeminist" Age* (London: Routledge, 1991).

But in addressing this problem, many feminist scholars have taken pains to theorize that the categories *women* and *woman*, and the notion of women's identity, have real material effects, genealogies, and ongoing social histories, and that "women" are continually being produced, situated, and "resignified" in relation to this history and these effects. Furthermore, historically constructed women may need (at various times and in various places) what Biddy Martin has called the "fiction" of identity, the strategic belief in the uneasy and provisional coherence of the categories *women, woman,* and *subjectivity* (the same way any socially subordinated group may need such a fiction or strategy) in order to wage political struggle for material survival and gains (Martin, "Feminism, Criticism, and Foucault," pp. 14–18). See also Butler, "Contingent Foundations," pp. 13–16, for an elaboration of the notion of resignification.

My approach to these dilemmas is to carefully historicize the meanings of *woman* and *women*; I see them as contingent, growing out of relationships with other meanings and historical events, and only temporarily fixed to particular definitions. In this way, all meanings of *woman* and *women* may be exposed and examined for their actual constructedness. And in this way also, the concept of "feminine subjectivity" (which, according to poststructuralist and postmodern theory, dangerously echoes the "subject" of bourgeois patriarchy) may be seen as a historical position for specific time- and situation-bound forms of action and agency. In this book, I want to make it clear that *women* refers to specific situationally generated groups rather than to a universal category, and also that political constructions of women's subjectivity, autonomy, and agency may be historically produced in relation to other discourses—for example, those of women's "objectification," "subordination," and "passivity." Notions of women's autonomy and agency and notions of a feminine and feminist subjectivity consequently may be seen as actions and positions emerging from particular historical discourses and configurations.

Much of the time, when I use the word *women*, I mean specifically the group of people constructed as "women viewers" (including myself) who watched *Cagney and Lacey* regularly in its first run, who were predominantly middle class and between the ages of twenty-five and sixty-four, predominantly (but not exclusively) white, and predominantly (but again, by no means exclusively) heterosexual. Many of the viewers' letters I discuss, for example, came from middle-class U.S., British, and Canadian women who appeared to fit this profile. Many quite explicitly defined themselves (at least in part) as "women" in relation to specific characteristics of the liberal women's movement in the United States, such as "independent," "career-oriented," "strong," and "not appendages of men." These terms (although in need of critique) offered the possibilities of power, action, and change to many viewers struggling to get beyond the limiting definitions and material conditions of sexual difference. (Many early liberal feminist terms need to be reexamined, especially from the viewpoints of class and race. "Career-oriented" and "not appendages of men," for example, may imply that white, upscale women are the norm for femininity.)

Some general works dealing with postmodernism, poststructuralism, and feminism include Alice Jardine, *Gynesis: Configurations of Woman and Modernity* (Ithaca, N.Y.: Cornell University Press, 1985); Chris Weedon, *Feminist Practice and Poststructuralist Theory* (Oxford: Basil Blackwell, 1987); Teresa de Lauretis, *Technologies of Gender: Essays on Theory, Film, and Fiction* (Bloomington: Indiana University Press, 1987); Meaghan Morris, *The Pirate's Fiancee: Feminism, Reading, Postmodernism* (London: Verso, 1988); Kaplan, ed., *Postmodernism and Its Discontents*; Toril Moi, "Feminism, Postmodernism, and Style: Recent Feminist Criticism in the United States," *Cultural Critique*, no. 9 (Spring 1988): 3–22; Weed, ed., *Coming to Terms*; Nancy Fraser, *Unruly Practices: Power, Discourse, and Gender in Contemporary Social Theory* (Minneapolis: University of Minnesota Press, 1989); Linda J. Nicholson, ed., *Feminism/Postmodernism* (London: Routledge, 1990); and Butler and Scott, eds., *Feminists Theorize the Political.*

14. Annette Kuhn, *The Power of the Image: Essays on Representation and Sexuality* (London: Routledge and Kegan Paul, 1985), p. 6. Kuhn says meanings "do not reside in images . . . [but] are circulated between representations, spectator and social formation."

15. Teresa de Lauretis, "Technology of Gender," in *Technologies of Gender*, pp. 1–30. Although I mainly use John Fiske's notion of primary and secondary texts (discussed in Chapter 1) when talking about TV programs and the texts—publicity, "promos" (short promotional advertisements for upcoming programs), and so forth—that surround them, I occasionally use the division "textual/extratextual." I perceive all the material as "textual," but I do want to maintain analytical divisions among the various "texts" in question. In using the word *texts*, however, I draw on Tony Bennett and Janet Woollacott's claim that texts are not stable objects but "sites around which the pre-eminently social affair of the struggle for the production of meaning is conducted" (*Bond and Beyond: The Political Career of a Popular Hero* [New York: Methuen, 1987], pp. 59–60).

16. Raymond Williams, *Television: Technological and Cultural Form* (New York: Shocken Books, 1974), pp. 78–119; Nick Browne, "The Political Economy of the Television (Super)Text," *Quarterly Review of Film Studies* 9 (Summer 1984): 174–82; John Ellis, *Visible Fictions: Cinema, Television, Video* (London: Routledge and Kegan Paul, 1982); James Collins, "Postmodernism and Cultural Practice," *Screen* 28, no. 2 (1987): 11–27; Lynne Joyrich, "Individual Response," *Camera Obscura*, nos. 20–21 (May–Sept. 1989): 193; Annette Kuhn, "Individual Response," *Camera Obscura*, nos. 20–21 (May–Sept. 1989): 215. Many of these scholars specifically attempt to differentiate television viewing from film viewing.

17. Charlotte Brunsdon, "Text and Audience," in Seiter et al., eds., *Remote Control*, p. 125.

18. The audience responses consist of a collection of 500 letters that I pulled arbitrarily from Barney Rosenzweig's files. They were written to Bud Grant (president of CBS),

Barney Rosenzweig, Tyne Daly, Sharon Gless, and Orion Television, primarily between 1982 and 1984. Although many of the letters indicate the writers' marital status and class, none refers to race or ethnicity. Many were written during a campaign to save *Cagney and Lacey* from cancellation in 1983. Others were sent during other stages of the program's history. The sample is very biased in favor of the series and its representations. This is not to imply that the letter writers should be seen as unidimensional; I just want to make clear that the letters have more commonalities than differences and were, for the most part, written explicitly as fan letters.

There are, of course, many pitfalls in using such ethnographic source material as audience letters (and, for that matter, interviews). There is the problem of taking what the letters say "at face value" and holding that up as the "truth" of the viewing experience. There is the additional trap, noted by Meaghan Morris, of using the people's voice as "the ethnographer's mask" (Morris, "Banality in Cultural Studies," in Patricia Mellencamp, ed., *Logics of Television: Essays in Cultural Criticism* [Bloomington: Indiana University Press, 1990], p. 23). I try to deal with these tricky issues by reading the discourses of the letters against contextual discourses such as those of the liberal U.S. women's movement, prime-time network television, and the backlash against feminism occurring at the time, and against the discourses of the texts to which they were a response. I also tried to let analytical categories emerge from the letters rather than superimposing my own on them from the outset; and I tried to be explicit about my own speculations, such as my discussion (in Chapter 5) of desire as a possible reason for viewers' (including my own) fascination.

I am mainly interested in how these letters participated in the construction of *Cagney and Lacey*; the terms in which the letter writers talked about the impact of the series on their lives; and the terms in which they understood themselves and constructed their experiences. This focus by no means settles the problem articulated by Morris but may somewhat diminish it.

19. The differences between spectators and social audiences will be discussed more fully in Chapter 5. Basically, by using *spectator* I want to signal the aspects of viewing that involve such dimensions as pleasure, identification, desire, and the ongoing constitution of subjectivity, including (but not limited to) gender.

CHAPTER ONE

1. To refer to the stake individuals and institutions have in their own particular meanings, I use the term *investment*, as it has been elaborated by Teresa de Lauretis and Wendy Hollway. De Lauretis defines investment as "something between an emotional commitment and a vested interest, in the relative power (satisfaction, reward, payoff) which that position promises (but does not necessarily fulfill). . . . Power is what motivates (and not necessarily in a conscious or rational manner) individuals' investments" (*Technologies of Gender: Essays on Theory, Film, and Fiction* [Bloomington: Indiana University Press, 1987], p. 16). Her discussion draws on Wendy Hollway, "Gender Difference and the Production of Subjectivity," in Julian Henriques, Wendy Hollway, Cathy Urwin, Couze Venn, and

Valerie Walkerdine, *Changing the Subject: Psychology, Social Regulation, and Subjectivity* (London: Methuen, 1984), pp. 228–52.

"Vulnerable" and "sympathetic" are the two terms used most often by the TV networks to describe what they want in women characters (from personal conversations with Terry Louise Fisher and Barbara Avedon, Feb. 1984, Los Angeles, Calif.).

2. Michael Leahy and Wallis Annenberg, "Discrimination in Hollywood: How Bad Is It?," *TV Guide*, 13–19 Oct. 1984, p. 14. According to Leahy and Annenberg, Orion TV hired women writers for 37 percent of its projects.

Articles in the mainstream press should be read with four things in mind. First, they provide examples of a particular critic's or journalist's own interpretation and thus figure as aspects of reception. Second, such articles often provide direct forums for program publicity. They may be "planted" by the public relations firm responsible for promoting a series, or they may offer program spokespeople (particularly producers and stars) free coverage in the form of interviews. Similarly, television reporters often reproduce the language of publicist-prepared press releases in their columns and stories about programs. Third, over the past forty years, particular ways of writing about television programs have become conventional, and TV critics often invoke Western culture's dominant strategy for evaluating popular fiction: reflection theory. They therefore tend to set a standard of "reality" for programs and characters whereby a program is "good" if it accurately reflects "reality" and if its characters are "real" or "true-to-life." And fourth, all press coverage, whether an unsolicited critical review or an industry plant, becomes what John Fiske refers to as "second-level" or "secondary" texts—part of the intertextual network that situates and influences future readings of the program itself (see note 26 below).

3. For more on poststructuralist feminism, see Introduction, note 13. For discussions and critiques of the taxonomy of feminisms employed here, see Alison M. Jaggar, *Feminist Politics and Human Nature* (Totowa, N.J.: Rowman and Allanheld, 1983); Katie King, "The Situation of Lesbianism as Feminism's Magical Sign: Contests for Meaning and the U.S. Women's Movement, 1968–1972," in *Communication* 9 (1987): 65–91.

4. Eileen Meehan, "Why We Don't Count: The Commodity Audience," in Patricia Mellencamp, ed., *Logics of Television: Essays in Cultural Criticism* (Bloomington: Indiana University Press, 1990), p. 129; Les Brown, *Television: The Business Behind the Box* (New York: Harcourt Brace Jovanovich, 1971), pp. 47–139; Todd Gitlin, *Inside Prime Time* (New York: Pantheon, 1983), pp. 203–20; Sally Bedell, *Up the Tube: Prime Time TV in the Silverman Years* (New York: Viking, 1981), pp. 31–104.

5. VHF means "very high frequency" and is distinguished from UHF, or "ultra high frequency." VHF stations produce stronger signals, which carry greater distances.

6. Jane Feuer, "Melodrama, Serial Form, and Television Today," *Screen* 25, no. 1 (1984): 15; Gitlin, *Inside Prime Time*, pp. 203–20. I am using the hybrid phrase "socially relevant" to describe the programs. See also Brown, *Television*; and Gitlin, *Inside Prime Time*.

7. CBS had attempted "relevant" programming in the early 1960s with *The Defenders* (1961–65), *The Nurses* (1962–65), and *East Side/West Side* (1963–64). But for a whole series of reasons, the practice did not "catch on." See U.S. Commission on Civil Rights, *Window Dressing on the Set: An Update* (Washington, D.C.: Government Printing Office, 1979), p. 2.

8. Lauren Rabinovitz, "Sitcoms and Single Moms: Representations of Feminism on American TV," *Cinema Journal* 29, no. 1 (Fall 1989): 3–19; Serafina Bathrick, "*The Mary Tyler Moore Show*: Women at Home and at Work," in Jane Feuer, Paul Kerr, and Tise Vahimagi, eds., *MTM: "Quality Television"* (London: British Film Institute, 1984), pp. 99–131; Bonnie J. Dow, "Hegemony, Feminist Criticism, and *The Mary Tyler Moore Show*," *Critical Studies in Mass Communication* 7 (Sept. 1990): 261–74; U.S. Commission on Civil Rights, *Window Dressing on the Set*, pp. 2, 3.

The overall history of television's representation of African American and other women of color is bleak. *Beulah* (1950–53), a situation comedy about a black maid in a white household, starred in succession two famous African American film actresses, Ethel Waters and Louise Beavers. (Hattie McDaniel had been slated to replace Waters but became ill.) When Beavers decided to leave and the show stopped production, the portrayal of black women on television virtually ceased until the late sixties, although Cicely Tyson played a secretary in *East Side/West Side* (1963–64). In 1968 *Julia*, influenced at least in part by the civil rights movement, starred Diahann Carroll as a widowed mother and a nurse. The depiction, although considered a "positive role" by the U.S. Commission on Civil Rights, was also criticized by black groups for "saccharine content and a distorted presentation of black family life" (see U.S. Commission on Civil Rights, *Window Dressing on the Set*, p. 1; Diana M. Meehan, *Ladies of the Evening: Women Characters of Prime-Time Television* [Metuchen, N.J.: Scarecrow Press, 1983], p. 157). *Star Trek* (1966–69) featured a black woman, Nichelle Nichols, in a supporting role as Lt. Uhura; and *Mannix* (1968–75) featured Gail Fisher as secretary Peggy Fair. In the 1970s, socially relevant sitcoms, primarily those of Norman Lear, reintroduced black characters to prime time.

After airing a number of comedies in the seventies that featured African American women (*The Jeffersons, Good Times, That's My Mama, What's Happening*, the short-lived *Baby, I'm Back*, and to some degree *Sanford and Son*), the networks decided to pull back on black programming, calling it financially too risky. They were reluctant to gamble that the majority-white audience would watch programs that starred black people (see Todd Gitlin, "Prime-Time Whitewash," *American Film* 9, no. 2 [Nov. 1983]: 36–38). *The Jeffersons*, featuring several black women, survived into the 1980s, and *Gimme a Break*, starring Nell Carter as a household manager/nanny for a white family, premiered in 1980. (*Benson*, about a black male household manager for a white governor, premiered in 1979. The other programs starring blacks were *Diff'rent Strokes* and *Webster*, both centering on young black boys adopted by white families.)

The runaway ratings success in 1984 of *The Cosby Show*, starring Bill Cosby, for a time put to rest the networks' fears about black programming and white audiences; Cosby's show also spawned a number of programs starring or featuring African American women. *Melba*, with Melba Moore, and *Charlie and Company*, which costarred Gladys Knight and featured Della Reese, are two examples of shows that did not make it past their first season. *227*, created by and starring Marla Gibbs (formerly of *The Jeffersons*), was one survivor of this burst of cloning; it not only featured a black woman as the main character but had several other black women as supporting characters and also represented the working class. *A Different World* joined the network schedule as a *Cosby* spinoff in 1987, and in the late eighties *Frank's Place*, *Family Matters*, *Fresh Prince of Bel Aire*, *Sugar and Spice*, and *Baghdad Café* also appeared. The early 1990s saw the addition of several new shows featuring African Americans (especially on the FOX network), but they continued to fall within the tradition of situation comedies.

The very few representations of Latina women included those in *9 to 5*, *AKA Pablo*, and occasionally *Chico and the Man*. Native American women occasionally appeared on *How the West Was Won*. A Japanese woman was featured on *The Courtship of Eddie's Father*, and Vietnamese women have appeared on *Night Court* and *China Beach*. Even the representation of white women has been very much homogenized. Since *The Goldbergs* (1949–54), starring Gertrude Berg, for example, Jewish women virtually disappeared from television until the character Rhoda was introduced on *The Mary Tyler Moore Show* in 1970.

9. Tartikoff is cited in Gitlin, *Inside Prime Time*, p. 72. Former Federal Communications Commissioner Nicholas Johnson corroborates Tartikoff's view and says that the "T & A" period was a direct response to pressures for the reduction of violence: The networks, impervious to the implications of sexism, replaced program violence with the displays of women's bodies (personal conversation, Madison, Wis., Feb. 1980).

10. *The Bionic Woman* is a program from this period in which a woman character, Jaime Sommers (played by Lindsay Wagner), is an active protagonist but is not cast in the extreme spectacle dimension of the other active women protagonists of the time.

11. Gitlin, *Inside Prime Time*, p. 73. See also Cathy Schwichtenberg, "*Charlie's Angels*: A Patriarchal Voice in Heaven," *Jump Cut*, no. 24/25 (1981): 13–16. In early 1950s television, women were sometimes showcased for their "spectacle" dimensions, such as dancers in variety programs.

Many women and women's groups protested the "spectacle" representations; the 18,000-member Association of Flight Attendants issued a statement about *Flying High* that said, "The script used every stereotype and cliché that has ever been used in a derogatory manner toward flight attendants. . . . We have worked so many years to dispel the mistaken image of flight attendants as sex goddesses and this program is a real setback in these efforts." In 1978 Kathleen Nolan, president of the Screen Actors' Guild, said, "Women . . . are desperately disheartened to be faced in 1978 with the disgraceful trash which is being transmitted in the guise that this is the American Woman" (U.S. Commission on Civil Rights, *Window Dressing on the Set*, pp. 5, 6).

12. Barbara Avedon, interview with author, Los Angeles, Calif., Feb. 1984; Barbara Corday, interview with author, Los Angeles, Calif., Feb. 1984; Barney Rosenzweig, interview with author, Los Angeles, Calif., Oct. 1983; Molly Haskell, *From Reverence to Rape: The Treatment of Women in the Movies* (New York: Holt, Rinehart and Winston, 1974).

13. Marjorie Rosen, "Cagney and Lacey," *Ms.*, Oct. 1981, pp. 47–50, 109.

14. Corday interview.

15. Ibid.

16. Rosen, "Cagney and Lacey," p. 49; Barbara Corday, "Dialogue on Film," *American Film* 10, no. 9 (July–Aug. 1985): 12; Avedon interview.

17. Rosen, "Cagney and Lacey," p. 49; Corday interview; Avedon interview.

18. Rosenzweig interview; Rosen, "Cagney and Lacey," p. 49; Avedon interview.

19. Rosen, "Cagney and Lacey," p. 49; Rosenzweig quoted in Lori Watson, "Women Get Buddy-Buddy in New Series," *Longmont Daily Times Call*, 3–4 Apr. 1982.

20. Rosen, "Cagney and Lacey," p. 49.

21. Ibid., p. 50; Corday, "Dialogue on Film," p. 2; Rosenzweig interview.

22. Rosenzweig interview; Avedon interview; Corday interview; Rosen, "Cagney and Lacey," p. 50. It is important, in examining the history of *Cagney and Lacey*, to consider the fact that Ted Post, an action director, was hired to direct the movie. As the series progressed, the "action" components of the scripts became almost totally subservient to the "interaction" components.

23. Sharon Rosenthal, "Cancellation of 'Cagney and Lacey' to Mean Loss of 'Rare' TV Series," *New York Daily News*, 3 June 1983.

24. Rosen, "Cagney and Lacey," p. 109. Some of the characteristics applauded by Rosen demonstrate the ways in which, at this particular point in the history of the American women's movement, advertising's definitions of women and those of the liberal women's movement could coexist without much trouble. Later in the 1980s it became harder to yoke together the discourses of the women's movement and advertising without encountering much conflict and contradiction. In the late 1970s and very early 1980s, the women's movement placed its greatest emphasis on equality in the labor force, primarily for white, heterosexual, middle-class women. But in the early 1980s, this emphasis began to shift to include women of color and lesbians.

25. *TV Guide*, 3–10 Oct. 1981, p. A-137.

26. V. N. Volosinov, quoted in Stuart Hall, "The Rediscovery of 'Ideology': Return of the Repressed in Media Studies," in Michael Gurevitch, Tony Bennett, James Curran, and Janet Woollacott, eds., *Culture, Society and the Media* (London: Methuen, 1982), p. 77; John Fiske, *Television Culture* (London: Methuen, 1987), pp. 84–85. See also Introduction, note 6. Fiske also describes a third-level or tertiary text, which is the discussion generated by viewers about the primary text or TV program itself.

Intertextuality refers to the "use of language that calls up a vast reserve of echoes from similar texts, similar phrasings, remarks, situations, characters" (Rosalind Coward and John Ellis, *Language and Materialism* [London: Routledge and Kegan Paul, 1977], p. 52). Intertextuality works to demonstrate both the multiplicity of meaning—its deferral onto and across many different texts—and also the ways that particular meanings, at particular historical moments, may "pile up" on one another and achieve a temporary discursive authority (Robert C. Allen, *Speaking of Soap Operas* [Chapel Hill: University of North Carolina Press, 1985], p. 61). See also Tony Bennett, "The Bond Phenomenon: Theorizing a Popular Hero," *Southern Review* 16, no. 2 (1983): 209, for a discussion of Pierre Machery's notion of "encrustation," which is also helpful here. See also Mimi White, "Television Genres: Intertextuality," *Journal of Film and Video* 38 (Summer 1985): 41–47, for a demonstration of the term as it applies to TV genres. Tony Bennett and Janet Woollacott use the term *inter-textuality* to refer to "the social organization of the relations between texts within specific conditions of reading" (*Bond and Beyond: The Political Career of a Popular Hero* [New York: Methuen, 1987], p. 45).

27. Barbara Basler, "Real Policewomen View the TV Variety," *New York Times*, 7 Oct.

1981; Howard Rosenberg, "'Cagney and (Uh) Lacey': A Question of a Pink Slip," *Los Angeles Times*, 23 June 1982, Calendar section.

28. Richard Turner, "The Curious Case of the Lady Cops and the Shots That Blew Them Away," *TV Guide*, 8–14 Oct. 1983, p. 52; "Gloria Gets Action," *Soho News*, 9 Mar. 1982.

29. "Meg Foster to Join Tyne Daly as CBS 'Cagney and Lacey' Duo," Filmways news release, 1982, Rosenzweig files; "Gloria Gets Action." Although Barbara Corday remained with the series as executive story consultant, Barbara Avedon left to pursue other writing projects.

30. Tom Bierbaum, "Steinem Takes Right Turn on TV Violence," *Daily Variety*, 2 Feb. 1982.

31. Bowden's Information Service, "Tyne Daly Returns to Detective Role," *The Leader Post*, 12 Mar. 1982; Barbara Holsopple, "Two New Series on Women: All Work, No Play," *Pittsburgh Press*, 25 Mar. 1982; Beverly Stephen, "Policewomen: TV Show on the Case," *Los Angeles Times*, 11 Apr. 1982; Bonnie Malleck, "Real Women at Last: Pinch-Hitter 'Cagney and Lacey' Is a Mid-Season Bonus," *Kitchner-Waterloo Record*, Apr. 1982.

32. Ed Bark, "Ratings May Kill Quality Cop Show," *Dallas Texas Morning News*, 1 Apr. 1982; Malleck, "Real Women at Last"; Bill Musselwhite, "No There's No Farm Raising Tiny Animals for Airlines," *Calgary Herald* (Alberta), 3 Apr. 1982.

33. The technique of mise-en-scène includes, among other things, the characters' body sizes, makeup, hairstyles, clothing, or costumes; character movement, gestures, and mannerisms; and use of props (see David Bordwell and Kristin Thompson, *Film Art: An Introduction*, 4th ed. [New York: McGraw-Hill, 1993], pp. 145–84).

34. Richard Hack, "TeleVisions," *The Hollywood Reporter*, 26 Mar. 1982; Musselwhite, "There's No Farm."

35. Turner, "Curious Case of the Lady Cops," p. 53; Rosenzweig interview; *TV Guide*, 3–10 Apr. 1982, pp. A-116–17. *Magnum, P.I.* was getting an average share of 38. When *Cagney and Lacey* aired, it pulled in a 25 share the first week and a 24 the second week. According to Rosenzweig, "At 9 o'clock all over America, 12 million people were getting up out of their seats *en masse* and walking away, or leaving the network."

36. Turner, "Curious Case of the Lady Cops," p. 54; Barbara Holsopple, "'Cagney and Lacey' Hanging by (Blond) Thread," *Pittsburgh Press*, 19 Nov. 1982, sec. B.

37. Turner, "Curious Case of the Lady Cops," p. 53. Harvey Shephard declined my requests for an interview.

38. "Itinerary for Tyne Daly and Meg Foster," public relations release from Brocato and Kelman, Inc., 27 Apr. 1982, Rosenzweig files.

39. Turner, "Curious Case of the Lady Cops," p. 54; Rosenzweig interview. After Meg Foster was released from her contract, she initially had difficulty getting other work. According to a United Feature syndicate article, before that time she "was an in-demand actress. But there was no official announcement of why she was fired, so people jumped to some pretty wild conclusions. . . . They want no part of a troublemaker." The article continues, "Later an official story came out and from then on Meg's offers picked up again" (Dick Kleiner, "TV Scout Sketch #1: Cagney and Lacey Situation, the Story behind Meg's

Ouster," week of 23 Aug. 1982, Rosenzweig files) Rosenzweig says he tried to save Foster's job by suggesting to CBS that they dye her hair blond (as a way of achieving character contrast with the also-brunette Daly). He admits, however, to giving in to the network rather quickly and making Foster the "scapegoat" in order to save the series (Rosenzweig interview). Foster later appeared as a district attorney on *The Trials of Rosie O'Neill*, starring Sharon Gless and produced by Barney Rosenzweig in the early 1990s.

40. Dave Kaufman, "CBS Ent Prez Grant Asks Crix for Fair Chance," *Daily Variety*, 25 May 1982; Richard Hack, "TeleVisions," *The Hollywood Reporter*, 28 May 1982, p. 6; Frank Swertlow, "CBS Alters 'Cagney,' Calling It 'Too Women's Lib,'" *TV Guide*, 12–18 June 1982, p. A-1.

41. Malleck, "Real Women at Last"; Alan W. Petrocelli, "Cagney and Lacey," *US*, 27 Apr. 1982, p. 46; Avedon interview. Meg Foster did not reply to my letters requesting an interview.

42. Jane Ardmore, "Who Is the Enemy?," draft of article for "Sunday Woman," 1982, Rosenzweig files; Sal Manna, "Cagney and Lacey on Trial," *Los Angeles Herald Examiner*, 22 Apr. 1982, sec. B.

43. My point here is that even though the programs presented "positive" portrayals of lesbians, the organizing principle of each story was that lesbianism is considered socially "deviant"—the point of the humor or drama.

44. Howard Rosenberg, "'Cagney and (Uh) Lacey.'"

45. Ibid., pp. 1, 7.

46. Rosenthal, "Cancellation of 'Cagney and Lacey'"; Holsopple, "'Cagney and Lacey' Hanging by (Blond) Thread."

47. Letters section, *TV Guide*, 10–16 June 1982, p. A-4.

48. Viewer letters, Rosenzweig files.

49. Frank Torrez, "TV Ratings," *Los Herald Examiner*, 2 July 1982; Sal Manna, "Sorry This Show Wasn't Seen," *Los Angeles Herald Examiner*, [1st week of July] 1982, sec. B.

50. Arnold Becker, quoted in Rosenberg, "'Cagney and (Uh) Lacey'"; John J. O'Connor, "'Cagney and Lacey'—Indisputably a Class Act," *The Patriot Ledger* (Quincy, Mass.), 5 July 1984; Tim Brooks and Earle Marsh, *The Complete Directory of Prime Time Network Television, 1946 to the Present*, 5th ed. (New York: Ballantine, 1992), p. 137. Although Corday and Avedon had wanted Sharon Gless for the part from the beginning, I found no evidence that Meg Foster was sacrificed in order to finally get Gless. Barbara Corday, however, contends that from the first time she saw Foster and Daly read a script together, she was sure they had made a mistake in casting. She recalls saying to Rosenzweig, "Oh, my God, this is a mistake." Corday believed that although Foster was a consummate actress, she played Cagney too much like Daly played Lacey. According to her, the Cagney part would have been played more upscale from the beginning of the series had not Foster inflected it with a more working-class interpretation (Corday interview).

51. Rick Du Brow, "Cagney and Lacey Hang Tough," *Los Angeles Herald Examiner*, 25 Jan. 1983, sec. C; "Analysis of Costs for CBS for 'Cagney and Lacey,'" prepared by *Cagney and Lacey* production offices, 1982, Rosenzweig files. Since the mid-1950s, advertisers had made it clear that they did not want their products associated with lower-class characters

and settings (see Erik Barnouw, *The Image Empire: A History of Broadcasting in the United States from 1953* [New York: Oxford University Press, 1970], pp. 5–8).

52. "Advertising and Promotion," from CBS Entertainment Division, 1982, Rosenzweig files.

53. "Review," *Daily Variety*, 28 Oct. 1982; Marilyn Preston, "If 'Cagney and Lacey' Fails, Other TV Women May Suffer," *Chicago Tribune*, 8 Nov. 1982; Howard Rosenberg, "The New Season," *Los Angeles Times*, 25 Oct. 1982, Calendar section.

54. Frank Torrez, " 'Cagney and Lacey' Has Integrity Intact," *Los Angeles Times*, 25 Oct. 1982, sec. D.

55. Gail Williams, "Review," *The Hollywood Reporter*, 1 Nov. 1982.

56. Carol Wyman, " 'Cagney and Lacey' Has Grown," *New Haven Register*, 24 Feb. 1983; Sharon Rosenthal, "Second-hand Roles Brought Actress Double Trouble," *New York Daily News* to the *Jacksonville (Florida) Times-Union*, 4 Nov. 1982, sec. E.

57. Candy Justice, "CBS Softens Show to Toughen Ratings," *Memphis (Tennessee) Scimitar*, 15 Nov. 1982.

58. Jim Butler, " 'Cagney and Lacey' Works Well," *Bryan (Texas) Eagle*, 7 Nov. 1982.

59. Michael Bandler, "Gless Is More," *American Way*, 22 Jan. 1985, p. 46.

60. Terrence O'Flaherty, "Women in the Line of Fire," *San Francisco Chronicle*, 11 Oct. 1983, sec. B; Gail Williams, "Review."

61. Viewer letters, Rosenzweig files.

62. Barbara Grizzuti Harrison, "I Didn't Think I Was Pretty: An Interview with Sharon Gless," *Parade Magazine*, 23 Feb. 1986, pp. 4–5. The word "readings" may be applied to film and televisual texts (programs) as well as to literary ones and emphasizes the particular ways in which individual viewers make sense of or interpret the text.

63. Caption for cover photo of Tyne Daly and Sharon Gless, *Los Angeles Herald Examiner*, 25 Jan. 1983; Du Brow, "Cagney and Lacey Hang Tough"; Elaine Warren, "Where Are the Real Women on TV?," *Los Angeles Herald Examiner*, 31 Oct. 1982, sec. E; Judy Mann, "Women on TV," *Washington Post*, 7 Jan. 1983; Laura Daltry, "Grandmother, What Big Role Models You Had!," *Los Angeles Times*, 28 Nov. 1982, Calendar section.

64. Larry Wood, " 'Cagney and Lacey' Doesn't Fit Policewoman Image," *Evansville Press*, 17 Nov. 1982.

65. Jerilyn Stapleton, personal interview with author, Feb. 1984, Los Angeles, Calif. The letter-writing campaign will be described in more detail in Chapter 2.

66. Such communities or networks (often based on exposure to similar cultural products such as films, TV programs, newspapers, magazines, novels, and so forth) give "participants" the language and analyses for articulating everyday life experiences. See Elizabeth Ellsworth, "Illicit Pleasures: Feminist Spectators and *Personal Best*," in Leslie G. Roman and Linda K. Christian-Smith with Elizabeth Ellsworth, eds., *Becoming Feminine: The Politics of Popular Culture* (Philadelphia, Pa.: Farmer Press, 1988), pp. 102–19; Jacqueline Bobo, " *The Color Purple*: Black Women as Cultural Readers," in E. Deidre Pribram, ed., *Female Spectators: Looking at Film and Television* (London: Verso, 1988), pp. 90–109.

67. The viewer letters quoted below were selected from correspondence in Barney Rosenzweig's files. See Introduction, note 18.

68. Gary Deeb, "Tube Watch," *Syracuse Post Standard,* 30 May 1983.

69. The *Sacramento Bee* used this phrase in printing a letter from Archie Brown, who was outraged at Deeb's column (date unknown, from Rosenzweig files).

70. Irene Baros-Johnson, letter to the editor, *Syracuse Standard Post,* 14 June 1983.

71. Terry Louise Fisher, interview with author, Feb. 1984. In April 1984, Susan McHenry wrote an article for *Ms.* about the revived show that discusses some of the history I have presented here ("The Rise and Fall—and Rise of TV's 'Cagney and Lacey,'" *Ms.,* Apr. 1984, pp. 23–25). See also Sue Reilly, "The Double Lives of Cagney and Lacey," *McCall's,* Apr. 1985, pp. 14, 20, 23; Mary Gordon, "Sharon Gless and Tyne Daly," *Ms.,* Jan. 1987, pp. 40, 41, 86–88.

72. Barney Rosenzweig, interview with author, Jan. 1984, Los Angeles, Calif.; Sharon Gless, interview with author, Mar. 1984, Los Angeles, Calif.

73. Judy Sabel, conversation with author, Feb. 1984, Los Angeles, Calif.; Rosenzweig interview, Oct. 1983; Joyce Sunila, "Are the Laceys Too Real for Television?," *Los Angeles Times,* Sunday Calendar section.

74. Personal observations, Feb. 1984; conversations with Eddie Barron, hairdresser for Tyne Daly, Feb. 1984, and with Tyne Daly, Mar. 1984, Los Angeles, Calif.

75. Personal observation, Feb. 1984; Avedon interview; Fisher interview; *60 Minutes,* CBS, Dec. 1984. According to Avedon, "sympathetic" means such things as showing women "in the kitchen"; to Terry Louise Fisher, it means showing them as "warm."

76. Karen Stabiner, "The Pregnant Detective," *New York Times Magazine,* 22 Sept. 1985, p. 104; Judith Michaelson, "Ironies in the Fired 'Cagney,'" *Los Angeles Times,* 14 Sept. 1983, Calendar section.

77. Mark Carlisle, "Cagney and Lacey Are Shaming the Men of America," *National Examiner,* 2 Apr. 1985, p. 21.

78. Bridget Smith, "*Cagney and Lacey,*" *Spare Rib,* no. 161 (Dec. 1985): 31. Another review, picking up from a different angle on some of the same contradictions as *Spare Rib,* described the representations as typically "Hollywood," emphasized the generally ludicrous character of police/crime genres, and saw Cagney and Lacey simply as female imports into the form. The protagonists, it said, were a "pair of female crime chasers who demonstrate that they can be just as dauntless, efficient, egotistical and generally silly as their male counterparts in Hollywood's Wonderful World of Crime" (O'Flaherty, "Women in the Line of Fire"). And a British reviewer said, "The hard-hittin', handbag-swinging New York police toughettes return to spit, bite and claw their way through TV's idea of the all-American criminal underworld" (Sarah Bond, "Tonight's Choice," 25 Sept. 1983, newspaper unknown, Rosenzweig files).

79. Exploitation topics use sensational—usually sexual or violent—subject material in order to attract an audience.

80. Sweep periods are times (usually one month, three times a year) during which the ratings companies survey all the television markets in the United States; this is when local stations get rated. Networks and affiliates usually engage in a practice called "hypoing" during the sweeps: they promote shows heavily and tend to air high-budget miniseries and "exploitation" programming.

81. Carol Cancila, "Cop Show Focuses on Breast Cancer," *American Medical News*, 8 Feb. 1985, pp. 2, 47.

82. Michael Ryan, "A Method in the Madness," *People*, 11 Feb. 1985, p. 96.

83. Kathryn C. Montgomery, *Target Prime Time: Advocacy Groups and the Struggle over Entertainment Television* (Oxford: Oxford University Press, 1989), pp. 201–15. Most of the direct pressure on the series in the instances I have discussed came from CBS programming executives. The activities of the Program Practices Department (the network "censors," called Standards and Practices at other networks) were less overt and consisted mostly of regular letters to the producers following the evaluations of scripts and script revisions. These letters delineated areas of concern, including language, wardrobe and sexuality, police procedures, commercial identification, and ethnic portrayals. Some of their aims were toning down obscenities; being sure, for example, that "Mary Beth's nightgown will not be unduly revealing"; certifying that most police actions were in accord with Los Angeles Police Department specifications; ensuring that the brand names of products were not identifiable; and preventing ethnic slurs. But at other times, as the example of "The Clinic" demonstrates, the Program Practices Department was a more active "censor" of the series (examples in letter from Christopher Davidson to Barney Rosenzweig, 12 Feb. 1982, Rosenzweig files).

84. Montgomery, *Target Prime Time*, p. 215; "An Episode of 'Cagney' under Fire on Abortion," Associated Press release, *New York Times*, 11 Nov. 1985.

85. CBS vice-president George Schweitzer, quoted in Nancy Hellmich, "Daly Defends 'Cagney' Show on Abortion," *USA Today*, 6 Nov. 1985, sec. D; NRLC president John Wilke, on *MacNeil/Lehrer News Hour*, PBS, 8 Nov. 1985.

86. Hellmich, "Daly Defends 'Cagney' Show on Abortion"; *MacNeil/Lehrer News Hour*, PBS, 8 Nov. 1985.

87. Judy Mann, "Cagney and Lacey, and Abortion," *Washington Post*, 15 Nov. 1985; Hellmich, "Daly Defends 'Cagney' Show on Abortion."

88. Celeste Michelle Condit, "The Rhetorical Limits of Polysemy," *Critical Studies in Mass Communication* 6, no. 2 (June 1989): 118.

89. Also, 12 April 1984 was declared Cagney and Lacey Day by Marion Barry, mayor of Washington, D.C., and by the Commission on Working Women.

90. Serita D. Stevens, *Cagney and Lacey* (New York: Dell, 1985); *Ms.*, Jan. 1987, cover; Gordon, "Sharon Gless and Tyne Daly," pp. 40, 41, 86–88. See also *Channels* 6, no. 6 (Oct. 1986): 39–59, esp. William A. Henry III, "*Cagney and Lacey*: No Copping Out," pp. 52–53.

CHAPTER TWO

1. Annette Kuhn calls this the "social audience," which she contrasts to the "spectator." "Social audience" assumes the a priori construction of gender (i.e., when a female viewer sits down to watch a TV program, she is *already* gendered). "Spectator" signals the fact that gender (as well as other human aspects) is partly constituted in and by the relationships of texts to viewers. Put another way, TV programs participate in the ongoing constitution of

gender in their spectators (Kuhn, "Women's Genres," in Christine Gledhill, ed., *Home Is Where the Heart Is: Studies in Melodrama and the Woman's Film* [London: British Film Institute, 1987], pp. 339–49). Chapter 5 deals with these concepts in more detail.

2. Charlotte Brunsdon, "*Crossroads*: Notes on a Soap Opera," in E. Ann Kaplan, ed., *Regarding Television: Critical Approaches—an Anthology* (Frederick, Md.: American Film Institute, 1983), pp. 76–83. Brunsdon refers to this connection as the "interplay of social reader and social text" (p. 77).

3. For another slant on this process, see Ien Ang, *Desperately Seeking the Audience* (London: Routledge, 1991), p. 41.

4. I use the word *promise* here to convey that when networks sell the Nielsen audience numbers to their advertisers, they are in effect promising those advertisers more viewers/ consumers (who, the networks and the ratings services claim, are "represented" by those numbers).

5. Dallas Smythe, "Communications: Blindspot of Western Marxism," *Canadian Journal of Political and Social Theory* 1, no. 3 (Fall 1977): 6. Smythe's article generated intense debate and criticism in the field. It was especially criticized for its economistic and unidimensional approach. Articles constituting the debate are Graham Murdock, "Blindspots about Western Marxism," ibid. 2, no. 2 (Spring/Summer 1978): 109–19; Smythe, "Rejoinder to Graham Murdock," ibid. 2, no. 2 (Spring/Summer 1978): 120–27; Bill Livant, "The Audience Commodity: On the 'Blindspot' Debate," ibid. 3, no. 1 (Winter 1979): 91–106; Sut Jhally, "Probing the Blindspot: The Audience Commodity," ibid. 6, nos. 1–2 (Winter/Spring 1982): 204–10; Livant, "Working at Watching: A Reply to Sut Jhally," ibid. 6, nos. 1–2 (Winter/Spring 1982): 211–15.

6. Eileen Meehan, "Why We Don't Count: The Commodity Audience," in Patricia Mellencamp, ed., *Logics of Television: Essays in Cultural Criticism* (Bloomington: Indiana University Press, 1990), pp. 117–37.

7. As early as the mid-fifties, television advertisers made it clear that they wanted their products associated only with upscale, noncontroversial programming and with "good-looking" characters and settings (see Erik Barnouw, *The Image Empire: A History of Broadcasting in the United States from 1953* [New York: Oxford University Press, 1970], pp. 5–8, 32–33). There have been programs featuring working-class characters—for example, *All in the Family, Good Times, Chico and the Man*, and *Roseanne*—but they have been few and far between.

8. One of the first successful advertising campaigns on television was that of Hazel Bishop lipstick. In 1950, before its TV campaign, the company was doing $50,000 in annual business; in 1952, after its television ads aired, sales climbed to $4,500,000 and continued upward. The Hazel Bishop "success story" was held up as an incentive for other advertisers to try the new ad forum, and TV rapidly developed as a medium for reaching an enormous sector of the women's market. Recurrent ads in *Advertising Age* in 1953, which also urged advertisers to try TV, featured a picture of a woman carrying a shopping bag loaded with products. The accompanying copy read, "She's Our Mighty Big Little Purchasing Agent" (Barnouw, *Image Empire*, p. 6; *Advertising Age*, many issues, 1953).

Car commercials may advertise "family" cars, in the selection of which women are considered to have the determining vote, or, since the late 1970s, they may target cars at the new "working women's market." They may also continue a tradition of automobile advertising, pioneered by Henry Ford in the 1920s, in which car campaigns are generally pitched to women even though men may actually buy the car (see Julie Chandler, "Ads for Women in Motion," *Advertising Age*, 26 July 1982, p. M-38).

Eileen Meehan, as mentioned above, stresses that what the networks actually sell the advertisers is the commoditized numbers only, and although I agree with her distinction, I am adding that the numbers carry with them the "promise" of millions of "real" consumers.

9. As its name implies, the target audience is the specific audience group that advertisers want to reach during a particular time of day or a particular historical period; this audience is basically defined by the demographics of age, sex, and income. All such target audiences need to be pinpointed by a ratings service like Arbitron or Nielsen.

10. Susan Horowitz, "Sitcom Domesticus," *Channels*, Sept./Oct. 1984, p. 22.

The Family Viewing Hour, which was introduced in the 1975–76 season, was a major factor in fragmenting prime-time viewing and changing the importance of women to the prime-time schedule. Instituted as a self-regulation measure by the National Association of Broadcasters (NAB) code, it required that the first hour of prime time be "free of themes that might be objectionable for child viewers" (see Muriel Cantor, *Prime-Time Television: Content and Control* [Beverly Hills, Calif.: Sage, 1980], p. 50). The measure was proposed and adopted by the networks in an effort to ward off regulatory agency interference in prime-time programming, which had, in the mid-seventies, been criticized for its violent content. Devoting a portion of prime time to programs unobjectionable for children promoted the production of child- and teen-oriented programs and stimulated the courting of this market by advertisers. Although the Family Viewing Hour (and the NAB code) are no longer legally operative, the practice in effect continues.

The introduction of nighttime sporting events such as ABC's *Monday Night Football* was another factor that contributed to the fragmentation of the prime-time audience—this time along gender lines. And the presence of multiple sets in a large percentage of U.S. homes added to this trend by allowing for a greater diversity of program viewing by different household members.

11. Jane Feuer, in a study of MTM Enterprises, has linked the notion of "quality audiences" to that of "quality programming." She claims that the TV and advertising industries' quest for an upscale, urban-minded audience in the 1970s made possible the emergence of an independent production company whose output was characterized by programs designed to reach this very audience. Feuer and her coauthors' characterization of MTM programming as "quality" in the sense of sophisticated has met with criticism. The general concept, however, is a useful and productive one, especially if the notion of "quality programming" is simply taken to mean programming designed by the industry with its particular quality audience in mind—and designed to provide advertisers with a rationale for programs that do not necessarily secure large gross numbers. See Jane Feuer, Paul Kerr, and Tise Vahimagi, eds., *MTM: "Quality Television"* (London: British Film Institute, 1984).

The Nielsen Company charts women in the following age clusters: 18–34, 18–49, 25–54, 35–64, and 55+. Since the late seventies and early eighties, it has been unclear which age groups actually spend the most. In the eighties, the 25- to 64-year-old group interested CBS and some advertisers, who felt that the buying power of people between 49 and 64 had been underestimated (see Karen Stabiner, "The Pregnant Detective," *New York Times Magazine*, 22 Sept. 1985, p. 103; and James Forkan, "Women Checking Out HOTEL," *Advertising Age*, 14 Nov. 1983, p. 10).

12. The production companies could argue this to the networks, and the networks could argue it to the advertisers. The networks, however, always feel more secure if a program draws in a number of "quality audiences" at the same time. *Cagney and Lacey's* place in the TV schedule would have been far less precarious had it managed to do so.

13. The period from the mid-1960s to the early 1980s was one of fundamental economic and social change for many women in the United States. During this time, the percentage of working women increased from 33 percent to 52 percent. The 1970s encompassed a decade of especially significant change that opened with about 31 million women (or 43 percent of all U.S. women sixteen years and older) in the labor force and ended with 43 million working women. The increase accounted for 60 percent of the growth of the entire U.S. labor force. The magnitude of these changes is underscored by the following comparative statistics: In 1981, 58 percent of all mothers with children under eighteen had jobs, compared with 28 percent in 1950 and 9 percent in 1940. The period was also one of great change in the area of education: In 1960, women received one-third of all bachelor's degrees; in 1980, the percentage had risen to nearly 50 percent; and in 1982, 54 percent of all undergraduates were women. See Laurie Ashcraft, "Ads Start to Roll with the Social Punches," *Advertising Age*, 26 July 1982, p. M-24; Lori Kesler, "Behind the Wheel of a Quiet Revolution," ibid., pp. M-11, M-12.

14. Elizabeth Nickles, "The Newest Mass Market: Women Go-Getters," *Advertising Age*, 9 Nov. 1981, p. 56.

15. Tina Santi, "The New Woman Market Is Here: How Do You Market to Her?," *Advertising Age*, 18 June 1979, p. 61.

16. Kate Lloyd Rand, "Stereotypes Don't Pay Today," *Advertising Age*, 26 July 1982, p. M-14.

17. Nickles, "The Newest Mass Market" (quotes); Elizabeth Nickles with Laura Ashcraft, *The Coming Matriarchy: How Women Will Gain the Balance of Power* (New York: Seaview Books, 1981); Rena Bartos, *The Moving Target: What Every Marketer Should Know about Women* (New York: Free Press, 1981). Two articles in *Advertising Age* discuss Nickles's and Bartos's books (Jennifer Alter, "Working Women 'Neglected' Study," *Advertising Age*, 4 May 1981, p. 50; Mary McCabe English, "A Cut above the Slice-of-Life Ads," ibid., 3 Oct. 1982, pp. M-9, M-11).

18. Some of the ads produced during this period, especially those portraying super-women who have high-powered careers and also deftly juggle the roles of mother, wife, and homemaker, provoked various responses, first of guilt and then of hostility, from readers and viewers. Advertisers countered by toning down the images, especially those of so-called "super-moms." This audience response illustrates how cultural texts have the

power to define femininity for readers and viewers—some women felt initial guilt that they did not measure up to the ideal "new woman"—but also demonstrates equally well that audience members are active in their reception and indeed do discriminate among discourses—they contested the ads and protested their implications.

19. Advertising's appeal to and construction of the upscale, professional segment of the working women's market may have, if only indirectly, influenced CBS's dissatisfaction with the representation of a lower-class, "street" Cagney and led to the subsequent changes in the character's class and appearance.

20. Harry Waters with David T. Friendly and George Hackett, "A Sex Change in Prime Time," *Newsweek*, 10 Jan. 1983, p. 75; Walter Karp, "What Do Women Want?," *Channels*, Sept./Oct. 1984, pp. 17–19; Alexis Greene, "What Do Women Want?," *American Film* 9, no. 5 (Mar. 1984): 61–63; Jodi Beckman, "From the Old . . .", *Advertising Age*, 26 July 1982, p. M-30; Cecilia Lentani, ". . . To the New," ibid.; Sara Stern, "Working to Meet Women's Multiple Roles," ibid., 3 Oct. 1985, p. 50.

21. Diane Mermigas, "It's 9:00 A.M.: Where Are America's Wives and Mothers?," *Advertising Age*, 3 Oct. 1983, pp. M-27–29; Judith Shandles, "A Forum for the Woman Next Door," ibid., pp. M-29–30; Charline Allen, "Radio Listens to an Increasingly Female Audience," ibid., pp. M-31–32.

22. Charlotte Brunsdon, "A Subject for the Seventies . . ." *Screen* 23, no. 3/4 (Sept./Oct. 1982): 22–28; Molly Haskell, "Women in the Movies Grow Up," *Psychology Today*, Jan. 1983, pp. 18–27; Richard Schickel, "Something's Missing in Hollywood," *Esquire*, June 1983, pp. 119–24; Roger Ebert and Gene Siskel, "For Celluloid Women, a Golden Age Ends," *Advertising Age*, 3 Oct. 1983, pp. M-22, M-26.

23. The episode in which Maude gets an abortion is particularly noteworthy.

24. Bob March, "Working Moms Trigger Late Night TV Shifts," *Advertising Age*, 8 Oct. 1979, p. 50; James Traub, "The World According to Nielsen," *Channels*, Jan./Feb. 1985, p. 70; Waters et al., "A Sex Change in Prime Time," pp. 72–75; conversation with David Woolfson, vice-president for business development, A. C. Nielsen Company, Mar. 1992.

25. Traub, "The World According to Nielsen," p. 70; Waters et al., "A Sex Change in Prime Time," p. 72; Colby Coates, "CBS Sweeps Key Women's Demographics," *Advertising Age*, 26 Jan. 1981, p. 79.

26. Waters et al., "A Sex Change in Prime Time," p. 72. Patricia Zimmerman makes the point that, even though the phenomenon of older women in prime time may be heavily motivated by target audience considerations, reference to advertising influences cannot replace textual analysis. It cannot, for example, account for *how* older women are represented in the narratives ("Good Girls, Bad Women: The Older Woman as Plot Point in Prime Time Soap Operas," paper presented at the Third International Conference on Television Drama, Michigan State University, 1983).

27. Meehan, "Why We Don't Count." I don't mean to assert that there is no correlation between ratings and audience "tastes," although Eileen Meehan certainly argues that point. However this relationship is much more complex than the industry allows, and the tortured history of innovative programs (many of which, when given enough time, have

gone on to be ratings "winners") clearly testifies to that complexity. For other discussions of this issue, see Ang, *Desperately Seeking the Audience*, p. 61.

28. For example, CBS's 1982 experience with Kimberly-Clark, Vidal Sassoon, Incorporated, and *Lou Grant* demonstrates that advertisers are wary of associating their goods with any program or figure (in this case the politically active Edward Asner) that is publicly controversial. Kimberly-Clark pulled its commercials from the series, and the president of Vidal Sassoon wrote to CBS, "We do not wish to have our products suffer because of an unfortunate association with a political issue" (Todd Gitlin, *Inside Prime Time* [New York: Pantheon, 1983], pp. 3–6). *Heartbeat, thirtysomething,* and *L.A. Law* all had trouble with networks and sponsors when religious groups protested episodes featuring lesbian and gay characters and story lines.

29. Whereas one of the ways a network makes money is by selling the audience commodity to advertisers in the first run of TV programs, the independent production company makes money on the sale of those programs in rerun or syndication, and therefore it wants to keep a series on the air as long as possible to ensure a profitable syndication venture. But often it has been the independent production companies that have taken creative risks and demonstrated that they can attract a smaller, more lucrative quality audience to the screen with innovative rather than formulaic programs.

30. Lori Watson, "Women Get Buddy-Buddy in New Series," *Longmont Daily Times Call,* 3–4 Apr. 1982, p. 17. As we saw in the previous chapter, Avedon, Corday, and Rosenzweig had originated the idea for *Cagney and Lacey* within the discourses of the liberal women's movement. As the property developed into a made-for-TV movie and a TV series, other members of the staff, such as coproducer P. K. (Patricia) Knelman, producer-writer Terry Louise Fisher, and actresses Meg Foster, Tyne Daly, and Sharon Gless, also spoke of the series in women's movement terms.

31. Rosenzweig and Arthur Krim, president of Orion Pictures, were negotiating about a *Cagney and Lacey* motion picture for theatrical release. Metromedia had offered to produce 20 episodes of the series for cable, but Rosenzweig declined because the package was too small.

32. See John Fiske, *Television Culture* (London: Methuen, 1987), pp. 314–19. Fiske draws on Pierre Bourdieu, "The Aristocracy of Culture," *Media, Culture, and Society* 2 (1980): 225–54.

33. Marjorie Rosen, "Cagney and Lacey," *Ms.,* Oct. 1981, p. 109; *Soho News,* 9 Mar. 1982; Sharon Rosenthal, "Cancellation of 'Cagney and Lacey' to Mean Loss of Rare TV Series," *New York Daily News,* 3 June 1983.

34. Beverly Stephen, "Policewomen: TV Show on the Case," *Los Angeles Times,* 11 Apr. 1982.

35. *Magnum, P.I.,* of course, drew a large women's audience. The scheduling of *Cagney and Lacey* after *Magnum,* however, seemed more of an attempt to offer the new program a good lead-in (with an already large audience) than it was a specific and concerted attempt to go after the working women's audience. In the Sunday night slot, the program got a 36 share and ranked number 7 in the overall ratings.

36. For articles on the "ladies' night line-up," see Ella Taylor, "Ladies' Night: CBS' Monday Night Mystique," *Village Voice*, 3 Dec. 1985, pp. 55–56; Pat Dowell, "Ladies' Night," *American Film* 10, no. 4 (Jan./Feb. 1985): 44–49. The working women's block will be delineated later in this chapter.

37. CBS promotional schedule, Oct. 1982, Rosenzweig files; Barney Rosenzweig quoted in *Daily Variety*, date unknown, ibid.

38. "*Cagney and Lacey*: Commercial Allocation," 4 Mar., 29 Oct., 27 Dec. 1982, Rosenzweig files.

39. During the 1970s, for example, the National Organization for Women listed yearly the ten advertisements it considered most derogatory to women and urged women to protest both the advertiser and the agency that produced the ad (S. Watson Dunn and Arnold Barban, *Advertising: Its Role in Modern Marketing* [Dryden Press, 1982], p. 90).

40. *Cagney and Lacey* had several publicity firms in its first few years as a series: Hanson and Schwam, Brocato and Kelman, and Rogers and Cowan.

41. Women working on police forces and as police detectives were, of course, "professional women" and were, comparatively speaking, well paid during these years, but my point is they did not fit in with the *image* of "the pretty vp swing along in a tailored suit and string tie" that the advertising industry was constructing at the period.

42. Rogers and Cowan to Orion Television, 8 Sept. 1982, Rosenzweig files.

43. The opening credits for the Foster/Daly series show the characters in uniforms. In the Gless/Daly opening credits, on the other hand, the characters are in streetclothes, and they appear in uniform only a couple of times in series episodes.

44. Rogers and Cowan to Barney Rosenzweig, 12 Oct. 1982, Rosenzweig files.

45. Rogers and Cowan to Orion Television, 8 Sept. 1982, ibid.

46. Ibid.

47. Rogers and Cowan to Barney Rosenzweig, 12 Oct. 1982, ibid.

48. Ibid.

49. Ibid.

50. Rogers and Cowan to Orion Television, 8 Sept. 1982, Rosenzweig files.

51. Rogers and Cowan, letter to national women's groups, 20 Oct. 1982, ibid.

52. Ibid.

53. Rogers and Cowan to Orion Television, 8 Sept. 1982, Rosenzweig files.

54. Patricia Bosworth, "The Arts: TV/Movies/Books," *Working Woman*, Nov. 1982, p. 214.

55. Rogers and Cowan was not acting in direct opposition to the network but simply according to its own strategies for gathering an audience of working women.

56. The cost of this effort was at least $100,000. See Elaine Woo, "Cagney and Lacey Fight for Survival," *Los Angeles Herald Examiner*, 17 Apr. 1983, sec. E; Rogers and Cowan to Barney Rosenzweig, 9 Apr. 1983, Rosenzweig files.

57. Tyne Daly quoted in Ev Skehan, "TV Star in Search of New Series," *Worcester Evening Gazette*, 18 Apr. 1983.

58. Susan Brower, "TV 'Trash' & 'Treasure': Marketing *Dallas* & *Cagney and Lacey*,"

Wide Angle 11, no. 1 (1989): 24–30. Plans for the publicity event are described in Rogers and Cowan to Barney Rosenzweig, 9 Apr. 1983, Rosenzweig files.

59. Rogers and Cowan, "An Open Letter from Sharon Gless and Tyne Daly," 25 Apr. 1983, Rosenzweig files.

60. Jerilyn Stapleton, "Cagney, Lacey: On the Block," *NOW L.A.*, May 1983, p. 13.

61. Richard Turner, "The Curious Case of the Lady Cops and the Shots That Blew Them Away," *TV Guide*, 8–14 Oct. 1983, p. 52.

62. CBS Print Department, memo to Barney Rosenzweig, 1 Apr. 1983, Rosenzweig files; *TV Guide*, 30 Apr.–6 May 1983, p. A-75 (other *TV Guide* ads for the series had small exploitation inserts in an otherwise nonexploitation ad); Jerry McNeely (TV producer/ writer/director), interview with author, Los Angeles, Calif., Feb. 1984.

63. Orion Pictures Company, interoffice memo, 27 Apr. 1983, Rosenzweig files.

64. Harvey Shephard quoted in Sal Manna, "Cagney and Lacey on Trial," *Los Angeles Herald Examiner*, 22 Apr. 1982, sec. B; Lee Margulies, "Campaign to Save Cagney and Lacey," *Los Angeles Times*, 20 July 1983; Turner, "Curious Case of the Lady Cops"; Tom Carson, "Police Persons," *Village Voice*, 3 Apr. 1984, p. 63; Tyne Daly quoted in Terry Ann Knopf, "Cagney and Lacey: Female Cops on Probation," *The Patriot Ledger* (Quincy, Mass.), 20 Apr. 1983.

65. Mark Lorando, "If Charlie's Angels Moved to Hill Street," *The Times-Picayune*, 20 Mar. 1983, "TV Focus"; Elaine Warren, "Where Are the Real Women on TV?," *Los Angeles Herald Examiner*, 31 Oct. 1982, sec. E.

66. Rick Du Brow, "*Cagney and Lacey*: The Reasons for Its Reappearance," *Los Angeles Herald Examiner*, 7 Dec. 1983; Barney Rosenzweig to viewer, 15 Apr. 1983, Rosenzweig files.

67. Barney Rosenzweig, form letter to viewers, May 1983, Rosenzweig files.

68. Margulies, "Campaign to Save Cagney and Lacey"; John J. O'Connor, "TV View," *New York Times*, 24 July 1983. At least four newsletters were distributed.

69. Elizabeth Ellsworth, "Illicit Pleasures: Feminist Spectators and *Personal Best*," in Leslie G. Roman and Linda K. Christian-Smith with Elizabeth Ellsworth, eds., *Becoming Feminine: The Politics of Popular Culture* (Philadelphia, Pa.: Falmer Press, 1988), pp. 102–19; Jacqueline Bobo, "*The Color Purple*: Black Women as Cultural Readers," in E. Deidre Pribram, ed., *Female Spectators: Looking at Film and Television* (London: Verso, 1988), pp. 90–109. The viewer letters quoted below were selected from correspondence in Barney Rosenzweig's files. See Introduction, note 18.

70. *Joanie Loves Chachi*, starring Scott Baio and Erin Moran, was a short-lived, preteen- and teenager-oriented spinoff from *Happy Days*.

71. See Beverley Alcock, "New York's Finest," *Spare Rib*, no. 186 (Jan. 1988): 24.

72. Viewer letter, Rosenzweig files. See also note 28 above.

73. Ellsworth, "Illicit Pleasures," p. 106.

74. In view of recent television studies that emphasize the semiotic power of the audience, these particular events provide a good example of such semiotic power actually taking on a social and material form.

75. See Turner, "Curious Case of the Lady Cops"; Gail Shister, "Boston Radio-Station

Owner Expected to Buy WWDB-FM," *Inquirer*, 25 Aug. 1983. Also, as another columnist wrote, "Tom Wyman (CBS' top honcho) [CBS chairman] is a fan of the show and when it was cancelled, he demanded an explanation of why it wasn't on the fall schedule" (George Maksian, " 'Cagney and Lacey' to Come Full Circle as Film," *New York Daily News*, 25 Aug. 1983). Rosenbloom committed the independent production company to its survival (in the same way that MTM Enterprises stood behind many of its "quality" programs that started out with shaky ratings).

76. *National NOW Times*, May–June 1984, p. 12; Kathy Bonk, "CAGNEY AND LACEY—Fate in CBS Hands Once Again," ibid., Apr. 1987, p. 5.

77. Du Brow, "*Cagney and Lacey*"; David Poltrack quoted in Fred Rothenberg, "Cagney and Lacey to Return," *Jackson Citizen Patriot*, 9 Feb. 1984, sec. B.

78. Stabiner, "The Pregnant Detective," p. 103.

79. Bill Dunlap, "Cagney and Lacey Put Badges on Line," *Broadcast Week*, 18 Apr. 1983, p. 24; Stabiner, "The Pregnant Detective," p. 103. The program's ratings and share averages were compiled and provided by Terri Luke of Nielsen Media Research. Information for 1987–88 was furnished by David Woolfson of the A. C. Nielsen Company.

80. Richard Turner, "CAGNEY Elbowed by WEST 57th—May Not Return," *TV Guide*, 4–10 Apr. 1987, p. A-3; Joseph Turow, *Media Systems in Society: Understanding Industries, Strategies, and Power* (New York: Longman, 1992), p. 91. Despite the fact that *Cagney and Lacey* did not inspire clones (with the exception of the short-lived, high-on-glamour *Partners in Crime* and the also short-lived *Code Name: Foxfire*), its presence and prestige most likely influenced the appearance of such working women–targeted, women-led programs as *Kate and Allie*, *Murder She Wrote*, *The Golden Girls*, *Designing Women*, *Heartbeat*, *China Beach*, *Murphy Brown*, and *The Trials of Rosie O'Neill*.

81. This area needs to be examined in more detail, because the push for quality audiences has allowed for a number of departures from conventional upscale characters, story lines, and mise-en-scène.

82. Ang, *Desperately Seeking the Audience*, p. 163.

CHAPTER THREE

1. John Fiske, *Television Culture* (London: Methuen, 1987), pp. 179–213, 216. Fiske refers to *Cagney and Lacey* as a mixture of "masculine" and "feminine" forms. According to him, masculine forms are "texts structured to produce greater narrative and ideological closure," whereas feminine forms are more open (more polysemic) and often present disruption without resolution. Although I have not adopted Fiske's notion of feminine and masculine forms, I do refer to *Cagney and Lacey* as a mixed form. Susan Brower also speaks of the program as a "generic hybrid" ("TV 'Trash' & 'Treasure': Marketing *Dallas* & *Cagney and Lacey*," *Wide Angle* 11, no. 1 (1989): 28).

As will become clearer in this and the following chapters, I use *women's form* and *women's program* to designate programs directed toward female audiences and involving subject matter and narrative structures that have become conventionally associated with women.

For a discussion of how the program incorporates elements of soap opera, see Beverley Alcock and Jocelyn Robson, "*Cagney and Lacey* Revisited," *Feminist Review*, no. 35 (Summer 1990): 45.

2. For the ways different readings "animate" different discourses of a text, see Christine Gledhill, "Pleasurable Negotiations," in E. Deidre Pribram, ed., *Female Spectators: Looking at Film and Television* (London: Verso, 1988), pp. 75–87.

3. Gaye Tuchman, "The Symbolic Annihilation of Women by the Mass Media," in Gaye Tuchman, Arlene Kaplan Daniels, and James Benét, eds., *Hearth and Home: Images of Women in the Mass Media* (New York: Oxford University Press, 1978), p. 11; U.S. Commission on Civil Rights, *Window Dressing on the Set: An Update* (Washington, D.C.: Government Printing Office, 1979), p. 9.

4. We must, of course, look both at the multiplicity involved in the representations of women in prime-time dramas and at the variety of interpretations they receive from women viewers. A "sexually excessive," "evil" woman such as Alexis (Joan Collins) in *Dynasty*, for example, may be interpreted by women viewers as a subversive character in a narrative that otherwise tries to domesticate and harness women's sexuality. Similarly, *Falcon Crest*'s Angela Channing (Jane Wyman), whose power in the public sphere causes her to be portrayed as a witch or "bitch," may also be read by women the way Tania Modleski interprets the daytime soap opera villainess. Angela Channing, in this reading, could offer great pleasure for women, because fictional engagement with her character provides vicarious revenge on a social order that represses women's power and sexuality. See Tania Modleski, *Loving with a Vengeance: Mass-Produced Fantasies for Women* (Hamden, Conn.: Archon Books, 1982), pp. 94–97; Janey Place, "Women in Film Noir," in E. Ann Kaplan, ed., *Women in Film Noir* (London: British Film Institute, 1980), p. 54.

Although women, as actresses and as active narrative subjects, have been very much absent from prime-time drama (especially before the mid-seventies), they have often been the stars and subjects of situation comedies. And in the history of women and sitcoms, inconsistencies, contradictions, and multiple readings are the rule. Three of early television's most popular programs were comedies that starred women. These series were *Mama*, about Norwegian immigrants living in San Francisco (considered to be the prototype of the TV domestic comedy or comedy/drama); *The Goldbergs*, about a New York Jewish family; and *Beulah*, about a black maid in a white household. They ran from 1949 to 1956 and together were a remarkable mixture of sexist, ethnic, and racist stereotypes. They positioned women well within the private, domestic sphere; two of the women were quintessential mothers, and one was a maid who served as "mother" to a white, middle-class household. However, the programs did represent a racial, ethnic, and age diversity that disappeared from television as the fifties and sixties progressed. They also displayed women as popular protagonists and active narrative subjects.

Comedies about single working women were also visible during television's early years— preceding, I would argue, the advertising industry's concerted targeting of the "upwardly mobile" middle-class family; these programs included *My Friend Irma* (1952–54), *Private Secretary* (1953–57), and *Our Miss Brooks* (1952–56). In the late fifties, working women sitcoms disappeared in favor of family sitcoms such as *Ozzie and Harriet, Father Knows*

Best, and *Leave It to Beaver*, which were themselves succeeded in the sixties by couples-oriented and fantasy comedies such as *The Dick Van Dyke Show, Pete and Gladys, I Dream of Jeannie*, and *Bewitched*. The single-working-women sitcoms did not reappear until the 1970s, with *The Mary Tyler Moore Show* and several other comedies spawned by TV's quest for the urban audience and for "relevance."

There are a number of inconsistencies and multiple meanings associated with the sitcom form. Even though women may be stars and subjects of situation comedies, their traditional limitation to a genre largely rooted in private domestic space may be seen as a confirmation that women's place and sexuality are viewed as domestic commodities. It also demonstrates both the constraints on women actresses and the circumscribed meanings of femininity: Women are portrayed primarily as dizzy housewives, dumb bunglers, crazy clowns, conniving secretaries, and zany, scatterbrained schemers. But as Patricia Mellen-camp suggests, the comedy of someone like Lucille Ball can provide a brilliant and delightful critique of women's confinement to the private sphere: Lucy is constantly trying to get out of the house and into show biz ("Situation Comedy, Feminism, and Freud: Discourses of Gracie and Lucy," in Tania Modleski, ed., *Studies in Entertainment: Critical Approaches to Mass Culture* [Bloomington: Indiana University Press, 1986], pp. 80–95).

It is also evident that sitcoms have consistently provided a space for the depiction of "women's sphere" in prime time. As Serafina Bathrick points out, the sitcoms are not only sources of great pleasure for women viewers but also representations of women's space, women's culture, and women's friendship (Bathrick, "*The Mary Tyler Moore Show*: Women at Home and at Work," in Jane Feuer, Paul Kerr, and Tise Vahimagi, eds., *MTM: "Quality Television"* [London: British Film Institute, 1984], pp. 99–131). And *Roseanne* and *Murphy Brown* demonstrate just how subversive and oppositional a woman actress/protagonist in a sitcom can actually be. In other words, women's virtual confinement to sitcoms by no means negates the power of their depictions to transgress or oppose conventional social and cultural norms. By my own rough count of sitcoms that aired between 1947 and 1990, there have been a total of 427—149 starring both women and men, 107 starring women, and 171 starring men. (The count is approximate.)

5. All of these are my own approximate counts. In defending the domination of prime time by men and male-oriented genres, the industry has usually claimed that it could not afford to gamble that men, too, would watch a program starring only women. Why women watch male-dominated narratives is, of course, another question. But some possible explanations surely include women's cultural heritage of male-oriented literature and films and the fact that women and girls read stories about men and boys in a variety of sometimes unpredictable ways—identifying, on the level of fantasy, with male heroes, being absorbed in the narrative intrigues, and so forth. Some women take pleasure in traditional representations of gender and others in the generation of oppositional interpretations and meanings.

One of the most promising areas for future investigation of this issue may be the examination of television viewing within the context of domestic leisure. As David Morley puts it, TV studies must attempt to "situate individual viewing within the household relations in which it operates and insist that individual viewing activity only makes sense inside of this frame." He further suggests that we must look to the ways in which TV is used by people "to construct occasions and viewing in which various types of interaction can be pursued." In this sense, many women throughout TV history may have wanted to organize "family" entertainment in the home: an activity that would keep husbands at home and engaged in male-oriented stories; involve the children and spare the need for babysitters; and promote a sense of shared pleasure. Lynn Spigel, in a different yet related vein, has argued that "the threat of sexuality/infidelity in the outside world can be contained in the home through its representation on television. Even while the husband neglects his wife and household chores to gaze at the screen woman, the housewife is in control of his sexuality insofar as his visual pleasure is circumscribed by domestic space." See David Morley, "Changing Paradigms in Audience Studies," in Ellen Seiter, Hans Borcher, Gabriele Kreutzner, and Eva-Marie Warth, eds., *Remote Control: Television, Audiences, and Cultural Power* (London: Routledge, 1989), p. 9; Lynn Spigel, "Installing the Television Set: Popular Discourses on Television and Domestic Space, 1948–1955," *Camera Obscura*, no. 16 (Jan. 1988), p. 40. See also Ann Gray, "Behind Closed Doors: Video Recorders in the Home," in Helen Baehr and Gillian Dyer, eds., *Boxed In: Women and Television* (New York: Pandora Press, 1987), pp. 38–54; Charlotte Brunsdon, "Women Watching Television," *MedieKultur* 4 (1986): 100–111.

6. The open structure, interlocking plots, and "indefinitely expandable middle" of soap operas, for instance, have been related to the fragmented time and mode of viewing by daytime women viewers, primarily "housewives" (Dennis Porter, "Soap Time: Thoughts on a Commodity Art Form," in Horace Newcomb, ed., *Television: The Critical View*, 3d ed. [New York: Oxford University Press, 1982], p. 89). See also Modleski, *Loving with a Vengeance*, pp. 85–109; Robert Allen, *Speaking of Soap Operas* (Chapel Hill: University of North Carolina Press, 1985), pp. 91–95.

7. Jane Feuer, "Genre Study and Television," in Robert C. Allen, ed., *Channels of Discourse, Reassembled: Television and Contemporary Criticism*, 2d ed. (Chapel Hill: University of North Carolina Press, 1992), pp. 135–60; Mimi White, "Television Genres: Intertextuality," *Journal of Film and Video* 38 (Summer 1985): 41–47; Lynne Joyrich, "All That Television Allows: TV Melodrama, Postmodernism, and Consumer Culture," *Camera Obscura*, no. 16 (Jan. 1988): 129–53; David Thorburn, "Television Melodrama," in Horace Newcomb, ed., *Television: The Critical View*, 4th ed. (New York: Oxford University Press, 1987), pp. 628–44; Horace Newcomb, "On the Dialogic Aspects of Mass Communication," *Critical Studies in Mass Communication* 1 (Mar. 1984): 42–43; Caren Deming, "*Hill Street Blues* as Narrative," *Critical Studies in Mass Communication* 2 (Mar. 1985): 1–22. It is, of course, also difficult to define film and literary genres, for the same reasons outlined for television by Feuer and White.

8. The program was always a mixed form. Others talk about this in different ways: Christine Gledhill, for example, discusses how the program interweaves discourses from the cop show, the buddy relationship, the woman's film, and the independent heroine figure ("Pleasurable Negotiations," p. 70). See also Danae Clark, "*Cagney & Lacey*: Feminist Strategies of Detection," in Mary Ellen Brown, ed., *Television and Women's Culture: The Politics of the Popular* (Newbury Park, Calif.: Sage, 1990), p. 119.

Although it is clear that much of television is suffused with melodrama, I specifically argue that *Cagney and Lacey's* adoption of more "women's program" elements was very much spurred on by the particular gender considerations I delineate. I want to thank Jackie Byars and Janet Staiger for discussions of this point.

9. The work of Cary Bazalgette, Geoffrey Hurd, and many of the scholars in *Screen Education's* Autumn 1976 issue on police programs has been invaluable to this examination. For a discussion of the conventional elements of police genres, see Cary Bazalgette, "Regan and Carter, Kojak and Crocker, Batman and Robin?," *Screen Education*, no. 20 (Autumn 1976): 54–65; Geoffrey Hurd, " 'The Sweeney'—Contradiction and Coherence," ibid., pp. 47–53. See also Hurd, "The Television Presentation of the Police," in Tony Bennett, Susan Boyd-Bowman, Colin Mercer, and Janet Woollacott, eds., *Popular Television and Film: A Reader* (London: British Film Institute, 1981), pp. 53–70.

10. David Marc, *Demographic Vistas: Television in American Culture* (Philadelphia: University of Pennsylvania Press, 1984), pp. 73–78; Tim Brooks and Earle Marsh, *The Complete Directory of Prime Time Network Television, 1946 to the Present*, 5th ed. (New York: Ballantine Books, 1992), p. 249. See Cary Bazalgette on the team partnerships and absence of women in the male cop's life ("Regan and Carter," pp. 63–65). Bazalgette also describes the way the police series is grounded in the "actuality of procedure." It is in this area he claims the genre makes its claims to realism (pp. 57–58).

11. See Brooks and Marsh, *Complete Directory*, p. 397.

12. These programs were the syndicated *Decoy* (1957), *Police Woman* (1974–78), *Get Christie Love* (1974–75), the police-related *Charlie's Angels* (1976–81), *Lady Blue* (half a season in 1985–86), *Cagney and Lacey* (1982–88), and *Amy Prentiss* (1974–75), which had a three-episode run as one of four revolving programs comprising NBC's *Sunday Mystery Movie*. Amy Prentiss, a white woman and widow, was chief of detectives in the San Francisco police department, truly an anomalous portrayal. For a few months in 1993, ABC aired a program called *Sirens*, featuring three women police officers.

13. *Ironside*, for example, which ran from 1967 to 1975, included a woman on a team with three men. *Mod Squad* (1968–73) grouped a white woman, an African American man, and a white man as young "hippie-type" police informers. In the last year of its twelve-year run, *Hawaii Five-O* added a woman police officer to its team; *T.J. Hooker* featured a woman police trainee who became an officer; and *Hill Street Blues* gradually developed its roles for women officers and featured a woman public defender as a major character. *Miami Vice* occasionally included two women detectives; *Hooperman* featured a woman as the precinct commander; and *Hunter* had a woman in a strong supporting role.

14. See Cary Bazalgette on the mentor relationship in *Kojak* ("Regan and Carter," pp. 59–61). For an early look at "professional families" on TV, see Horace Newcomb, *TV: The Most Popular Art* (New York: Anchor, 1974), pp. 117–26.

15. See Bazalgette, "Regan and Carter," pp. 59–61.

16. See John Dennington and John Tulloch, "Cops, Consensus, and Ideology," *Screen Education*, no. 20 (Autumn 1976): p. 39.

17. Hurd, "Television Presentation of the Police," pp. 59–60. Cary Bazalgette speaks of women in the genre as having "low status" ("Regan and Carter," p. 64). In a *People* article

by Jeff Jarvis, Locklear is quoted as saying that on *T.J. Hooker*, "Everyone thought I didn't look busty enough. So they had me wear a padded bra." She goes on to say they also wanted her to wear "padded panties," and she had to insist that she should not wear a bikini in one serious dramatic scene (*People*, 7 May 1984, pp. 158–62). It is Diana Meehan who points out that the character of Eve on *Ironside* was often used as "decoy" and as secretary (*Ladies of the Evening: Women Characters of Prime-Time Television* [Metuchen, N.J.: Scarecrow Press, 1983], p. 76).

18. Geoffrey Hurd describes women in the genre as vamps, career girls, molls, and mothers ("Television Presentation of the Police," pp. 59–60).

19. I use the term *deserving* to underscore the narratives' portrayal of events and the implications they make about the women's characters. Although my use is ironic, I have not put the term in quotes each time I employ it in the text.

20. Brooks and Marsh, *Complete Directory*, p. 102.

21. Frank Furillo and public defender Joyce Davenport eventually married, separated, and reunited in the course of the series. See Bazalgette, "Regan and Carter," pp. 64, 65; Hurd, "Television Presentation of the Police," p. 60. Hurd discusses the separation of the police protagonists from significant relationships with women and the male world that emerges. Bazalgette discusses the surrogate marriages of male partners.

22. See Bazalgette, "Regan and Carter," p. 57.

23. See Rick Altman, "A Semantic/Syntactic Approach to Film Genre," *Cinema Journal* 23, no. 3 (Spring 1984): 6–18; George Gerbner, "Cultural Indicators: The Case of Violence in Television Drama," *Annals of the American Association of Political and Social Science* 338 (1970): 69–81; Bazalgette, "Regan and Carter," pp. 54–65; Hurd, "Television Presentation of the Police," pp. 59–60. Rick Altman has devised a schema for genre study that combines what he calls a "semantic" and a "syntactic" approach. The semantic elements of a genre are the "easily identifiable elements of a genre's vocabulary." These include the conventions and iconography of a genre such as characters, locations, props, sets, and types of shots—what I am calling the "conventional generic elements." A genre's "syntax," according to Altman, refers to the "genre's specific meaning bearing structures."

24. The relationship between Starsky and Hutch contains a good deal of fairly blatant homoeroticism.

25. *Hooperman*, unlike the other series, has a half-hour format. It is atypical of the genre, falling into a category that has recently been called the "dramady" (comedy and drama). Hooperman's position, in addition, has been described by other male characters on the show as the "women's view" on police work.

26. Dennington and Tulloch, "Cops, Consensus, and Ideology," pp. 39–40.

27. For another look at male and female power as they relate to these issues, see Lorraine Gamman, "Watching the Detectives: The Enigma of the Female Gaze," in Lorraine Gamman and Margaret Marshment, eds., *The Female Gaze: Women as Viewers of Popular Culture* (London: Women's Press, 1988), pp. 16–18.

28. Phillip Drummond talks about the way that "villainy" in police genres is "deprived of characterial continuity," whereas "legality is allied with continuity of character, the law authorizing the perpetuity of the character, and the character responding by humanizing

and personalizing the instance of the law. Empirical relations with law enforcement thus displace conceptual relationships with the symbolic-field of law" ("Structural and Narrative Constraints and Strategies in 'The Sweeney,'" *Screen Education*, no. 20 [Autumn 1976]: 25). Drummond's comments provide the springboard for my discussion of the conflation of the individual hero and the Law.

29. On Kojak as a "compassionate cop," see Richard Patterson, "'The Sweeney': A Euston Films Production," *Screen Education*, no. 20 (Autumn 1976): 12; on identification, see Hurd, "Television Presentation of the Police," p. 58; and on *Kojak* and family aspects of U.S. cop shows, see Bazalgette, "Regan and Carter," pp. 59, 61. T.J. Hooker, Kojak (despite his toughness), and some of the protagonists from *Hill Street Blues* fall into the "squad room family" category.

30. This comment should be understood in context: The priest who was raped hears the confession of her rapist. Even though she knows the rapist confessed to her as a way of putting her in a bind, she refuses to testify against him because it would violate the seal of the confessional. Hooker, therefore, speaks out against "church" in this context. He does, however, attend church in the final sequence to hear the priest's first sermon.

31. See Bazalgette, "Regan and Carter," p. 63.

32. For more on this aspect, see Fiske, *Television Culture*, pp. 198–223, esp. p. 210.

33. Jane Gallop, *Feminism and Psychoanalysis: The Daughter's Seduction* (Ithaca, N.Y.: Cornell University Press, 1982), p. 14.

34. The syndicated *Decoy* negotiated femininity and the police genre by stressing the heroine's maternal aspects and her maternal way of dealing with police tasks. The series *Lady Blue* (1985) attempted to put one woman in the role of the protagonist cop. She was very much the subject of rough physical action and was billed as "ABC's Dirty Harriet" (*TV Guide*, 21–27 Sept. 1985). Although conventionally attractive, she was not exploited by the series as a sex object. She was, however, like her 1970s predecessors, often linked with a father/mentor cop, McNichols. In this way, her autonomous subjectivity was modified. The program lasted only a few months. (*Honey West*, a program in the related private detective genre, ran in the 1965–66 season.)

35. See the discussion of Julia Kristeva in Toril Moi, *Sexual/Textual Politics: Feminist Literary Theory* (London: Methuen, 1985), p. 165. Hooperman's commanding officer was a woman.

36. For a discussion of the notion of "masquerade," see Mary Ann Doane, "Film and the Masquerade: Theorising the Female Spectator," *Screen* 23, nos. 3–4 (Sept.–Oct. 1982): 74–88. See also Meehan, *Ladies of the Evening*, pp. 73–84.

37. Meehan, *Ladies of the Evening*, p. 82. John Fiske, in fact, has read *Charlie's Angels* as oppositional. According to him, "the patriarchy which was deeply inscribed in the series . . . was challenged by the aggressiveness and success of the women detectives, and many women have reported to me that their pleasure in this was strong enough to overwhelm the patriarchal frame" (Fiske, *Television Culture*, p. 189).

38. Marjorie Rosen, "Cagney and Lacey," *Ms.*, Oct. 1981, p. 50; Peter Farrell, "Women Cops: You've Come a Long Way," in "TV Click," *Sunday Oregonian*, 26 Dec. 1982. Farrell

says, however, that "the early episodes were just what Rosenzweig promised they would not be: 'We're not Starsky and Hutch in drag,' he said then and says now."

39. For a discussion of *Cagney and Lacey* and masquerade, see Clark, "*Cagney and Lacey*," p. 131.

40. Frank Swertlow, "CBS Alters 'Cagney,' Calling It 'Too Women's Lib,'" *TV Guide*, 12–18 June 1982, p. A-1.

41. I am purposely using *deviance* here to emphasize the point of view inscribed in the network's comments.

42. Barney Rosenzweig, quoted in "'Cagney, Lacey' Axes Foster, Plans to Stress Women's Angle," *Daily Variety*, 26 May 1982, Rosenzweig files; "*Cagney and Lacey* Bible," 1982, Rosenzweig files. Many television series have "Bibles," which contain the background histories of the characters and background information on the story and settings. Bibles can ensure continuity and offer guidelines to writers.

43. "*Cagney and Lacey* Series Format," 4 Dec. 1981, Rosenzweig files.

44. Over the course of the next three chapters I will be talking about "women's program" subject matter and "women's issues" subject matter. "Women's issues" is the more specific of the two phrases. By it, I mean serious social issues that have become identified, in television programming, as being of specific concern to women; these include rape, wife battering, sexual harassment, abortion, and breast cancer. "Women's program" subject matter covers these issues but also includes others, such as male/female relationships, "infidelity," child molestation, child pornography, teenage suicide, teenage and married spouses' homosexuality, family murders, sexually transmitted diseases, prostitution, and eating disorders. Certain issues such as pornography, incest, and prostitution, depending on their treatment, fall under either category. Later in this chapter, I will define more fully and discuss the implications of "women's-issues" subject matter.

45. A shot/reverse shot sequence representing dialogue between two characters contains a series of edited-together, alternating camera shots. The first shot, for example, may show Cagney looking to the right of the frame, the second shows Lacey (to whom Cagney is talking) looking to the left of the frame, the third shows Cagney (to whom Lacey is talking) looking to the right, and so forth.

46. *Cagney and Lacey* budgets, 3 Oct., 22 Nov. 1983, Rosenzweig files.

47. The episode about the visit of Detective Deedee, the Hollywood cop, employs a strategy common to all genres: the framing of *other* representations (especially genre-bound ones) as "fictional" or "unrealistic" in order to buttress the "reality" of the program itself.

48. The notion of the extended "precinct family" underlies many of these stories.

49. Paramount intercommunication from Barney Rosenzweig to Fred Freiberger, "RE: 'Beyond the Golden Door,'" 17 Feb. 1982, Rosenzweig files.

50. An out-of-house writer is one who is not on staff or part of the production team.

51. April Smith, Filmways Productions memorandum, "RE: Treatment for 'Witness to an Incident,'" 15 July 1982, Rosenzweig files.

52. Paramount intercommunication from Barney Rosenzweig to Fred Freiberger, "RE: 'Beyond the Golden Door,'" 24 Feb. 1982, Rosenzweig files.

53. Rona Barrett, *The Barrett Report* 2, no. 1 (5 Jan. 1983); Barney Rosenzweig, interview with author, Oct. 1983; personal telephone conversation with April Smith, Los Angeles, Calif., Jan. 1984.

54. Orion Pictures Company interoffice memo, 27 Apr. 1983, Rosenzweig files.

55. Barney Rosenzweig and Richard Rosenbloom to CBS, 1983 [exact date unknown], Rosenzweig files.

56. Terry Louise Fisher, interview with author, Los Angeles, Calif., Feb. 1984.

57. Notes from personal observation and discussion with Terry Louise Fisher and Peter Lefcourt, Los Angeles, Calif., Feb. 1984. "Melodrama" is used here in its popular rather than its technical sense.

58. Terry Louise Fisher quoted in Kathy MacKay, "New Focus on Prime-Time TV," *Mississippi Valley Airlines Magazine*, Dec. 1984, p. 43. Thanks to Russell Merritt for providing me with this source.

59. Judine Mayerle, "Character Shaping Genre in *Cagney and Lacey*," *Journal of Broadcasting and Electronic Media* 2 (Spring 1987): 133–51. Mayerle viewed seventy-five episodes of the series and compared the screen time devoted to "professional time" ("involvement in police detective work") and "personal time." She found that as the series progressed, "there was a gradual shift from episodes having 25 percent personal screen time to those having close to 50 percent screen time. By the 1985–86 season, 10 of the 20 episodes had at least half the total screen time dramatizing personal discourse" (p. 139). See also Cathleen Schine, "Real Women . . . Don't Always Shoot Straight," *Vogue*, Aug. 1984, pp. 75–76.

60. Peter Lefcourt, Terry Louise Fisher, and Steve Brown were producers for the 1984–85 season. During the 1985–86 season, a number of different people served as producers, including Steve Brown, Liz Coe, Ralph Singleton, and Patricia Green. During the 1986–87 season, Ralph Singleton and Georgia Jeffries produced, and Shelley List and Jonathan Estrin were supervising producers. Ralph Singleton produced during the 1987–88 season, and Shelley List and Jonathan Estrin were again supervising producers.

61. Ien Ang also talks about Cagney as a "melodramatic heroine," and Beverley Alcock and Jocelyn Robson speak of her as being "brought to heel." See Ien Ang, "Melodramatic Identifications: Television Fiction and Women's Fantasy," in Mary Ellen Brown, ed., *Television and Women's Culture: The Politics of the Popular* (Newbury Park, Calif.: Sage, 1990), p. 88; Alcock and Robson, "*Cagney and Lacey* Revisited," p. 45.

62. In this sense, my interpretation of *Cagney and Lacey*'s mixed form differs from that of John Fiske, who says that "in *Cagney and Lacey* the masculine 'end' of the narrative is often neglected in favor of a feminine emphasis on the process by which that end is achieved" (*Television Culture*, p. 216). Also, Danae Clark talks about the text's refusal to separate the public and private aspects of the characters' lives ("*Cagney and Lacey*," p. 124). I am not, however, arguing that this edge-or-bite-by-default is the only or best way a mainstream series could pose a challenge to conventional femininity.

63. Lorraine Gamman also writes that Cagney and Lacey's difference did not translate into "otherness" ("Watching the Detectives," p. 16).

64. As we have seen, *Cagney and Lacey*'s textual shifts involved a number of dimensions,

each of which could be pursued in more detail (the relationships between women and comedy or women and melodrama, to name only two). I am focusing on the exploitation dimension here because it was so fundamental to the shifts and is so particularly troubling. On exploitation and made-for-TV movies, see Laurie Schulze, "The Made-for-TV Movie: Industrial Practice, Cultural Form, Popular Reception," in Tino Balio, ed., *Hollywood in the Age of Television* (New York: Unwin Hyman, 1990), pp. 351–76.

65. Jim Mintz, "The Hot Sell: How TV Turns on the Viewers," *Channels*, May–June 1984, pp. 24–30; Jerry McNeely (television producer/writer), interview with author, Los Angeles, Calif., Feb. 1984. An article by James Forkan describes the pains ABC took with the "taboo" subject addressed in *Something about Amelia*; he categorizes it with movies about the "seamy side" of life ("ABC says 'Amelia' Will Sell," *Advertising Age*, 12 Dec. 1983, p. 2).

66. Schulze, "Made-for-TV Movie," p. 366.

67. John J. O'Connor, " 'Cagney and Lacey'—Indisputably a Class Act," *The Patriot Ledger* (Quincy, Mass.), 5 July 1984; Tyne Daly in *USA Today*, 11 Feb. 1985, quoted in John Fiske, "*Cagney and Lacey*: Reading Character Structurally and Politically," *Communication* 9 (1987): 418.

68. Schulze, "Made-for-TV Movie," p. 370; viewer letters, 1983, Rosenzweig files. Quotes in the following paragraphs are also from these viewer letters.

69. Virginia Castleberry, "Battling for Battered Wives," *Dallas Times Herald*, 1 May 1983, sec. H; Beverly Stephen, "TV Show Brings Home Tragedy of the Battered Wife," *New York Daily News*, 21 Apr. 1983. According to Beverly Stephen, some hesitations were voiced by women who had screened the episode at Lincoln Center. "Although the women who work with this problem were happy to see it portrayed in a way that challenges some of the old stereotypes, they expressed concern that the battering cop was not arrested." The NYPD assistant commissioner for legal matters, Rosemary Carroll, is quoted by Stephen as saying, "Now officers are required to make an arrest if a felony has been committed" (p. 46).

70. Other viewers wrote about what other specific episodes meant to them. Concerning "Burnout," the 1983 episode in which Lacey has a minor breakdown and disappears for a day and a night, one said, "I just finished watching the show where Mary Beth is on the edge of a nervous breakdown. It was good. I've been there a few times and I know how it feels and what can send you there." And another, "I cried through the entire show being able to identify so completely with her dilemma. I found the show extremely good and did not take my eyes from it for a moment. The human emotions expressed were fantastic, and so true to life." After the broadcast of the two-part episode on Lacey's breast cancer in 1985, Tyne Daly and the program's offices were overwhelmed with responses. In a *Cagney and Lacey* newsletter, Daly wrote, "I am grateful to all of you who shared by letter the history of your personal struggles and I am grateful if you feel I represented some of these struggles with honesty and realism" ("*Cagney and Lacey* Fall Newsletter," 1985).

71. These qualities were shared by many made-for-TV movies of the time.

72. I am speaking here about the conscious, as opposed to any unconscious, responses

these programs may have engendered, and I include myself as part of the audience I am discussing.

73. On soap operas, see Modleski, *Loving with a Vengeance*, pp. 85–114; Charlotte Brunsdon, "*Crossroads*: Notes on a Soap Opera," in E. Ann Kaplan, ed., *Regarding Television—Critical Approaches: An Anthology* (Frederick, Md.: American Film Institute, 1983), pp. 76–83; Allen, *Speaking of Soap Operas*; Ellen Seiter, "Promise and Contradiction: The Daytime Television Serials," *Film Reader* 5 (Winter 1982): 150–63. On melodramas, see Mary Ann Doane, *The Desire to Desire: The Woman's Film of the 1940s* (Bloomington: Indiana University Press, 1987); Linda Williams, " 'Something Else Besides a Mother': *Stella Dallas* and the Maternal Melodrama," *Cinema Journal* 24, no. 1 (Fall 1984): 2–27; Christine Gledhill, "The Melodramatic Field: An Investigation," in Gledhill, ed., *Home Is Where the Heart Is: Studies in Melodrama and the Women's Film* (London: British Film Institute, 1987), pp. 5–39; Ien Ang, *Watching "Dallas": Soap Opera and the Melodramatic Imagination* (London: Methuen, 1985); Jackie Byars, *All That Hollywood Allows: Re-Reading Gender in 1950s Melodrama* (Chapel Hill: University of North Carolina Press, 1991); Joyrich, "All That Television Allows." On sitcoms, see Mellencamp, "Situation Comedy, Feminism, and Freud"; Bathrick, "*The Mary Tyler Moore Show*"; Lynn Spigel, "From Domestic Space to Outer Space: The 1960s Fantastic Family Sit-Com," in Constance Penley, Elisabeth Lyon, Lynn Spigel, and Janet Bergstrom, eds., *Close Encounters: Film, Feminism, and Science Fiction* (Minneapolis: University of Minnesota Press, 1991), pp. 205–23. On women fans of *Star Trek*, see Constance Penley, "Brownian Motion: Women, Tactics, and Technology," in Constance Penley and Andrew Ross, eds., *Technoculture* (Minneapolis: University of Minnesota Press, 1991), pp. 135–61; Henry Jenkins, "*Star Trek*, Rerun, Reread, Rewritten: Fan Writings as Textual Poaching," *Critical Studies in Mass Communication* 5, no. 2 (June 1988): 85–107; Camille Bacon-Smith, *Enterprising Women: Television Fandom and the Creation of Popular Myth* (Philadelphia: University of Pennsylvania Press, 1992).

74. This is not to say that exploitation topics are indigenous or natural to women's programming, but simply that relationship is highly complex and the subject matter is conceived differently by the industry and by a good many of its viewers.

CHAPTER FOUR

1. See John Fiske, *Television Culture* (London: Methuen, 1987), pp. 84–99; Annette Kuhn, *Women's Pictures: Feminism and Cinema* (London: Routledge and Kegan Paul, 1982), p. 137. In an interview, Barbara Avedon reflected on how subtly and almost imperceptibly these changes begin to occur. She spoke specifically about the evolution from Harvey Lacey's problem with impotence in the made-for TV movie to Harvey and Mary Beth's eventual active sex life—the most active of any married couple on TV. Avedon was not happy with these changes (Barbara Avedon, interview with author, Los Angeles, Calif., Feb. 1984).

2. Elaine Warren, "Where Are the Real Women on TV?," *Los Angeles Herald Examiner*, 31 Oct. 1983, sec. E. The quotations that follow are also from this article.

3. *TV Guide*, 16–22 Jan. 1988, cover; Gloria Steinem, "Why I Consider *Cagney and Lacey* the Best Show on TV," ibid., pp. 4–6.

4. Most of the feminism of the original series derives from the U.S. liberal women's movement. I refer to this as "general" because it is represented as addressing large social issues, not just those issues that are cast as specific to women and only resolvable at the level of the individual woman.

5. Paramount intercommunication from Barney Rosenzweig to Fred Freiberger, 10 Mar. 1982, Rosenzweig files.

6. Ibid.; Paramount intercommunication from P. K. (Patricia) Knelman to Fred Freiberger, 21 Mar. 1982, Rosenzweig files; Sal Manna, "Sorry This Show Wasn't Seen," *Los Angeles Herald Examiner*, [1st week of July] 1982, sec. B.

7. Although "heavy-handed" and "didactic" were the words used by some of the press at the time to criticize the series's handling of feminism, it is also important to remember that much of that feminism is bound to seem dated from a 1990s perspective.

8. "Hooker gear" is the phrase used in the scripts to refer to the type of costumes and behaviors (Hollywood's notion of prostitutes) described in Chapter 3.

9. "*Cagney and Lacey* Bible," 1982, Rosenzweig files.

10. "The City Is Burning" created a sensation in the press because of its "shocking" language. See "In a Shocker Show, *Cagney and Lacey* Tests Limits with the Most Vicious Racial Slurs Ever Heard on TV," *People*, 5 Oct. 1987, pp. 62–64. For more on this episode, see Susan Brower, "TV 'Trash' & 'Treasure': Marketing *Dallas* & *Cagney and Lacey*," *Wide Angle* 11, no. 1 (1989): 27.

11. The "naturalness" of Lacey's motherhood is also analyzed. In the same episode that examines Cagney's daughterhood, the protagonists interrogate a pregnant and scared female suspect. The dialogue, with a tag-line joke, goes as follows:

Cagney: All she had to do is mention the baby and you turned into a tower of Jell-O.
Lacey: Just what is it you think this frightened pregnant girl can tell us about these
     completely masked bank robbers?
Cagney: You're such a snob. You think I can't understand how that girl feels, just
     because I'm not a member of the great fraternity of motherhood?
Lacey: I think you mean sorority, don't you?
Cagney: Yeah, I guess I do.

12. Howard Rosenberg, "The New Season," *Los Angeles Times*, 25 Oct. 1982, Calendar section; Barbara Holsopple, "Two New Series on Women: All Work, No Play," *Pittsburgh Press*, 25 Mar. 1982, sec. B.

13. Viewer letters, Rosenzweig files. Quotes from viewers in succeeding paragraphs also come from this selection.

14. A good example of these objections is Bridget Smith, "*Cagney and Lacey*," *Spare Rib*, no. 161 (Dec. 1985): 31.

15. "*Cagney and Lacey* Bible," 1982.

16. April Smith quoted in Bob Knight, "'Grant' Grad Tries New Series," *Variety*, 27 Oct. 1982, p. 66. Sharon Gless said the series was "humanist," and she did not want to call it "feminist" because this was "limiting" (quoted in Lorraine Gamman, "Watching the

Detectives: The Enigma of the Female Gaze," in Lorraine Gamman and Margaret Marsh-ment, eds., *The Female Gaze: Women as Viewers of Popular Culture* [London: Women's Press, 1988], p. 25).

17. Susan Faludi, *Backlash: The Undeclared War against American Women* (New York: Anchor Books, 1991), pp. xvii, xix, xxi.

18. Given that the series was a prime-time network presentation, it should be no surprise that the explicit feminism was never fully developed. See Cathleen Schine, "Real Women . . . Don't Always Shoot Straight," *Vogue*, Aug. 1984, pp. 75–76.

19. Frank Swertlow, "CBS Alters 'Cagney,' Calling It 'Too Women's Lib,'" *TV Guide*, 12–18 June 1982, p. A-1.

20. I use the word *victim* to underscore network prime time's way of presenting women as victims in such narratives. Although I will not continue to put the term in quotes as I use it in the text, I do not see the women in any of these situations as characterized by the helplessness that "victim" normally implies.

21. In one episode, aired on 16 December 1985, Cagney takes temporary command of the squad, and Petrie overtly challenges the other male detectives on not being able to take orders from a woman:

Petrie [to Isbecki]: You have trouble taking orders from a woman, admit it. [To all the male detectives] You all do.

Isbecki: You gotta be kidding. I love women. Ask anybody in my little black book.

Newman: Anybody who grew up with my mother and my four sisters had to be a feminist.

Petrie: Right. That's why you mentioned Cagney's eyes.

Newman: So, I'm a feminist and a nice guy.

Petrie: It wasn't nice, Newman, it was a come-on.

Isbecki: I do not have a problem working for a woman. I think women can be very competent once they learn how to deal with power.

Newman: I'm sure some women are terrific commanders.

Carassa: If they're not out to prove something.

Isbecki: I would work for a woman any day. As long as they have their hormones under control.

Petrie: Oh no!

22. Mimi White speaks of the (circumscribed) "competing voices" in *Cagney and Lacey* ("Ideological Analysis and Television," in Robert C. Allen, ed., *Channels of Discourse, Reassembled: Television and Contemporary Criticism*, 2d ed. [Chapel Hill, University of North Carolina Press, 1992], p. 184).

23. For more on characters as bundles of traits, see David Bordwell and Kristin Thompson, *Film Art: An Introduction*, 4th ed. (New York: McGraw-Hill, 1993), p. 68.

24. And even though supervising producer Shelley List and story editor Kathryn Ford said that their policy was to avoid hard-line statements that would alienate the audience, they also said they were committed to keeping the women's perspective and described their orientation as "definitely feminists" (Beverley Alcock, "New York's Finest," *Spare Rib*, no. 186 (Jan. 1988): 24.

25. Lorraine Gamman also writes about what she calls the "mockery of machismo" in the series ("Watching the Detectives: More on *Cagney and Lacey*," *Spare Rib*, no. 187 (Feb. 1988): 6.

26. See Tim Brooks and Earle Marsh, *The Complete Directory of Prime Time Network Television, 1946 to the Present*, 5th ed. (New York: Ballantine, 1992), p. 137.

27. Petrie passed the exam as well but had to wait for a sergeant's spot to become available. Lacey also passed the exam toward the end of the series but never assumed a command position.

28. This ambiguous feminism also surfaces in an episode in which she says to Lacey, "We're equal in everything except perhaps peeing in the woods," and another one in which she refers to God as "She."

29. During another episode, the squad members set Isbecki up with a blind date who is actually a transvestite, and Cagney taunts Isbecki the following morning, saying, "You and Ronnie make a perfectly beautiful couple." Isbecki responds, "Actually, she reminded me a lot of you. Only I think you make the better man." To which Cagney, never to be outdone, says, "Thank you, Victor, but really, you give me way too much credit. Around here I don't have that much competition."

30. For most of the series, the narratives support the Laceys' "role reversals," but during the 1987–88 season, in which Harvey, Jr., takes Oliver North and Rambo as his heroes and enlists in the Marine Corps, Harvey, Sr., says it might not have happened if he "had been more of a man and hadn't worn the apron in the family." There are also various periods during which Harvey's contracting work picks up and he is more involved in public-sphere activity; and there is one period in which he begins making a lot of money.

31. When, for example, in the first Foster/Daly episode, Lacey decides to wear her "hooker gear" home, she says to Cagney, "I thought I'd give Harvey something to go with the tuna bake tonight." And if an "experimental" sexual practice is ever discussed at the precinct, Lacey knows about it and appears to have tried it.

32. In a 1987 episode in which Lacey and Cagney dress as "hookers," Lacey says about high heels: "The man who invented these was into cruel and unusual punishment." Cagney, however, replies, "I hate to ruin your fun, but he was a she—Catherine de Medici—and she didn't have to work or walk." Daly also tried to play Lacey as a "blocky" body-type character. She visualized squareness and solidity when preparing for the role (personal conversation with Tyne Daly, Los Angeles, Calif., Mar. 1984).

33. Estrin's comments were made to Angela Spindler-Brown during a 1987 interview (personal discussion with Angela Spindler-Brown).

CHAPTER FIVE

1. Thanks to Charlotte Brunsdon and Biddy Martin for their discussions of this chapter. "Spectator positions" are spaces offered to a viewer by the text, positions from which the narrative makes sense and from which the viewer may identify with on-screen characters. Following Louis Althusser, we may also say that a text calls out to or hails a viewer to take

up particular positions (interpellation). Although the phrase *spectator positions* and the term *spectator* have been widely critiqued, I am using them to emphasize the point that television programs, along with myriad other things, are involved in the ongoing process of subject construction. However, I do not intend for *spectator* to signal only the ongoing process of *gender* construction (although that is my primary focus). Rather, I use the word to indicate the ways in which media texts may play an active part in addressing human subjects on many dimensions such as race, class, gender, and ethnicity, to name the most salient. Texts offer up many positions and viewers may shift among them.

2. Susan Sheridan, *Grafts: Feminist Cultural Criticism* (London: Verso, 1988), p. 4. Feminist writings that interpret the program as feminist or important to feminism include Judine Mayerle, "Character Shaping Genre in *Cagney and Lacey*," *Journal of Broadcasting and Electronic Media* 2 (Spring 1987): 133–51; Gloria Steinem, "Why I Consider *Cagney and Lacey* the Best Show on TV," *TV Guide*, 16–22 Jan. 1988, pp. 4–6; Jim Hillier, "*Cagney and Lacey*: Negotiating the Controversial in Popular Television," paper presented at the Second International Television Society Conference, London, July 1986; Jackie Byars, "Reading Feminine Discourse: Prime-time Television in the US," *Communication* 9 (1987): 289–303; Lorraine Gamman, "Watching the Detectives: The Enigma of the Female Gaze," in Lorraine Gamman and Margaret Marshment, eds., *The Female Gaze: Women as Viewers of Popular Culture* (London: Women's Press, 1988), pp. 8–26; Gamman, "Watching the Detectives: More on *Cagney and Lacey*," *Spare Rib*, no. 187 (Feb. 1988): 6–7; John Fiske, "*Cagney and Lacey*: Reading Character Structurally and Politically," *Communication* 9 (1987): 399–426; Christine Gledhill, "Pleasurable Negotiations," in E. Deidre Pribram, ed., *Female Spectators: Looking at Film and Television* (London: Verso, 1988), pp. 64–89; Danae Clark, "*Cagney & Lacey*: Feminist Strategies of Detection," in Mary Ellen Brown, ed., *Television and Women's Culture: The Politics of the Popular* (Newbury Park, Calif.: Sage, 1990), pp. 117–33; Ien Ang, "Melodramatic Identifications: Television Fiction and Women's Fantasy," in Brown, ed., *Television and Women's Culture*, pp. 75–88; Celeste Michelle Condit, "The Rhetorical Limits of Polysemy," *Critical Studies in Mass Communication* 6, no. 2 (June 1989): 103–22 (I discussed Condit's reservations Chap. 1); Beverley Alcock, "New York's Finest," *Spare Rib*, no. 186 (Jan. 1988): 22–25 (Alcock also discusses the problems for feminist representations of women in the series and cc...ends that there is "no real sense of the construction of the female spectator"); Beverley Alcock and Jocelyn Robson, "*Cagney and Lacey* Revisited," *Feminist Review*, no. 35 (Summer 1990): 42–53 (likewise discusses problems with the text's feminism as noted in this chapter); Bridget Smith, "*Cagney and Lacey*," *Spare Rib*, no. 161 (Dec. 1985): 31 (maintains that the series "offers nothing" for feminists); Mimi White, "Ideological Analysis and Television," in Robert C. Allen, ed., *Channels of Discourse, Reassembled: Television and Contemporary Criticism*, 2d ed. (Chapel Hill: University of North Carolina Press, 1992), pp. 181–87 (discusses problems in the series's representation of women and also the positive aspects concerning its representation of women's solidarity).

3. Alcock and Robson, "*Cagney and Lacey* Revisited," p. 44; Gamman, "Watching the Detectives: More on *Cagney and Lacey*," p. 6; Gledhill, "Pleasurable Negotiations," p. 72.

4. I want to thank Robert Allen for a discussion of these issues.

5. Teresa de Lauretis has examined how gender becomes absorbed subjectively by individuals ("The Technology of Gender," in *Technologies of Gender: Essays on Theory, Film, and Fiction* [Bloomington: Indiana University Press, 1987], p. 13). Judith Butler describes the "performance" of gender (*Gender Trouble: Feminism and the Subversion of Identity* [New York: Routledge, 1990], pp. 24–25, 134–41). Judith Mayne, drawing on the work of Linda Gordon, argues that many of these competing claims need to be held in tension (*Cinema and Spectatorship* [London: Routledge, 1993], pp. 75–76). See also Linda Gordon, "What's New in Women's History," in Teresa de Lauretis, ed., *Feminist Studies/Critical Studies* (Bloomington: Indiana University Press, 1986), p. 22.

6. Annette Kuhn, "Women's Genres," in Christine Gledhill, ed., *Home Is Where the Heart Is: Studies in Melodrama and the Woman's Film* (London: British Film Institute, 1987), pp. 343–44. For other discussions of these issues, see Jackie Byars, *All That Hollywood Allows: Re-reading Gender in 1950s Melodrama* (Chapel Hill: University of North Carolina Press, 1991), pp. 29–37; Charlotte Brunsdon, "Pedagogies of the Feminine: Feminist Teaching and Women's Genres," *Screen* 32, no. 4 (Winter 1991): 371–73.

7. Kuhn, "Women's Genres," p. 347.

8. "Regime of pleasure" comes from ibid., p. 344. When I talk about what it meant to be a woman in the 1980s Western world, I am not implying that the category is a homogeneous one. I am simply saying that specific groups of historically constituted women were defined by and participated in overlapping practices and discourses (as well as many other divergent ones).

9. Gledhill, "Pleasurable Negotiations," p. 67. Gledhill's formulations about the meanings of "women's history," "experience," and "discourse," which will be taken in up this chapter, must be read in relation to the previous note and also in relation to another of Gledhill's comments: "Female cultural practices do not operate in some free 'feminine' space, they are produced from the different social and psychic positions of women within an overall complex of social relations and discourses" ("The Melodramatic Field: An Investigation," in Gledhill, ed., *Home Is Where the Heart Is*, p. 35). They also, of course, may never be seen as existing apart from the influence of dominant ideology.

10. Gledhill, "Pleasurable Negotiations" (quote, p. 76).

11. Ibid., p. 66. Gledhill is paraphrasing Laura Mulvey, "Visual Pleasure in Narrative Cinema," *Screen* 16, no. 3 (Autumn 1975): 6–18.

12. I should add that the social discourses in question get taken up into the text and transformed by it in ways that make them very specific to the text per se. The many changes that *Cagney and Lacey* underwent make it clear that the textual figure of woman is not only something culturally and historically specific but also something quite specific at a particular historical moment or place in the text itself.

13. "Common sense" is used here in the sense elaborated in the Introduction, note 2.

14. Gledhill, "Pleasurable Negotiations," p. 73.

15. Annette Kuhn, *Women's Pictures: Feminism and Cinema* (London: Routledge and Kegan Paul, 1982), p. 136.

16. Ibid., p. 73.

17. Gledhill, "Pleasurable Negotiations," pp. 76–77.

18. "1980s women" is a phase that appears often in the fans' letters.

19. A realist film or TV program does, in fact, work to achieve a mimetic effect—to create a reproduction of reality and further the belief that TV or film is a "window on the world" or a mirror held up to reflect reality. In realist film or TV, "a coherent narrative time and space is set up by means of continuity editing, and sound and image support one another in the construction of a transparent, readable and credible fictional world" (Kuhn, *Women's Pictures*, p. 142). It is crucial, however, to remember that in speaking about realism and mimesis I do not mean the text's ability to represent reality per se. As John Fiske says, we do not call a text realistic because it reproduces reality but "because it reproduces the dominant sense of reality. . . . Realism is not a matter of any truth to reality but of the discursive conventions by which and for whom a sense of reality is constructed" (Fiske, *Television Culture* [London: Methuen, 1987], p. 21).

Richard Dyer writes of the history, in fan literature, of speaking about stars as "real" or authentic. He says, "It is the star's really seeming to be what s/he is supposed to be that secures his/her star status, 'star quality,' or charisma. Authenticity is both a quality necessary to the star phenomenon to make it work, and also the quality that guarantees the authenticity of the other particular values a star embodies (such as girl-next-door-ness, etc.). It is this effect of authenticating authenticity that gives the star charisma" ("*A Star Is Born* and the Construction of Authenticity," in *Star Signs: Papers from a Weekend Workshop* [London: BFI Education, 1982], p. 14). Dyer is also quoted in Steven Cohen, "Masquerading as the American Male in the Fifties," in Constance Penley and Sharon Willis, eds., *Male Trouble* (Minneapolis: University of Minnesota Press, 1993), pp. 223–24. I am demonstrating and arguing for the *specific ways* "real" was used to describe Cagney and Lacey's authenticity for particular fans.

20. From one point of view, these viewers' responses can be seen as simply emerging from Western culture's dominant reading strategy for realist texts—reflection theory. Such a strategy has been problematic for feminism and television studies because it assumes that television is a neutral vehicle for reflecting "real life" and thus overlooks real life's socially constructed and ideological character. It also overlooks the ideological, industrial, and mediational aspects of all representational practices, including television, film, and literature.

In the late 1970s and 1980s, a popular approach to the question of women and representation was "image analysis," which was based in reflection theory and relied on the methodology of content analysis. Scholars using this approach looked for positive images of women in media texts and often invoked the terms *real* and *role model* to underscore the portrayals they found valuable. But the image analysis approach has also proved troublesome for feminist media analysis because it extracts images of women from their narrative and generic contexts and valorizes new, potentially prescriptive portrayals as alternative or oppositional ideals. Old images of women, in other words, are replaced with someone's version of new and better ones. Positive image analysis has, for example, designated representations of professional women on TV as "positive" by virtue of the women's professionalism alone, without analyzing the functions of the characters in the overall narrative and without examining the middle-class, Western, white bias evident in such a choice.

Because they are so ingrained in our culture's reading practices, aspects of reflection theory and positive image analysis probably figure in the letter writers' designation of *Cagney and Lacey* as "real," just as they figure in many of our immediate readings, but my examination of realism here offers additional explanations for what the viewers might be signaling. See also Diane Waldman, "There's More to a Positive Image Than Meets the Eye," in Patricia Erens, ed., *Issues in Feminist Criticism* (Bloomington: Indiana University Press, 1990), pp. 13–18.

21. I do want to make it clear that I am not devaluing the work of women who choose to stay at home to raise children or tend to the running of a household.

22. Joyce Sunila, "Are the Laceys Too Real for Television?," *Los Angeles Times*, Sunday Calendar section; viewer letters, Rosenzweig files. I have included Sunila's comments in this section on viewer letters because they so directly relate to the matter under discussion.

23. Gledhill, "Pleasurable Negotiations," p. 79.

24. See Introduction, note 13.

25. According to John J. O'Connor, "The chemistry between Daly and Gless is irresistible, by turns street-smart sassy and movingly intimate. The balance there, in terms of admirably professional teamwork is just about perfect" (" 'Cagney and Lacey'—Indisputably a Class Act," *The Patriot Ledger* [Quincy, Mass.], 5 July 1984).

26. Mayerle, "Character Shaping Genre in *Cagney and Lacey*," p. 139.

27. Cagney also went undercover as a nun. See Mary Ann Doane, "Film and the Masquerade: Theorising the Female Spectator," *Screen* 23, nos. 3–4 (Sept.–Oct. 1982): 74–88. For another look at masquerading and *Cagney and Lacey*, see Clark, "*Cagney and Lacey*," p. 131.

28. In 1986 a policewoman, Faverty, began appearing in a minor role. Beverly Faverty (both the actress's and the character's name) was actually Sharon Gless and Tyne Daly's personal assistant. In 1987 Merry Clayton appeared as Detective Verna Dee Jordan.

29. de Lauretis, "The Technology of Gender," p. 26.

30. A long shot is one in which the entire human figure is in the frame. A long take is a shot that is held on the screen for an extended period of time.

31. Much of this analysis of the "Jane" scenes comes from discussions with Charlotte Brunsdon and Biddy Martin.

32. We can see in the TV friendships of women such as those on *Kate and Allie, The Golden Girls, Designing Women*, and *Heartbeat* a bonding that also emerges out of the social conditions of the characters—the need for affordable housing and the running of women's businesses. We can also see how the representation of these friendships points to the formation of alternative "families" and consequently interrogates, usually on a tacit level, conventional social and cultural discourses regarding "the family." *Cagney and Lacey*, however, is fairly unique in that it consistently, and sometimes quite explicitly, calls attention to the discourses and conventions that inform the material conditions (a male-dominated workplace) under which the characters' friendship was founded.

33. Mary Beth's relationship with Harvey is often described by the letter writers with such phrases as "the best portrayal of a marriage I have ever seen." One fan wrote to Tyne Daly, "I somehow identify with your character Lacey. Being the wife of an active duty

military man, and mother of five children, I can appreciate Lacey's independence and yet devotion to her husband and children."

34. There were some disagreements between Tyne Daly and the writers over how Lacey would react on particular issues pertaining to motherhood. In the episode entitled "Baby Broker," for example, Daly thought that Lacey would severely chastise the mother who had abandoned her deaf baby at birth. Terry Louise Fisher thought Lacey would be more sympathetic to the mother.

35. A social and political issue on which Lacey manifests an initial conservative reaction, seemingly emanating from her motherhood, involves AIDS—she wants to take her baby out of a daycare center where one of the children has been diagnosed with the virus. By the end of the episode, Harvey has convinced her that the risks are virtually nonexistent.

As the series progressed, Harvey Lacey became the most consistently left-of-liberal character on prime-time TV. He was completely fascinated with conspiracies involving the U.S. government, including the Christic Institute's findings on Iran-Contra, and he often barraged Lacey with political information and his condemnations of CIA activities and U.S. policy in general.

36. Gless objected to the fur because she did not see it as "Cagney" (personal conversation with Sharon Gless, Los Angeles, Calif., Feb. 1984).

37. During the period in which I observed on the set, Tyne Daly was adamant about not having Lacey use incorrect grammar. "She's not stupid," Daly said.

38. In the 1985 two-part breast cancer program, the cop-story segment involves an African American single mother, Mrs. Taggert, and her young son Kevin, who is running drugs for older kids. Because Mrs. Taggert works during the day and is not there when Kevin comes home from school, Cagney wants to have custody of the boy assigned to the state. Lacey persists, throughout the program, in making her partner face the complexity of the situation: "I was a latch-key kid," she says. To which Cagney replies, "This is different." And Lacey responds, "Why? Because I'm white?" Later in the program, Mrs. Taggert confronts Cagney, saying, "I know you look at me and you think I'm nothing. Well, let me tell you something. From where I started I'm doing okay. . . . But you go around judging me. . . . What gives you the right to tell me that I'm not a good enough mother to my own son? . . . I made the best home that it was humanly possible for me to make." By the end of the episode, while Lacey is in the hospital preparing for surgery, Cagney "comes around" and testifies on behalf of Mrs. Taggert's fitness as a mother. (The stereotyped portrayal of African Americans is obvious here.)

39. Although this facet was only occasionally touched upon, the characters' different class and political backgrounds affected their divergent reactions to racism. As noted in the previous chapter, Lacey was actively and publicly antiracist, while Cagney's more ambivalent relationship to racism was underscored in several episodes, including "The City Is Burning." In that episode, for example, Lacey gets an interracial neighborhood group together to discuss and deal with tensions. And, as mentioned in note 37, she was quick to challenge the racist implications of her partner's remarks about Mrs. Taggert. In the final episode of the series, when Samuels tells the protagonists he never liked Inspector Mar-

quette (a black man), he quickly adds, "Do you think I'm prejudiced, Lacey?" To which she replies, "No more than the rest of us."

40. The episode about Cagney's sexual harassment is a particularly jarring and cruel example of the differences between the characters. Although Lacey has offered Cagney her support, Lt. Samuels leaves Cagney to fend for herself. She is pictured alone in the frame shot, and, as Mimi White has pointed out, she is also positioned in front of the bars of the precinct windows ("Ideological Analysis and Television," p. 154). The next scene shows Harvey and Mary Beth dancing romantically on the roof of their apartment building. The final frame freezes on the Laceys.

On the "subject-in-process," see Julia Kristeva, "Signifying Practice and Mode of Production," *Edinburgh Magazine*, no. 1 (1976): 64–76. See also Chris Weedon, *Feminist Practice and Poststructuralist Theory* (Oxford: Basil Blackwell, 1987), p. 165.

41. Michael Ryan, "A Method in the Madness," *People*, 11 Feb. 1985, p. 92; Karen Stabiner, "The Pregnant Detective," *New York Times Magazine*, 22 Sept. 1985, p. 83; Howard Rosenberg, "Grace under Pressure in 'Cagney and Lacey,'" *Los Angeles Times*, 25 Feb. 1985; Tyne Daly quoted in Fred Robbins, "This TV Star's Also High on Family Life," *Today Plus* (a publication of the *Wisconsin State Journal* and *Capital Times*), 22 Jan. 1986.

42. In the spring of 1990, a female fan, obsessed with Sharon Gless/Chris Cagney, broke into a home the actress used as an office (Gless was not there), where, the press reported, she wanted to kill herself in front of Gless. The tabloid *Star's* headlines read "Cagney and Looney," with the subheadline "TV star Sharon Gless tells of her terror as rifle-wielding lesbian fan storms Hollywood home." (Gless actually made a very few considered and respectful comments about fans who become pathologically obsessed with TV characters.) The title over the actual article read, "Kamikaze Lesbian Storms Sharon Gless Home" (*The Star*, 17 Apr. 1990).

43. Alcock, "New York's Finest," p. 25; comedy act performed at the Pied Piper, Provincetown, Mass., Summer 1988, as reported by Elizabeth Ellsworth (personal conversation with author, Madison, Wis., Aug. 1988); Walta Borawski, "'Cagney and Lacey' Blows the AIDS Show," *Gay Community News*, 3–9 Apr. 1988, p. 16.

44. Personal discussions with various lesbian viewers, 1984–90.

45. Jackie Byars, "Gazes/Voices/Power: Expanding Psychoanalysis for Feminist Film and Television Theory," in E. Deidre Pribram, ed., *Female Spectators: Looking at Film and Television* (London: Verson, 1988), p. 125.

46. Personal discussions with lesbian viewers, 1984–90.

47. Laura Mulvey has argued that the relay of looks set up in classical Hollywood cinema is the main mechanism for engendering identification with male protagonists and desire for female characters on the screen. This whole process, of course, in Mulvey's analysis, assumes and constructs a male spectator ("Visual Pleasure in Narrative Cinema"). See also Jackie Stacey, "Desperately Seeking Difference," *Screen* 28, no. 1 (Winter 1987): 59.

For a description of a shot/reverse shot, see Chapter 3, note 45. For other readings of *Cagney and Lacey* and the "female gaze," see Gamman, "Watching the Detectives: The Enigma of the Female Gaze"; Clark, "*Cagney and Lacey.*"

48. The network, I would maintain, was not setting out consciously to recuperate the representations of women; it was proceeding according to its own vested interests in meanings that were functional for its own operations.

49. Mary Ann Doane, for example, writes of the way femininity in patriarchal culture is constituted as a "pathological condition" (*The Desire to Desire: The Woman's Film of the 1940s* [Bloomington: Indiana University Press, 1987], p. 36).

CONCLUSION

1. Patrice Petro, "Mass Culture and the Feminine: The 'Place' of Television in Film Studies," *Cinema Journal* 25, no. 3 (Spring 1986): 17.

2. Lynn Spigel, *Make Room for TV: Television and the Family Ideal in Postwar America* (Chicago: University of Chicago Press, 1992); Mary Beth Haralovich, "Individual Response," *Camera Obscura*, nos. 20–21 (May–Sept. 1989): 178.

3. See Janet Bergstrom, "Enunciation and Sexual Difference," in Constance Penley, ed., *Feminism and Film Theory* (London: Routledge, 1988), pp. 178–81.

4. Jacqueline Bobo, "*The Color Purple*: Black Women as Cultural Readers," in E. Deidre Pribram, ed., *Female Spectators: Looking at Film and Television* (London: Verso, 1988), pp. 90–109.

5. *The Cosby Show, 227, Frank's Place, Cagney and Lacey, Roseanne*, and *Designing Women* are some noteworthy examples of such shows.

6. Barbara Corday, interview with author, Feb. 1984; Herman Gray, "Recodings: Possibilities and Limitations in Commercial Television Representations of African American Culture," *Quarterly Review of Film and Video* 30, nos. 1–3 (1991): 117–30.

7. Knelman was with the series from the beginning and, among other things, was responsible for a good deal of the postproduction work on the episodes.

8. One viewer letter read, "The story lines are terrific, and it is refreshing to see women and racial minorities portrayed in less stereotyped roles."

9. Clayton was hired, however, just as Carl Lumbly, who played the African American Detective Petrie, left the series.

10. Josie was played by Jo Corday, a former vaudeville performer and the mother of Barbara Corday.

11. See Kate Oberlander, "Network Group Hits Boycotts," *Electronic Media*, 5 Aug. 1991, p. 4; "TV News: New Emphasis on Gay Themes," *TV Guide*, 17–23 Aug. 1991, pp. 25–26.

12. For a critique of feminist appropriations of Anita Hill, see Kimberlé Crenshaw, "Whose Story Is It Anyway?: Feminist and Antiracist Appropriations of Anita Hill," in Toni Morrison, ed., *Race-ing Justice, En-gendering Power: Essays on Anita Hill, Clarence Thomas, and the Construction of Social Reality* (New York: Pantheon, 1992), pp. 402–40. Other "girls with guns" movies included *V. I. Warshawski* and *La Femme Nikita*.

CAGNEY & LACEY

"A CRY FOR HELP"

Written by Chris Abbott & Terry Louise Fisher

FINAL DRAFT, MARCH 18, 1983

CAST

CHRIS CAGNEY	SHARON GLESS
MARY BETH LACEY	TYNE DALY
BERT SAMUELS	AL WAXMAN
HARVEY LACEY	JOHN KARLEN
VICTOR ISBECKI	MARTIN KOVE
PAUL LA GUARDIA	SIDNEY CLUTE
MARCUS PETRIE	CARL LUMBLY

CHARACTER ACTORS

DESK SERGEANT

NORMA

ROSE

EDITH

BRENT NELSON

MICK SOLOMON

ED RUSKIN

PHYLLIS NELSON

ALEJANDRO

OBIE

MUSEUM CURATOR

JOE KLOTZMAN

SETS

INTERIOR:

14th PRECINCT
    SQUAD ROOM
    LADIES' ROOM
    INTERVIEW ROOM
    SAMUELS'S OFFICE
    SPECIAL FRAUDS DIVISION
    PROPERTY ROOM
    BOOKING AREA
RUSKIN ENTERPRISES, INC.
BEDROOM
INTERNATIONAL CARRIERS TERMINAL
    BOARDING AREA
    SECURITY CHECKPOINT
    AIRPORT SECURITY
NELSON HOUSE
CAGNEY/LACEY CAR
LACEY APARTMENT
    LACEY BEDROOM
    LACEY LIVING ROOM
INTERROGATION ROOM—
    RIKER'S ISLAND
PROPERTY ROOM—RIKER'S ISLAND
SHELTER FOR BATTERED WIVES
    WAITING ROOM

EXTERIOR:

NEW YORK STREET
POLICE VEHICLE
HOT DOG STAND
KENNEDY AIRPORT
14th PRECINCT
NELSON HOUSE
LACEY APARTMENT BLDG.
CAGNEY/LACEY CAR
SHELTER FOR BATTERED WIVES
PARKING BAY

ACT ONE

FADE IN:

I   INT. SQUAD ROOM—DAY

LACEY sits at her desk sipping the first cup of morning coffee.
CAGNEY hobbles in on a cane.

LACEY

    Late date, Christine?

CAGNEY grins a Cheshire-cat kind of smile as she sits down.

LACEY

    This is the one who took you parachuting, right?

CAGNEY

    Right.

LACEY

    And hang gliding the week before when you racked up your leg?

CAGNEY

    I really like this one.

LACEY

    Uh huh. Aside from a strong death wish does he have any other
    qualifications?

CAGNEY

    He's gorgeous.

LACEY

    How did I know.

CAGNEY

    And an incurable romantic. Last night he had the dessert chef at
    Chez Robaire bake this into a souffle for me.

She pulls a gold chain out of her handbag and dangles it in front of
LACEY.

LACEY

    It's nice.

CAGNEY

    Yeah, but I don't really know him well enough. I have to send it
    back.

ISBECKI appears, a cup of coffee in his hand. He swoops the chain
from CAGNEY.

ISBECKI

    Guy must be a real loser. Has to buy you presents to get a date.

CAGNEY

Get out of here, Isbecki.

She grabs the chain back from him.

ISBECKI

What do you think he paid for something like that? Fifty, seventy-five bucks?

CAGNEY

I couldn't care less and it's none of your business.

ISBECKI

Only gift I ever have to give a chick is me.

CAGNEY

Take me off your Christmas list.

ISBECKI winks and leaves. CAGNEY hefts the chain in her hand appraisingly.

CAGNEY

(continuing)

At least twelve grams of gold here. A hundred-fifty bucks, the very least.

LACEY

(teasing her)

But you couldn't care less.

CAGNEY

(defensive)

I'm sending it back.

Before LACEY can respond, PETRIE interrupts their conversation.

PETRIE

That Ponzi scheme you've been working on? Three more victims just walked in.

He hands them a file and turns to point out three little old ladies. In the b.g. the PHONE RINGS.

2   CAGNEY AND LACEY'S POV

NORMA, ROSE and EDITH. Three ladies in their sixties, one middle-class, now struggling to make it on Social Security.

2A   RESUME ANGLE

ISBECKI calls out:

ISBECKI

A phone call for you, Lacey.

LACEY
(to CAGNEY)
I'll catch up with you in the interview room.

CAGNEY moves toward the Ladies' Room. LACEY answers the phone.

LACEY
(continuing; into phone)
Detective Lacey, 14th Squad.

INTERCUT with woman.

2B   INT. BEDROOM—DAY

It's a darkened room. We are CLOSE on a WOMAN. She is 35, careworn. Her face is obscured by shadows, but we can make out that it is bruised.

WOMAN
I can't stand it anymore. I have to talk to someone.

LACEY
Yes, ma'am.

WOMAN
(building hysteria)
You won't believe me. You'll stick up for *him*. I know you will.

LACEY
(impatient)
I'm sorry, ma'am. Do you wish to report a crime?

WOMAN
My doctor told me it was *my* problem. He gave me tranquilizers.

LACEY
Excuse me, ma'am? What is the problem?

WOMAN
My husband beats me.

LACEY
We'll send an officer right over. What's the address?

WOMAN
No. No—No police. That would only make things worse.

LACEY
Is your husband there now?

WOMAN
No.

LACEY
Let me give you a number to call, they'll find a shelter for you.

LACEY's looking for a number, no response.

LACEY

(continuing)

Here it is, hello? Are you there?

WOMAN

(quietly)

Just tell me what'll happen to him if I turn him in. See, my husband, he's a . . . What's the use. Forget it.

She hangs up. LACEY is a bit baffled, but not terribly concerned. Detectives get lots of strange calls.

CUT TO:

3   INT. INTERVIEW ROOM—DAY

CAGNEY is at a table with NORMA, ROSE and EDITH. LACEY enters, somewhat preoccupied by the phone call.

ROSE

You, you're young yet. You wouldn't understand about setting aside for your old age.

EDITH

Then I say she's living in a dream world. She thinks she's going to make it on Social Security? I gotta laugh.

CAGNEY

(looking at file)

We've been investigating this Mr. Ruskin.

NORMA

(interrupting)

You should spit when you say his name. This Mr. Ruskin, he said he was a real estate investor and he promised me a 50 percent return on my investment. Guaranteed.

CAGNEY

How much money did you give him?

NORMA

Ten thousand dollars. Money I'd saved, a nickle here, a dime there. At first the checks came in every month, like clockwork. $416 a month—the difference to me between living like an animal and living like a human being. He asked if I had any friends interested . . .

EDITH

Better she should have kept her mouth shut.

(beat)

Not that I'm blaming anyone.

ROSE

I gave him $12,000. For awhile it was just like Norma said. A miracle. Then the funny stuff started. First the check was a few days late—then a week.

EDITH

Then nothing at all for the last two months. Every time we call they say he's out.

CAGNEY and LACEY look at each other.

NORMA

I can't tell you how bad I feel. Like a criminal.

ROSE

You didn't twist our arms. He seemed very sincere to me.

EDITH

Well not to me. I smelled something fishy right off. Didn't I tell you, Norma, the penthouse office, rings on every finger. Someone's paying for all that, I said. But Norma said he was okay. So—I lost everything.

(beat)

Not that I'm blaming anyone.

NORMA

Please, officers, is there something you can do?

CUT TO:

3A   ONE POLICE PLAZA—ESTABLISHING—DAY (STOCK)

3B   INT. HALLWAY—DAY

CAGNEY and LACEY walk down hallway passing a sign indicating Special Frauds Division.

CAGNEY

How come we have to hold our strategy meetings here? Why can't Solomon and Nelson ever come up to the 14th?

LACEY

Rank has its privileges.

CAGNEY

That's what I'm talking about. You and Brent Nelson graduated from the Academy together, so how come he's got two grades on you?

LACEY

I would say . . . sexual discrimination?

CAGNEY

(playing along)

Why didn't *I* think of that?

LACEY

In all fairness, he's a smart man, Christine. Number one in our class.

CAGNEY

Well I hope Number One's come up with something for us today. I can't face another destitute widow.

CUT TO:

4   OMITTED

5   INT. SPECIAL FRAUDS DIVISION—DAY

CAGNEY and LACEY sit across the desk from BRENT NELSON (35, good-looking, "too refined" in appearance to be a cop), and his partner, MICK SOLOMON (40, big, gruff and crass).

CAGNEY

(to BRENT)

Here's the files on the three new victims.

She slaps the files onto the desk.

MICK

(to CAGNEY)

I finally figured out who it is you remind me of. My ex-wife. Number three. I mean, around the eyes.

BRENT

Solomon . . .

MICK shrugs, CAGNEY ignores him.

CAGNEY

(to BRENT)

Have you heard back from the I.R.S.?

MICK

The I.R.S. connections are mine. I'm seeing what I can do. I'm checking with the S.E.C. too.

BRENT

Sure. You'll turn it over to the Feds and we'll lose Ruskin on some lousy Securities technicality.

MICK

    You kidding? Mick Solomon always gets his man.
    (leers at CAGNEY)
    And usually his woman.

LACEY

    You still got a tail on Ruskin, right?

MICK

    (nodding yes)
    I thought he'd make a run for it by now.
    (more)

MICK

    (continuing)
    I like when they run. It's good evidence for a collar.

LACEY

    So, let's make the guy nervous. See what he does.

CAGNEY

    I could go in to see him. Undercover.

BRENT

    You're a little young for his usual investor.

CAGNEY is one step ahead of him.

CAGNEY

    Poor Mom. She lost everything she had.

                                                    CUT TO:

6   OMITTED

7   INT. RUSKIN ENTERPRISES, INC.—DAY
    ED RUSKIN's office is very luxurious in garish, nouveau riche style.
    Prominently displayed are gilt framed photos of offices, hotels,
    apartment complexes, etc., all depicting RUSKIN's real estate
    holdings.
    ED RUSKIN, an ordinary looking man, but dramatic in dress and
    style, has a penchant for gold jewelry—neck chains, pendants,
    bracelets, and a ring on every finger.
    CAGNEY sips coffee while RUSKIN paces the floor, all but tearing his
    hair out.

RUSKIN

    I can't stand it that I've caused your lovely mother even a second's
    discomfort.

CAGNEY

You have been very hard to reach and she hasn't received a payment in two months.

RUSKIN

(interrupting)

What can I say? Cash flow. That's all it is, a tiny cash flow problem. The escrow on the sale of the hotel on Grand Cayman got held up by the fluctuating interest rate. But it's sure to close by the end of the week at a 300 percent profit to investors.

CAGNEY

Perhaps you could show me the paperwork on the hotel sale?

RUSKIN

Of course. Of course.

He waves a thick file at her; replaces it on his desk out of her reach.

RUSKIN

(continuing)

Now, will you do one little thing for me? Will you reassure that lovely mother of yours.

CAGNEY

I wonder if you could make your books available . . .

RUSKIN

Absolutely no problem. My auditors are working on them right now. I'll have a statement for all the investors by the end of the month.

The INTERCOM on his phone BUZZES.

He picks up.

RUSKIN

(continuing)

Yes.

(beat)

Right. Right away. Fabulous.

He hangs up, a big smile on his face.

RUSKIN

(continuing)

Stupendous news. I've just closed on an office building in Juneau. An absolute give-away price.

He stands.

RUSKIN

(continuing)

If you'll excuse me I have papers to sign.

He takes her hand, stares meaningfully into her eyes as he presses it.

RUSKIN
(continuing)
By the way—if you've got a little money saved up, I could possibly get you into the Juneau deal.

SCENES 8, 9, 10 OMITTED

10A INT. BOOKING AREA—DAY
CAGNEY & LACEY enter from the back door. CAGNEY remembers something. She pulls a paperback book from her purse.

CAGNEY
Oh Mary Beth. I've been meaning to ask you. You ever read this kind of thing?

She hands LACEY the lurid-looking book.

LACEY
"Love's Savage Harvest," by Brianna Dumain. One of those corny romances?

CAGNEY
Yeah. A friend of mine wrote it and I have to say something, so I was kind of hoping you'd read it for me.

LACEY
Me? Why don't you read it?

CAGNEY
I can't get through it.
(teasing her)
But housewives like this stuff.

LACEY
(rising to the bait)
Thanks a lot, Christine.

CAGNEY
That's a joke.

LACEY
Almost funny.

CAGNEY
Please, Mary Beth. What am I going to say to my friend. Can't you just try? Please, as a favor.

LACEY
I'll try. It's gotta be better than television.

CAGNEY

Great. Thanks.

She stuffs the book into LACEY's purse and smiles at her as LACEY pushes open the door to the squad room and stops dead in her tracks, staring at CAGNEY's desk (we can't see what she sees).

LACEY

(awestruck)

What in the world is that?

CUT TO:

II   OMITTED

IIA   INT. SQUAD ROOM—NIGHT

CAGNEY is on the phone. There is a huge ice sculpture of a dolphin on her desk. You can barely see CAGNEY's head over it. ISBECKI can't believe it.

ISBECKI

An ice sculpture?

CAGNEY

(into phone)

Ruskin's so good at his con, I don't know if I made him nervous or not . . .

ISBECKI

So the guy sent you something you couldn't return.

CAGNEY ignores ISBECKI.

CAGNEY

(continuing into phone)

Yes, I know I make you nervous, Solomon.

ISBECKI

You should have kept the gold chain.

He leaves.

CAGNEY

(continuing into phone)

Thanks anyway. You're married already and five is my unlucky number.

She hangs up.

LACEY

I take it Detective Solomon just proposed.

CAGNEY

The guy almost makes Isbecki look good.

(looks at sculpture)

What am I going to do with a thousand pounds of ice?

LACEY

I know this is all very romantic, Christine. But what you really need is a guy with his feet on the ground.

CAGNEY

Like who?

LACEY

Like Harvey.

CAGNEY

Great, he's married and I even like his wife.

LACEY

I'm just giving you examples. Brent Nelson.

CAGNEY

He's married too.

LACEY

And I like his wife.

(beat)

Petrie.

CAGNEY

Could you come up with some *un*-married examples.

LACEY proceeds to think.

CAGNEY

(continuing)

Take your time.

The PHONE RINGS.

CAGNEY

(continuing)

Detective Cagney, 14th.

(beat)

Solomon, take "no" for an answer.

(beat)

Oh. Okay. We'll meet you there.

CAGNEY gathers up her stuff.

CAGNEY

(continuing)

C'mon, Mary Beth. Ruskin's ordered a limo. He's on the way to the airport.

LACEY
   (gathering her stuff)
   Albert Schweitzer.
CAGNEY
   He's dead.

                                                            CUT TO:

12   OMITTED

13   EXT. KENNEDY AIRPORT—ESTABLISHING—NIGHT (STOCK)

                                                            CUT TO:

14   INT. INTERNATIONAL CARRIERS TERMINAL—NIGHT
BRENT greets CAGNEY and LACEY inside the door. The following
conversation continues on the run as they race through the airport.
LACEY
   How are we going to arrest him? We don't have enough probable
   cause for a collar.
BRENT
   We wait 'til he gets on the plane—shows consciousness of guilt.
They badge their way through Security Control.
CAGNEY
   Where do you think he's going?
BRENT
   Probably South America. Maybe Switzerland.
They SKID to a halt as they reach . . .

15   MICK SOLOMON
Who is standing in the newsstand in the gift shop, pretending to
browse. There is a display of sunglasses and floppy sun hats with "I
(love) New York" on them.
MICK
   (to CAGNEY)
   Hi, beautiful lady.
CAGNEY
   Where is he?
MICK
   (slight nod of head)
   Bar.
They look.

16   THEIR POV
      FIFTY FEET AWAY ED RUSKIN is alone at a table, nursing a drink.
      LACEY (O.S.)
          Is he gonna recognize you?

17   ANGLE ON THE FOUR DETECTIVES
      CAGNEY
          I'll take care of it.
      She moves to the counter.
      LACEY
          Where's his luggage?
      MICK
          He didn't bring any, but if that overcoat of his is lined with cash,
          he's not going to need anything else.
      ANNOUNCER (V.O.)
          Flight 401 for Zurich now boarding at Gate 7.
      BRENT
          Look . . . he's moving . . . let's go!
      CAGNEY hurries to join them, now wearing glasses and hat.

18   ED RUSKIN
      leaves a couple of bills on the table, stands and leaves the cocktail
      lounge. He passes a few feet in front of the four detectives (they're all
      very busy looking at magazines). Once he's past them, they tail him
      at a discreet distance into the . . .

19   CORRIDOR
      RUSKIN's pace picks up and so does theirs. The passengers line up at
      Gate 7, but RUSKIN continues past. RUSKIN winds his way through
      the crowd and the detectives are in hot pursuit. Another plane is
      arriving at Gate 10.

20   ANGLE—CAGNEY AND LACEY
      Look at each other.

21   ANGLE
      ED RUSKIN stops. He waves. He waits. A man carrying a suitcase
      (ALEJANDRO) walks forward. The two men shake hands.

22   ANGLE—CAGNEY AND LACEY

CAGNEY

    Great, he's not going anywhere, he's picking somebody up.

23   THE FOUR DETECTIVES

do their best to fade into the woodwork, as RUSKIN and ALEJANDRO turn around and head back out toward the entrance of the airport.

                    CUT TO:

24   OMITTED

24A   INT. SQUAD ROOM—NIGHT

CAGNEY and LACEY enter, tired, dejected. The ice sculpture is a puddle in its container on CAGNEY's desk. SAMUELS catches them near the door, file in hand.

SAMUELS

    Where's Ruskin? I thought you were bringing him in.

LACEY

    Wild goose chase.

They walk toward their desks.

CAGNEY

    We got to the airport just in time to see him pick up a friend, then we had a nice two hour drive in rush hour traffic as we followed them back to his office. We still don't have enough for a collar, and I'm out eighteen dollars for this dumb disguise.

LACEY

    (noticing, annoyed)

    Not to mention your dolphin has melted all over our desks.

SAMUELS

    La Guardia took another victim's report while you were gone. A seventy-two-year-old widow. Lost everything she had.

LACEY grabs up some paper towels and starts wiping up around the container. The PHONE RINGS in the b.g. ISBECKI picks up.

LACEY

    This guy's worse than the one who sent you the turtle.

CAGNEY

    The snapping turtle? Remember that?

They start to laugh.

LACEY

    When it got loose in the men's room?

The two women are laughing like crazy.

ISBECKI

Lacey. Telephone.

It takes LACEY a second to choke down her laughter.

LACEY

Detective Lacey, 14th Squad.

INTERCUT with:

24B   THE WOMAN

WOMAN

I just called to tell you he's not going to do it again.

LACEY

I'm sorry, what? I don't understand.

WOMAN

My husband . . . he's never going to hurt me again.

LACEY

You called earlier?

WOMAN

I bought a gun. If he lays a hand on me, I'm going to kill him.

LACEY

Please, don't hang up. We can't help you unless . . .

WOMAN

(bitter)

Help me? You won't help me. He's one of you. He's a cop.

LACEY

A cop?

ON LACEY'S REACTION, WE . . .   FADE OUT.

END OF ACT ONE

ACT TWO

FADE IN:

24C INT. SQUAD ROOM—NIGHT

LACEY still has her hand on the phone. She's concerned. LACEY throws out the wet towels.

LACEY

She says she's a cop's wife. Claims her husband's beating her, and she's bought a gun.

CAGNEY

Let's get over there.

LACEY

She wouldn't give me her name or address.

CAGNEY

This is a potential homicide/suicide here. Let's go talk to the lieutenant.

LACEY

Talk about what? Two hysterical phone calls?

CAGNEY

Regulations say we have to turn a cop like this in to his superior officer.

LACEY

Regulations only apply when you know who's doing it.

CAGNEY

Why are you dragging your feet on this?

LACEY

Because we don't have anything. But we can go in there. The lieutenant'll make a nice, little speech about the brotherhood of cops, and tell us to sit on it.

CUT TO:

25 OMITTED

25A INT. SAMUELS'S OFFICE—NIGHT

SAMUELS

I want you to find the bastard and nail him.

CAGNEY

Yes, sir.

CAGNEY
(to BRENT)
I'm leaving.
PHONE RINGS, BRENT picks up.
BRENT
Special Frauds, Detective Nelson.
MICK
(to CAGNEY)
Wait, wait, wait, wait. I called you over here for a reason.
BRENT
Mick, it's your wife.
MICK
Dammit.
(flashing anger; into phone)
I told you I'd call you later. I don't care.
He hangs up—turns the charm to CAGNEY.
MICK
(continuing)
You wanna be there for the Ruskin collar, right.
CAGNEY
(nods "yes")
It's my case.
MICK
He's gonna run any minute. I figure we could wait him out together.
CAGNEY
I'll wait with Lacey.
MICK
You'll have a lot more fun with me.
She starts out.
MICK
(continuing)
I'll order in dinner.
She walks out. MICK turns to BRENT.
MICK
(continuing)
She likes me. I can tell.

CUT TO:

SCENES 29, 29A, 30 OMITTED

CAGNEY enters, throws her purse on her desk. SAMUELS is in his office working. The other detectives are out.

CAGNEY

I can't stand that man.

LACEY has some news for her.

LACEY

Listen to this, Christine. I got a copy of the tape from Communications.

She turns on a tape recorder.

MAN (V.O.)

Fourteenth Precinct.

WOMAN (V.O.)

I'd like to speak to Mary Beth Lacey, please.

MAN (V.O.)

Hold on.

LACEY snaps off the machine.

LACEY

The cop's wife. She asked for me by name.

CAGNEY

You recognize the voice?

LACEY

(shaking her head "no")
I've listened to it over and over. I got a printout of all the guys in the precinct who are married. I'm going over it, but I can't believe it's one of ours. Petrie? You believe he's hitting Claudia? Davidson? Coleman?

PETRIE walks in, goes over to his desk. CAGNEY and LACEY are suddenly awkward.

CAGNEY

(quietly)
Nobody ever thinks it's somebody they know, Mary Beth. But one out of four guys hit their wives.

LACEY

(angry)
Don't quote me statistics, here. I'm talking about people.

CAGNEY

So am I. Chances are, one of those people is hitting his wife. I don't think the guys should know what we're working on.

LACEY throws down her pencil. She knows CAGNEY's right but it's so hard to accept. CAGNEY sits down at her desk.

CAGNEY
(continuing; terse)
Brent says Ruskin's getting ready to run. I said we'd stay by the phone.

LACEY
So we'll stay.

CAGNEY
If you want, you can go home to Harve and the boys.

LACEY
I'll stay.

CAGNEY
I'm going to miss my date.

LACEY
(quiet)
We could order in a pizza.

CAGNEY
Great. Those fancy nouvelle cuisine sauces never agree with me anyway.

CUT TO:

31   OMITTED

31A   CLOSEUP—PIZZA CRUST
is tossed down onto a now-empty pizza box.

31B   PULL BACK
to see the remains of the pizza. LACEY has the yellow pages out in front of her. She's checking the gun stores. She is also holding "Love's Savage Harvest" in front of her, reading during the times she's on hold. CAGNEY has the telephone in her hand, a soft drink can in the other. She sips from the can, then murmurs into the phone. Except for SAMUELS, who is still working in his office, the other detectives have gone home.

CAGNEY	LACEY
Ooooh . . . this wine is fabulous. Mouton Charlemagne '71 is my absolute favorite.	. . . and I'm checking hand gun registrations for the last two weeks. Yes, I'll hold.

LACEY reads, CAGNEY bites into a potato chip.

CAGNEY	LACEY
(continuing)	(continuing; into phone)
This duckling is exquisite. So crispy.	Yes, I'm here. All right.

The PHONE RINGS. LACEY looks at CAGNEY who ignores it. LACEY punches it up, letting her other call go.

CAGNEY	LACEY
(continuing)	(continuing)
No dessert, darling. I couldn't eat another bite. Oh . . . that's not dessert.	Fourteenth Squad, Det. Lacey . . . yes, Mick. You got a gate number? We'll meet you there.

She hangs up.

LACEY
    (continuing)
    Christine . . . airport.

CAGNEY
    Damn. Okay.
    (into phone)
    Hold that thought. To be continued. Bye.

CAGNEY grabs up her hat and glasses. The two race out the door, LACEY still clutching her book.

LACEY
    (indicating book)
    Right at the exciting part.

CAGNEY
    Me, too.

                                      CUT TO:

32   EXT. KENNEDY AIRPORT—ESTABLISHING—NIGHT (STOCK)

33 & 34 OMITTED

34A   INT. INTERNATIONAL CARRIERS TERMINAL—NIGHT—CLOSE
    on a NEWSPAPER. CAGNEY and LACEY sit down on either side of the paper. CAMERA PULLS OUT TO REVEAL BRENT as he lowers the paper. CAGNEY and LACEY are on either side of him. He speaks quietly to them. CAGNEY's in hat and glasses.

BRENT

It's for real this time. He's ticketed for Quito, Ecuador and he's got a bag that he's not letting out of his sight.

He nods in the direction where RUSKIN is pacing. They look.

35   THEIR POV

In the waiting area ED RUSKIN is nervously pacing and staring out the window at the airfield. MICK is standing nearby, ostensibly engrossed in his newspaper.

ANNOUNCER (V.O.)

Intercontinental Flight 307 for Quito, Ecuador will be boarding at Gate 17.

RUSKIN turns toward the gate, then changes his mind. He turns, looks for something.

36 & 37 OMITTED

38   ANOTHER ANGLE

To include our detectives. RUSKIN briskly strides toward the men's room. He passes right past the detectives. Never too engrossed to stare at a pretty woman, he notices CAGNEY. There's something about that face—even behind dark glasses. He feigns indifference and continues on toward the men's room. The detectives' heads turn, oh so subtly to follow him. He turns around quickly and catches them looking. His step picks up.

CAGNEY

Damn. He recognized me.

And RUSKIN's off and running. As he passes our detectives, he throws the suitcase at them.

CAGNEY

I've got the bag! You get him!

LACEY, MICK and BRENT take off after RUSKIN.

39   RUSKIN races down the corridor shoving his way through the crowd.

40   THE THREE DETECTIVES, BRENT, LACEY & MICK

in pursuit, attach their badges as they run.

BRENT, LACEY & MICK

Halt! Police.

Passersby hug the wall and shriek. MICK tackles RUSKIN.

MICK

Ed Ruskin, you're under arrest.

RUSKIN

You can't arrest me. I'm going on a vacation.

MICK

No problem. I know a lovely resort up the river. Plan on twenty years.

CUT TO:

41   INT. AIRPORT SECURITY—LATER

The four detectives sit in the glassed-in office with the head of airport security. CAGNEY is still clutching ED RUSKIN's unopened suitcase, which is on the floor next to her. In the b.g., outside the office, we see RUSKIN being led away by N.Y.P.D. uniformed officers.

CAGNEY

(to LACEY)

I never held a million dollars in my hands before.

She lifts the suitcase onto the table.

CAGNEY

(continuing)

Weighs less than I thought it would.

BRENT

Well okay, Airport Security's here to witness this now. Let's open it up.

CAGNEY clicks the locks. MICK is practically breathing down her neck.

MICK

One million bucks. Hello you pretty green things . . .

The bag snaps open. And everyone just stares. It's filled with socks and underwear. They dump everything out. Socks and underwear. Two shirts, a pair of pants, and socks and underwear. ON THEIR REACTION . . .

FADE OUT.

END OF ACT TWO

ACT THREE

FADE IN:

42   INT. SAMUELS' OFFICE—DAY

The next day. CAGNEY, LACEY, and SAMUELS are holding the "post-mortem."

SAMUELS

> He takes all his money out of the bank and he goes directly back
> to his office. From there he goes to the airport with a one-way
> ticket to Quito, Ecuador. So where's the money?

CAGNEY

> Two hundred bucks on him. That's all he had.

SAMUELS

> Doesn't make sense.

PETRIE sticks his head in the door.

PETRIE

> Excuse me . . . your real estate fraud victims are waiting for you.

LACEY

> Thanks. We'll be right there.

CAGNEY

> Guy doesn't leave the country with two hundred bucks.

They turn to leave.

SAMUELS

> Lacey—how you doing on finding that cop?

LACEY

> I've called every gun dealer in the city. If she bought the gun
> legally, we can match up the registration with our personnel files.
> Alice Martinez is doing a computer run for me.

SAMUELS

> I'll call her, tell her it's top priority.

LACEY

> Thank you, sir.

CUT TO:

43 & 44 OMITTED

45   INT. SQUAD ROOM—CLOSE—DAY

On the book "Love's Savage Harvest."

EDITH (O.S.)

My cousin reads these. She tells me they're nothing but smut. It's all smut these days. Movies, television, books. All smut.

46 ANOTHER ANGLE

To reveal the three ladies at LACEY's desk. CAGNEY and LACEY are approaching them.

ROSE

Well, if you think it's bad for me, Edith.

EDITH

I wouldn't want to tell you what to do, dear.

At that moment, CAGNEY and LACEY join them.

CAGNEY

(surprised; pleased)

Oh—you're reading Brianna Dumain's book?

ROSE practically flings it back onto LACEY's desk.

ROSE

Not me! It's smut!

LACEY, a tad embarrassed, puts the book away in a desk drawer.

EDITH

We heard on the news you arrested Ed Ruskin. We came to get our money.

CAGNEY and LACEY exchange a glance.

CAGNEY

I'm afraid we haven't recovered the money, yet.

NORMA

(concerned)

You haven't?

(a bright idea)

Have you checked with his bank? It's probably still there.

A quick look between LACEY and CAGNEY. They don't want to hurt the ladies' feelings. They treat their questions seriously.

LACEY

He withdrew all his funds before he tried to leave the country.

NORMA

Then it must be at his house.

LACEY

Believe me, Mrs. Fisher, we're searching everywhere for it.

ROSE

(wanting to get in her two cents worth)

His office?

LACEY nods.

NORMA

His car.

CAGNEY

We've tried his car.

EDITH

A mistress. He's probably got a mistress. Check her place.

LACEY

We'll look everywhere, ma'am.

ROSE is very upset.

ROSE

I don't know how I'll pay my rent next month if you don't find that money.

If CAGNEY and LACEY had thought the women amusing, ROSE's concern brings home the sobering truth.

LACEY

We'll find it, ma'am.

                                                              CUT TO:

SCENES 46A THRU 48A OMITTED

48B   INT. BOOKING AREA—DAY—CLOSE

on candy bar machine. PULL BACK to see CAGNEY get a candy bar. We FOLLOW HER through the doors into the . . .

48C   SQUAD ROOM

as she walks back to her desk.

48D   ANOTHER ANGLE

MICK SOLOMON is talking to LACEY. We see CAGNEY approaching them in the background.

MICK

I've never seen such a deadbang case. The Hotel De—
(he can't pronounce it)
Somethingorother . . . on Grand Cayman . . . owned by Letty Corporation.

LACEY

So it's not Ed Ruskin's?

MICK

Not technically. His mother is Letty Corporation.

LACEY

So it is Ed Ruskin's.

MICK

His and ten other people's . . . each of whom think they own 25%.

He looks up at CAGNEY as she joins them, sniffs the air.

MICK

(continuing)

What is that perfume? You're driving me wild.

CAGNEY

Eau de chocolate.

LACEY

(showing report to CAGNEY)

Ruskin's sold two hundred and fifty percent of this hotel.

MICK

That's the small potatoes. He really cleaned up on this office building in Juneau.

CAGNEY

(annoyed)

That's the one he tried to sell me!

MICK

Owned by . . .

LACEY

Let me guess. Letty Corporation.

MICK

(turns to LACEY)

You got it.

LACEY

I suppose there are a few other investors in this property, too.

MICK

He sold 500%.

SAMUELS comes out of his office. He looks troubled.

CAGNEY

You can prove this?

MICK

The case is solid. We have the man. We have the crime. Now where the hell is the money?

SAMUELS walks over to their desk.

LACEY

Lieutenant . . . you're going to want to see this.

SAMUELS

(to SOLOMON)

Where's your partner?

MICK

Out with the flu. It's going around.

SAMUELS nods.

SAMUELS

Could I see the two of you in my office a minute. If you'll excuse us, Detective Solomon?

MICK

Sure, I'm through here.

SAMUELS walks into his office as MICK gathers up his things.

MICK

(continuing to CAGNEY)

Call me later if you want to put in some overtime.

CAGNEY's really had it.

CAGNEY

Enough, Solomon.

He winks at her, leaves. CAGNEY follows LACEY toward SAMUELS's office.

49   INT. SAMUELS'S OFFICE

As CAGNEY and LACEY enter, SAMUELS rips the piece of paper off the pad.

CAGNEY

We got Ruskin dead to rights.

SAMUELS

Alice Martinez found your wife beater.

He hands the paper to LACEY. CAGNEY looks over her shoulder.

LACEY

Brent Nelson! That can't be!

SAMUELS

Wife's name Phyllis?

LACEY looks at him.

LACEY

Yes.

SAMUELS

There's a .38 snubnose registered in her name.

LACEY

He'd never hit her. I've never even seen him angry.

SAMUELS

It was the same thing with my partner. Jekyll and Hyde.
(beat)
Solomon said Nelson's out with the flu.

CAGNEY

He's home and she's got a gun.

SAMUELS

You two check it out.
They're out the door.

CUT TO:

50 EXT. HOUSE—DAY

CAGNEY and LACEY's car pulls up in front of a tract house which looks just like the one next to it. The houses are packed close together.

SCENES 50A THRU 50D OMITTED

50E EXT. HOUSE—DAY

As CAGNEY and LACEY exit the car and approach the house.

CUT TO:

51 ANGLE—AT THE DOOR—DAY

CAGNEY rings the bell. There's no answer. They wait a minute, ring again. Still no response. CAGNEY starts looking for a way in.

LACEY

Ring one more time.

CAGNEY goes to do so, but at the same time, the door opens. BRENT is there in his bathrobe. He looks disheveled. Sick, hung over, who can tell? He's surprised to see them.

BRENT

What are you two doing here?

CAGNEY and LACEY are wary. They don't want to tip their hand.

CAGNEY

We wanted to talk to you about Ruskin. Can we come in?

BRENT

You should've called. I have the flu. I don't think you want to get too close to me.

LACEY

(easygoing)

That's okay. If I haven't gotten it from the kids by now, I'm not
going to get it.

She walks right past BRENT into the house. CAGNEY follows. BRENT
closes the door behind them.

CUT TO:

SCENE 51A OMITTED

52 INT. HOUSE—DAY

The place is spotless, except that a lamp is knocked over and the
pillows from the sofa are tossed about. LACEY looks for any sign of
PHYLLIS. The door to the bedroom is closed.

LACEY

Must be great to have a house. Harvey and I've been thinking
about buying.

BRENT is clearly not pleased about their being there.

BRENT

I'd show you around, but the place is a mess.

LACEY

Phyllis here? I'd love to see her.

BRENT is getting edgy.

BRENT

What'd you want to talk to me about?

CAGNEY

Solomon's linked Letty Corporation to Ruskin.

BRENT

(annoyed)
He called me. Let's talk about it tomorrow. I'm really feeling rotten.

LACEY

I'm sorry. We shouldn't have gotten you out of bed. You're right.
Why don't we say a quick hello to Phyllis and get out of your way.

BRENT

You'll have to do that another time. She isn't here.

He's not giving them anything. LACEY can't help but wonder if
PHYLLIS is behind that closed door. She can't leave without finding
out.

LACEY

Harve's such a baby. I can never leave him alone when he's sick.

BRENT

She's out getting me some cough medicine.

LACEY

Then, she'll be back soon.

BRENT

I don't mean to be rude, but I'm in no condition for company.
CAGNEY and LACEY look at each other. How can they stay? At that
moment, the front door opens, a woman we'll come to know as
PHYLLIS enters. She's wearing dark glasses to cover a black eye. She
stiffens when she sees LACEY.

LACEY

Phyllis?

PHYLLIS doesn't say anything.

BRENT

You remember Mary Beth Lacey, Phyllis. This is her partner,
Christine Cagney.

CAGNEY

Hello.

PHYLLIS stands dead still.

LACEY

(gentle)

How are you, Phyllis?

PHYLLIS

(scared; to BRENT)

I got your cough medicine. You'd better take some right away.
BRENT notices her anxiety.

BRENT

Right away? You trying to get rid of me?

PHYLLIS

No.

BRENT

(ominous)

Something wrong, Phyl? Or, you want to talk girl talk with Mary
Beth.

PHYLLIS can hear the veiled threat.

PHYLLIS

I'm worried about your cough, is all.

He puts his arm around her.

BRENT

(to MARY BETH, there's an edge to his voice)

Isn't she the best little wife in the world. I'll go take my medicine,
Phyl. Leave you to your friends.

He goes out of the room. PHYLLIS still can't move. LACEY and CAGNEY are worried that he'll reappear. They talk quietly, fast.

LACEY

(gently)

Phyllis, we know you've been calling.

PHYLLIS

(very frightened; low voice)

I don't know what you're talking about.

CAGNEY

(also quietly)

You don't have to stay here. You can come with us. We'll help you find a place to stay.

PHYLLIS

(denying)

This is my home. Why would I leave?

LACEY

Brent.

PHYLLIS

Brent and I are very happy. Please . . . you'd better go.

It doesn't look like LACEY and CAGNEY are going to go.

PHYLLIS is too frightened of what they're asking her to do. She can't take the responsibility. She calls out to BRENT.

PHYLLIS

(continuing)

Brent! Mary Beth is just leaving. You want to say goodbye?

He appears in the doorway. He doesn't say anything. He doesn't have to. LACEY tries to keep it real light, but we can still feel the threat.

LACEY

(directly to PHYLLIS)

Give me a call, sometime. I'd love to get together.

PHYLLIS

I'm . . . pretty busy.

LACEY's heart sinks. She nods.

LACEY

Let's go, Christine.

They leave together. PHYLLIS still doesn't move.

CUT TO:

SCENE 52A OMITTED

53   EXT. HOUSE—DAY
      As they get into the car.

SCENE 53A OMITTED

54   INT. THE CAR
      CAGNEY sits behind the steering wheel, frustrated, not knowing what
      to do.
      CAGNEY
        She never took off her sunglasses, but it looked to me like she had
        a shiner.
      LACEY
        We can't drag her out of there if she doesn't want to go.
      CAGNEY
        At least he knows we're onto him.
      LACEY looks at her.
      CAGNEY
        (continuing)
        Maybe we scared him off.
      LACEY
        Maybe we pushed him over.
      CAGNEY
        Let's stick around a few minutes. Make sure no fireworks start.
      LACEY
        (sure)
        Okay. We'll both feel better.
      They settle into the car and watch the house.
      CAMERA PULLS BACK to see the car outside the house. HOLD and . . .

                                                          FADE OUT.
                          END OF ACT THREE

ACT FOUR

FADE IN:

55   EXT. LACEY APARTMENT BUILDING—ESTABLISHING—DAY

CUT TO:

56   INT. LACEY BEDROOM—DAY

It is early morning. LACEY is sitting up in bed, awake. The alarm goes off. HARVEY reaches over and shuts it off. He turns over, sees that MARY BETH is already awake. "Love's Savage Harvest" is sitting open against her, but she's staring out into space.

HARVEY

That must be some book.

LACEY

Hmmm?

HARVEY

You're up before the alarm.

LACEY

Oh. I couldn't sleep.

HARVEY

What?

She nods.

LACEY

How could they both stand there and pretend like nothing's happened?

HARVEY

Some people can't talk about their troubles, Mary Beth. They get all locked up in a picture of how they're supposed to be.

LACEY

Who thinks they're supposed to beat up their wife? What kind of "picture" is that?

HARVEY

Take another look at that book. The hero—a tough guy, right? And sometimes he pushes his woman around and she loves it. Am I wrong?

LACEY

Are you telling me Phyllis likes to get hit? That I don't believe.

HARVEY

Mary Beth—if I hit you, you'd leave me.

"A CRY FOR HELP"   293

LACEY

Not everybody's me, Harve. I know I've got a job. I can take care of myself. Not every woman knows that.

HARVEY

Give me a break, would you? If the woman stays—I say she's got a problem.

                                                                    CUT TO:

56A   INT. 14TH PRECINCT/LADIES' BATHROOM—DAY

LACEY is washing her hands. CAGNEY enters.

CAGNEY

You won't believe who just called.

LACEY

Phyllis Nelson?

CAGNEY

Brent. We're supposed to meet him and Solomon over at Riker's Island at ten o'clock.

LACEY

What?

CAGNEY

Says he has an informant over there who's going to tell us where Ed Ruskin has stashed his money.

LACEY

Did he say anything about Phyllis?

CAGNEY

Nothing. He acted like everything was hunky-dory.

LACEY

Well, maybe it is.

CAGNEY

(sarcastic)

Oh sure. Phyllis seemed just swell to me yesterday.

LACEY

Maybe we should butt out.

CAGNEY

I see. You think she got that shiner by walking into a door.

LACEY

I don't know for sure. Harve says if he's hitting her and she stays, it's her choice and it's none of our business.

CAGNEY

I can't believe you're saying this.

LACEY

What can't you believe? A, we don't have hard evidence Brent has ever laid a hand on her. And B, if he has—I gotta ask myself why. What's Phyllis' part in this? What's she done to him?

CAGNEY

(incredulous)

What's she done to him? There is nothing, I mean nothing, justifies a man hitting a woman.

LACEY

That's all very easy for us to say, but we're not there. We don't know what happens.

CAGNEY takes just a moment; makes the decision.

CAGNEY

You remember Jeremy?

LACEY

Of course I remember him. I never understood why you let that one get away.

CAGNEY

I'll tell you why. He hit me.

(beat, she admits the whole truth)

No, Mary Beth, he beat me up. Once, that's all it took.

LACEY

Christine, you never told me.

CAGNEY

Not something I like to talk about.

LACEY

Why?

CAGNEY

According to him, he had a very good reason.

LACEY

Which was what?

CAGNEY

It doesn't matter. There are no reasons. Lots of excuses, but no reasons . . . Jeremy apologized and he swore that it would never happen again. And I loved him. And I left him anyway, Mary Beth. 'Cause you don't hit. If a man's got a problem, he can talk, or if he's too mad, he can walk out. But he doesn't hit. Ever.

This hits LACEY hard.

LACEY

I'm going to call Phyllis, make sure she's okay.

CUT TO:

SCENES 57 THRU 59 OMITTED

59A   EXT. PARKING BAY—DAY
CAGNEY and LACEY walk toward their car.
LACEY
   She couldn't have been nicer or more polite. She kept insisting
   that they're okay. That she's okay.
CAGNEY
   But?

60   INT. INTERROGATION ROOM—RIKER'S ISLAND—DAY
BRENT is sitting slouched in a chair, unhappy. MICK is talking to
BRENT's informant, OBIE. MICK is incredulous. LACEY has a hard time
looking at BRENT.
MICK
   You wanna run that past me again?
OBIE
   Ruskin says the money's right under your noses.
CAGNEY
   That's it? That's where he stashed it?
OBIE
   Yeah.
MICK
   (sarcastic)
   The man's a gold mine of information.
OBIE
   (expectantly)
   So . . . what do I get for helping you?
MICK
   Ten years in Sing-Sing. That's if you're lucky.
   (to CAGNEY and LACEY)
   Come on, let's get out of here.
CAGNEY and LACEY and MICK file out. BRENT hangs back. He's cold,
hard, angry.
BRENT
   (to OBIE)
   You burned me, man. You're through.
OBIE knows better than to respond.

61   INT. PROPERTY ROOM—DAY

The four detectives are going through RUSKIN's personal property once again. BRENT is agitated, looking over the list. MICK is sitting on a chair, leaning up against a wall. CAGNEY is going through RUSKIN's wallet. LACEY is looking at the jewelry. CAGNEY and LACEY are some distance from each other.

MICK

    What a waste of time.

LACEY

    He says it's right under our noses. It's worth a try going through this stuff again.

BRENT

    (upset)
    It's gotta be here.

MICK teases BRENT.

MICK

    Of course it is. Would a Brent Nelson informant lie?

BRENT bristles, doesn't say anything.

LACEY

    Look at this. The man had a ring for every finger, a couple of gold bracelets. A gold medallion. Add it up. How much could it be?

CAGNEY

    (still engrossed in her own investigation)
    Any stones?

LACEY

    No.

CAGNEY

    Three hundred apiece . . . five hundred, maybe.

LACEY

    So, five thousand total.

MICK

    Great! We're only $995,000 short. And change. But what the heck. I love to spend my day off at Riker's Island.

BRENT

    I don't need the cheap sarcasm, partner.

MICK

    No, no, I mean it. I can't thank you enough for schlepping us out here.

BRENT has had enough.

BRENT

You want to work on this case yourself? Fine.

He storms out of the room.

MICK

Man can't take a little ribbing.

CAGNEY and LACEY know it could be more serious than that.

LACEY

(to CAGNEY)

I'm going after him.

MICK stands up.

MICK

He's my partner. Finish up here. We'll meet you back at the
fourteenth.

CAGNEY and LACEY watch him leave.

CAGNEY

What if he doesn't cool off before he gets home? He'll take it out
on Phyllis. We've got to turn him in to I.A.D.

LACEY

Let's give him a chance to do it himself. We'll talk to him the
minute we get back.

CAGNEY

Yeah. Okay.

CAGNEY tries to turn her attention back to RUSKIN's property. But
she knows it's a wild goose chase.

CAGNEY

(continuing)

It's not here.

LACEY

What?

CAGNEY

Whatever we're looking for that's worth a million bucks. It's not
here.

LACEY nods. Her mind is obviously more on BRENT than on the
money.

CUT TO:

62   EXT. FOURTEENTH PRECINCT—ESTABLISHING—DAY (STOCK)

63   INT. SQUAD ROOM—DAY

There are socks and underwear strewn all over CAGNEY's desk. CAG-
NEY and LACEY are at LACEY's desk. They're ripping the lining of
RUSKIN's suitcase open with a knife. ISBECKI picks up one of the
pairs of socks.

ISBECKI

   Maybe these socks belonged to George Washington or
   something. Worth a fortune. Collector's item.

CAGNEY can't believe what she's hearing. She looks up at him.

CAGNEY

   (annoyed)
   Very creative, Isbecki.

He grins.

ISBECKI

   Just trying to be helpful.

LA GUARDIA wanders over.

LA GUARDIA

   You'd be amazed at the things people collect. I went to an
   exhibition and sale last spring . . . antique shoe hooks, collar
   stays, and corsets. But no socks.

CAGNEY can't even begin to think of a response. LA GUARDIA walks
away.

THE TELEPHONE RINGS. PETRIE picks up. LACEY has pulled the lining
away from the suitcase.

PETRIE

   (into the phone)
   Fourteenth squad. Detective Petrie.

LACEY

   (to CAGNEY)
   Nothing. What else is right under our noses?

PETRIE

   (to CAGNEY & LACEY)
   Which one of you wants to talk to Mick Solomon?

CAGNEY points to LACEY. LACEY takes the phone.

LACEY

   Hello, Mick. Yeah, cardboard.

CAGNEY

   And George Washington's socks.

LACEY

That's all I know. I thought you and Brent were coming here.
She looks up at CAGNEY, worried.
LACEY

(continuing)
How long ago did you leave him? I see. Yeah, sure. We'll talk to you tomorrow.
She hangs up. She starts gathering her things.
LACEY

(continuing; to CAGNEY)
Brent got into a fight in a bar. Mick told him to go sleep it off at home.
CAGNEY

I'm right behind you.
LACEY is on her way out the door. CAGNEY grabs up her things and hurries after her.

CUT TO:

64   INT. NELSON HOUSE—DAY

BRENT has hold of PHYLLIS and is hitting her. She tries to avoid his blows, but can't. She's sobbing, yelling out to him. He's drunk.
PHYLLIS

You promised you wouldn't hit me again. You promised.
He doesn't even hear her. He shouts accusations back at her.
BRENT

And you promised to love, honor, and obey. Where's the honor, Phyllis? You made me look like a fool. What kind of wife are you?
PHYLLIS

I didn't do anything, Brent. Please!
BRENT

You called them, didn't you? You called them and shot off your big mouth. You want everybody to feel sorry for you so you make up lies about me.
She finds the strength to break away from him.
PHYLLIS

I've got a gun. I'll use it. I swear to God. Stay away from me.
BRENT

Poor Phyllis. Poor, poor Phyllis.
PHYLLIS

Stay away from me!

He hits her, she goes over the sofa, comes up bleeding, goes for her gun.

CUT TO:

65   EXT. HOUSE—DAY

As CAGNEY and LACEY's car arrives. They run to the front door. They can hear the sounds of the argument inside.

PHYLLIS (v.o.)
(hysterical)
Don't come any closer! I'll kill you. I will!

BRENT (v.o.)
(angry again)
You're going to pay for this, Phyllis. You're going to be sorry you were ever born.

LACEY pounds on the door.

LACEY
Let us in! Right now!

PHYLLIS (v.o.)
I mean it! Get away Brent.

LACEY
Open the door.

CAGNEY
(to LACEY)
We gotta break in. Stand back.

CAGNEY breaks the glass on the front door and they let themselves into the house.

66   INSIDE

PHYLLIS is still holding him off with the gun. LACEY moves over to her. CAGNEY has her hand on her gun.

LACEY
Give me the gun, Phyllis.

CAGNEY
(yelling)
Get away from her, Nelson. Right now.

He turns and looks at CAGNEY through a drunken haze.

BRENT
This is family business. Stay out of it.

BRENT moves toward LACEY and PHYLLIS.

CAGNEY

You don't take one more step. You understand me?

He looks at her. He's enraged. But he's not going to argue with her.

LACEY

(to PHYLLIS)

You all right? You're coming with us.

PHYLLIS breaks down and starts to sob. LACEY physically maneuvers her toward the door.

BRENT

(low; dangerous)

Where are you taking my wife?

LACEY

You've got until eight o'clock tomorrow morning to turn yourself into I.A.D.

BRENT

Phyllis.

LACEY

If you don't, I will.

CAGNEY and LACEY take PHYLLIS and leave. BRENT watches, disbelieving, then with a cry of rage and fear:

BRENT

Phyllis!

CUT TO:

67   EXT. LACEY BUILDING—ESTABLISHING—NIGHT (STOCK)

CUT TO:

68   INT. LACEY BEDROOM—NIGHT

LACEY and HARVEY are in bed asleep. We hear someone POUNDING on their FRONT DOOR. They wake up, startled, look at each other.

CUT TO:

69   INT. LACEY LIVING ROOM—NIGHT

HARVEY and LACEY, robes on, come hurrying into the living room. They can hear someone shouting outside their door.

BRENT (O.S.)

Open up, dammit! I know you're in there.

HARVEY looks through the peep hole.

HARVEY

(to LACEY)

It's Brent Nelson.

BRENT (O.S.)

Where's my wife? I know she's in there!

HARVEY

(to LACEY)

You go back in the bedroom. I'll handle it.

LACEY

This is my problem, Harve.

She goes for her gun. She stands flush against the wall, signals HARVEY to open the door. BRENT comes in. He's more drunk than before.

LACEY

(continuing)

Put your gun on the floor.

He turns and looks at her.

LACEY

(continuing)

Don't act crazy, here, Brent. Put your gun on the floor.

He reaches into his coat, undoes his gun, puts it carefully on the floor. HARVEY picks the gun up off the floor. HARVEY, JR., comes in and rushes over to MARY BETH, holding her.

BRENT	LACEY
(angry, low)	(to HARVEY, JR.)
Where is she?	Down the hall and shut the door.
HARVEY	HARVEY, JR.
She isn't here.	(scared)
	Mom!
	LACEY
	Now, Harve!

HARVEY, JR., leaves.

BRENT

How would you like it if someone came in here and took Mary Beth away from you? What would you do?

LACEY

You're upsetting my children. I want you out of here.

BRENT

(angry)

But it's okay for you to bust into my house. Stick your nose into my business.

LACEY

You were beating her!

BRENT

That's a lie!

LACEY

(incredulous)

I saw her face. How can you deny it?

BRENT is momentarily stopped, but not for long.

BRENT

She . . . I . . . maybe I pushed her a little. Once.

LACEY

Don't lie to me anymore, Brent.

He turns to HARVEY.

BRENT

You know what it's like. You come home tired, under a lot of pressure, she starts whining about this thing, that thing. I've just seen a man with his face blown away and she's complaining because the washing machine's broke down. All I want is a little dinner and peace and quiet.

HARVEY just looks at him. BRENT turns to LACEY. She's impassive also.

BRENT

(continuing; anguished)

Why are you all blaming me?! It's not my fault! It's not my fault! They just stare at him. He breaks down.

BRENT

(continuing)

Oh God, Phyl. I'm sorry. I'm so sorry.

He starts to sob. LACEY and HARVEY look at each other. They have all kinds of mixed feelings for this man. There's a sense of the dam finally bursting.

CUT TO:

70   INT. SQUAD ROOM—DAY

LACEY is in good spirits as she comes into the squad room.

CAGNEY is holding a ring, examining it. She looks up at LACEY.

LACEY

I talked to Phyllis this morning. She's doing okay. I told her we'd stop by the shelter in a couple of days to see her.

CAGNEY

Good. So we go to I.A.D. now?

LACEY

It's taken care of. Brent turned himself in voluntarily.

It's a relief to CAGNEY as well.

LACEY's attention is caught by CAGNEY's ring.

LACEY

What do you have there? Another bauble from your mystery
man?

CAGNEY

Yeah. Too bad I have to send it back.

ISBECKI, lurking nearby, is quick to appraise it.

ISBECKI

Why's that? Looks like he got it in a gumball machine.

CAGNEY

Shows what you know, Isbecki. It happens to be worth a fortune.

LACEY hefts it by hand.

LACEY

Come on. Even I know the stuff goes by weight.

CAGNEY

Unless it's 400 years old. This is 24 karat gold. See how soft it is.

LACEY bounces the ring in her hand a bit, testing the weight. It
reminds her of something.

LACEY

Ruskin's jewelry.

She looks up at CAGNEY. CAGNEY doesn't get it.

LACEY

(continuing)

Those rings I asked you about yesterday? They were all like this.

CUT TO:

71   INT. PROPERTY ROOM—RIKER'S ISLAND—DAY

CLOSE on a magnifying glass, magnifying one of Ruskin's rings.

CURATOR (O.S.)

$125,000, even in a depressed market.

72   ANOTHER ANGLE—TO REVEAL

CAGNEY and LACEY talking to a MUSEUM CURATOR who is appraising
the jewelry.

LACEY

For one ring?

CURATOR

It's Minoan.

(he goes through some of the others for them)

This one's Chinese . . . Han Dynasty. I'd take this one to be Mayan. This is a remarkable collection.

LACEY

Where would Ruskin get them? You can't buy them from a museum.

CURATOR

(a chuckle)

Oh, my, no. Antiquities like these are generally sold on the black market.

LACEY

(to CAGNEY)

Ruskin's friend at the airport.

CAGNEY

The South American connection. They must have made the switch at his office.

LACEY

I know at least three ladies who are going to be very happy. I don't think Edith ever expected to get her money back.

CAGNEY

Not that she was blaming anybody.

On LACEY's expression . . .

CUT TO:

73   SHELTER FOR BATTERED WIVES—ESTABLISHING—DAY

CUT TO:

74   INT. WAITING ROOM—DAY

PHYLLIS is ushering CAGNEY and LACEY into a waiting room. There are four or five other women, various ethnic groups, and a half dozen children.

PHYLLIS

I always thought . . . if I loved Brent enough . . . I could fix him. You know what I mean? Make him feel better about himself so he wouldn't hit me.

(the realization)
But I can't. I can't do it for him.
She falls silent.

LACEY
(gently: information)
He's getting help from the Department.

PHYLLIS looks at her.

PHYLLIS
Yeah, I know he turned himself in.

CAGNEY
You spoke to him?

PHYLLIS
No, I can't yet. I'm afraid he'll talk me back into the house.

She looks away again. There's something she wants to tell them. She tries:

PHYLLIS
(continuing)
I know how tough police work has been on Brent. And I'm glad . . . I'm really glad he's getting help. And maybe he'll change. Maybe he will. And maybe he won't. But I've got to do what I can to make sure I'm okay—without him.

LACEY nods.

LACEY
You're doing fine.

CUT TO:

74A EXT. PARKING BAY—DAY
CAGNEY and LACEY get out of their car, walk toward Precinct. LACEY is pulling "Love's Savage Harvest" out of her purse.

LACEY
I keep forgetting to give this back to you.

CAGNEY
You finished it?

LACEY
I told you I would.

CAGNEY
Well? What did you think?

LACEY
I hated it.

CAGNEY

Really?

LACEY

All the way up to four o'clock in the morning when I finally
finished it.

CUT TO:

75 INT. BOOKING AREA—DAY

as they come in.

CAGNEY

You couldn't put it down.

LACEY

Right.

CAGNEY

But you hated it.

LACEY

Right.

CAGNEY

Right.

We FOLLOW them into . . .

76 THE SQUAD ROOM

ISBECKI stops them just inside the door.

ISBECKI

Someone here to see you, Cagney.

They look over at CAGNEY's desk.

77 THEIR POV

An incredibly handsome man lounges about at her desk.

78 RESUME ANGLE

He practically takes LACEY's breath away.

LACEY

(to CAGNEY)

Your mystery man?

CAGNEY nods.

ISBECKI

(a little petulant)

Why do you waste your time with these losers?

CAGNEY smiles at him. She and LACEY walk over to the desk.

The mystery man, JOE KLOTZMAN, smiles up at them.

JOE

I know I'm a little early . . .

CAGNEY

Mary Beth Lacey, I'd like you to meet Brianna Dumain.

LACEY is flabbergasted.

LACEY

You're Brianna Dumain?

He flashes a 100-watt smile.

JOE

Sometimes. Though my mother knows me as Joe Klotzman.
You've read my books?

LACEY

Well, not really.

JOE

You ought to try them. You might like them. Christine reads all
my books the minute they come off the press.

This interests LACEY very much.

LACEY

Oh?

JOE

Yes. I know I can count on her for an honest opinion.

CAGNEY

(realizing they're headed for trouble)
We'd better be getting out of here. We'll be late for our dinner
reservations.

LACEY

Don't rush off. I'd like to hear your honest opinion of "Love's
Savage Harvest."

JOE

(to CAGNEY; pleased)
You finished it?

LACEY

Stayed up all night. Couldn't put it down. Isn't that what you
said, Christine?

CAGNEY

(a sick smile)
That's right.

LACEY

Tell him your favorite parts.

CAGNEY

(to LACEY)

Could I see you in the conference room a moment?

JOE

I'd really like to hear what you have to say.

There's a moment of silence. Then:

LACEY

She had no favorite parts.

JOE

What?

LACEY

She loved the entire book. Every page. Every line.

JOE

(to CAGNEY)

You're wonderful.

CAGNEY shoots LACEY a thankful look.

JOE

(continuing)

You're going to love this little Russian restaurant I've found.

He starts to usher CAGNEY off. CAGNEY gives LACEY a "thumbs up,"
which LACEY returns. LACEY smiles after them, gets an idea, sits
down, dials a phone number.

LACEY

Hi Harve. Whattaya say we get a sitter tonight and go dancing. I
don't know. I'd kind of like a date with my number one guy.

(she grins)

Me, too.

(a squeal)

Harvey!

As she laughs, we HOLD and . . .

FADE OUT.

THE END

ORION TV PRODUCTIONS, INC.
CAGNEY & LACEY
"A Cry for Help"
Prod. #635-124
SHOOTING SCHEDULE

EXEC. PRODUCER:	BARNEY ROSENZWEIG	SHOOTS:
SUPERVISING PROD:	DICK ROSENBLOOM	
EXEC. IN CHARGE		MONDAY, MARCH 21, 1983
OF PRODUCTION:	STAN NEUFELD	THRU
PRODUCER:	HARRY SHERMAN	TUESDAY, MARCH 29, 1983
PRODUCER/WRITER:	STEVE BROWN	
PRODUCER/WRITER:	TERRY LOUISE FISHER	
DIRECTOR:	BARBARA PETERS	
UNIT PROD. MGR.:	BOB BIRNBAUM	
IST ASST. DIR.:	BILLY RAY SMITH	
2ND ASST. DIR.:	STEVE ROSENBLOOM	TOTAL PAGES: 61⅞

DATE	SET/SCENES	CAST	LOCATION
IST DAY MONDAY 3/21/83	INT. SQUAD ROOM	#1 LACEY #2 CAGNEY	2630 LACY STREET
	Sc. 30A Day–2 pgs	#4 SAMUELS #5 PETRIE	PROPS Tape recorder Cassette
	I can't stand that man.	ATMOS. Squad rm. atmos.	Pencil
	INT. SQUAD ROOM	#1 LACEY #2 CAGNEY	AS ABOVE
	Scs. 24A, 24Bpt Night—1⅝ pgs	#4 SAMUELS #6 ISBECKI	PROPS Puddle of water
	Tired and dejected.	ATMOS. Squad rm. atmos.	

DATE	SET/SCENES	CAST	LOCATION
	INT. SQUAD ROOM	#1 LACEY	AS ABOVE
		#2 CAGNEY	
	Sc. 24C		PROPS
	Night—⅝ pg	ATMOS.	Wet towels
		Squad rm. atmos.	
	What was that all about.		
	INT. SAMUELS'S OFFICE	#1 LACEY	2630 LACY STREET
		#2 CAGNEY	
		#4 SAMUELS	
	Sc. 25A	#7 LA GUARDIA	
	Night—1⅛ pgs		
	I want you to find that bastard.		
	INT. SQUAD ROOM	#1 LACEY	AS ABOVE
		#2 CAGNEY	
	Sc. 11A	#6 ISBECKI	PROPS
	Night—2⅛ pgs		Ice sculpture
		ATMOS.	"Dolphin"
	Solomon calls.	Squad rm. atmos.	

END OF 1ST DAY—TOTAL PAGES: 8⅝

DATE	SET/SCENES	CAST	LOCATION
2ND DAY TUESDAY 3/22/83	EXT. PARKING BAY Sc. 74A Day—⅞ pg	#1 LACEY #2 CAGNEY	2630 LACY STREET PROPS Book VEHICLES C&L car Parking bay autos
	EXT. PARKING BAY Sc. 59A Day—⅝ pg She says she's okay.	#1 LACEY #2 CAGNEY	AS ABOVE VEHICLES C&L car Parking lot autos
	INT. SQUAD ROOM Sc. 63 Day—1⅝ pgs	#1 LACEY #2 CAGNEY #5 PETRIE #6 ISBECKI #7 LA GUARDIA ATMOS. Squad rm. atmos.	AS ABOVE PROPS Socks Underwear Suitcase (Ruskin's)
	INT. SAMUELS'S OFFICE Sc. 42 Day—1⅛ pgs Holding post mortem.	#1 LACEY #2 CAGNEY #4 SAMUELS #5 PETRIE ATMOS. Squad rm. atmos.	AS ABOVE

DATE	SET/SCENES	CAST	LOCATION
	INT. SAMUELS'S OFFICE Sc. 49 Day—⅞ pg We got Ruskin dead to rights.	#1 LACEY #2 CAGNEY #4 SAMUELS ATMOS. Squad rm. atmos.	AS ABOVE PROPS Paper pad
	INT. SQUAD ROOM Sc. 70 Day—1⅛ pgs He turned himself in.	#1 LACEY #2 CAGNEY #6 ISBECKI ATMOS. Squad rm. atmos.	AS ABOVE PROPS Ring
	INT. SQUAD ROOM Scs. 31A, 31B Night—1 pg	#1 LACEY #2 CAGNEY #4 SAMUELS	2630 LACY STREET PROPS Book—"Loves Savage Harvest" Soft drink Pizza Glasses
	INT. LADIES' ROOM Sc. 56A Day—2⅞ pgs Guess who called.	#1 LACEY #2 CAGNEY	AS ABOVE SP. EFX Running water

END OF 2ND DAY—TOTAL PAGES: 10

DATE	SET/SCENES	CAST	LOCATION
3RD DAY WEDNESDAY 3/23/83	INT. WAITING ROOM Sc. 74 Day—1 pg Have you heard from Brent.	#1 LACEY #2 CAGNEY #17 PHYLLIS ATMOS. 6 Women 6 Kids	11643 GLENOAKS BLVD. PACOIMA, CA PROPS Toys—etc.
	INT. INTER- NATIONAL TERMINAL Scs. 14, 15, 16, 17, 18, 19, 20, 21, 22, 23 Night—2⅞ pgs Ruskin picks up Alejandro.	#1 LACEY #2 CAGNEY #14 BRENT #15 MICK #16 RUSKIN ATMOS. 11 Airport per- sonnel 29 N.D. travel- lers w/change & baggage	13246 WEIDNER STREET PACOIMA, CA PROPS Drink Money
	INT. INTER- NATIONAL TERMINAL Scs. 34A, 35, 38, 39, 40 Night—1⅛ pgs Pickup Ruskin.	#1 LACEY #2 CAGNEY #14 BRENT #15 MICK #16 RUSKIN STUNT/DOUBLES St Dbl Mick St Dbl Ruskin ATMOS. 11 Airport per- sonnel 29 N.D. travellers	AS ABOVE PROPS Newspaper Bags Glasses Suitcase—Rus- kin's

DATE	SET/SCENES	CAST	LOCATION
	INT. AIRPORT SECURITY	#1 LACEY	AS ABOVE
		#2 CAGNEY	
		#14 BRENT	
	Sc. 41	#15 MICK	
	Night—⅝ pg	#16 RUSKIN	
	Open Ruskin's	ATMOS.	
	suitcase	2 Uniform cops	

END OF 3RD DAY—TOTAL PAGES: 6⅞

DATE	SET/SCENES	CAST	LOCATION
4TH DAY THURSDAY 3/24/83	EXT. NELSON HOUSE	#1 LACEY	112 SO. KINGSLEY
		#2 CAGNEY	LOS ANGELES, CA
	Sc. 65		
	Day—⅝ pg		PROPS Gun
	Break glass.		
			VEHICLES C&L car

	EXT. NELSON HOUSE	#1 LACEY	AS ABOVE
		#2 CAGNEY	
		#14 BRENT	VEHICLES
	Scs. 50, 50E, 51, 53, 54		C&L car
	Day–2 pgs		
	C & L check on Phyllis.		

DATE	SET/SCENES	CAST	LOCATION
	INT. NELSON HOUSE	#1 LACEY	AS ABOVE
		#2 CAGNEY	
		#14 BRENT	PROPS
	Sc. 52	#17 PHYLLIS	Lamp
	Day—3⅛ pgs		Pillows
			Glasses—Phyllis's
	Brent with flu.		
	END ACT III		
	INT. NELSON HOUSE	#1 LACEY	AS ABOVE
		#2 CAGNEY	
		#14 BRENT	PROPS
	Scs. 64, 66	#17 PHYLLIS	gun
	Day—2⅞ pgs		
			MAKEUP
	Brent beats		Black eye
	wife—C & L		Blood
	break in.		
			SP. EFX
			Break door glass
	INT. NELSON BEDROOM	#17 PHYLLIS	AS ABOVE
			PROPS
	Sc. 2B		Telephone
	Day—⅞ pg		
	My husband—he beats me.		
	INT. NELSON BEDROOM	#17 PHYLLIS	112 SO. KINGSLEY LOS ANGELES, CA
	Sc. 24B		
	Night—⅛ pg		
	He's not going to do it again.		
	END ACT I		

END OF 4TH DAY—TOTAL PAGES: 9⅜

DATE	SET/SCENES	CAST	LOCATION
5TH DAY FRIDAY 3/25/83	EXT. HOT DOG STAND Sc. 10 Day—1 pg What did Ruskin have to say—gives book.	#1 LACEY #2 CAGNEY	650 SO. SPRING STREET, LOS ANGELES, CA PROPS Book—"Loves Savage Har- vest" Prospectus VEHICLES C&L car
	INT. RUSKIN ENT. Sc. 7 Day—1⅞ pgs Cagney goes to Ruskin's office.	#2 CAGNEY #16 RUSKIN	AS ABOVE PROPS Coffee File Rings Neck chains Pendants Bracelets Prospectus
	INT. SPECIAL FRAUDS DIV. Sc. 28 Day—2 pgs Talk about bank account.	#2 CAGNEY #14 BRENT #15 MICK ATMOS. 1 Civilian 1 Uniform cop 1 Plainclothes	AS ABOVE PROPS Bank statements

DATE	SET/SCENES	CAST	LOCATION
	INT. SPECIAL FRAUDS DIV.	#1 LACEY #2 CAGNEY #14 BRENT	AS ABOVE
	Sc. 5 Day—1⅛ pgs	#15 MICK	PROPS Police files Guns for officers
	We don't have anything on Ruskin.	ATMOS. 2 Plainclothes 2 Civilians 1 Uniform cop	
	INT. HALLWAY	#1 LACEY #2 CAGNEY	AS ABOVE
	Sc. 3B Day—⅝ pg		
	On way to Frauds Div.		
	INT. INTERROGA-TION RM.	#1 LACEY #2 CAGNEY #14 BRENT	650 SO. SPRING STREET, LOS ANGELES, CA
	Sc. 60 Day—⅝ pg	#15 MICK #20 OBIE	
	Says the money is under their nose.		

END OF 5TH DAY—TOTAL PAGES: 8⅛

DATE	SET/SCENES	CAST	LOCATION
6TH DAY MONDAY 3/28/83	INT. PROPERTY ROOM Sc. 61 Day—2⅜ pgs What a waste of time.	#1 LACEY #2 CAGNEY #14 BRENT #15 MICK	2630 LACY STREET PROPS Wallet Jewelry
	INT. PROPERTY ROOM Scs. 71, 72 Day—1 pg Buy only on the Black Market.	#1 LACEY #2 CAGNEY #21 CURATOR	AS ABOVE PROPS Ruskin's jewelry
	INT. INTERVIEW ROOM Sc. 3 Day—1⅝ pgs Tell of the money they gave Ruskin.	#1 LACEY #2 CAGNEY #11 NORMA #12 ROSE #13 EDITH	AS ABOVE
	INT. SQUAD ROOM Scs. 1, 2, 2A, 2Bpt Day—3⅜ pgs Fifty dollar rule, three ladies enter.	#1 LACEY #2 CAGNEY #5 PETRIE #6 ISBECKI #11 NORMA #12 ROSE #13 EDITH ATMOS. Squad rm. atmos.	AS ABOVE PROPS Coffee Gold chain Cane

DATE	SET/SCENES	CAST	LOCATION
	INT. SQUAD ROOM	#1 LACEY	AS ABOVE
		#2 CAGNEY	
	Scs. 45, 46	#11 NORMA	PROPS
	Day—2 pgs	#12 ROSE	Book
		#13 EDITH	
	My cousin reads these.	ATMOS.	
		Squad rm. atmos.	

END OF 6TH DAY—TOTAL PAGES: 10⅜

DATE	SET/SCENES	CAST	LOCATION
7TH DAY TUESDAY 3/29/83	INT. BOOKING AREA/SQUAD ROOM	#1 LACEY	2630 LACY STREET
		#2 CAGNEY	
		#6 ISBECKI	PROPS
	Scs. 75, 76, 77, 78, 79	#22 KLOTZMAN	Book
	Day—3⅞ pgs		
	Someone to see you.		

	INT. BOOKING AREA/SQUAD ROOM	#1 LACEY	AS ABOVE
		#2 CAGNEY	
		#4 SAMUELS	
		#15 MICK	
	Scs. 48B, 48C, 48D	ATMOS.	
	Day—2⅛ pgs	Squad rm. atmos.	
	Deadbang case.		

DATE	SET/SCENES	CAST	LOCATION
	INT. LACEY'S LIVING RM.	#1 LACEY #3 HARVEY #14 BRENT	AS ABOVE PROPS
	Sc. 69 Night—2 pgs		Gun
	Brent looking for wife.		

	INT. LACEY'S BEDROOM	#1 LACEY #3 HARVEY	AS ABOVE
	Sc. 68 Night—⅛ pg		
	Pounding wakes them up.		

	INT. LACEY'S BEDROOM	#1 LACEY #3 HARVEY	AS ABOVE PROPS
	Sc. 56 Day—1⅞ pgs		Book Clock
	That must be some book.		

END OF 7TH DAY—TOTAL PAGES: 9⅞

DATE	SET/SCENES	CAST	LOCATION
STOCK SHOTS	ONE POLICE PLAZA Scs. 3A, 27A Day—2/8 pg ESTABLISHING.		
	EXT. KENNEDY AIRPORT Scs. 13, 32 Night—2/8 pg ESTABLISHING.		
	EXT. LACEY APARTMENT Sc. 67 Night—1/8 pg ESTABLISHING.		
	EXT. SHELTER FOR BATTERED WIVES Sc. 73 Day—1/8 pg ESTABLISHING.		

END OF STOCK SHOTS—TOTAL PAGES: 6/8

INDEX

In this index, *Cagney and Lacey* is abbreviated throughout as *C&L*.

A. C. Neilsen Company, 13–14, 72, 102. *See also* Neilsen ratings

A&W (sponsor), 77

Abatemarco, Frank, 125, 127

Abbott, Chris, 128

ABC (network), 14, 19, 65, 211 (n. 2); and working women's audience, 9, 26–27, 72, 85, 90; cancellation of *Heartbeat* by, 32, 208. See also *Monday Night Football*

Abortion, 49, 51, 209, 232 (n. 23); on *C&L*, 11, 55, 57–59, 62, 192

Action: as element of police genre, 77, 105–6, 109, 114, 223 (n. 22). *See also* Violence

Adam-12 (TV program), 110

Advertising (TV), 8, 65–66, 73, 104, 106, 213 (n. 6); women as consumers, 2, 65–73, 95, 104, 106, 205; for *C&L* programs, 21–24, 29, 35, 85, 88–90, 138; and class, 65, 225 (n. 51), 229 (n. 7); representation of women, 77, 231 (n. 18); and *C&L* fans, 98–99, 103. *See also* Target audience; Working women's audience

Advertising Age, 68, 229 (n. 8)

Affirmation: in *C&L*, 176, 178

"Affirmative Action" (*C&L* episode), 127, 154

African American men: in production of *C&L*, 26, 150, 151, 207; in police genre, 111, 114; in *C&L*, 149–50, 256 (n. 9)

African American women: TV representation of, 14–16, 68, 118, 221 (n. 8), 237 (n. 4); advertising interest in, 67–68, 70–71; in *C&L*, 68, 128, 200–201, 207, 254 (n. 38)

Age: target audiences specified by, 66–67, 72, 102–3, 230 (nn. 10, 11), 232 (n. 26); on TV, 72, 205; in *C&L*, 207. *See also* Youth audience

AIDS, 196, 254 (n. 35)

AKA Pablo (TV program), 222 (n. 8)

Alcock, Beverley, 169–70, 235 (n. 71), 237 (n. 1), 244 (n. 61), 248 (n. 24)

Alcoholism: in *C&L*, 55, 127, 132, 184, 194

Alice (TV program), 14, 77, 104

Alice Doesn't Live Here Anymore (film), 13, 71, 175

Alive and Well (cable TV program), 71

Allen, Robert C., 213 (n. 5), 223 (n. 26), 239 (n. 6), 246 (n. 73), 250 (n. 4)

All in the Family (TV program), 14, 31, 104, 229 (n. 7)

All My Children (TV program), 32

Althusser, Louis, 249 (n. 1)

Altman, Rick, 114, 115

American Film Institute, 100

American Girls (TV program), 15, 107

American Home Products (sponsor), 66, 77

American Medical News, 56

American Women in Radio and Television Award, 139

Amos 'n' Andy (TV program), 15

Amy Prentiss (TV program), 110

Ang, Ien, 104, 229 (n. 3), 233 (n. 27), 244 (n. 61), 246 (n. 73)

Ann-Margret, 19

Appearances: changes in Lacey's and Cagney's, 5, 9, 35–38, 48–49, 52, 61–62; Lacey's and Cagney's, in early advertising, 21, 35; press on Foster's/Daly's, 28, 30–34; and cultural stereotypes of women, 42–43; attempts to save Foster's job through change in, 225 (n. 39)

Arbitron ratings, 230 (n. 9)

Archie Bunker's Place (TV program), 77

Arden, Eve, 16

Ardmore, Jane, 31

Arthur, Karen, 207

Ashcraft, Laura, 69

Asian Americans, 67; TV representations of, 111, 114, 222 (n. 8)

Asner, Edward, 233 (n. 28)

A-Team, The (TV program), 96

Audience. *See* "Audience commodity"; "Commodity audience"; "Quality" audiences; Social audience; Spectator(s); Target audience; Viewers; Working women's audience

"Audience commodity," 65, 73, 74, 90, 103

Avedon, Barbara: as *C&L* creator, 5, 16–20, 26, 224 (n. 29); on Foster, 30–31; on female characters, 51, 220 (n. 1); on Gless, 225 (n. 50); on *C&L* changes, 246 (n. 1)

Avon (sponsor), 77

Baby, I'm Back (TV program), 221 (n. 8)

"Baby Broker, The" (*C&L* episode), 130, 254 (n. 34)

Bacon-Smith, Camille, 140

Baghdad Café (TV program), 222 (n. 8)

Ball, Lucille, 183, 238 (n. 4)

"Bang, Bang, You're Dead" (*C&L's* first episode), 6, 119, 123, 148–49

Baretta (TV program), 110, 116

Baros-Johnson, Irene, 227 (n. 70)

Barr, Tony, 49, 51

Barrett, Michele, 215 (n. 11)

Barrett, Rona, 88, 127

Barron, Eddie, 227 (n. 74)

Barry, Marion, 100

Bartos, Rena, 69

Basler, Barbara, 25

Bathrick, Serafina, 14, 238 (n. 4)

Battering. *See* Wife-beating

Bazalgette, Cary, 114, 116, 240 (nn. 9, 10, 14, 17)

"Beauty Burglars" (*C&L* episode), 126

Beauvoir, Simone de, 28–29

Beavers, Louise, 221 (n. 8)

Becker, Arnold, 32

Bennett, Tony, 218 (n. 15), 223 (n. 26)

Berg, Gertrude, 222 (n. 8)

Bergstrom, Janet, 256 (n. 3)

"Better than Equal" (*C&L* episode), 147–52

Beulah (TV program), 15, 221 (n. 8), 237 (n. 4)

Beverly Hillbillies, The (TV program), 13

Bewitched (TV program), 238 (n. 4)

"Bible," 243 (n. 42); *C&L's*, 121, 150, 154

"Biological Clock" (*C&L* episode), 49–51

Bionic Woman, The, 107, 222 (n. 10)

Blue Knight, The (TV program), 110, 113

Bobo, Jacqueline, 44, 94, 206

Body Language (radio program), 71

Bogle, Donald, 14

Borawski, Walta, 196

Bordwell, David, 214 (n. 6), 224 (n. 33), 248 (n. 23)

Bosworth, Patricia, 84

Breast cancer: *C&L* episodes on, 52, 55–57, 136, 157, 160, 184, 196–97, 207, 245 (n. 70), 254 (n. 38)

Broadway Department Stores, 84

Brocato and Kelman (publicity firm), 29–30, 234 (n. 40)

Brower, Susan, 86, 236 (n. 1)

Brown, Archie, 227 (n. 69)

Brown, Georg Stanford, 26, 111, 151, 207

Brown, Steve, 127–28, 155, 157, 244 (n. 60)

Browne, Nick, 7

Brunsdon, Charlotte, 8, 64, 187, 239 (n. 5), 246 (n. 73), 249 (n. 1)

Bryan (Texas) Eagle, 39

Bryant, Gay, 79

Buddy movies. See *Cagney and Lacey:* female friendship in; Partnership

Budget: for *C&L* made-for-TV movie, 20; for "feminization" of Cagney, 35; for "save *C&L*" campaign, 85; for *C&L* episodes, 124

"Burnout" (*C&L* episode), 49, 128, 245 (n. 70)

Burstin, Michael, 145

Bush administration, 2, 59, 208. *See also* Women's movement: backlash against

Butch Cassidy and the Sundance Kid (film), 16

Butler, Judith, 211 (n. 1), 212 (n. 4), 216 (n. 13), 251 (n. 5)

Byars, Jackie, 196, 240 (n. 8), 246 (n. 73)

Cable television: rise of, 4, 66–67; *C&L* rights sold to, 5; economics of, 65; as threat to network TV, 71, 208. *See also* Narrowcasting

Cagney, Charlie (character), 35, 57, 120, 127, 192

Cagney, Christine (character), 17; characterization, in Swit movie, 5, 20, 21, 25, 149, 161–62, 215 (n. 10); characterization, in Foster/Daly series, 5, 25–35, 39, 41, 149–50, 152–53, 156, 161–62, 215 (n. 10); sexuality, 5, 32, 51–52, 127, 132, 190–91, 197; characterization, in Gless/Daly series, 5, 35–36, 38–39, 41, 46, 51–52, 61–62, 79, 95, 121, 150, 154, 161–66, 177, 181, 193–95, 215 (n. 10); and class, 5–6, 32, 35, 232 (n. 19); politics, 36, 52, 149–51, 157–60, 191–92; as role model, 46, 74; pregnancy scare, 49–51, 58; ambition, 51, 52, 163–64; relationship with father, 120, 152–53, 192; alcoholism of, 127, 132, 184, 194. *See also* Appearances; Characterization

Cagney and Lacey (TV program): as case study of femininity construction, 2, 4–9; made-for-TV movie version, 4, 5, 13, 16–25, 72, 74, 76, 90, 118, 119, 147, 149, 153, 197, 215 (n. 10); representation of women in, 4, 8, 9, 16–37, 84, 91–92, 105–6; original script, 4, 13, 16–19; premier and series run, 5; target audience, 5, 8, 66, 73–85, 121, 128, 134, 140, 174; 1988 cancellation, 5, 103; genre of, 5, 105, 108–9, 118–41, 181, 198; female friendship in, 5–6, 16–17, 20–21, 28–29, 31, 34, 41–43, 45, 62, 77, 83, 119, 121, 143, 176, 179–98; unique aspects of, 5–7, 27–28, 42, 44, 107, 119–20, 142, 166, 174, 184, 202, 240 (n. 12), 253 (n. 32); first and last episodes, 6, 119, 123, 148–49, 199–201; as feminist project, 9, 20–21, 44–45, 119, 142–67, 169, 209; relationship between characters and audience, 9, 25, 45–46, 74–75, 93–101, 104, 109, 172–82, 189–203, 206, 245 (n. 70); pressure for weekly series, 20–21, 25, 75; Foster/Daly series, 25–36, 38, 72, 75–77, 85, 108, 122, 123, 125, 127, 140, 147, 149–50, 153, 156, 161–66, 184; changes in opening sequences, 36–37, 234 (n. 43); Gless/Daly series, 36–49, 73, 76–85, 122, 123, 125, 143, 153–54, 194; 1983 cancellation, 46–47, 85–92, 129; awards won by, 48, 59, 135, 139; sponsors, 77; shift from action to interaction in, 77, 105–6, 121, 123–24, 130–31, 183–84, 223 (n. 22); contradictory images of femininity in, 89–90, 133–39, 161–66, 174, 177–85, 189–95; as test case for other shows, 92; fan club, 94, 98, 100; 1987 possible cancelling of, 100–101; influence on other TV programs, 103, 236 (n. 80); "Bible" for, 121, 150, 154, 243 (n. 42); episode structure, 121–22, 124–27, 132; subversive power of, 175–77, 205; role of women in producing, 207. *See also* Breast cancer; Budget; Cagney, Christine; CBS;

Lacey, Mary Beth; Pregnancy scare; Talking; Viewers; names of actresses, characters, creators, and episodes

Cagney and Lacey (Stevens), 59

"Cagney and Lacey Day" (Washington, D.C.), 100

Carby, Hazel, 216 (n. 13)

Carnation (sponsor), 77

Carroll, Diahann, 68, 221 (n. 8)

Carroll, Rosemary, 245 (n. 69)

Carson, Tom, 92

Carson Pirie Scott, 84

Carter, Nell, 221 (n. 8)

Castleberry, Virginia, 138

CBS (network), 65, 139, 211 (n. 2); executives' ambivalence toward *C&L*, 6, 29–35, 49–52, 57–59, 61–62, 73, 85, 92, 99, 120, 194, 228 (n. 83); concern about representation of women, 7, 10–11, 29–35, 38, 41–42, 52, 145, 156, 198, 256 (n. 48); and working women's audience, 9, 13–15, 26–27, 63, 72, 73, 76–77, 94–95, 99, 172; O and O's of, 13–14, 81; selects *C&L* as made-for-TV movie, 19–20; promotion of *C&L*, 21–24, 35, 172; and Foster/Daly *C&L* series, 25–30; removes Foster from series, 30–35, 38, 96, 121, 148, 224 (n. 39); hires Gless, 35–37; attempts to cancel Gless/Daly series, 43–44, 47–48; cancels *C&L* in 1983, 46–47, 85–92, 129; seven-episode trial run of Gless/Daly series, 48, 99–100, 129–31; renews *C&L* after seven-episode trial run, 52; Program Practices Department, 57; affiliates, 58, 81, 102; cancels *C&L* in 1988, 103. *See also* Budget; Prime-time network TV; Promotions; Television

CBS Radio Network, 81

Channels magazine, 59

Characterization: instead of feminism in *C&L*, 161–66, 167, 169; audience's pleasure in *C&L*'s, 172–73, 177–85; differ-

ences between Lacey and Cagney, 182, 189–95, 198

Charlie and Company (TV program), 221 (n. 8)

Charlie's Angels (TV program), 6, 15, 16, 20, 27–28, 107, 110, 117, 118, 183

Chicago Sun Times, 97

Chico and the Man (TV program), 104, 222 (n. 8), 229 (n. 7)

China Beach (TV program), 107, 183, 222 (n. 8), 236 (n. 80)

CHiPs (TV program), 110

Chrysler (sponsor), 77

"City Is Burning, The" (*C&L* episode), 150–51

Clark, Danae, 239 (n. 8), 244 (n. 62)

Class: changes in depiction of Lacey's and Cagney's, 9, 35, 52, 61, 62, 121, 194, 225 (n. 50), 232 (n. 19); TV's treatment of working class, 32, 51, 104, 221 (n. 8), 229 (n. 7); TV's preference for portrayal of middle class, 65–68, 104, 225 (n. 51), 237 (n. 4); and feminism in *C&L*, 151–53, 155, 166; differences between Cagney and Lacey, 191–93; TV's constraints on, 205; advertisers and, 225 (n. 51), 232 (n. 19)

CLASS (*Cagney and Lacey* Appreciation of the Series Society), 98, 170

Clayton, Merry, 68, 207, 253 (n. 28)

"Clinic, The" (*C&L* episode), 57–59

Clothing. *See* Appearances; Mise-en-scène

Coca-Cola (sponsor), 77

Coe, Liz, 244 (n. 60)

Coleman, Sergeant (character), 157, 158

Colgate-Palmolive (sponsor), 68

"Collective alternative interpretations," 94

Collins, James, 7

Color Purple, The (film), 206

Columbo (TV program), 110, 116

Comedy: as element in *C&L*, 108, 121, 132, 140. *See also* Situation comedies

Coming Matriarchy, The (Nickles and Ashcraft), 69

Commercials. *See* Advertising

"Commodity audience," 65, 73, 230 (n. 8)

"Community of heightened consciousness," 44, 94

Condit, Celeste Michelle, 58–59

Confessions of a Married Man (made-for-TV movie), 90

Conrad, Robert, 125

Consumers, 2, 64, 65–73, 95, 205

Context. *See* Social context

Contraception, 49, 51, 59

Contradictions: in *C&L*'s images of femininity, 88–90, 133–39, 161–66, 174, 177–81; in nature of TV, 204–5

Controversiality: in TV programming, 73, 82, 99, 208, 233 (n. 28)

Coping With (radio program), 71

Corday, Barbara: as *C&L* creator, 5, 16–20, 26, 102, 224 (n. 29); as *C&L* production team member, 49, 51, 52, 212 (n. 2); *C&L* promotion by, 78, 80; on difficulties of changing TV, 207; on Foster, 225 (n. 50)

Corday, Jo, 256 (n. 10)

Cosby, Bill, 221 (n. 8)

Cosby Show, The (TV program), 68, 207, 221 (n. 8), 256 (n. 5)

Country programs, 13–14

Courtship of Eddie's Father, The (TV program), 222 (n. 8)

Crais, Robert, 125, 126, 127

Crawford, Joan, 16, 72, 145

Crime Syndicated (TV program), 109

"Cry for Help, A" (*C&L* episode), 85–90, 128, 129, 138, 139, 157

Cultural feminism, 12, 54–55

Daily Variety, 30, 77, 85

Dallas (TV program), 6, 49, 72, 77, 177, 199

Dallas Times Herald, 138

Daltry, Laura, 42

Daly, Tyne: portrayal of Lacey, 5, 34, 48–49, 52, 245 (n. 70), 254 (nn. 34, 37); *C&L* promotions by, 20, 21, 29–30, 58, 75, 78–82, 85–86, 100, 138; casting as Lacey, 20, 95; chemistry with Foster, 28, 34, 41; appearance, 28, 48–49, 165; on portrayal of female friendship in *C&L*, 31; chemistry with Gless, 45, 98, 253 (n. 25); Emmy awards, 48, 49, 59; views, 57, 92, 136, 193; pregnancy, 132

Dan August (TV program), 110

Date rape, 55, 132. *See also* Rape

"Date Rape" (*C&L* episode), 128, 137, 157, 158–61

Daughters: father-identified, 118; Cagney as, 120, 152–53, 192

Daytime TV viewership, 71. *See also* Soap operas

Decoy (TV program), 117, 240 (n. 12)

Deeb, Gary, 6, 46–47, 55, 62

Deedee, Detective (character), 124

Defenders, The (TV program), 220 (n. 7)

De Lauretis, Teresa, 7, 185–86, 205–6, 212 (n. 3), 219 (n. 1), 251 (n. 5)

Delvecchio (TV program), 110

Deming, Caren, 108

Dennington, John, 115, 240 (n. 16)

Department stores, 64, 83–84

Designing Women (TV program), 99, 103, 183, 236 (n. 80), 253 (n. 32), 256 (n. 5)

Desire, 104, 195–98

Dickinson, Angie, 17, 28, 43, 84, 117, 118

Dick Van Dyke Show, The (TV program), 238 (n. 4)

"Differently oriented interests," 214 (n. 6)

Different Story, A (film), 30

Different World, A (TV program), 207, 221 (n. 8)

Diff'rent Strokes (TV program), 221 (n. 8)

Dirty Harry (film), 116

"Discursive authority," 3, 7, 8, 61, 169, 172

Doane, Mary Ann, 242 (n. 36), 246 (n. 73), 256 (n. 49)

Documentary style: of police genre, 109

Dominus, Jerome, 101, 102

Donahue (TV program), 20, 71, 75, 96

Donehey, Daniel, 57

Dory (character). *See* McKenna, Dory

Double address: to women, 77, 83–84

Dow, Bonnie, 14

Dowell, Pat, 234 (n. 36)

Dragnet (TV program), 109, 110, 114

Drama(s) (TV): relative lack of female protagonists, 11, 15–16, 73, 83, 107, 110–12; *C&L* awarded Emmy for best, 59; domination by male protagonists, 106–8, 179; female protagonists in police, 110, 117–20, 242 (n. 34). See also *Cagney and Lacey*; Police genre

"Dramady," 241 (n. 25)

Drummond, Phillip, 241 (n. 28)

Duke, Bill, 207

Dukes of Hazzard, The (TV program), 94, 96

Duracell (sponsor), 77

Dyer, Richard, 252 (n. 19)

Dynasty (TV program), 6, 35, 68, 177, 199, 237 (n. 4)

East Side/West Side (TV program), 220 (nn. 7, 8)

Eastwood, Clint, 110, 116

Ehrmann, Paul, 126

Eighties Woman, The (cable TV program), 71

87th Precinct (TV program), 114

Ellis, John, 7

Ellsworth, Elizabeth, 44, 94, 255 (n. 43)

Emmy Awards, 48, 49, 59, 100, 207

England: *C&L*'s reception in, 6–7, 54–55, 97, 98

Entertainment Tonight (TV program), 31, 85

Equal Rights Amendment (ERA), 32, 35, 143, 147–52

Essence magazine, 70–71

Estrin, Jonathan, 166, 244 (n. 60)

Ethnicity: in *C&L*, 128, 149–51, 195; on TV, 205, 222 (n. 8), 237 (n. 4). *See also* Jewish women; Race; Women of color

Evans, Linda, 35

Evansville (Indiana) Press, 43

Exploitation advertising: for *C&L*, 21–24, 88–90, 129, 138

Exploitation topics: in *C&L* programming, 47, 55–57, 106, 107, 128–34, 140, 153, 155–61, 167; *C&L*'s competition with, 105–6, 135; and women's programming, 134–41; definition of, 227 (n. 79). *See also* Made-for-TV movies

Fairclough, Henry, 54

Falcon Crest (TV program), 6, 199, 237 (n. 4)

Faludi, Susan, 1, 154

Families: lack of, in police genre, 109, 114; precinct, 110, 116, 124–25; alternative, 253 (n. 32)

Family Matters (TV program), 222 (n. 8)

Family Viewing Hour, 230 (n. 10)

Fans, 94, 98, 100. *See also* Spectator(s); Viewers

Fantasy: in *C&L*, 199–200

Farrell, Peter, 242 (n. 38)

Father Knows Best (TV program), 237 (n. 4)

Faverty, Beverly, 253 (n. 28)

Federal Communications Commission, 13

Feldman, Ed, 16, 17

Female bonding: on TV, 182–83. See also *Cagney and Lacey*: female friendship in

Female gaze, 196–97, 255 (n. 47)

Female protagonists. See *Cagney and Lacey*: unique aspects of; Drama(s)

Female subjectivity, 216–18 (n. 13). *See also* Subjectivity

Femininity: society's struggle over meaning of, 4; varied meanings of, on TV, 21–24, 30–37, 52–62, 107, 140–41, 143–45, 171, 181–95, 198–201, 205, 231 (n. 18); discomfort with Foster's, 30–35, 39, 41; struggle over, among press and viewers, 37–48, 75–76; discomfort with Gless's, 84; contradictory images in *C&L*, 88–90, 133–39, 161–66, 174, 177–81, 189–98. *See also* CBS; Women

Feminism: impact on TV, 4; prime-time TV's representations of, 9, 16, 72–73; camps within, 12–13, 216 (n. 13); *C&L's* engagement with, 26, 27, 30, 32, 35–36, 38, 47, 48, 52, 61, 74–75, 95–97, 139, 142–67, 169, 176–77, 209; diminution of, in *C&L*, 35, 38, 48, 61, 153–61, 168–69, 176; as hook for working women's audience, 75, 84–85, 201–2; problems with exploitation topics, 135–36, 155–61; "explicit general," 147–55, 166–69, 176, 247 (n. 4); "women's issue," 155–61, 167, 176; "tacit or ambiguous," 161–66, 167, 169, 176; theoretical aspects of, 216 (n. 13). *See also* Women's movement

Feminization. *See* Appearances

Femme Nikita, La (film), 256 (n. 12)

Feuer, Jane, 14, 108, 230 (n. 11)

"Fiction of identity," 217 (n. 13)

Films: women in 1970s, 13, 71

Filmways: as *C&L* production company, 5, 16, 17, 19; *C&L* publicity by, 26, 29–30. *See also* Orion Television

Fisher, Gail, 221 (n. 8)

Fisher, Terry Louise: on feminism in *C&L*, 48, 130, 155, 161; as *C&L* production team member, 49–51, 127–31, 157, 212 (n. 2), 244 (n. 60); on female characters, 220 (n. 1), 227 (n. 71), 254 (n. 34)

Fiske, John, 246 (n. 1); on text levels, 22, 218 (n. 15), 220 (n. 2), 223 (n. 26); on "masculine" and "feminine" forms, 236

(n. 1), 244 (n. 62); on *Charlie's Angels*, 242 (n. 37); on realism, 252 (n. 19)

Flamingo Road (TV program), 72

Flying High (TV program), 15, 107, 222 (n. 11)

Fonda, Jane, 144

Force. *See* Action; Law; Violence

Ford, Kathryn, 161, 196

Ford Motor Company (sponsor), 66

Foster, Meg, 225 (n. 41); portrayal of Cagney, 5, 25–35, 39, 41, 149–50, 152–53, 161–62, 215 (n. 10); chemistry with Daly, 28, 34, 41; *C&L* promotions by, 29–30, 75, 86; CBS's removal of, 30–35, 38, 96, 121, 148, 224 (n. 39)

Foucault, Michel, 205, 212 (nn. 4, 5)

FOX (network), 4, 65, 66–67, 103, 222 (n. 8)

Frank's Place (TV program), 222 (n. 8), 256 (n. 5)

Freebie and the Bean (film), 16

"Freeze" (original *C&L* script), 4, 13, 16–19

Freiberger, Fred, 147

Fresh Prince of Bel Aire (TV program), 222 (n. 8)

Friday, Joe (character), 109

Friedan, Betty, 30

Friedman, Sonya, 71

Friendship. *See Cagney and Lacey:* female friendship in

From Reverence to Rape: The Treatment of Women in the Movies (Haskell), 16

From Washington: Citizen's Alert (cable TV program), 71

Gallop, Jane, 116

Gamman, Lorraine, 241 (n. 27), 244 (n. 63), 247 (n. 16), 249 (n. 25), 255 (n. 47)

Gangbusters (TV program), 109

Garland, Beverly, 117

Gay Community News, 196

Gay Media Task Force, 35, 62

Gays: on TV, 190, 233 (n. 28). *See also* Lesbianism

Gender: construction of, by TV, 2, 63–104, 106–7, 171–72, 176–77, 205–6; and prime-time TV, 106–7, 230 (n. 10); "performance" of, 212 (n. 4). *See also* Femininity; Masculinity; Men; Woman; Women

"Gender trouble," 2, 211 (n. 1)

General Foods (sponsor), 66, 77

General Mills (sponsor), 66

Genre: mixed nature of *C&L*'s, 5, 105, 108–9, 118–41, 181, 198; role in construction of gender, 105–41. *See also* Drama(s); Police genre; Situation comedies; "Woman's program"

Gerbner, George, 241 (n. 23)

Get Christie Love (TV program), 15, 16, 107, 110, 117, 118

Gibbs, Marla, 221 (n. 8)

Gilbert, Bruce, 144

Gillette (sponsor), 77

Gimme a Break (TV program), 221 (n. 8)

Girlfriends (film), 71, 175

"Girls with guns" movies, 209

Gitlin, Todd, 14, 16, 221 (n. 8), 222 (n. 11)

Gleason, Michael, 144

Gledhill, Christine, 181, 202, 205, 246 (n. 73); on cultural "negotiation," 3, 173, 176–77; on female media friendships, 180, 182, 189; on police genre, 239 (n. 8)

Gless, Sharon: portrayal of Cagney, 5, 38–39, 41, 95, 121, 150, 161, 165, 193, 215 (n. 10), 254 (n. 36); selection to portray Cagney, 20, 35, 225 (n. 50); other roles, 39, 225 (n. 39); lesbian fans of, 41–42, 62, 255 (n. 42); chemistry with Daly, 45, 98, 253 (n. 25); on 1983 cancellation of *C&L*, 47; appearance, 48, 61–62, 121; Emmy awards for, 59; *C&L* promotions

by, 78–82, 85–86, 100, 138; on feminism in *C&L*, 154, 247 (n. 16)

Gloria (TV program), 73, 145

Goldbergs, The (TV program), 222 (n. 8), 237 (n. 4)

Golden Girls, The (TV program), 32, 103, 183, 236 (n. 80), 253 (n. 32)

Goldsmith, Judy, 100, 138

Gomery, Douglas, 213 (n. 5)

Good Times (TV program), 14, 15, 104, 221 (n. 8), 229 (n. 7)

Gordon, Linda, 251 (n. 5)

Gordon, Mary, 227 (n. 71)

Grace Kelly (made-for-TV movie), 90

Gramsci, Antonio, 205, 213 (n. 6)

Grant, Bud, 93, 95, 101

Graves, Teresa, 16, 117, 118

Gray, Ann, 239 (n. 5)

Gray, Herman, 207

Green, Patricia, 131, 207, 244 (n. 60)

Green Acres (TV program), 13

Gunsmoke (TV program), 13

Hairstyles. *See* Appearances; Mise-en-scène

Hall, Stuart, 211 (n. 1), 213 (n. 6)

Hanes (sponsor), 77

Hanson and Schwam (publicity firm), 234 (n. 40)

Haralovich, Mary Beth, 205

Haskell, Molly, 16

Hawaii Five-O (TV program), 110–14, 116, 240 (n. 13)

Hazel Bishop lipstick, 229 (n. 8)

Heartbeat (TV program), 32, 99, 107, 183, 208, 233 (n. 28), 236 (n. 80), 253 (n. 32)

"Heat" (*C&L* episode), 207

Hee Haw (TV program), 13

Hegemony, 7, 213 (n. 6)

Helene Curtis (sponsor), 77

Heterosexuality: in *C&L*, 36, 120, 132, 162, 190, 197–98. *See also* Marital status; Marriage; Sexuality

Hierarchical relationships: in police genre, 110, 114, 119–20, 242 (n. 35)

Highway Patrol (TV program), 109, 110, 114

Hill, Anita, 209

Hill Street Blues (TV program), 94; lesbians in, 32; women characters, 32, 111, 117, 240 (n. 13); mixed genre of, 108, 114–15; precinct "families" in, 110, 242 (n. 29); minority protagonists, 111; writers of, 125, 126; precinct design in, 185; marriage in, 241 (n. 21)

History: "realist" approaches to, 213 (n. 5). *See also* Social context

Hollway, Wendy, 219 (n. 1)

Hollywood: representations of women by, 16, 19, 113

Hollywood Reporter, 30, 38, 85

Holsopple, Barbara, 34, 247 (n. 12)

Holt, Laura (character), 144–45

Homoeroticism: in *C&L*, 42, 62, 176, 195–98; in *Starsky and Hutch*, 241 (n. 24)

Homophobia: and Foster's removal from *C&L*, 30–34

Honey West (TV program), 242 (n. 34)

Hooperman (TV program), 115; African American male protagonists, 111; women characters, 111, 117, 240 (n. 13); unique aspects, 241 (n. 25)

Horowitz, Susan, 230 (n. 10)

Hotel (TV program), 32

"Hotline" (*C&L* episode), 123

Howard Beach (N.Y.) incident, 150

How the West Was Won (TV program), 222 (n. 8)

Humanitarian Award, 139

Humanitas Award, 59

Hunter (TV program), 111, 240 (n. 13)

Hurd, Geoffrey, 111, 240 (n. 9), 241 (n. 18)

Identification: of audiences with *C&L* characters, 45–46, 74–75, 104, 109, 172, 175–82, 189–203, 245 (n. 70); of Law with cop/hero, 115–17

I Dream of Jeannie (TV program), 238 (n. 4)

I Love Lucy (TV program), 183, 238 (n. 4)

Image analysis, 178

Incest, 135

In Living Color (TV program), 207

Interest groups: and cultural construction of women, 2; impact on *C&L*, 6, 11, 16, 37, 132–43, 147, 166–67, 169–70, 177, 199, 206; on *C&L*'s handling of exploitation topics, 137–39

"Interpretive community," 44

Intertextuality, 24, 145, 223 (n. 26)

In the Heat of the Night (TV program), 111

Intimate Agony (made-for-TV movie), 90

Investment(s): in femininity, 7, 41–42; in "audience," 73–75, 92–93; cooperation between various, 86; definition of, 219 (n. 1)

Ironside (TV program), 110, 111, 240 (n. 13)

Isbecki, Detective Victor (character), 125, 152, 157, 158, 161, 165, 249 (n. 29)

It's My Turn (films), 71

It Takes Two (TV program), 73, 143, 145

Jaggar, Alison M., 220 (n. 3)

"Jane Doe" (*C&L* episode), 128

Jeffersons, The (TV program), 14, 77, 221 (n. 8)

Jeffries, Georgia, 244 (n. 60)

Jenkins, Henry, 140

Jewish women: on TV, 222 (n. 8), 237 (n. 4)

"Jiggle" era: of TV, 15–16, 28, 107, 117, 118

Joanie Loves Chachi (TV program), 95, 235 (n. 70)

Job discrimination: in *C&L*, 6

Johnson, Nicholas, 222 (n. 9)

Johnson and Johnson (sponsor), 66

Jones, James Earl, 111

Jordan, Detective Verna Dee (character), 207

Josie (character), 207

Joyrich, Lynne, 7, 108, 246 (n. 73)

Judd for the Defense (TV program), 14

Julia (film), 13, 71, 175

Julia (TV program), 14, 221 (n. 8)

Justice, Candy, 39

Kate and Allie (TV program), 31, 100, 103, 183, 236 (n. 80), 253 (n. 32)

Kellerman, Sally, 18

Kellogg's (sponsor), 99

Kidder, Helen, 33–34

Kimberly-Clark (sponsor), 233 (n. 28)

King, Katie, 220 (n. 3)

Knelman, Inspector (character), 164, 185, 186–87, 189

Knelman, P. K. (Patricia), 50, 148, 207, 212 (n. 2)

Knight, Gladys, 221 (n. 8)

Knots Landing (TV program), 77

Koch, Ed, 86

Kodiak (TV program), 114

Kojak (TV program), 110, 116, 185

Kove, Martin, 54

Krim, Arthur, 100

Kuhn, Annette, 2–3, 7, 205, 218 (n. 14), 246 (n. 1); on production of gender, 64, 171–72; on openness, 167; on "new women's cinema," 175–76, 252 (n. 19); on "discursive authority," 212 (nn. 4, 5)

Lacey, Harvey (character), 5, 125, 132, 157, 165, 184, 190, 197, 246 (n. 1), 254 (n. 35). *See also* Marriage

Lacey, Mary Beth (character), 17; casting of, 5; sexuality, 5, 190–91, 197, 246 (n. 1); class of, 5–6; characterization in Foster/Daly series, 27, 33; characterization in Gless/Daly series, 36, 39, 46, 61–62, 79, 154, 165–66, 177, 181, 193–95; politics, 36, 119–20, 150–52, 155, 157–61,

191–92; nervous breakdown, 49, 128, 245 (n. 70); as mother, 120, 132, 190, 191, 247 (n. 11); pregnancy, 132, 164, 184; career, 191, 249 (n. 27). *See also* Appearances; Breast cancer; Characterization; Marriage; Role reversals

Ladd, Cheryl, 34

"Ladies' night" line-up, 76–77, 121

Lady Blue (TV program), 240 (n. 12), 242 (n. 34)

LaGuardia, Detective (character), 125, 157

L.A. Law (TV program), 48, 127, 208, 233 (n. 28)

Lane, Jeffrey, 125, 126–27

Lansing, Sherry, 19

Latinos/Latinas: on *C&L*, 57, 68, 152, 207; advertising's interest in, 67; on TV, 111, 114, 222 (n. 8)

Laverne and Shirley (TV program), 104, 183

Law: depiction in police genre, 115–20, 133–34

Lear, Norman, 14, 221 (n. 8)

Learned, Michael, 6, 92

Leave It to Beaver (TV program), 238 (n. 4)

Lefcourt, Peter, 49, 51, 129–31, 212 (n. 2)

Legs (made-for-TV movie), 129

Lesbianism: TV representations of, 1–2, 31–32, 208, 225 (n. 43); attempts to shield *C&L* from connotations of, 11, 41; association with Foster, 30–34; spec *C&L* script on, 196; sponsors of TV representations of, 233 (n. 28). *See also* Femininity; Gless, Sharon: lesbian fans of; Homophobia; Viewers: lesbian

Lever Brothers (sponsor), 66, 77

Liberal women's movement, 12, 223 (n. 24). *See also* Women's movement

Lifetime (cable channel), 5, 66

Line-Up, The (TV program), 110

List, Shelley, 161, 244 (n. 60)

Little Gloria (made-for-TV movie), 90

Locklear, Heather, 111
"Long shot," 253 (n. 30)
"Long take," 253 (n. 30)
Los Angeles chapter (NOW), 43–44, 87–88, 100
Los Angeles Commission on Assaults on Women, 139
Los Angeles Herald Examiner, 6, 31, 38, 42, 143
Los Angeles Police Department, 25, 33–34, 78, 79
Los Angeles Times, 25, 33–34, 42, 57, 93, 178, 193
Lou Grant (TV program), 99, 125, 127, 233 (n. 28)
Love Boat (TV program), 81
Luke, Terri, 236 (n. 79)
Lumbly, Carl, 256 (n. 9)

McDaniel, Hattie, 221 (n. 8)
McDonald's (sponsor), 77
MacGruder and Loud (TV program), 110
McHenry, Susan, 227 (n. 71)
Machery, Pierre, 223 (n. 26)
McKenna, Dory (character), 52, 127, 162–63
McMillan and Wife (TV program), 110, 111
McNeely, Jerry, 235 (n. 62), 245 (n. 65)
MacNeil/Lehrer News Hour (TV program), 58
Macy's, 84
Made-for-TV movies: as *C&L*'s competition, 43, 74, 85, 90, 95, 129; as women's prime-time TV fare, 72, 135, 136; *C&L* promos on, 77. *See also* Exploitation topics; titles of specific made-for-TV movies
Magazines. *See* Women's magazines
Magnum, P.I. (TV program), 29, 76
Mainstream press. *See* Press
Makeup. *See* Appearances; Mise-en-scène
Male protagonists: domination of TV dramas, 106–7, 108, 110–11, 114

Mama (TV program), 107, 237 (n. 4)
Mandela, Winnie, 59
Mann, Judy, 42, 58
Manna, Sal, 31
Mannix (TV program), 221 (n. 8)
Marc, David, 240 (n. 10)
Margulies, Lee, 93
Marital status: in *C&L*, 9, 32, 46, 51–52, 62, 161–63, 190; and pregnancy, 49; in police genre, 109, 114, 116; of sitcom characters, 237 (n. 4). *See also* Marriage
Marquette, Inspector (character), 200, 201
Marriage: in *C&L*, 27, 35, 46, 52, 162–63, 165, 182, 190, 197, 246 (n. 1), 253 (n. 33). *See also* Marital status
Martin, Biddy, 216 (n. 13), 249 (n. 1), 253 (n. 31)
Mary Tyler Moore Show, The (TV program), 14, 183, 222 (n. 8), 238 (n. 4)
Masculinity: *C&L*'s depiction of, 148–49, 152–53, 161, 164–65
*M*A*S*H* (TV program), 14, 16, 20, 76
Masterpiece Theatre (TV program), 96
Matter of Choice, A (film), 58
Maude (TV program), 14, 232 (n. 23)
Mayberry RFD (TV program), 13
Mayerle, Judine, 131, 183
Mayne, Judith, 251 (n. 5)
Medical Center (TV program), 31
Medical profession: and *C&L*'s breast cancer episodes, 55–57, 160
Meehan, Diana, 118, 241 (n. 17)
Meehan, Eileen, 13, 65, 73, 230 (n. 8)
Melba (TV program), 221 (n. 8)
Mellencamp, Patricia, 238 (n. 4), 246 (n. 73)
Melnik, Dan, 19
Melodrama, 140; as element of police genre, 108, 240 (n. 8); as element of *C&L*, 121, 130–31; and realism, 176–77
Men: "shaming of," by Cagney and Lacey, 52–54; power in police genre, 115–18; bodies, 116–20; characterization on

C&L, 157. *See also* Male protagonists; Masculinity; Viewers: male; names of male characters

Mentors. *See* Partnership

MGM, 19

Miami Vice (TV program), 110, 111, 115, 116, 240 (n. 13)

Mildred Pierce (film), 16

Mise-en-scène: in *C&L*, 28, 33, 123–24; definition of, 214 (n. 6), 224 (n. 33). *See also* Appearances; Squad room settings; Women's room

"Mr. Lonelyhearts" (*C&L* episode), 126–27

Modleski, Tania, 217 (n. 13), 237 (n. 4), 239 (n. 6), 246 (n. 73)

Mod Squad (TV program), 14, 111, 240 (n. 13)

Mohanty, Chandra, 216 (n. 13)

Monday Night Football (TV program), 76–77, 85, 90, 102, 230 (n. 10)

Montgomery, Kathryn C., 57

Moonlighting (TV program), 100, 103

Moore, Mary Tyler, 14, 183, 222 (n. 8), 238 (n. 4)

Moore, Melba, 221 (n. 8)

Mord, Marvin, 66

Morita, Pat, 111

Morley, David, 213 (n. 6), 214 (n. 6), 238 (n. 5)

Morris, Meaghan, 219 (n. 18)

Morrison, Toni, 211 (n. 1)

Mothers Against Drunk Driving (made-for-TV movie), 90

Moving Target, The: What Every Marketer Should Know about Women (Bartos), 69

Ms. magazine: as part of liberal women's movement, 12, 70–71; as *C&L* promoter, 20, 25, 26, 59, 75, 79

MTM Enterprises, 14, 230 (n. 11), 236 (n. 75)

"Multi-accentuality" of TV representations, 214 (n. 6)

Mulvey, Laura, 255 (n. 47)

Murder She Wrote (TV program), 107, 236 (n. 80)

Murphy Brown (TV program), 209, 236 (n. 80), 238 (n. 4)

My Friend Irma (TV program), 237 (n. 4)

Narrative structures: and gender, 108, 121–41; open, 143, 167–69, 175–76, 189–98, 206

Narrowcasting, 4, 66–67, 104

National Abortion Rights Action League (NARAL), 11, 58, 62

National Black Feminist Organization, 15

National Committee on Working Women, 59

National Examiner, 6, 52, 62

National Gay Task Force, 11

National NOW Times, 6, 47, 87, 100–101

National Organization for Women (NOW): support for *C&L*, 6, 43–44, 47, 57, 83, 100, 138; as part of liberal women's movement, 12, 58; Los Angeles chapter, 43–44, 87–88, 100; on offensive ads, 234 (n. 39)

National Right to Life Committee (NRLC), 11, 57–58, 62

Native American women: on TV, 222 (n. 8)

NBC (network), 65, 95, 208, 211 (n. 2); and competition for working women's audience, 9, 85, 90

Negotiation: of definitions and discourses, 3; over representations of women in *C&L*, 8, 172–74, 203; definition of, 213 (n. 6). *See also* Femininity

Neilsen markets, 81–82

Neilsen ratings: changes in sample for, 13–14, 72; of *C&L* made-for-TV movie, 25, 29; of Foster/Daly *C&L* series, 27, 29, 30, 31, 34; of Gless/Daly *C&L* series, 39, 43, 48, 52, 66, 85, 87, 90–91, 95, 96, 100, 101–3, 129; sweep periods,

55, 227 (n. 80); as promise of consumers, 65, 229 (n. 4); and target audiences, 73, 230 (n. 9); and program cancellations, 99

Network Television Association, 208

Newcomb, Horace, 108, 240 (n. 14)

Newhart (TV program), 76

New Haven Register, 39

Newspapers. *See* Press

Newsweek magazine, 72

New York City Police Department, 5, 17, 25, 86

New York Daily News, 33, 39, 138

New York Times, 24–25, 93, 101–2, 136

New York Times Magazine, 52, 193

Nichols, Nichelle, 221 (n. 8)

Nickles, Elizabeth, 69

Night Court (TV program), 222 (n. 8)

9 to 5 (film), 26, 71

9 to 5 (TV program), 26, 29, 73, 143–44, 222 (n. 8)

Nolan, Kathleen, 222 (n. 11)

NOW. *See* National Organization for Women

NOW L.A., 87–88

NRLC. *See* National Right to Life Committee

Nurse (TV program), 6, 92, 107

Nurses, The (TV program), 215 (n. 8), 220 (n. 7)

"O and O's," 13–14, 81

O'Connor, John J., 93, 136, 253 (n. 25)

Ohara (TV program), 111

One Day at a Time (TV program), 14, 77

"One of Our Own" (*C&L* episode), 126

On the Move (radio program), 71

"Open and Shut Case" (*C&L* episode), 128, 139, 157

Openness: of TV representations, 182, 189–95, 198, 214 (n. 6). *See also* Narrative structures

Orion Pictures Company, 90–91, 100

Orion Television: as *C&L* production company, 5, 58, 236 (n. 75); representation of women by, 11; viewer support for, 34; and creation of women's audience, 63, 73–74, 76–78, 82; on *C&L*'s ratings, 73–74, 128–29; publicity campaigns by, 85, 90–91. *See also* Filmways; Rosenbloom, Richard

Our Miss Brooks (TV program), 237 (n. 4)

Ozzie and Harriet (TV program), 237 (n. 4)

Paley, William, 93

Paris (TV program), 111, 113

"Parting Shots" (*C&L* episode), 207

Partnership: as element of police genre, 109, 110, 114, 117–18, 240 (n. 12). *See also Cagney and Lacey*: female friendship in

Patterson, Richard, 242 (n. 29)

Penley, Constance, 140

People magazine, 57, 193

Pepsi (sponsor), 66

Pete and Gladys (TV program), 238 (n. 4)

Petitions: for reinstatement of *C&L*, 97–98

Petrie, Detective Marcus (character), 124–25, 149–52, 157, 249 (n. 27), 256 (n. 9)

Petro, Patrice, 204

Petticoat Junction (TV program), 13

Phyllis Schlafly Reports (newsletter), 148

Pittsburgh Press, 34

Plainclothesman, The (TV program), 109

Planned Parenthood, 11, 58

Pleasure: viewers', in *C&L*, 7, 42, 44–45, 74–75, 94, 104, 109, 170, 172, 174, 175, 180, 182, 184, 195–98; women's, in police genre, 118; viewers', in TV programs, 206; women's, in sitcoms, 238 (n. 4). *See also* "Regime of pleasure"

PM Magazine (TV program), 85

Police genre: *C&L* as, 5, 7, 9, 54, 105, 106,

118–41, 181, 199–201, 215 (n. 9); and
gender, 107–20; characterization in,
111–14, 116; changes in Gless/Daly
C&L, 121–41. *See also* Policewomen;
"Woman's program"

Police procedure: as element of police
genre, 109, 114, 119, 240 (n. 10)

Police Woman (TV program), 15, 17, 84,
107, 110, 117, 118

Policewomen: public relations involving,
78, 81; *C&L*'s portrayal of, 86–87, 118–
20; TV portrayals of, 111–13, 117–20. *See
also* Los Angeles Police Department;
New York Police Department; Working
women

Politics: alternative, 104, 175, 206, 242
(n. 37). *See also* Cagney, Christine: politics of; Feminism; Lacey, Mary Beth:
politics of

Poltrack, David, 66, 101–2

Polysemy, 7, 214 (n. 6), 216 (n. 13)

*Popcorn Venus: Women, Movies, and the
American Dream* (Rosen), 20

"Pop Used to Work Chinatown" (*C&L*
episode), 152–53

Post, Ted, 20, 118, 223 (n. 22)

Postmodernism, 216 (n. 13)

Poststructuralist feminism, 12–13, 181–82,
216 (n. 13)

Powell, Norman, 19

Power: and media portrayals of women,
6–7; police genre's depiction of white
male, 115–18, 133–34; shift in depiction
of, 150–51; and "investment," 219 (n. 1)

"Power" (*C&L* episode), 164, 186–89

Precinct families: in police genre, 110, 116,
124–25

Pregnancy scare: in *C&L*, 49–51, 58, 62

Prentiss, Paula, 18

Press: and cultural construction of
women, 2; interest in representation of
women, 7, 8, 9, 11, 37–43, 49, 62, 182;
C&L publicity in, 24–25, 220 (n. 2);

on Swit/Daly and Foster/Daly *C&L*,
27–28, 31, 32, 33–34, 74, 148, 153; on
diminution of *C&L*'s feminism, 38, 153;
and creation of working women's audience, 63, 74–76, 80, 92, 93, 99–100,
103, 104; women's pages of, 64, 78–79,
81–82, 86–87. *See also* names of specific
newspapers and reporters

Prime-time network TV, 211 (n. 2); and
cultural construction of women, 2–3,
8–9, 63–73, 108, 204; competition for
audience, 4, 9, 25, 71; conventions for
female characters, 7, 92, 95–96, 99,
103–4, 178–81, 220 (n. 1), 237 (n. 4);
"women's programming" during, 72–
73, 134–39; fragmented viewing of, 76,
230 (n. 10); males on, 106–7; feminism
on, 166–67; use of character differences
by, 190; different investments in, 213
(n. 6). See also *Cagney and Lacey*; CBS;
Controversiality; Target audience;
Working women's audience; names of
TV programs and genres

Private Benjamin (TV program), 76

Private Secretary (TV program), 237
(n. 4)

Private-sphere stories, 107, 238 (n. 5). *See
also* Women's room

Procter and Gamble (sponsor), 66, 77, 99

Production companies: and cultural construction of women, 2; role in television, 104, 213 (n. 6), 233 (n. 29). *See also*
Filmways; Orion Television

Production team(s): and cultural construction of women, 2, 8; *C&L*'s, 11,
48–52, 62, 68, 100, 147–52, 193–94, 197,
212 (n. 2); and creation of women's
audience, 63, 74, 104, 172; and "save
C&L" campaign, 86; and female
friendship in *C&L*, 182; components
of, 213 (n. 6). *See also* names of individuals on *C&L*'s production team

Professional women. *See* Target audience

Promotions: for *C&L*, 6, 20, 21, 29–30, 36, 58, 75–87, 100, 138
Prostitutes: representations in police genre, 111, 113–14
PTA, 15, 117
Publicity: for *C&L* made-for-TV movie, 20–25; for Foster/Daly series, 26; for Gless/Daly series, 35, 64, 76–85. *See also* Promotions
Publicity firms: and cultural constructions of women, 2, 8; and creation of women's audience, 63, 78–85, 104, 172; and "save *C&L*" campaign, 86, 100; role in television, 104, 213 (n. 6); and mainstream press, 220 (n. 2). *See also* Brocato and Kelman; Publicity; Rogers and Cowan
Public-sphere stories: on TV, 106–8, 118, 178

"Quality" audiences: definition of, 66; and Orion Television, 74, 90; TV's consideration of, 101–4; number of, 137, 231 (n. 12)
Quality programming, 95, 230 (n. 11)
Quayle, Dan, 209

Rabinovitz, Lauren, 14
Race: in *C&L*, 18, 59, 62, 149–53, 155, 166, 195, 254 (nn. 38, 39); TV's emphasis on white, 66–68, 70, 73, 88; and TV advertising, 67–68, 70; on prime-time network TV, 106. *See also* Ethnicity
Radical feminism, 12, 54–55
Radio: and working women's audience, 71, 81
Radio Advertising Bureau, 71
Radway, Janice, 208
Rage of Angels (made-for-TV movie), 88, 90
Rand, Kate Lloyd, 69
Rape, 209; on *C&L*, 55, 132, 137, 157–61
Rashād, Phylicia, 68

Ratings. *See* Neilsen ratings
Readings, 226 (n. 62). *See also* Text(s)
Reading the Romance (Radway), 208
Reagan, Ronald, 44. *See also* Reagan administration
Reagan administration, 2, 26, 59, 139, 143, 208. *See also* Women's movement: backlash against
"Real" depictions (of women), 11, 25, 28, 42, 43, 46–47, 49, 74, 97, 177–81, 183–85, 201, 220 (n. 2), 245 (n. 70)
Realism: as element of police genre, 109, 114, 198, 240 (n. 10); in women's texts, 175–77; in film or TV, 252 (n. 19)
Realist approaches: to history, 213 (n. 5)
Reception, 220 (n. 2). *See also* Press; Spectator(s); Text(s); Viewers; Women's movement
"Recreational Use" (*C&L* episode), 127
Reese, Della, 221 (n. 8)
Reflection of life: TV as, 178, 214 (n. 6), 220 (n. 2)
"Regime of pleasure," 172, 203
Reilly, Sue, 227 (n. 71)
Religious groups: TV pressures by, 32, 208
Remembrance of Love (made-for-TV movie), 90
Remington Steele (TV program), 73, 96, 143–44
Reruns, 233 (n. 29)
Rhoda (TV program), 14
Rich and Famous (film), 71
Ride, Sally, 71
Riley, Denise, 216 (n. 13)
Robbins, Fred, 193
Robson, Jocelyn, 169–70, 237 (n. 1), 244 (n. 61)
Rogers and Cowan (publicity firm), 6, 76, 78–87
Role reversals: women as cops, in *C&L*, 16, 19, 32, 42, 92, 119; Harvey's and Mary Beth's, 27, 165
Rolle, Esther, 14–15

Rookies, The (TV program), 110, 111

Rose, Tricia, 211 (n. 1)

Roseanne (TV program), 1, 104, 208, 229 (n. 7), 238 (n. 4), 256 (n. 5)

Rosen, Marjorie, 20–21, 75

Rosenberg, Howard, 25, 33–34, 57, 193, 247 (n. 12)

Rosenbloom, Richard, 11, 20, 21, 75, 100, 129, 138, 236 (n. 75)

Rosenthal, Sharon, 33, 39

Rosenzweig, Barney, 78, 100, 102; as *C&L* executive producer, 5, 25, 34, 127–29, 201 (n. 2); on creation of *C&L*, 16–20, 118; as *C&L* production team member, 26, 48–49, 51, 121, 125, 212 (n. 2); on CBS's lack of support for *C&L*, 29–30; told to disinvite Steinem, 35; *C&L* publicity efforts of, 43–44, 57–58, 74, 76, 85, 92–94, 99, 138; on breast cancer episodes, 56–57; and women of color on *C&L*, 68, 88; on *C&L* fans, 74; on politics in *C&L*, 127–28, 147–48, 154; on Foster/Daly series, 224 (n. 35); and Foster, 225 (n. 39)

Rubin, Gayle, 212 (n. 3)

Ryan, Michael, 193

Ryan's Hope (TV program), 125, 127

Sabel, Judy, 48

St. Elsewhere (TV program), 32, 95

Sally Jessy Raphael Show, The (TV program), 71

Samuels, Lieutenant (character), 6, 119, 124, 148–49, 152, 157, 159, 164, 185, 200, 201

Sanford and Son (TV program), 104, 221 (n. 8)

Santi, Tina, 68–69

Scarecrow and Mrs. King (TV program), 100, 130

Schlafly, Phyllis: *C&L* character based on, 34–35, 147–49

Schulze, Laurie, 135, 136

Schwichtenberg, Cathy, 222 (n. 11)

Scott, Joan W., 216 (n. 13)

Screen Actors' Guild, 222 (n. 11)

Script development, 49–59, 121–22, 124–27, 132, 147–52. *See also* Text(s); titles and subjects of *C&L* episodes

Sears (sponsor), 77

Secrets of Midland Heights (TV program), 72

Seiter, Ellen, 246 (n. 73)

Sensationalism. *See* Exploitation topics

Sex: on TV, 15–16. *See also* Exploitation advertising; Exploitation topics; "Jiggle" era; Spectacle

"Sex/gender system," 3, 212 (n. 2)

Sexism, 149–53, 155, 166

Sexual harassment: *C&L* episodes on, 52, 55, 132, 255 (n. 40)

Sexuality: in *C&L*, 9, 32, 51–52, 165. *See also* Heterosexuality; Homoeroticism; Lesbianism

"Sexually excessive" women: in police genre, 111–12, 114, 117, 118

Shea, Patt, 126

Shephard, Harvey, 6, 29–30, 92, 99, 100, 101, 102

Sheridan, Susan, 169

Shot/reverse shot sequences, 197, 243 (n. 45)

Simon and Simon (TV program), 95, 96

Singleton, Ralph, 50, 212 (n. 2), 244 (n. 60)

Single women. *See* Marital status

Sirens (TV program), 240 (n. 12)

Situation comedies (sitcoms): depiction of women in, 11, 103; "socially relevant," 14, 71; as women's preserve, 107, 140, 237 (n. 4); female friendship in, 183. *See also* Comedy

60 Minutes (TV program), 52, 77, 96

Smith, April, 78, 80, 125–27, 154

Smith, Bridget, 54–55, 247 (n. 14)

Smythe, Dallas, 65

Soap operas, 96; on prime-time TV, 72; as element of police genre, 108; as element of *C&L*, 121, 125–27; and "women's programming," 140, 237 (n. 1); narrative structure, 239 (n. 6)

Soap Talk (radio program), 71

Social audience: Kuhn's definition of, 170, 171, 228 (n. 1); for *C&L*, 172, 202–3

Social context: of television programs, 3, 7, 171–74, 204–9; of *C&L*, 13–16; and meaning of "women," 216 (n. 13)

Social discourses: mediated by television, 214 (n. 6)

Socialist feminism, 12–13

"Socially relevant" programming, 14, 31–32, 71, 220 (n. 7)

Social order: depiction in police genre, 115–17

Solidarity: in *C&L*, 185–89, 198, 200, 201. *See also* Female bonding; Partnership

Something about Amelia (made-for-TV movie), 135

Sonya (cable TV program), 71

Spare Rib (journal), 6–7, 54–55

Spectacle: use of female bodies as, 16, 17, 118, 209, 222 (n. 10)

Spectator(s), 8; production of gender in, 108, 170–72, 205; *C&L*'s appeal to, 170–77; defined, 219 (n. 19), 228 (n. 1), 250 (n. 1). *See also* Audience; Spectator positions; Viewers

Spectator positions: offered by *C&L*, 202–3; defined, 249 (n. 1)

Spigel, Lynn, 205, 239 (n. 5), 246 (n. 73)

Spindler-Brown, Angela, 249 (n. 33)

Sportswoman (cable TV program), 71

Squad car scenes, 109, 186

Squad room settings, 109, 110, 114, 185, 186. *See also* Women's room

Square Pegs (TV program), 76

Stabiner, Karen, 101–2, 193

Stacey, Jackie, 255 (n. 47)

Staiger, Janet, 240 (n. 8)

Stam, Robert, 214 (n. 6)

Stanwyck, Barbara, 72

Stapleton, Jerilyn, 44, 87–88

Starsky and Hutch (TV program), 92, 110, 111, 113–14, 116, 118

Star Trek (TV program), 140, 221 (n. 8)

Steinem, Gloria, 143; as part of liberal women's movement, 12, 147, 152, 159, 161; as *C&L* promoter, 20, 25–27, 75, 86, 138, 145; proposed appearance on *C&L*, 35, 148

Stephen, Beverly, 138

Stevens, Serita Deborah, 59

"Street Scene" (*C&L* episode), 152

Streets of San Francisco, The (TV program), 110, 111–13, 114

"Struggle over meanings," 2–3, 211 (n. 2)

Subjectivity: Lacey's versus Cagney's, 181, 193–95, 198–201; female, 217 (n. 13)

Sugar and Spice (TV program), 183, 222 (n. 8)

Sunila, Joyce, 178

Supermarkets, 66

Sutter, Lynn (character), 200–201

Swanson, Dorothy, 98–99

Swit, Loretta: portrayal of Cagney, 5, 20, 21, 25, 149, 161–62, 215 (n. 10); *C&L* promotions by, 20, 21, 75

T.J. Hooker (TV program), 110, 111, 112, 113, 116, 240 (n. 13)

Talking: importance in *C&L*, 6, 77, 105–6, 121, 123–24, 130–31, 183–84, 223 (n. 22)

Tampax (sponsor), 77, 99

"T&A" era. *See* "Jiggle" era

Tandem Productions, 14

Target audience: women as, 2, 65–67, 134–35, 205, 213 (n. 6); for *C&L*, 5, 73–85, 101–3, 108, 121; professional women as, 35, 52, 59, 64, 69–70; mail from, 46; attempts to reach beyond, 143; definition of, 230 (n. 9). *See also*

Narrowcasting; "Quality" audiences;
Working women's audience
Tartikoff, Brandon, 15
TAT Productions, 14
Taylor, Ella, 234 (n. 36)
"Technology of gender," 7, 218 (n. 15)
Television: as institution, 3, 65, 104,
134–39, 204–9, 213 (n. 6); as flow, 7–8;
multiple roles for women in, 64–104;
role of programming on, 65; impact of
audience pressure on, 206–7; domestic
viewing of, 238 (n. 5), 239 (n. 6). *See
also* Advertising; Cable television; CBS;
Prime-time network TV; Target audience; Text(s); Viewers; Working
women's audience
Television and Radio Age magazine, 68
Text(s), 3, 214 (n. 6); second-level, 22, 24,
63–64, 75, 85, 119, 145, 220 (n. 2), 223
(n. 26); contradictory nature of *C&L's*,
49–59, 106, 134–40, 161–67; changes in
C&L's, 49–59, 125–28; oppositional
readings of mainstream, 75, 104, 168–
203, 206, 242 (n. 37); construction of
gender in, 108, 170–74; increasingly
"open" nature of *C&L's*, 143, 167–69,
175–76, 189–98, 206; third-level, 145,
223 (n. 26); definition of, 218 (n. 15).
See also Genre; Script development;
Spectator(s)
That's My Mama (TV program), 221 (n. 8)
Thelma and Louise (film), 1, 209
thirtysomething (TV program), 103, 233
(n. 28)
Thompson, Kristin, 214 (n. 6), 224
(n. 33), 248 (n. 23)
Thorburn, David, 108
Thorn Birds, The (TV miniseries), 85, 90
Thornton, Lieutenant (character), 194
Three's Company (TV program), 15, 95
Toft, Harland, 54
Toma (TV program), 110, 113
Tonight Show, The (TV program), 85

Torrez, Frank, 38
Toyota (sponsor), 77
Trapper John, M.D. (TV program), 29
Trials of Rosie O'Neill, The (TV program),
107, 225 (n. 39), 236 (n. 80)
Tucker's Witch (TV program), 77
Tulloch, John, 115, 240 (n. 16)
Turnabout (TV program), 20, 39
Turning Point, The (film), 13, 71
Turow, Joseph, 103
TV Guide: C&L advertising in, 21–24,
29, 35, 85, 88–90, 138; on *C&L*, 30, 32,
102–3, 145; viewer letters on *C&L* in,
34, 92, 97
Twentieth Century–Fox, 14, 19
Two on the Town (TV program), 85
Two-shots, 197
227 (TV program), 103, 183, 207, 256
(n. 5)
Tyson, Cecily, 221 (n. 8)

Universal, 20
Unmarried Woman, An (film), 13, 71, 175
Upjohn (sponsor), 77
US magazine, 30

V (TV miniseries), 129
Variety magazine, 154
Victims: use of term, 248 (n. 20). *See also*
"Women in distress"
Vidal Sassoon (sponsor), 233 (n. 28)
Videocassette recorders, 4
Viewers, 8, 218 (n. 18); and cultural construction of women, 2, 205, 214 (n. 6),
231 (n. 18); of *C&L*, 5, 8, 74–75, 93–94,
102, 174, 217 (n. 13); interest in representation of women, 6, 7, 32, 44–47,
52, 62, 103, 153, 169–70, 172–81, 184,
189, 195–98, 201–2, 206; change in
Neilsen sample of, 13–14; on Foster's
removal, 33, 34–35, 41; on Gless, 41; lesbian, 42, 62, 174, 176, 195–98, 206;
male, 45, 98, 102, 137, 180, 238 (n. 5);

on Deeb, 47; and creation of working women's audience, 63, 104, 172; on exploitation topics, 137–39; on Laceys' marriage, 253 (n. 33). *See also* Affirmation; Desire; Identification; Pleasure; Working women's audience

Viewers for Quality Television, 99

Village Voice, 92

Violence: on TV, 15, 117, 137, 153, 230 (n. 10); in police genre, 112–13, 115, 119, 155–61; in *C&L*, 160, 191, 196, 199–200. *See also* Action; Exploitation advertising; Exploitation topics

V. I. Warshawski (film), 256 (n. 12)

Vogue magazine, 131, 133, 155

Volosinov, V. N., 214 (n. 6), 223 (n. 26)

Voters for Choice, 58

Wagner, Lindsay, 222 (n. 10)

Wait until Mom Gets Home (made-for-TV movie), 90

Waldman, Diane, 253 (n. 20)

Wallace, Michele, 211 (n. 1)

Warner Bros., 14

Warren, Elaine, 6, 42, 143–44, 145

Washington Post, 42, 58

Waters, Ethel, 221 (n. 8)

Waters, Harry, 72

Webster (TV program), 221 (n. 8)

Weed, Elizabeth, 216 (n. 13)

Weiss, Harriett, 126

Welch, Raquel, 19

What's Happening (TV program), 221 (n. 8)

White, Mimi, 108, 215 (n. 10), 223 (n. 26), 248 (n. 22), 255 (n. 40)

Who Will Love My Children? (made-for-TV movie), 90

Wife-beating: *C&L* episodes on, 55, 85–87, 128, 129. *See also* "Cry for Help, A"

Wilke, John, 58

Williams, Clarence III, 111

Williams, Ethel, 100

Williams, Gail, 38

Williams, Linda, 246 (n. 73)

Williams, Raymond, 7

Williams, Samm-Art, 150

"Witness to an Incident" (*C&L* episode), 126

WKRP in Cincinnati (TV program), 15

Woman: TV struggle over meaning of, 2–3, 4, 202–3; definition of, 3, 7, 173, 212 (n. 3), 216 (n. 13), 251 (n. 8). *See also* Femininity; Women

Woman's Day (cable TV program), 71

"Woman's program": *C&L* reconstructed as, 5, 9, 121–41, 181, 198–99, 215 (n. 9); on prime-time TV, 72–73; definition of, 236 (n. 1), 243 (n. 44). *See also* "Women's issues"

Woman to Woman (cable TV program), 71

Women: media representations of, 1–3, 11, 13–16, 19, 42–43, 95–96, 213 (n. 6), 220 (n. 1); as TV target audiences, 2, 7, 35, 52, 59, 64–67, 69–70, 134–35, 205, 213 (n. 6); as consumers, 2, 65–73, 95, 106, 205; definition of, 3, 7, 212 (n. 3), 216 (n. 13); as portrayed in *C&L*, 5–8, 21–24, 27–28, 30–35, 42–43, 120–41; as TV writers, 11; as protagonists on TV dramas, 11, 15–16, 73, 83, 107, 110–12, 117–20, 242 (n. 34); "exploitation" in *C&L*, 47, 55–57, 88–90, 107; multiple roles in television, 63–104, 207; changing demographics of, 67, 68–70, 231 (n. 13); "sexually excessive," in police genre, 111–12, 114, 117, 118. *See also* Age; Exploitation topics; Femininity; "Real" depictions (of women); Woman; "Women in distress"; Women of color; Women's bodies; Women's movement; Working women; Working women's audience

Women against Pornography, 12

"Women in distress": in *C&L*, 5, 21, 132, 136, 140, 153, 215 (n. 10); prevalence on

TV, 15, 167; in police genre, 111–12, 114, 117, 118

Women in the Workplace (radio program), 71

Women of color: representations on *C&L*, 59, 207; *C&L*'s appeal to, 174. *See also* African American women; Asian Americans; Latinos/Latinas; Native American women

Women's audience. *See* Working women's audience

Women's bodies: on TV, 117–18, 165. *See also* Appearances; Exploitation topics; Sex; Spectacle

Women's culture: and TV constraints, 104, 238 (n. 4)

Women's form. *See* "Woman's program"

"Women's issues": in *C&L*, 122, 124, 128, 129–36, 155–61, 169; definition of, 243 (n. 44)

Women's magazines, 64, 70–71, 78–79, 83–84

Women's movement: backlash against, 2, 4, 15, 16, 26, 37, 73, 103, 139, 154–55, 167, 168, 199; contributions to cultural understanding, 2–3, 4, 44–45; impact on definitions of femininity, 4, 13, 117; influence on *C&L*, 6, 11, 16, 37, 48, 132–43, 147, 166–67, 169–70, 177, 199; support for *C&L*, 6, 11, 26–27, 75–76, 86–88, 99–101, 103, 145, 169, 206; interest in depiction of women, 7, 9; camps in, 12–13; *C&L* viewers generally a part of, 44, 178, 217 (n. 13); and creation of working women's audience, 63, 71, 74, 78, 94, 97, 104, 172; advertising's use of, 69–70, 84–85. *See also* Feminism; *Ms.*

magazine; National Organization for Women

Women's organizations, 64, 82–83

Women's Pictures (Kuhn), 175–76

Women's room (*C&L* setting), 183, 185–87, 200–201

Wonder Woman (TV program), 15, 107

Wood, Larry, 43

Woolfson, David, 236 (n. 79)

Woollacott, Janet, 218 (n. 15), 223 (n. 26)

Work: Lacey's and Cagney's attitudes toward, 51, 52, 163–64, 191, 249 (n. 27); female solidarity at, 185–89

Working Mother (cable TV program), 71

Working Woman magazine, 69, 70, 79, 84

Working women: on TV, 14, 37–38, 72–73, 77, 78; in *C&L*, 26, 27, 51, 52, 163–64, 185–89, 191. *See also* Policewomen

Working women's audience: TV's attempts to attract, 4, 9, 25, 67–85, 213 (n. 6), 215 (n. 7); *C&L* aimed at, 5, 8, 66, 75–85, 121, 128, 134, 140, 174; creation of, 9, 63–94, 100–104, 105; banding together of, 94–101. *See also* Exploitation topics; Target audience

WOWT-TV (Omaha, Nebr.), 58

Wyman, Carol, 39

Wyman, Tom, 93, 236 (n. 75)

York, Peggy, 33–34

You! Magazine (cable TV program), 71

Youth audience, 66–67, 71, 103, 230 (n. 10)

Zimbalist, Stephanie, 144–45

Zimmerman, Patricia, 232 (n. 26)